DANGEROUS INTIMACY

DANGEROUS INTIMACY

*The Untold Story of
Mark Twain's Final Years*

Karen Lystra

University of California Press · Berkeley, Los Angeles, London

Frontispiece. Lyon, Twain, and Ashcroft at Stormfield in
a photo Twain used for Christmas postcards in 1908.

REPRINTED BY PERMISSION, MTP.

University of California Press
Berkeley and Los Angeles, California

University of California Press, Ltd.
London, England

© 2004 by the Regents of the University of California

Library of Congress Cataloging-in-Publication Data

Lystra, Karen.
    Dangerous intimacy : The untold story of Mark Twain's
final years / Karen Lystra.
        p.   cm.
    Includes bibliographical references and index.
    ISBN 0-520-23323-9 (cloth : acid-free paper)
    1. Twain, Mark, 1835–1910—Last years.   2. Twain, Mark,
1835–1910—Relations with private secretaries.   3. Twain,
Mark, 1835–1910—Relations with women.   4. Twain, Mark,
1835–1910—Finance, Personal.   5. Authors, American—19th
century—Biography   7. Lyon, Isabel, 1863–1958. I. Title.

PS1332.L97   2004
818'.409—dc22   2003018999

Manufactured in the United States of America

13   12   11   10   09   08   07   06   05   04
10   9   8   7   6   5   4   3   2   1

The paper used in this publication is both acid-free and totally
chlorine-free (TCF). It meets the minimum requirements of
ANSI/NISO z39.48–1992 (R 1997) (*Permanence of Paper*).

For Paul Zall and Bob Middlekauff,
accomplished scholars and generous friends
and
in memory of Martin Ridge who,
like Mark Twain,
was courageous to the end

CONTENTS

Preface   ix

Acknowledgments   xvii

A Note on Names   xxi

1. Mark Twain—and Sam's Women   1

2. Heartbreak   20

3. Rearranging the Household   45

4. Looking for Love   59

5. A Pact with the Devil   80

6. Life in the Sanitarium   88

7. Someone to Love Him and Pet Him   100

8. A Viper to Her Bosom   110

9. Innocence at Home   123

10. Stormfield   134

11. An American Lear   146

12. Illusions of Love   159

13. Unraveling   171

14. The Exile Returns   179

15. Confrontation   191

16. A Formidable Adversary   199

17. False Exoneration   207

18. The Funniest Joke in the World   218

19. Melting Marble with Ice   234

20. The End of My Autobiography   243

Epilogue: How Little One May Tell   263

Notes   275

Index   325

PREFACE

In the spring of 1987 I was invited to serve as co-editor of a set of documents that had been recently acquired by the Henry E. Huntington Library in San Marino, California. The library had purchased diaries kept by Mark Twain's youngest daughter, Jean Clemens, from the estate of her sister's secretary, Phyllis Harrington. Though the diaries chronicle only four of the last ten years of her life, those were years in which Jean struggled with severe epilepsy and endured a variety of treatments at her family's behest, including an extended stay in a private sanitarium. My work in American nineteenth-century social and cultural history provided a helpful background for reading the diaries in the context of their period, especially in understanding the position of young women of the time.

What I found in the diaries was a compassionate, lonely woman in her twenties, frustrated by all the ways that her disease had interfered with her life. Jean's writing showed her to be a sensitive, kindhearted person who loved horseback riding and dancing and who participated joyfully in almost any outdoor sport or activity. Her intelligence and sense of fun, her tenderness for the downtrodden, her quick but forgiving temper, and her low self-esteem and hunger for love combined to touch me deeply. In order to understand her more fully, I went looking for the wider context of her life, in particular the life of her father.

At that point, I shared the common American images of Mark Twain: the Missouri boyhood captured in *The Adventures of Tom Sawyer*, the Mississippi riverboat pilot (where the measure of river depth—"mark twain," or two fathoms—gave him his pseudonym), the Western adventurer and journalist, the hugely successful novelist, and finally the charmingly irascible lecturer and raconteur, wisely and wittily challenging the absurdities of everyday life. Indeed, thanks to the one-man show the actor Hal Holbrook has performed for some fifty years, many Americans feel they almost know Mark Twain and cherish his quintessentially American humor, with its basic urge to get even with petty despots and expose the cant of hypocrites.[1]

The private life of Mark Twain—or, more properly, of Samuel Lang-horne Clemens—is more obscure. That there was a darker, more deeply cynical face to his humor is evident in much of his later writing, especially in the desolate satire of human cruelty, greed, and selfishness of *Letters from the Earth* and the evident heartlessness of fate and the universe in *No. 44, The Mysterious Stranger.* This has led to the widely accepted view that Twain in his late sixties and early seventies, especially after the death of his wife in 1904, was a downcast, cheerless old man. And, indeed, most of the writers and scholars who have made his life and work the subject of many books and documentaries portray his old age as depressed, despairing, and possibly incompetent.

When I began to research the life of Mark Twain, I expected that the basic biography of such a popular icon, over ninety years after his death, would be incontestable. Every inch of his life should have been minutely sifted—or so I thought. Yet on the strength of what I had learned from Jean's diaries and my first foray to the Mark Twain Papers, the vast depository for Twain's private papers and manuscripts at the Bancroft Library of the University of California, Berkeley, I felt at first uncomfortable and ultimately strongly at odds with the traditional interpretation of Twain presented by the standard biographies. Of course, the vast majority of public facts and events of this period have been established: Twain's whereabouts delineated; the characters of his life story sketched; even his tangle of manuscripts has been well sorted out. But, as I went beyond the biographies, the plot line of his private life in his last years began to seem woefully incomplete to me. Most of the manuscripts and other primary sources I consulted in my research have been available for some time, but the more I studied them, the more I became convinced that they simply could not be examined closely or placed next to one another chronologically without revealing an entirely new picture of Twain's final years. There was a "hidden" story yet to be told in the life of Mark Twain.

I came to see the tragedy of Jean Clemens as the key to the story of Twain's later life, even though she was the person who, ironically, had the least control over events. That Jean had epilepsy and that she spent several years in virtual exile from her home after her mother died was set forth in all the biographies, but in them the details of the rest of her life remain sketchy at best. The most important biographer of Twain's last ten years has characterized Jean as "the daughter Mark Twain wanted to forget" and asserts that as Jean's epileptic attacks became more violent, she attempted to kill the family's housekeeper, Katy Leary.[2] Twain, according to this account, banished Jean from his household because of her assault on Katy. Having met Jean through her diaries, I found this claim startling, raising questions about the state of her mental health and about the connection between epilepsy and violence.

Of course, Jean, like many diarists, might simply have refused to put powerful and frightening emotions on the page, but *nothing* in her diaries had suggested to me unmanageable anger, "homicidal" aggression, or any form of mental illness. I went to the secondary literature on epilepsy—including both the social history of the disease and the results of current clinical research. Scientific opinion is firm: there is absolutely no physiological connection between epilepsy and violence directed against another person. Nonetheless, the belief that epilepsy caused homicidal behavior had been widespread in the nineteenth century—and it had obviously not been put to rest in the twentieth.

Thus I found myself on the trail of a mystery, which I set out to solve with the sleuth's process of deduction. (Like many investigators, I uncovered much more than I had expected.) The claim that Jean attempted murder has never been challenged. Who, I wanted to know, originally thought Jean Clemens was a homicidal killer and why? The accusation had apparently been made by Isabel Lyon, who was Twain's secretary from 1902 to 1909. Her papers, including her diaries, are part of the Mark Twain Papers, housed in the Bancroft Library. In reading those diaries there, both the original and a typescript version, I found the entry in her Daily Reminder for January 27, 1906, where she writes that Jean had struck Katy Leary in "a burst of unreasoning rage," with the intent to kill. But by that date her diaries also revealed that the forty-two-year-old Lyon had fallen deeply in love with her seventy-year-old employer. She would eventually use all her wiles to try to get him to marry her. In studying the original diaries, I could see that many revisions had been made, as if Lyon had spent time in later years revisiting and rethinking her life with Mark Twain. Most changes were trivial, but some more substantive emendations related to the charge against Jean. Judging Lyon's truthfulness and sincerity thus became central to untangling this narrative. Was she a victim of late-nineteenth-century culture, which taught her to fear persons with epilepsy? How much influence did she have over Twain's decisions—and Jean's life—and how did she use it? And these questions led me to what was perhaps the most important one: Did Mark Twain believe that his daughter was potentially homicidal?

To answer this, I turned to Twain's own unpublished account of his later life, which is also held in the Mark Twain Papers at the Bancroft Library. This remarkable 429-page manuscript, written in 1909 and known among scholars as the Ashcroft-Lyon manuscript, in reference to Lyon and Twain's business manager, Ralph Ashcroft, opened an entirely new perspective in my research. For all its faults—not least of which is its lack of organizational structure—this forceful, sharp-edged, and often courageous autobiography may be Twain's most important confessional writing. (It should not be confused with the published autobiographical "chapters" that appeared in *The North American Review* in 1906 and 1907 and that were republished in 1990 as *Mark Twain's Own Autobiography*.)

In the Ashcroft-Lyon manuscript, Twain recounts the tale of an amazing plot, abetted by his own folly, weakness, and vulnerability to the flattery and lies of his secretary and business manager, who became his confidants and who, he says, thought "I couldn't help myself; that all in good time they would be indisputably supreme here, & I another stripped & forlorn King Lear."[3] Twain charges that Lyon sought to exile Jean from his house forever and confesses that as a widowed father he had failed—to the point of betrayal—to confront his daughter's condition and to live up to his parental responsibility. Yet he furiously repudiates any characterization of his youngest daughter as "crazy." He also accuses his secretary and business manager of financial skullduggery once Jean was out of the way.

I was puzzled. Twain's charges, with the exception of embezzlement in connection with building his house in Redding, Connecticut, do not figure in the biographies. Why had they been rejected? Why would a man of Twain's enormous vanity make such humiliating confessions if they were not true? Yet those who have examined the Ashcroft-Lyon manuscript closely have essentially dismissed it. Some suggest that Twain was close to paranoid fantasy, while others more charitably hint that he was losing his grip on reality as he slid into depression and despair.

Twain's accounts are most often simply discounted in favor of his secretary's version of events, put forward in her diaries and also in a series of interviews that appeared in the *New York Times* after she was fired.

It thus became important to determine whether Mark Twain in his seventies was still a rational man fully in possession of all his mental faculties or a senile old fool who defamed two loyal and caring employees. I wanted to check every fact that could be verified independently. One important source was a professional audit of Twain's finances ordered by his lawyers in 1909, after Lyon and Ashcroft had been dismissed. I closely studied this voluminous ledger-sheet, and as I pored over it for the record of his financial dealings, I found evidence to support Twain's case. I also found other illuminating documents, including a much-contested power-of-attorney, drafted by Ralph Ashcroft, as well as letters, private contracts, and a memorandum written by Ashcroft in defense of Lyon and himself. Ashcroft also did two revealing interviews with the *New York Times* that help to clarify his role.

Many other details that could not be verified externally were examined for internal consistency. Here Jean's diaries and letters were critically important because she—unlike Twain, who wrote for an "Unborn Reader," or Ashcroft and Lyon, who sought more immediate vindication—was not campaigning for a place in history. She wrote of events with a directness, openness, and guilelessness that were extremely helpful in sorting out the claims and counterclaims between her father and his employees. I also appreciated the value of the diaries for their depiction of the experience of a person with epilepsy in the early twentieth century, when effective treatment was still decades away, and for their rare glimpse at life inside a private sanitarium of the day, where men and women with financial means voluntarily sought a cure for the incurable. Although these did not bear directly on my questions about Twain and Lyon, I saw them as an important part of the larger story of Twain and his family.

I also drew on three other important primary sources: a memoir by Twain's middle daughter, Clara; the first biography of Twain, by Albert Bigelow Paine; and Katy Leary's memoir, as told to Mary Lawton, a friend of Clara. What I found most telling in these books is the near invisibility of Isabel Lyon, as if she had been purged by common consent. Clara Clemens wrote *My Father, Mark Twain* in 1931; it is a cheerful account of her family life that studiously ignores Lyon and Ashcroft. After her mother's death, Clara largely lived away from the family home as she struggled to establish an independent identity in the glare of her father's celebrity. Her absence left the stage open for the growing intimacy between Twain and Lyon, and some have attributed the tensions that developed in the household to Clara's jealous perception of Lyon as a rival for her father's affection. But Clara's separate life was largely dependent on her father's ample financial support, and her motivations for ultimately intervening actually revolved around money. After the deaths of Jean and Twain, Clara became the guardian of the family story.

Albert Bigelow Paine was invited by Twain to act as his official biographer in 1906 and became a member of Twain's inner circle, essentially a member of the household. He had to wage a struggle to retain his position, however, in the face of Lyon's increasing control over Twain's life. In *Mark Twain: A Biography*, published in 1912, Paine made a single reference each to Ashcroft and Lyon in 1,587 pages. He was following the wishes of Clara, who successfully imposed a fifty-year blackout on information about her father's life with his secretary and business manager. In Katy Leary's oral history, *A Lifetime with Mark Twain*, published in 1925, much that is relevant has clearly been censored by Clara's friend Mary Lawton, who conducted and transcribed the interviews with Katy. Leary is nonetheless a vital witness to the events that unfolded in the Clemens household.

At the end of my research I found I had a story I could not walk away from—a *Rashomon*-like tale of the family triangle involving Twain, Lyon, and Jean, each with his or her recounting of events. But for this tale there were other witnesses as well. Indeed, I decided I could write this book in large part because the record of private thoughts and feelings was so rich. One challenge of telling a dramatic nonfiction story is how to get inside the feelings and motivations of the main characters without inventing monologues and dialogues. So many members of Twain's inner circle were on the record that I could give every participant a voice, allowing each to speak his or her mind directly from within the available documents. I believe the story as I re-create it here presents each of these powerful voices fairly. I believe, as well, that it contains many enduring elements: a disabled child, a May-December romance, the vulnerabilities of age and aging, the vanity of success, the power of prejudice, the loneliness everyone seeks to overcome, the longing for love at any age, and the barriers that seem to keep people apart, including (or especially) parents and children. The story has a universal attraction: although it is rooted in the specific history of one remarkable family, it functions as an emotional sampler of the precarious balance of love and pain that motivates us all.

ACKNOWLEDGMENTS

To paraphrase the words of a famous fictional character, authors often depend on the kindness of strangers. They also rely heavily on their friends. Acknowledgments are born of the gap between this dependence and the paltry means most writers have to repay their debts.

The generosity of large numbers of people, and of the institutions in which they work, have helped see this book into print. Time to write is the most precious gift a teacher can receive, and two institutions have been especially instrumental in giving me this time. First is the Henry E. Huntington Library in San Marino, California, which supported my work with a Summer Research Stipend in 1995 and then became the home for my National Endowment for the Humanities Grant in 1999–2000. Roy Ritchie, Director of Research at the Huntington, encouraged me to set my sights on a full year off from teaching and other responsibilities. The National Endowment for the Humanities provided the financial means. And the long-term fellows at the Huntington added sociability and discernment to my year of intellectual nirvana.

Many people who work at the Huntington were supportive of my project, including Alan Jutzi, Curator of Rare Books, Carolyn Powell, Assistant to the Director of Research, and Virginia Renner, now retired from her position as the Head of Reader Services. I also thank the current Head of Reader Services, Romaine Ahlstrom, and her staff, including Christopher Adde, Jill Cogen, Susi Krasnoo, and Mona Shulman, for the many courtesies that make working at the Huntington so satisfying. Sarkis Badalyan presides over the daily entry and exit into the library with gentle grace.

Scholars who work at the Huntington are called *readers*. Many readers too numerous to mention listened to snippets of my work with interest. One of my favorite parts of the day at the Huntington was lunch, where lively dialogue, social commentary, cultural and political observations, and humorous repartee gave me a boost for meeting the intellectual demands of the afternoon.

The second institution that has been especially supportive of my research is also the place where I teach: California State University, Fullerton. Without the support of former Dean of Humanities and Social Sciences Don Castro, Associate Dean Kurt Swanson, and their administrative assistant, Bunny Casas, as well as my department chair, Jesse Battan, I would not have been able to take a full year off to work on the book. The university also supported my research on this book with two Summer Faculty Research Awards and a semester of sabbatical leave.

Another institution that has been central to this project is the Mark Twain Papers at the University of California, Berkeley. The director, Robert Hirst, took time out from his demanding schedule to explain the intricacies of Twainian copyright. He generously granted me permission to quote from unpublished manuscript sources and also allowed me to reproduce photographs from the collection. Over the years, other scholar-editors at the Mark Twain Papers have been helpful, including Victor Fischer, Kenneth Sanderson, and Robert Pack Browning.

The University of California Press believed in my book, beginning with the reassuring support of Jim Clark, the now-retired director, and his assistant, Mari Coates. Mary Severance skillfully assumed responsibility for the book during the later stages of editing and production. I have been blessed with an extraordinary editor, Ellen F. Smith, whose commitment and dedication to the craft of writing is priceless. She was indefatigable in her efforts to improve my work and pushed me to dig for the telling little detail as well as to strive for the most exacting clarity of exposition. She polished off the rough spots and pushed for changes that at times no doubt saved me from myself. I am especially grateful for her work on my preface, which helped to get at the heart of my intentions. Her probing questions and guidance on matters of style and content have combined to make this a better book.

Several friends have made unique contributions to my project. Paul Zall introduced me to Jean Clemens's diaries and took seriously my ambition to write a book on Twain. He allowed me to use a partial typescript of Jean's diaries that he had banged out on his venerable Remington typewriter. Leila Zenderland and Allan Axelrad read a draft of my manuscript and made suggestions that improved the final work, even if I did not always follow their advice. Bob Middlekauff read a later draft and gave me valuable assistance in the late stages of my project. He has been a wise friend and an astute critic. Sherwood Cummings read the penultimate draft with the eye of a careful editor. Carol Pearson used her exceptional experience and skill to create an outstanding index.

I was also a grateful beneficiary of the editorial skills of Martin Ridge. Martin's nitty-gritty suggestions came at a crucial stage in the writing process. I am indebted to him for this, as well as for his incisive intelligence, unfailing humor, and generosity of spirit. Even his expressions of cantankerous exasperation with my fretting were somehow reassuring. Martin's death on September 22, 2003, has left his friends with a great vacancy, a hollow space that will not be easily filled; he had a rare kindness that he combined with a razor-sharp intellect, an ever youthful curiosity, and a fierce dedication to the craft of writing history. He took unselfish delight in furthering the work of younger scholars and his legacy is reflected in their accomplishments as well as in his own. He will be greatly missed.

Several people shared the names of their agents and editors, which I gratefully acknowledge. These include: Joan Bromberg, Richard and Marilyn Buel, Michael Fellman, Donna Munker, Walter Nugent, and Charles Royster. Other friends and colleagues—Tom Madden, Carol Srole, Sarah Stage, Brian Stryer, Joan Waugh, Sean Wilentz—invited me to speak on my Twain project at seminars, conferences, and university lecture series. They provided an invaluable opportunity to take my findings "on the road." Finally, I had one conversation with Ellen Dwyer years ago about my project that has continued to inspire me. Her admirable scholarship on epilepsy allowed me to resolve some key dynamics in Twain's inner circle.

I wish to thank my colleagues in the American Studies Department at California State University—Allan Axelrad, Jesse Battan, Leila Zenderland (again); also Wayne Hobson, John Ibson, Michael Steiner, Pamela Steinle, Terry Snyder, and Scott Tang—for valuing my work and for making research and writing an integral part of our collective endeavor. Students who enrolled in my Mark Twain seminar shared their insight and enthusiasm for Twain's work as well as their disillusionment and frustration with some of his life choices. I have also been the grateful beneficiary of the questions, advice, and encouragement of Douglas Temple, a member of the staff at Fullerton. Even his daily trivia question, which I hardly ever got right, has cheered me on my way.

Many other friends provided encouragement through their questions, enthusiastic observations, and cheerful assumption that the book was going to be worth reading. These include: Norma Almquist, Lanny Amigo, Austin Briggs, Sharon Calhoun, Barbara Donagan, Mary Felstiner, Debbie Girkin, Pat Haley, Bob Hine, Colleen Jaurretche, Barry Menikoff, Lois Nettleship, Jean Nichols, Judy Raftery, Bunny Serlin, Geoff Shrager, and Lucy Steiner. Their encouragement and empathy has been a great boon.

Pat and Jim McPherson took me on a road trip to visit Hartford, Connecticut, to tour the house where Twain lived in his prime. We also went to Elmira, New York, Twain's summer home for twenty years. Making a pilgrimage to his gravesite in Elmira, where his entire family is buried, was a moving experience, and visiting these landmarks with the McPhersons was a highlight of my work on Twain.

"To write is to sit in judgment on oneself," a wise author once remarked. One is lucky to have family and friends who are sympathetic and who temper their expectations with affection. My parents, Jim and Lily Lystra, are among the most unselfish and generous-minded people I have ever met. Their unfailing support has been sustaining. My siblings, Torrey Lystra and Gaylen Mollet, and their spouses, Carol Lystra and Ralph Mollet, have always taken an open and nonjudgmental approach to my work.

Finally, I wish to express my appreciation for all the scholars in the field of Mark Twain criticism, biography, and textual editing whose work I have drawn on and in many cases cited in my notes. I know very few of you personally, and I sometimes disagree with your interpretations of Twain's late years, but your labors on Twain have made my biography possible, and I salute you.

A NOTE ON NAMES

TELLING A BIOGRAPHICAL STORY in an essentially novelistic style—and, even more, writing about the private life of a man who is universally known by his pseudonym but whose intimates would never have called him by it—presents a problem: What form of the "characters'" names should one use? Because the story is a family one, in which many of the actors share the same surname and all would have addressed each other by given names or other family pet names and designations, I have chosen to refer to the women of the Clemens household by their first names, including Katy Leary. Isabel Lyon, who was almost invariably referred to as "Miss Lyon," is generally designated as "Lyon." I use "Mark Twain" to refer to the writer and public persona when appropriate, but for the man himself I use "Sam" or "Clemens," according to the context.

CHAPTER 1

Mark Twain — and Sam's Women

IN 1895 MARK TWAIN was one of the most famous men in the world. At the age of sixty, he was celebrated as the author of *The Adventures of Tom Sawyer, The Adventures of Huckleberry Finn,* and other novels for adults and children as well as a great number of short stories and non-fiction sketches and articles. He was perhaps equally renowned as a lecturer, a second—and sometimes more lucrative—career he had pursued in parallel with his writing since the 1860s. Twain held strong views on many issues, from anti-imperialism to copyrights for authors. His opinion was constantly in demand, and he never hesitated to offer it. He knew a long list of celebrities, including Bram Stoker, Bret Harte, Ulysses S. Grant, P. T. Barnum, Harriet Beecher Stowe, and James Whistler. He had also met, among many others, Robert Browning, Lewis Carroll, Charles Darwin, Rudyard Kipling, William James, Grover Cleveland, Winston Churchill, and the Prince of Wales.

In both his lectures and his written works, Twain seemed to capture a quintessentially American spirit, a mix of sly humor, cynicism, affirmation, and plain speech that felt both unique and universal and that captivated audiences in the United States and Europe. With his extroverted nature and his evident enjoyment of life and his own performance in it, he managed to combine pessimism and optimism in such a way that people often missed—or could choose to miss—the depth of the bite beneath the laughter. This, one suspects, just made Mark Twain that much more popular. Shrewd enough to observe that "My books are water; those of the great geniuses are wine. Everybody drinks water,"

Samuel Langhorne Clemens, the man behind the pseudonym, clearly relished his celebrity.[1]

In 1895 Sam Clemens had reason to feel blessed in his private life as well. Although the previous five years had been clouded by financial difficulties and ultimate bankruptcy, brought on by Sam's penchant for extravagant living and bad investments, his family had never been less than comfortable. Beyond material wealth, he could look back on twenty-five years of married life confident in the love of his wife and three daughters. Oddly enough, for all Mark Twain's identification with a rough-and-tumble image of America, Sam Clemens had lived most of those years in an ornately Victorian New England home, sharing domestic contentment with a household of women who helped him with his work, catered to his needs, and were a continual source of amusement and happiness.

———

Samuel Clemens and Olivia Langdon were married on February 2, 1870, at the Langdon family home in Elmira, New York. The couple settled briefly in Buffalo and in 1871 moved to Hartford, Connecticut, where they lived for the next twenty years. With her dark brown hair, regular features, and angelic smile, Livy, as she was affectionately called by her friends and family, was the picture of an ideal Victorian wife. By almost all accounts, Sam and Livy had an exceptionally successful marriage. "How I do want you at home Darling," she wrote to him in their second year of marriage. "I am so thankful that I do want you—you are a dear little man—I am grateful that my heart is so filled with love for you." "Lecturing is hateful," Sam acknowledged during that absence, "but it *must* come to an end yet, & *then* I'll see my darling, whom I love, love, *love*."[2]

Olivia Clemens has often been cast as a Victorian prude, ever vigilant to quash the frankness of ideas and language Mark Twain was famous for. This interpretation originated with Van Wyck Brooks's publication in 1920 of *The Ordeal of Mark Twain,* in which he claimed that from the moment Sam married Livy, his artistic integrity was compromised: "[I]n his case the matrimonial vow had been almost literally reversed and it was he who had promised not only to love and honour but also to obey." According to Brooks—and the many critics who followed in his footsteps—Livy became Twain's chief censor, tragically squelching the virile westerner with her "infantile" taste and Victorian conformity. Yet, interestingly, the private Sam Clemens was much more emotionally reserved than his wife. She expressed her affection for him in kisses, caresses, and verbal endearments, which he freely admitted were "always an astonishment to me." His daughter Clara remembered that her father was quite bashful about expressing physical affection. He would stand near his wife and surreptitiously take her hand, squeezing it devotedly, yet appear embarrassed if his children noticed.[3]

Although she had a weak heart and was often ill, Livy was a woman with a cheerful disposition and an unusual endowment of both common sense and sympathy. Sam's closest literary friend, the novelist and critic William Dean Howells, described her as the loveliest person he ever knew: "the gentlest, the kindest, without a touch of weakness; she united wonderful tact with wonderful truth." She had an extraordinary capacity for compassion without seeming patronizing or self-aggrandizing. "[I]f there was any forlorn and helpless creature in the room Mrs. Clemens was somehow promptly at his side or hers," Howells observed; "she was always seeking occasion of kindness to those in her household or out of it." He also portrayed her as a woman so generous that she could even embrace rebellion against the social conventions she had once approved. Sam persuaded her to give up formal Christianity, a remarkable step for a well-bred lady of the time. And though she protested, Livy readily forgave her husband's swearing. According to Katy Leary, who became the Clemenses' housekeeper in Hartford, Twain was free in the privacy of his home "to say anything and everything that he wanted to—no matter what it was." (In exactly what terms he could say it might sometimes be under dispute.) Livy decided when they were first married "that his home was going to be a place where he could say and do what he wanted." She was committed to other people's rights, Katy observed, "even if they was her husband's."[4]

Missing from some accounts of Livy's nature is the quality that, according to Howells, allowed her to appreciate the "self-lawed" genius of her husband: a sense of humor. One morning Sam was in the bathroom, where he usually did not get through a shave without a string of profanity. Taking the necessary precautions, he had shut the door to allow for his usual expressions of annoyance. The shave went smoothly, but after he put on his shirt, he realized that a button was missing. He tossed the shirt out the window and put on another, and then another, only to discover that buttons were missing on all three shirts. "I augmented my language to meet the emergency," he reported, "and let myself go like a cavalry charge." It was then that he realized the door was open. Livy had been lying in bed the entire time. As he crept into the room and met her gaze, she responded by imitating his "latest bathroom remark," but with a "velvety" expression that he said was "absurdly weak and unsuited to the great language."

"There, now you know how it sounds," she exclaimed.

"Oh Livy, if it sounds like *that* I will never do it again!"

"Then she had to laugh herself," Twain remembered. "Both of us broke into convulsions, and went on laughing until we were physically exhausted and spiritually reconciled."[5]

Livy did have a strong sense of what was proper—and Sam thoroughly enjoyed tempting his wife to laugh at something that shocked her at the same time. One day, after they had been married many years, a reporter arrived for a scheduled interview. Livy went in to announce the reporter and found her husband in bed, where he often worked. "Youth," she addressed him by her favorite nickname, "don't you think it will be a little embarrassing for him to find you in bed?"

"Why, if you think so, Livy," came the deliberate reply, "we could have the other bed made up for him."[6]

Because of her reputation for cultivated prissiness, Livy unfairly shoulders blame as censor of her husband's writing, but Mark Twain was himself deeply committed to guarding his public persona well before he met Livy. To this end he had enlisted Mrs. Mary Mason Fairbanks, a matron he met on the journey that he transformed into his first best-seller, *Innocents Abroad,* to educate him in matters of taste and refinement. "I acknowledge—I acknowledge—that I *can* be most laceratingly 'funny without being vulgar,'" Twain wrote in 1868 to Fairbanks, whom he almost always addressed as "Mother." His toast to "Woman" at a grand banquet the night before was "frigidly proper in language & sentiment," he reported. "*Now* haven't I nobly vindicated myself & shed honor upon my teacher & done credit to her teachings?" he asked her only half in jest. Mother Fairbanks had convinced him to make some alterations to *Innocents Abroad,* including the deletion of "offensive" language, such as slang terms and colloquialisms that might be considered vulgar, as well as "improper" allusions, such as seeing underneath ladies' skirts on the ascent of Vesuvius. Although her influence began to wane after her star pupil was married, she continued to lobby for his respectability. "I'm just crazy to have him write one book of polite literature," Fairbanks admonished Livy in 1872. "I want him to show the world more of his rich, brilliant imaginings."[7]

Twain regularly turned as well to William Dean Howells—himself a popular writer, a perceptive critic, and the respected editor of the *Atlantic Monthly*—for editorial advice. Howells was no less vigilant than Livy or Mrs. Fairbanks when it came to certain public proprieties, and Twain always accepted his editorial changes without a murmur. "His proof-sheets came back each a veritable 'mush of concession,'" Howells noted approvingly. "If you wanted a thing changed, very good, he changed it; if you suggested that a word or a sentence or a paragraph had better be struck out, very good, he struck it out." Howells routinely struck out the profanity in Twain's magazine pieces, observing that "Now and then he would try a little stronger language than *The Atlantic* had stomach for."[8]

Twain also tricked his unsuspecting wife in her role as his editor. At Quarry Farm, the family's summer home in Elmira, New York, Livy would sit on the porch and read her husband's manuscripts aloud to the children, with pencil at the ready. "[T]he children would keep an alert and suspicious eye upon her right along," Twain chuckled, "for the belief was well grounded in them that whenever she came across a particularly satisfactory passage she would strike it out." He would often deliberately create offensive passages or what he called "felicitously atrocious" remarks to entertain himself and the children, who would vigorously protest their deletion. "Now and then we gained the victory and there was much rejoicing," he confessed. "Then I privately struck the passage out myself."[9]

———

Livy was known as a grand hostess. The Clemenses had built a large and luxuriously appointed home in Hartford, and they entertained regularly with lavish dinner parties for twelve people or more. "They used to have the most beautiful dinners that I ever heard of before or since," Katy remembered. "To them dinners we always had a fillet of beef and ducks as a rule, canvasback, they called them." She also recalled serving sherry, claret, and champagne, plus ice cream shaped like cherubs, flowers, and little angels. Among those invited were Hartford neighbors such as Charles and Susan Warner and family friends such as the Howellses and Joseph and Harmony Twichell. (Twichell was the minister who had married Sam and Livy.) Many luminaries were invited, such as the famous actors Henry Irving and William Gillette; the renowned explorer Sir Henry Stanley and his wife, Dorothy Tenant, a well-known English artist; and George Robinson, the governor of Connecticut, and his wife. Sam would ask his guests to tell stories and always delighted in satisfying their entreaties for tales from Mark Twain.[10]

In an episode that reveals much about the household, Katy Leary recalled that Livy's sense of propriety was sometimes tested at these dinner parties by the butler, George. He regularly laughed out loud at all the stories and jokes that were told during dinner. In fact, he was always the first to roar at a funny line. George had other faults as well, among them his penchant for stretching the facts. Livy's patience finally snapped one day, and she fired him. The next morning she came down to breakfast to discover that the butler was at his usual post at the breakfast table.

"Why, George, I discharged you yesterday, didn't I?" she asked with some surprise.

"Well, yes, Mrs. Clemens," George replied, "you did, but I know you really couldn't get along without me, so I thought I'd just stay right on anyway."

For a more inflexible, humorless woman that would have been the last straw, but George continued to work for the family and left them after eighteen years of service only when they closed the Hartford house.[11]

———

Sam and Livy had four children. The short life of their only son, Langdon Clemens, was one of the few shadows across their early years together. Langdon was born prematurely on November 25, 1870, and was always sickly. In June 1872, a little more than two months after the birth of his sister Olivia Susan on March 19, he died of diphtheria. Sam always believed that he was to blame for Langdon's death. "I have always felt shame for that treacherous morning's work," he confessed thirty-three years later in his published autobiography, "and have not allowed myself to think of it when I could help it." He had let the covers slip off the child during a long drive in an open carriage in April. A bad chill did not kill his son, though Sam's feelings of guilt may have intensified his grief. Both parents found some antidote for loss in their new baby, and she soon became, in Sam's words, "our wonder and our worship."[12]

The Clemenses' second daughter, Clara Langdon, was born on June 8, 1874. While Susy was a malleable child, Sam affectionately called Clara "the sassmill," noting her irreverence and lack of deference to authority. Six years later, a third daughter was born, on July 26, 1880. Although she was named after her paternal grandmother, Jane Lampton, this was a strictly ceremonial legacy, for the youngest child was called Jean from birth. Sam joked that she had replaced her mother as "No. 1" in the stock-quotations on her sisters' "Affection Board." "I have dropped from No. 4, and am become No. 5," he quipped. "Some time ago it used to be nip and tuck between me and the cats, but after the cats 'developed' I didn't stand any more show."[13]

As in all things domestic, Sam left the training of his children to their mother and was ruled by Livy's judgment. She was a judicious parent who believed that the purpose of punishment was to warn against future transgressions. Sam remembered vividly Susy hitting her sister Clara with a shovel or stick. According to her mother's guidelines, Susy was allowed to impose a penalty on herself. As Sam recalled later with a pang, she chose, after much deep thinking, to miss her first hayride because, she reasoned, "other things might not make me remember not to do it again."[14]

Thus Livy set the tone for the warm and orderly existence the family enjoyed. In Hartford Livy and Sam breakfasted late, around eleven, according to Katy, except for the few years when, rather than hiring tutors, Livy acted as her children's governess. After breakfast, Sam retired to the billiard room where he worked or played his favorite game until dinner. (These were the years in which he wrote and published *Tom Sawyer, The Prince and the Pauper, Life on the Mississippi, Huckleberry Finn,* and *A Connecticut Yankee in King Arthur's Court,* as well as many articles, sketches, and short stories.) He never took lunch but would sometimes sit with his children and chat or read aloud during their meal. Livy attended to her domestic duties or the children's lessons in the family schoolroom. The whole family gathered for dinner around six o'clock. "Mrs. Clemens always put on a lovely dress for dinner," Katy remembered, "even when we was alone, and they always had music during dinner." George, the butler, would crank up the music box they had brought back from Switzerland, and the family would listen to its repertoire of nine pieces while they ate. In the library after dinner, there might be charades or Sam would read aloud to his brood— perhaps Browning or Dickens or Mark Twain. The children were sent to bed around nine. Then Livy would take tea and Sam a hot toddy while they talked until their day ended around ten. Entering their bedroom, Livy often found a pile of manuscript pages on her nightstand. It was her husband's habit to deposit his day's work by the side of her bed, and she always read and edited his drafts before she went to sleep.[15]

Much the same routine was followed during the summers at Quarry Farm in Elmira. At about ten o'clock, Twain went to his study, an octagonal room shaped like a Mississippi riverboat pilothouse, which was completely separated from the main house by a winding path and about twenty stone steps. There he worked contentedly in isolation until five, seldom taking any break in the middle of the day. After dinner, which was routinely on the table by six o'clock, he would read his daily output aloud to the whole family. Or he might play chess or cards with Theodore Crane, his brother-in-law, while Livy read other authors aloud to the group. Sam, keeping one ear cocked, would often throw out humorous comments on the author's style, especially Jane Austen, whom he always enjoyed criticizing.[16]

Sam seemed to take endless delight in his young daughters, Susy in particular. In his published autobiography, he gave most of the attention to Susy, describing her as a happy child, who was given to searching out "the hidden meanings of the deep things that make the puzzle and pathos of human existence." "Susy was a dreamer, a thinker, a poet and philosopher," he wrote, and he admired these qualities—along with her temper, claiming that once she learned to govern it, her character was stronger and healthier for its presence. By contrast, Clara was practical, plucky, and physically brave. Susy remembered how three-year-old Clara stood stoically while her mother dug a sliver out of her hand with a needle. "Why Clara! You are a brave little thing!" Livy exclaimed. Clara responded, "No bodys braver but God!" Her courage stood her in good stead, for Clara seemed accident prone, surviving a crib fire, a toboggan crash at eleven, in which she seriously injured her ankle, and other misadventures. And unlike Susy, who took punishment to heart, Clara often found a way to turn discipline into fun. One day Livy, frustrated by previous efforts at reform, decided to lock Clara in a closet for a period of solitary confinement. After waiting half an hour in worried and anxious anticipation, the mother finally flung open the closet door to set the prisoner free, only to discover that Clara had built a fairy cavern and requested permission to spend the rest of the day in solitary.[17]

A friend once remarked that "Susy was made of mind, and Clara of matter." After Motley, one of their kittens, died, another family friend predicted that Susy would be "wondering if this was the *end* of Motley and had his life been worth while," whereas Clara would be interested in making certain that Motley received a "creditable funeral."[18]

The girls were born into a household that found constant ways to amuse itself. Impromptu charades were almost a nightly passion after Susy and Clara reached the age of five or six. The two sisters acquired stagecraft and acting skills from this experience, which they drew on later in life. They also took music and dancing lessons and learned to embroider. According to Clara, she was especially enthusiastic about piano and Susy was interested in voice. Katy recalled that Clara wanted to become a piano teacher and gave her and George a few practice lessons. Susy wrote plays at ten and twelve that she and the other children would perform. They especially enjoyed playing Elizabeth and Mary, Queen of Scots, with their mother's gowns. "It was grand to see the queens stride back and forth," their father wrote, "and reproach each other in three-or-four syllable words dripping with blood."[19]

Six years younger than her nearest sibling, Jean was unable to participate fully in many of their escapades. But her sisters kindly included her in their homegrown plays, in which Jean had a single function: to sit silently at a tiny table and draft death warrants for the other girls to sign. "Familiarity with daily death and carnage had hardened her to crime and suffering in all their forms," her father reminisced, "and they were no longer able to hasten her pulse by a beat." When there was a lull, the three-year-old would fall asleep. Still, Sam cautioned, "It was a really important office, for few entered those plays and got out of them alive."[20]

The Clemens children shared a love of animals, and over the years they had an assortment of pets, including cats, dogs, and donkeys. On one occasion Sam decided to show his girls how to ride Kadichan, the pet donkey they had at Quarry Farm. One sister always had to walk ahead with a bag of crackers to coax the recalcitrant animal to move at all, and the girls would argue over whose turn it was to ride or to walk with the crackers. One day Sam grew tired of listening to their bickering and decided to intervene. "I'll make that creature do his work," he said with a determined look. He mounted the pet donkey—and soon found himself dumped in the long grass in front of the quadruped. "The whole transaction lasted only a second," Clara remembered many years later, concluding gleefully: "A DONKEY had gotten the best of our father!"[21]

Jean's passion for animals led her to become an accomplished horsewoman. The most athletic of the girls, she was attracted to a variety of other vigorous outdoor activities and sports as well. In this, she resembled Clara in her practicality more than Susy in her intellectuality. Indeed, one of the most memorable stories about her childhood revolves around her lack of interest in reading. When she was nine, Jean was invited to a dinner party at the Murray Hill Hotel in New York. The child actress Elsie Leslie, also nine, was one of the guests. Jean was awed by the ease with which Elsie participated in the grown-up conversation. By contrast, she was silent and had nothing to contribute. But finally "Tom Sawyer" was mentioned and Jean spoke up, deliberately grabbing the conversational spotlight.

"I know who wrote that book—Harriet Beecher Stowe!"[22]

Sam saw his youngest daughter's character "from the beginning" as "orderly, steady, diligent, persistent." He also noted that she had a facility for languages. (All the children were tutored in French and German, and their German nurse, Rosa, initiated them into her language in the nursery.) He might have added headstrong to his portrait of Jean's character, for he recalled that she had once precipitated a vigorous argument over the merits of returning home or continuing to follow some cows to their pasture. After demolishing her arguments for pursuing the cows, the satisfied father expected compliance. Instead, she barked sharply in German: "Wir werden nichts mehr darüber sprechen! [We will say nothing more about it!]" Charmed by her defiance, Sam continued their expedition. Jean was then four years old.[23]

Sam was not the only keen observer of family life. True to her intellectual bent, Susy remarked, after watching her three-year-old sister bring a cat to their father, "Jean has found out already that mamma loves morals and papa loves cats." Sam chuckled appreciatively in retrospect, calling it "another of Susy's remorselessly sound verdicts." At thirteen, Susy further won the admiration of her father when, entirely on her own initiative, she embarked on a project to write his biography. "I remember that time with a deep pleasure," he mused. The value of Susy's biography, in his eyes, was her unselfconscious honesty. His eldest daughter, as he wryly acknowledged, did not get "overheated" when she was evaluating his life. "He...gradually picked up enough education," Sam quoted Susy appreciatively, "to enable him to do about as well as those who were more studious in early life." Susy's frank appraisals made her compliments all the more endearing. As an adolescent, she admired her father's looks (with, she said, the exception of his teeth), his humor, and his goodness. She was especially impressed by his ability to tell impromptu stories on demand. But as Sam remarked, she used no "sandpaper" on him. "He has the mind of an author exactly," Susy wrote, "some of the simplest things he cant understand."[24]

While neither parent deliberately set out to favor Susy, both were especially close to her. When she was a teenager, Susy and her father used to promenade daily in the library of their Hartford house. With arms around each other's waists, they would pace up and down the room discussing politics, philosophy, or family intimacies. Susy and her mother were also close. Twain wrote that they were "passionate adorers of each other," which also aptly described his relationship to their eldest child.[25]

———

During her years at the Hartford house, Katy Leary came as near as could be to being part of the Clemens family. "Green as a monkey" she recalled herself at age twenty-four, when, not long after Jean's birth, she left her Irish immigrant family in Elmira to keep house for Sam and Livy. Indeed, Katy's mother was reluctant to let her go and only agreed after an interview with Mrs. Clemens, who volunteered to act *in loco parentis*.[26] Livy, who was sixteen years older than Katy, became a great influence in the housekeeper's life.

In a memoir dictated in 1925, Katy looked back on the years in Hartford with great satisfaction and did not appear to think of her faithful service as self-sacrificing. She loved the Clemens family as if they were "my own people," her telling phrase. "[T]hey was just as considerate of me as they was of one of themselves," she affirmed. Hospitalized once with pneumonia, Katy was showered with attention and concern by her "family." "[D]o you *work* for this family, or are you *adopted* by them or what? I can't make it out!" one of the nuns asked her during her hospital stay. To Katy, such observations were proof of the special intimacy she shared with her employers. She gave up the prospect of a husband and a house of her own to stay with them. "So you can see how much I loved the family," she later explained. Though she loved them all, Mrs. Clemens was first in her affections. "I told her everything—all my secrets," she remembered, adding slyly, "though I didn't have many to tell then."[27]

Katy was hired as Mrs. Clemens's maid, but her service soon knew no limits. Sam would often wake in the middle of the night with an idea and race to the billiard room to write. Worried that he would catch cold, Katy, who had been a seamstress before Livy hired her, introduced Sam to long nightshirts, which she made in all sorts of colors and fabrics, including flannel, always trimmed down the front in red or blue or pink. "You see, he was comfortable all the rest of his life with those nightshirts," the spinster chuckled, "so I don't think I have lived in vain. I've made *one* man comfortable, anyway."[28]

She performed other personal tasks for the comfort of her employers. Afraid of going bald, Sam felt that a scalp massage every day would keep his hair from falling out. He would ring at a certain time each morning, and Katy would massage his head. They kept up this practice until he died. She also took great pleasure in brushing out Livy's long brown hair at bedtime—and in the intimate conversations they had then. "She would teach you a lot, just from being herself, you know," Katy reflected in later years.[29] Livy did not tutor merely by example; she gave her maid books to read and discussed ideas with her in their nightly talks.

Livy directed her household staff, which numbered as many as seven, with gentle firmness—and, as in the case of the butler who refused to be fired, with some generosity. Sam practiced a contrasting style. After Katy took over the job of dusting in the billiard room, where Twain wrote, they skirmished regularly over his manuscripts. Whenever something could not be found, Twain would call her to task. She recalled a typical confrontation.

"Katy, what did you do with all that manuscript I left on the table last night?"

"I didn't do anything with it; I didn't touch it," she replied. "Isn't it where you left it?"

"No," he answered. "No, I suppose it's burned! *You* burned it this morning! That's what you've done—burned it!"

"Well," she said, "I'll look on the table. It wasn't there this morning when I come up. There was no manuscript on that table—only them few letters."

"Well, it was on that table when I left last night, Katy!" Clemens insisted. "Well, you burned it—I know you did! It's gone, anyway. It's lost—burned!! That's the end of it!"

Around dinnertime, while Katy was fixing Livy's hair, Sam came out of the bathroom and gave her a wink that she could see in the dressing table mirror. "I found it, Katy," he said sheepishly.

"What's that? What is it?" Livy asked in confusion. Sam muttered that it was nothing; Katy was not so easily placated.

"Oh, Mrs. Clemens!" she sighed, "if it wasn't for *you,* I'd be on my way back to Elmira to-night, because he accused me of taking his manuscript, burning his manuscript and destroying it! I told him I knew he'd find it—and he has. He's all the time scolding me for burning his manuscript."[30]

Livy chided her husband, but Katy and Mr. Clemens had to settle this quarrel themselves. They had a "good many tough fights," in her words, before Twain called a permanent truce. She knew she had finally won his trust when he chose to ship the precious manuscript of *Tom Sawyer* to her when he mailed it to Hartford from the summer home at Quarry Farm. She proudly remembered his words: "I knew if I sent it to *you* it would be all right!"[31]

After the duo stopped fighting about Twain's manuscripts, they regularly argued about religion. Never intimidated, Katy held her own, if she did not actually best him on this score, and steadfastly refused to accept that Mark Twain was an atheist. "I know you do believe the way I do: you believe there *is* a God, no matter what you say! I know it," she maintained. And when Father Hardy, her parish priest, characterized *A Connecticut Yankee in King Arthur's Court* as an atheistic, anti-Catholic book, Katy bristled. "Why, he doesn't say any more about the Catholic religion than any other," she informed Father Hardy, who admitted that he had not read the "awful" book. "When he wrote that book he was trying to put down 'higher authority,' so one man was just about as good as another," Katy lectured the priest. "He said the low man (as he called it) was just as good in the sight of God as the King."[32]

Katy's confidence in her literary opinion was based on an unimpeachable source, her Mrs. Clemens, but she shared her employer's disdain for the artificial hierarchy of society. "He used to think all men was equal if their hearts was right," she reported approvingly, "and he said so in one of his books." Reminiscing about time spent in Europe and the ranking of servants there, she recalled, "Upper housemaid, under housemaid; upper chambermaid, under chambermaid; upper and under everything! It made me laugh, for I didn't take my position very lofty, you know."[33]

Sam also often made her laugh. He would sometimes have fun at her expense but she was not insulted. "I'd say," she remembered, " 'Well, I don't know how to say it right'—then he'd say, 'Why, *of course* you don't, Katy!' And then he'd tell me *how* to say it and explain everything to me—all the little things I didn't understand." Katy never felt like an inferior, even when she was the butt of one of her boss's jokes. Fun-loving and quick-witted, she appreciated Twain's humor for several reasons. He always turned "everything into a joke," she said, but "he never played bad jokes on people, and never disappointed them, either." He hated meanness.[34]

Katy was as shrewd and tough-minded as she was sentimental. Although she might say in a moment of supreme nostalgia that all of her life with the Clemens family was happiness, her memories of the pain and grief she eventually shared with each of them were just as powerful. "Sometimes it all seems just like an accident, things come out so queer," she mused, "—the sad and the funny get all mixed up and it's hard to tell what it's all about anyway."[35] Regardless of "what it's all about," Katy was "always there," as Sam once remarked—with help and comfort and a much-needed dose of common sense.

———

Sometime around 1890 another woman entered Sam's life. Isabel Van Kleek Lyon was the daughter of Charles H. Lyon Sr., a college professor at Columbia who wrote Greek and Latin textbooks. Little is known about Lyon's early life. She had a sister and a brother and was particularly close to the brother, who died of an overdose of morphine after making a disastrous marriage and falling into gambling and heavy drinking. She believed that he had committed suicide.[36] After her father's death in the late 1880s, Lyon—unmarried and without other family or an independent income to rely on—was forced to support herself and her mother by her wits and charm, which appear to have been considerable. Few occupations were open to unmarried middle-class women in the Gilded Age. Lyon knew no shorthand, could not type, and had acquired no specialized training. Little wonder then that she became a governess to the children of privilege, for what she did possess were the diction and manners of her employers and the ability to offer ingratiating service to those who, under other circumstances, might have been peers.

Lyon met Mark Twain when she delivered a package to the Clemenses at the behest of their friends and neighbors, the Whitmores, who employed her at the time. At a party not long after that, the Whitmores invited the governess to join their guests for whist, a fashionable card game of the time. Attractive, vivacious, and shrewd, she stole the show in Hartford that night. Partnered with Clemens, who may have maneuvered his pairing with the appealing governess, Miss Lyon created a buzz at her table with a daring ploy that threatened to unhinge the more conservative players. She trumped Clemens's ace to get into the game and proceeded to win every trick. When at the end of the evening, he was invited to return, he replied: "I'll come if I can play with the little governess."[37] No one then could have guessed the role "the little governess" was to play in his life.

———

By 1891, life in Hartford was drawing to a close. Sam had been finding writing more difficult and less remunerative. The Clemenses' extravagant lifestyle and Sam's misguided efforts to make himself a "businessman" had the family at the edge of financial disaster. Among other failed investments he had poured hundreds of thousands of dollars into the prototype of an automatic typesetting machine that would ultimately prove unworkable.[38] Even before the financial crisis, however, the family's life had begun to change as Susy and Clara grew from girls to young women.

In the fall of 1890, Susy had left home to attend Bryn Mawr College. At first she was homesick, but in time she adjusted to life away from her papa. In February 1891 Sam wrote his friend Howells that she was beginning to love Bryn Mawr—"to my regret." Fellow students admired her voice, and Susy was given the leading role of Phyllis in the student production of *Iolanthe*. Perhaps this was the origin of her ambition to become an opera singer. She also decided to call herself Olivia, an indication she was seeking an identity that would separate her from childhood. Moreover, she made at least one friend, Louise Brownell, whom she deeply loved.[39]

That Susy ultimately cut short her first year at Bryn Mawr is puzzling in light of what would seem to be her growing independence. Grace King, a Southern writer who was a friend of the family, claimed that "a very short time proved the utter impossibility of hard study for Susy." But this seems an odd reaction for the one daughter who everyone agreed was a "born" intellectual. Perhaps Susy was afraid of her new emotional freedom, including her attachment to Louise.[40] It is also possible that she left college without completing her first year to help ease the family's financial crisis and was simply too proud ever to admit it.

Sam's solution to their financial crisis was to embark on an extended tour of Europe to reduce the family's expenses. In early June 1891 he and Livy closed up their Hartford home and set sail with their three daughters. The faithful Katy traveled with them for the first three months but was sent home that winter as an economy measure. The family would not return until 1895—and never to the house in Hartford. Initially, both Sam and Livy sought relief for their rheumatism at the fashionable Aix-les-Bains baths and then at Marienbad. They were accompanied by Jean and Livy's sister, Susan Crane, while Susy and Clara briefly attended a boarding school in Geneva.[41]

During those first months abroad, while Livy was in Berlin to scout rooms for the family, Sam invited Clara to take her mother's place at a military ball in Marienbad. She was thrilled to attend her first formal dance. The next day one of the officers, who had asked her to dance, called at breakfast. At lunchtime, he was seated at the next table, and he managed that arrangement at dinner also. Sam was livid and decided to keep Clara away from the dining room altogether. Katy was under orders to bring meals to Clara in her room. When Livy returned, Sam poured forth his tale of parental woe, only to be greeted by peals of laughter from his wife, who found her husband's conventions ludicrous. "The donkey and I had scored one," Clara gloated, harking back to the pet who had likewise showed up her self-righteous father.[42]

The family spent the winter in Berlin, where Sam was in bed for a month with terrible bronchitis and severe rheumatism in his writing hand. Seeking a better climate for their health in the spring, they went to the French Riviera, Rome, Venice, Florence, and the baths at Bad Nauheim. By the end of the summer of 1892, however, Livy was much worse, suffering severe headaches and a swollen face and neck. After they returned to Florence that fall, she began to improve, and Sam found the peace and serenity to write *Tom Sawyer Abroad* and some short travel sketches for magazines. He also began work on two other novels: a draft of *Puddn'head Wilson*, which was published in 1894, a work that slyly subverts notions of race in America and was a commercial failure; and twenty-two chapters of *Personal Recollections of Joan of Arc,* which appeared in 1896 and which he considered his best work (an opinion uniformly dismissed by modern critics).[43]

In Europe with her family, Susy was restless and unhappy, writing her friend Louise in June 1893 from Florence that she sometimes lacked enough "raison d'être." "She was ever seeking something, craving something, she could not find," Grace King observed; "and meeting only disappointment." Like many ambitious women of privilege in the late nineteenth century, despite the benefits of money and position, including education and travel, Susy's future opportunities were primarily defined by marriage and family. She carried the additional burden of being the child of a celebrity. She told King about a court ball in Berlin where she had received attention only as the daughter of Mark Twain. She was a young, blond beauty who had donned a fashionable silk dress for the occasion, and then failed to attract admirers on her own terms. Little wonder that she was bitterly disappointed.[44]

Susy had a happier time in England, where she visited with her friend Louise, and she spent a gratifying month in Paris in 1893, where she consulted a famous voice teacher, Madame Marchesi. She reported that Marchesi said "some pleasant and unexpected things about my voice but insisted she could do nothing with me in my present state of health." Her singing teacher recommended a year of farm life and outdoor activities to improve her overall physical condition, which Susy planned to undertake when she returned to the United States. (According to Katy, Marchesi's advice to Susy was intended to "get her chest stronger, because if she could do that, she'd have more volume to sing with.")[45]

Clara went to school in Berlin and also studied piano for two winters. Though accompanied by a governess, she delighted in the balls, receptions, and dinners she attended without her parents' supervision. Sam characteristically chided her in one letter for being the only female in a room full of attentive German officers.[46]

As for Jean, she found herself uprooted at age eleven from the stable home she had known all her life, to be dragged around the world for three years by a mother and father full of anxiety about money and uncertain of their own future. Her principal identity during these years was as a passionate defender of animals against abuse. She joined humane societies in every country they visited and was especially diligent in guarding against the mistreatment of horses. Clara too took up the cause, and she and Jean acquired blue cards from the Society for the Prevention of Cruelty to Animals soon after they arrived in Paris in 1893. The cards entitled them to stop the beating of any horse on a public street. One day Sam was on his way to a social function, and his daughters carded their driver for beating his horse. Finally persuaded to lay down his whip, the driver could barely get the horse to walk. "Girls, you can drive the other two blocks alone," their exasperated father shouted as he jumped out of the carriage. "I wouldn't go to hell at such a pace."[47]

During his time in Europe, Sam made many crossings to New York, sometimes for extended stays, while his family remained behind. While in America, he met frequently with Henry Huttleston Rogers, a vice president with Standard Oil and a Mark Twain fan who became his financial adviser and the architect of his future solvency. In August of 1893, Sam sailed for New York with Clara, who had a persistent cough that, it was hoped, would respond to an ocean voyage.[48] While Clara soon returned to Europe, Sam's stay lasted until April 1894. It was at this time that Rogers advised him to declare voluntary bankruptcy in order to stave off his creditors. In another piece of advice that was to prove invaluable, Rogers had all of Twain's copyrights assigned to Livy, declaring her one of the principal creditors, and thus saved what may have been their most valuable asset.

Livy's reaction to her husband's failure is illuminating. "You say Mr. Rogers has said some caustic and telling things to the creditors," she remarked in the midst of these negotiations, "I should think it was the creditors place to say caustic things to us." Livy combined the moral uplift that was prescribed as a duty of Victorian women with her unique sense of self. "My darling, I cannot have any thing done in my name that I should not approve," she admonished her husband. "I feel that we owe those creditors not only the money but our most sincere apologies that we are not able to pay their bills when they fall due."[49] Neither Mark Twain nor Standard Oil intimidated Mrs. Clemens.

Moreover, she had a keen understanding of her husband. "Do not for one moment [let] your sense of our need of money get advantage of your sense of justice and generosity," she warned. "Dear sweet darling heart!" she cajoled. "You will not throw this aside thinking that I do not understand will you?" In the midst of adversity, however, she did more than hector her husband on ethics. "[I]f failure comes we shall not be cast down and you must not allow yourself to be," she wrote reassuringly from Europe. "You know I love you yourself, much more than anything that you may be able to give me." Given her delicate health, Livy's stamina throughout this crisis was remarkable. With the skill of a ringmaster, she managed to balance her children's needs, her husband's career and celebrity, and the financial rebuilding necessitated by Twain's disastrous investments. She lightened these heavy domestic burdens—and those of her husband—with quiet certainty and affirmation. "Good night," she told him in 1894, "yours in the deepest love of my heart."[50]

CHAPTER 2

Heartbreak

IN MAY 1895, the Clemens family returned to the United States and their summer home in Elmira, New York. There Sam made preparations for an extended lecture tour that he hoped would raise the money needed to clear his bankruptcy. In fact, perhaps partly in response to Livy's scruples, he had undertaken to repay all his debts in full. (Early in the previous year he had estimated that his debt was $160,000, an astounding figure for the period.) Livy and Clara were to travel with him. Taking to heart Madame Marchesi's recommendations about her health, however, Susy chose to remain with Theodore and Susan Langdon Crane, her uncle and aunt, at Quarry Farm. Undoubtedly, she also hoped to see her friend Louise Brownell, who was now back in America working on an advanced degree. Jean was to attend school in Elmira. Katy rejoined the family at Quarry Farm, where she stayed to take care of Jean and Susy.[1]

When the train carrying Sam, Livy, and Clara pulled away from the Elmira station on July 14, 1895, the two remaining sisters waved good-bye to their determined parents.[2] Jean and Susy would make Quarry Farm their home for almost a year. Perched on a hilltop, with an expansive view of the river and distant hills, the farm must have seemed like a safe haven after several years of wandering abroad. Jean in particular enjoyed the rural atmosphere, where she had the freedom to express her athletic self.

———

Mark Twain's lecture tour began in the United States, with stops in twenty-two cities in five weeks. On August 23, Sam, Livy, and Clara set sail from Vancouver, British Columbia, across the Pacific to Australia,

New Zealand, India, and Africa. Clara recalled that people in her father's audiences were capable of "laughter that spread into uproars of mirth." Twain was so skilled that even she and her mother were often "struck afresh with the humor of each performance."[3]

Clara had especially vivid memories of India, where Twain lectured from January to April 1896. She recalled it as a romantic world of elephants, camels, princes, exotic silks, velvets, and jewels, punctuated by mundane, but surprisingly regular brawls at railway stations between private servants and official porters. And she remembered how funny her father looked perched upon an elephant, his uneasy expression framed by gray curls sticking out from under his birch-bark umbrella hat. She loved the gentleness and spirituality of their Indian hosts and admired their self-mastery. So did her father, who, after looking at the men and women kneeling in worship beside the holy waters of the river Ganges, exclaimed: "They spend hours like this while we in America are robbing and murdering."[4]

———

In February the first of two devastating blows that would strike the Clemenses in 1896 changed life forever for Jean and her family. While at school the fifteen-year-old Jean had a major seizure. The diagnosis was epilepsy, a condition in which erratic electrical signals in the brain create a variety of disabling symptoms, including grand mal (tonic-clonic) seizures with loss of consciousness and convulsions of the arms and legs and petit mal, or nonconvulsive, seizures with brief lapses of consciousness. Jean suffered from both. Although today most epilepsy can be controlled by medication, in 1896 there was no effective medical intervention.[5]

There were, however, theories and regimens for treatment. Dr. M. Allen Starr, the New York physician in charge of Jean's care, prescribed a daily dose of 1–1½ teaspoons of bromide, a sedative with a depressive effect on the central nervous system—and the potential to poison in high enough doses. Starr also recommended a restricted diet: meat only once a day, no sweets, generous servings of green vegetables and fruits, plus 1½ quarts of water daily. He urged regular exercise and purgatives to avoid constipation. "There is nothing to do in an attack but to keep her quiet, loosen her dress, put a spoon between her teeth, and cool cloths to her head," Dr. Starr advised Jean's worried aunt. "The attack is not harmful or dangerous," he counseled, "tho' disagreeable to see."[6]

Jean's parents did not rush home to be with her. Perhaps reassured by Aunt Sue or calmed by the counsel of Dr. Starr, they focused on repaying the debt and pushed on with Twain's lecture schedule. What effect this parental choice had on Jean is unclear. In any case, although she probably had several grand mal seizures during the spring, her attacks tapered off by mid-May.[7] The travelers meanwhile enjoyed the charms and endured the rigors of the tour—the latter, according to Clara, included cockroaches, snakes, stifling heat, and unpalatable food. Twain took many notes for another travel book, which was published in 1897 as *Following the Equator.* From India Sam, Livy, and Clara went to South Africa and finally arrived in England in July 1896, where they joyously anticipated that Susy and Jean would soon join them.[8]

––––––

During that time, Susy had begun practicing Mental Science, a less structured version of Christian Science, an interest that had been sparked by a meeting with her old governess, Mary Foote, who was a practitioner and proselytizer of this philosophy. Sam and Livy heartily approved; Katy was unimpressed but held her tongue. Susy had become bored with country life, and after less than half a year she went to New York City for a change of pace. There she stayed with old family friends and sought new friends among other avid practitioners of Mental Science and Spiritualism. Restless or perhaps homesick, she moved on to visit friends in Hartford and then returned to Elmira in the spring. She finally landed in Hartford for the summer, where she stayed with old family friends, the Warners, who were sympathetic to Mental Science. Katy rented a little apartment, and Susy practiced her singing there. When word came that the family on the U.S. side were to set sail for London in a week to rejoin the others, Katy hurried to Elmira to pack up Jean, who was still at the farm. She returned to Hartford only to find that Susy had fallen suddenly and seriously ill. Susy stubbornly insisted that she wanted no doctor, nor any medicine, only treatment by her spiritualist. "No!" replied the level-headed Katy, who thought Susy's spiritualist was a "pirate" and who had enough authority to intervene. "Nobody will treat you but the doctor." She rushed out to get the family doctor, who diagnosed Susy's illness as spinal meningitis.[9]

Katy had already moved Susy into the old Hartford house and was by her side night and day. Susy would take medicine from no one else. She suffered raging fevers, which produced pain and delirium. Pacing the floor and scribbling hallucinatory notes, she imagined her companion was La Malibran, a famous Parisian mezzo-soprano of the early nineteenth century, who had died at twenty-eight after being thrown by a horse.[10]

On August 15, Livy's brother, Charley Langdon, sent a cablegram to the family in Southampton, indicating Susy was very ill but was expected to recover slowly. Livy immediately decided that she and Clara would cross the Atlantic while Sam remained behind to attend to the house and other business in England. At about noon on August 16, 1896, Susy went blind; an hour later she spoke her last word. Another cablegram to Guildford, England, on August 18 informed Sam that "Susy was peacefully released today." Clara and Livy had already set sail, and Sam could only send a heartbroken letter that Livy would not get until after she arrived: "If I were only with you—to be near with my breast and my sheltering arms when the ship lands & Charley's tears reveal all without his speaking. I love you, my darling,—and I wish you could have been spared this unutterable sorrow."[11]

Livy and Clara, anxious and depressed for their entire voyage, arrived in New York on August 22. They were preparing to disembark when the captain asked to see Clara. He handed her a newspaper with the bold headlines: "Mark Twain's Eldest Daughter Dies of Spinal Meningitis." Clara relived the moment: "The world stood still. All sounds, all movements ceased. Susy was dead. How could I tell Mother?"[12] Susy had been twenty-four.

Katy, too, dreaded her first encounter with Livy. "I could hardly bear to look at Mrs. Clemens just at first," she remembered. "It was something awful when she turned to me and held out her hands and said, 'Katy, Susy's gone—Life has killed her!'"

"Oh, Mrs. Clemens, no!" Katy cried. "No, she just died. God wanted her—and so she died."

Katy's religious determinism offered little comfort to the anguished mother in that desolate moment. The balm Livy needed was more intimate. She asked Katy to repeat all the little things that had occurred before Susy died. On the last night, Katy told her, Susy "put her arms around my neck, and rubbed down my face with her two little hot hands, and she laid her cheek against mine, and she whispered 'Mamma, mamma, mamma!'" Livy asked her to repeat that story many times in the early hours of her grief. "I was crying then. I was crying so I couldn't speak; so I just held her hands and she held mine, and I tried to brace her up that way," Katy recalled. "I didn't think Mrs. Clemens could live then. Her heart almost broke in front of our eyes."[13]

———

After Susy's funeral, Livy, Clara, Jean, and Katy sailed for England, where they spent the rest of 1896. Sam took his two surviving daughters for walks by the river or into Regent's Park. But "everywhere," Clara concluded sadly, "we met an atmosphere of world-loneliness." Clara claimed that when she was growing up she never realized her older sister was the favored child. Susy's death may have made that distinction clear at last to her and added a bittersweet dimension to the experience of mourning. "It was a long time before anyone laughed in our household," Clara recalled. Jean, whose life had already been turned inside out by epilepsy and who had watched helplessly as her grief-stricken mother and sister returned to America too late to do anything but bury Susy, was as gloomy as the rest of the family. As a diversion, no doubt, she took lessons in woodcarving, which became a lifelong hobby.[14]

Following a quiet spring in London, Sam settled his family on the shores of Lake Lucerne, amidst the beauties of Switzerland, where they endured the one-year anniversary of Susy's death. This was not an easy summer for the grieving parents, who were forced as well to cope with the downturn in their youngest daughter's health. At some point in the previous year, Livy had taken the opportunity to talk to Dr. Starr. Although the New York specialist said that a complete recovery was improbable, he had offered a slim and tantalizing hope: he believed that if their daughter's convulsions could be staved off for a year, the family might expect a cure.[15]

Jean had been taking a daily dose of bromide since her first grand mal seizure in February 1896, and her attacks had stopped several months before she was reunited with her family. In the summer of 1897, however—three months beyond the doctor's indicator mark for recovery—

Jean suffered two grand mal seizures. These were the first grand mal attacks that either Sam or Livy had witnessed, and it must have been a shock. For fifteen months Jean had been seizure-free, a year had passed since Susy's death, and they had nurtured a hope that illness and despair were behind them. That hope was now crushed.[16]

At the end of September 1897, the family moved to Vienna, where Jean had no convulsions for three months. Clara had persuaded her parents to favor Vienna because she could study with the famed piano teacher Theodore Leschetitkzy. Clara's passion for music was not diminished by her family tragedies. Influenced by the American singer Alice Barbi, her friend, Clara announced she was switching her musical efforts from piano to voice in the summer of 1898. (According to Katy, however, Clara was frustrated at the piano by her small hands.)[17]

Unfortunately, Jean had another grand mal seizure on January 2, 1898. A Viennese specialist increased her bromide to two doses a day, with three to six doses for "extraordinary emergencies." "He warned us to be cautious in the use of this poison," Sam acknowledged, "& we were careful to obey." But the consequence of his advice was devastating for parents and daughter alike. From January 2, 1898, to July 11, 1899, Sam and Livy watched Jean obsessively for any sign of an impending attack. Compelled to treat their adolescent daughter with clinical objectivity, they subjected the poor girl to unceasing scrutiny and themselves to unwavering vigilance. "It was like watching a house that was forever catching fire," Sam reflected, "& promised to burn down if you ever closed an eye." "The signs of coming trouble," possible indicators of petit mal, that they watched for were painfully intimate gestures: a sudden loss of facial expression, "as if a light had been blown out"; the cessation of speech for the briefest of moments, perhaps in midsentence; nervous gestures of fingers and hands, as if their daughter were searching for something they knew she could never find.[18]

But the Clemenses' burden did not end at mere observation. They had to time the intervals between her symptoms and adjust her medication. If her petit mal occurred sporadically, Sam reported that "nothing was done," but "if they came at brief & shortening intervals, & amounted to half a dozen within an hour, an extra bromide-powder was administered." If the shortened intervals continued, they added more doses of the deadly poison—up to five on two occasions and the absolute limit of six during three fearsome episodes of repeated petit mal.[19] The toll on Jean was also great—never able to twitch without being intimately scrutinized, she virtually became her disease at times in the eyes of parents striving to save her from what they could not.

For fourteen and a half months, Sam and Livy kept a daily record of fingers picking nervously and aimlessly, of hands searching for a phantom pin in dress or bed clothes, of the briefest cessation of speech in midsentence, of eyes suddenly blank.[20] On guard day and night for the smallest changes in Jean's behavior, her parents felt rewarded for their strenuous watchfulness so long as they avoided a major attack. But on March 19, 1899, Jean had a grand mal seizure. In her father's revealing metaphor, the house burned down.

After the massive effort of her parents to ward off an attack, Jean must have experienced not just the physical blow but a deep sense of loss and failure. Little wonder that her self-image was shattered. Sam and Livy, beaten and defeated, probably experienced a similar sense of having failed, as they had somehow failed Susy. "There was nothing for us to do," Sam admitted bleakly, "but go on watching & dosing, & wait for the end."[21] Despairing of any progress, they ceased their record keeping if not their vigilance.

————

Not all was misery during their Viennese sojourn. For one thing, by January 1898 Sam had managed to pay off all his bankruptcy debts. And Mark Twain's celebrity remained undiminished. During those two years, the family received visitors in a steady stream, generally from five o'clock in the evening on. Clara invited her famous piano teacher to a dinner party, and he asked permission to bring two former students. A man of many talents, Leschetitzky spoke almost without interruption for three hours and awed even Mark Twain with his oratorical skills. Clara was more impressed by the "unusual intellectual gifts" of his students, who she said held "the fixed attention of the other guests at dinner, when Leschetitzky stopped to take his breath." One of them, the Russian pianist Ossip Gabrilowitsch, would eventually become her husband. Katy remembered "lots of officers for beaux" who came every day to pay court to Clara as well.[22]

In Clara's memory, however, callers came almost exclusively to see her father, who did not always appear, sometimes preferring to write or take long walks instead. Clara dreaded making the announcement that Mark Twain was absent, knowing the intense disappointment it would create in the faces of those whose wandering eyes rarely rested for long on her. And if the event was "graced by his presence," she remembered some years later, "my existence was on the level of a footstool—always an unnecessary object in a crowded room."[23]

Still, as Clara recognized, she also benefited from the two-edged sword of her father's celebrity. One morning, on a day of celebration in Vienna, Sam and his daughters left their hotel early to check out the festivities. When they returned, a huge crowd had gathered across the street from their hotel, hoping to catch a glimpse of the emperor and his procession. With much effort, they succeeded in swimming through the crowd, only to discover that armed guards blocked their path to the hotel. Suddenly a mounted policeman came charging up: "For God's sake, let him pass," he said to the patrolman on foot. "Don't you see it's Herr Mark Twain?" Clara acknowledged that she felt as important as if she were a member of the royal family.[24]

But there was no doubt who was king. If, as Sam maintained, music eventually developed Clara's latent spiritual and intellectual side, she still sometimes felt overpowered by her father's intellect, never sharing in that special bond that Susy and Sam had enjoyed. Clara often heard a warning voice inside her head that she mimicked in her memoir: "Take care. He may appear to be harmless, but without action or words he can smother you dead, smother you with the mere greatness of his intellect."[25] This warning voice only grew stronger in her young adulthood.

———

Having heard of a Jonas Henrik Kellgren, a Swedish osteopath who had some success with epilepsy patients, in July 1899 the family left London, where they had been for several months, in pursuit of a new cure. They spent the summer in Sanna, Sweden, where the whole family took treatments at Kellgren's sanitarium, including Clara, who had been advised by Susy's old mentor, Madame Marchesi, that she was not yet strong enough to embark on her newly chosen career as a singer. The stay was a welcome respite for Sam and Livy. Responsibility for Jean was on the shoulders of the professional staff, and her parents could relax.[26] Jean, in turn, was released from the constant pressure of parental scrutiny.

Curious and open to nontraditional medicine, Sam also took daily treatments that summer and kept a health diary. He wanted to observe the Kellgren technique, he explained, and also "get myself freshened up for work." Sam's routine included resistance exercises for his arms and legs, stretching and bending, body kneading and massage, and other carefully prescribed movements. He came to believe that fifteen minutes of Kellgren's physical manipulations were worth two hours of exercise in an ordinary gymnasium.[27]

His enthusiasm for Kellgren's treatment extended to his daughter's condition. Kellgren divided sufferers into two types—those who inherited the disease and those whose symptoms resulted from injuries—and he believed he could cure the latter. The family thought Jean's case fit this type, recalling that she had fallen and hit her head when she was ten and had lain unconscious for three hours. One patient with epilepsy told Sam that Kellgren had cured her disease in two summers. Sam longed for the same result for his daughter and was thrilled by Jean's early progress, noting an improvement in his youngest daughter's disposition after only four days. He credited the Kellgren treatment for transforming her from a moody, irritable, willfully negative person to someone cheerful, lively, cooperative, and in "brisk health."[28]

The Kellgren treatment was indeed the cause of this change, for it stopped her daily dose of bromide. In higher dosages such as Jean had been taking in Vienna, bromide can produce many negative side effects, including apathy, irritability, memory failure, intense headaches, and withdrawal. The positive result of ending Jean's bromide regimen was immediate, and it was enhanced by the mandatory exercise and massage, games, dances, hiking, picnicking, and other outdoor activities that Jean loved.[29]

Although Sanna was a welcome relief for her body, she did not share her father's optimism and found no matching curative for her soul. Epilepsy had taken a deep toll on her personal life, and even without the effects of bromide, the fact of the disease left Jean less than "cheerful" at heart. No real friends, no demonstrable talent, and abominable health was how she self-consciously summarized the causes of her melancholy the following year. Except for sixteen months in the United States—and those marked by the onset of her disease and Susy's death—she had been a virtual gypsy since 1891, living in Vienna, Berlin, Paris, Florence, Switzerland, and London. Clara, despite her own demons, seemed to thrive under these peripatetic conditions, acquiring admirers, making friends, and attracting numbers of beaux. Jean by contrast counted herself friendless; at twenty she had neither suitors nor intimates of either sex.[30] Beyond the torments of the disease itself, she was acutely aware of society's fear and disparagement of persons with epilepsy.[31] ("I always could get on better with an animal than I could with a person," she wrote defensively.) She had come to see herself as unattractive and talentless as well. "Is it going to be my miserable lot never to really love & be loved?" "That would be too dreadful," she lamented, "and would offer another fair reason for suicide."[32]

If Jean was keenly aware of epilepsy's harmful effects on her own life, it is doubtful that she fully understood the negative effects on her father, and those effects have generally been overlooked by others as well. The deepening of Twain's famous melancholy and pessimism about the "damned human race" is most often associated with Susy's death in 1896. Certainly this was a dreadful blow to both parents, but the family had already suffered a blow with the onset of Jean's epilepsy just six months before. Although Sam never discussed Jean's epilepsy in the tragic language he used to describe the loss of his eldest daughter, he wrote a chronicle of Jean's "illness," not for publication, in which he expressed feelings of fierce frustration, raging powerlessness, and bone-weary tension, strikingly captured in his metaphor of a house forever threatening to burn down if he closed an eye.[33]

Although Livy bore the brunt of Jean's disease within the family, Sam had required of himself unrelenting vigilance and sacrifice, as he revealed in a comment written at the Kellgren treatment center. "The attack due at midnight did not occur," he noted with evident relief. "No *petit mal* yesterday and none today. Jean is in good spirits and brisk health. For once the approach of attack-time gave us no solicitude. We provided no night-watch last night, and went to bed at the usual hour and to sleep without uneasiness and without any conversation about the probabilities."[34] Sam and Livy could temporarily pass their anxious burden to others.

In the fall of 1899, following their summer in Sweden, the family settled in London to continue Jean's treatments at Kellgren's main clinic, which was located there. But after a year of disappointing results, Sam and Livy decided to return to America. Whatever their other reasons, they were plainly tired of European life. Perhaps spurred by his anticipated homecoming, Twain had a creative burst during the summer months, working on a fantasy about a Satanic visitor to earth, a theme he had been exploring for some years and would continue to develop. Nonetheless, he was weary of being rootless after nine years of travel. "The poor man is willing to live anywhere," Livy wrote, "if we will only let him 'stay put.'"[35]

"If I ever get ashore," Twain quipped to reporters waiting for him to alight on American soil on October 15, 1900, "I am going to break both of my legs so I can't get away again." His entire family shared his enthusiasm at being home. "America! America! It was wonderful to be there again," Clara exclaimed. The family decided to settle in New York; they could not face their old Hartford home without Susy.[36]

Mark Twain, welcomed to his country as a celebrity, was immediately showered with unstinting admiration and the fawning attention of press and public. His reception was like an unending party where more and more guests arrived every hour and no one ever left. As host of this grand bacchanal, Twain seemed never to weary. He plunged into the banquet circuit with enthusiasm. "Old friends and new crowded into our parlor," Clara said, "and made us feel we had lost much by staying away from home so many years." Twain especially rejoiced in the companionship of his old friend William Dean Howells: the luncheons, the talks, the excursions, the politics, the jokes. Both men joined in hearty condemnation of the Boer war and America's imperialism in the Philippines and took public stands denouncing President McKinley's policies. "[W]e are old fellows," Howells described his camaraderie with Twain to his sister, "and it is pleasant to find the world so much worse than it was when we were young."[37]

But Twain's political essays were more than exercises in curmudgeonly humor; they were serious efforts to change the direction of American foreign policy. Soon after reaching American soil, he became vice president of the Anti-Imperialist League of New York. In February 1901 he published "To the Person Sitting in Darkness," a scathing critique of American imperialism. Twain tackled head-on the most important geopolitical issue of his day: American (and European) exploitation of less powerful countries based upon a spurious sense of cultural and racial superiority. He also attacked a high-ranking missionary for demanding money from locals during the Boxer Rebellion. One literary critic aptly described the essay as "great propaganda becomes great art." When he was criticized by some clergymen for his attack on missionaries, Twain felt compelled to reply to his detractors. Before he left New York for the summer, he finished his satirical rebuttal, "To My Missionary Critics," in which he suggested that the American Board of Commissioners for Foreign Missions, which had justified certain pecuniary actions in China on the grounds of local custom, change the ten commandments and bring them up to date: "*Thou Shalt not steal*—except when it is the custom of the country."[38]

With many old family friends now just a carriage ride away, social invitations for the Clemens daughters arrived in flurries that first autumn. They attended dinner parties at the home of Dr. Clarence Rice, their father's physician and family friend, and one in their father's honor given by Henry Huttleston Rogers. Clara had a new voice teacher and continued to pursue her musical career. At the same time she felt herself strongly attracted to the pianist Ossip Gabrilowitsch, who was now also in the United States, but she worried that marriage would be incompatible with her career. Nevertheless, Gabrilowitsch, who made his American debut on November 11, 1900, at Carnegie Hall, sought to spend as much time with Clara as his concert schedule and her inclination would allow. Katy carried messages back and forth between his hotel and her home, deliberately assisting the budding romance.[39]

Meanwhile, in the diary she began keeping after the family settled into their new home at 14 West 10th Street, Jean expressed her delight in Gabrilowitsch's Carnegie Hall concert. She recorded many trips to the theater and her passion for opera. She also enjoyed a reception at Delmonico's for her father, given by the Association of American Authors. And she participated in almost all the activities of the month-long social whirl that followed their return.[40]

But some invitations came exclusively to Clara, leaving feelings in the household unsettled. Howells's daughter Mildred, called "Pilla," asked

Clara for a Sunday entertainment but snubbed Jean. "Mamma thought it queer," Jean confided to her diary, and "I think it's horrid of her." Why Mildred Howells was "extraordinarily rude"—Jean's characterization of her behavior—cannot be told for certain, but the incident was not unique. Four days earlier Jean had noted, "Mamma seemed to think, just as I had that it was very impolite in Miss Foote to ask Clara to go with her to the theater in my presence without saying a word about my going with them."[41]

Clearly, a climate of hostility and mistrust surrounded epilepsy in the late nineteenth and early twentieth centuries. In 1903, Congress would pass an immigration law that added epileptics, along with the insane, beggars, and anarchists, to the list of immigrants to be turned away at Ellis Island. Negative stereotypes of viciousness, criminality, cunning, and immorality long associated with epilepsy remained virulent.[42] In the face of prejudice that cast people with epilepsy as moral and physical degenerates, Jean's intimate circle kept her condition to themselves, but this still did not spare her from feelings of ostracism.

Prejudice is often a companion of fear. Although families seldom feared the epileptic, they almost always feared the stigma that the disease imparted to the sufferer and sometimes to the entire family. Social attitudes inevitably mold parental strategies of freedom or restriction. Certainly Livy struggled against the stigma of her daughter's disease, but one thing is certain: she refused to give in to the isolation that can be epilepsy's worst side effect. If concealment of the condition was the family's preferred strategy for dealing with Jean's epilepsy, Livy still insisted upon a normal role for her daughter in their active social calendar and kept Jean tightly integrated into the family circle. Forced by her illness to leave an afternoon tea, Jean was able to rejoin her family for dinner but then excused herself early after getting angry at her mother and sister. "A little later Mamma came up here," she reported, "and without really saying anything I could see that she wished to make up so I said I might come down at nine thirty & play cards. I didn't want to a bit. All I wanted to do was to sit still & cry, but I knew that I would not be allowed to remain alone so after Clara had come in to see about my coming down stairs I finally went." The remedy was effective. "I am not sorry I did go," Jean confessed, "because I felt for the time being a trifle less melancholy."[43]

For the summer of 1901 Sam took his family to Lower Saranac Lake in the Adirondacks. There they were visited by Howells's son John, who, as Howells later wrote his old friend, reported that Sam was "only partially satisfied with the universe, whence I infer that you think it has not improved since I last saw you." Mark Twain's particular dissatisfaction then was with the condition of ex-slaves and their children. That summer at the lake he wrote an extraordinary satire, "The United States of Lyncherdom," in which he put forth a plan to stop what he called "this epidemic of bloody insanities." American missionaries in China, he suggested, should return to their homeland where there was much greater need for their services. "O kind missionary, O compassionate missionary," Twain implored, "leave China! Come home and convert these Christians!" Worried about book sales in the South, however, he never published this essay, hoping someone else would write the book on lynching that he foreswore.[44]

In October 1901, as if to cement both their fame and their friendship, Yale University granted honorary doctorates to Doc Howells and Doc Clemens, as the "old fellows" began to call each other. Sam had rented a baronial mansion in Riverdale, a fashionable area of the Bronx overlooking the Hudson, and the two friends were now a "time-table's length away." But the timetable held no sway over Doc Clemens, who commanded a train from gatemen and train starters no matter the scheduled arrival or departure. Twain always had to stop off at the men's room, Howells noted gleefully to a mutual friend, with "me dancing in the corridor, and holding his train for him. But they would not let it go without him, if it was the Chicago limited! What a fame and a force he is!" Writing to the same friend some months later, Twain returned the compliment: "Old Mr. Howells was here day before yesterday, on his way to a reception, for he is very gay and societous. It was raining like hell. I never saw such an indiscourageable old dude. But he is sweet & lovely as ever."[45]

In a house that boasted a dining room sixty feet long and thirty feet wide, Sam was back to operating in his usual style—careless of personal finances and ready once again to believe in rags-to-riches investment schemes. He was touting Plasmon, the wonder protein powder that eventually cost him $50,000. "He was apt," Howells observed sagaciously, "for a man who had put faith so decidedly away from him, to take it back and pin it to some superstition, usually of a hygienic sort." But after paying off his creditors, his friend chuckled, "he had to do something with his money." From Riverdale, Clara went twice a week into New York for her singing lesson, and in the spring she traveled to Paris to see Ossip Gabrilowitsch. While she was away, Howells talked Clemens into renting a summer house in York Harbor, Maine, in 1902.[46]

Living only a 40-minute trolley ride apart in Maine, the old "dudes" regaled each other regularly—telling stories and sharing their manuscripts. Twain continued work on *Which Was It?,* a novel he had begun in the summer of 1899 and returned to at Saranac Lake, Riverdale, and now again at York Harbor. In this story Twain's protagonist becomes a robber and a murderer who struggles with the burden of a guilty conscience and especially fears exposure at the hands of his mulatto servant.[47] The longest of his unfinished novels, it relied on a device that Twain repeated obsessively in his late fiction: the main character only dreams his catastrophes. Perhaps the author wished that he could as readily banish his own intimate afflictions.

————

At the time, Sam was coping with a personal strain that he did not share with Howells, choosing instead to take another friend into his confidence. "Then I saw it," he told Henry Rogers in July 1902, in a rare revelation. "I have seen it only three times before, in all these five fiendish years." The "it" was one of Jean's grand mal seizures, objectified and abstracted from the person of his daughter. Blaming her seizures for creating the "fiendish" qualities of those years, his phrasing conferred a loathsome quality on his daughter's illness.[48] And even allowing for his peripatetic lifestyle, the claim that he had witnessed only three of Jean's attacks is astonishingly low. Self-conscious avoidance appears to be the likely reason, for Jean was having grand mal seizures almost every three weeks that summer, and he was painfully aware of this.

Still, there were indications that Sam was not simply keeping away. "Papa has gout rather badly," Jean had written two years earlier, "but when he heard me jump upstairs, I was cussing my luck to Katie, he came right up to see if I had fainted." ("Fainted" was Jean's euphemism for a grand mal seizure.) This was hardly the response of an avoider. The fact that he witnessed so few attacks may have been truly coincidental, but his response to Jean's seizures has been characterized as repulsion.[49] More likely his feelings were wildly mixed, and sometimes shame was the dominant emotion.

Sam had made use of Henry Rogers's yacht to transport his family to York Harbor. Ostensibly this was so they could travel in comfort and style, but his deeper motive was to avoid any public exposure of his daughter's epilepsy. It would have been "the equivalent to being in hell," he confided to Rogers, in thanking him for making their seclusion possible. "The scare and anxiety would have been unendurable." He believed that in fact he and Livy had held off a seizure during an exhausting vigil while on board. Revealing what may be another reason he actually saw so few attacks, he gave most of the credit to his wife, who was "alert, and up the most of the time two nights—and I helped," he added, "after a man's fashion—and so the convulsion was staved off."[50] A "man's fashion" is undefined, but clearly this division of labor was a fateful constant in his response to Jean's illness and allowed him perhaps to submerge her suffering in her mother's.

"It comes near to killing Mrs. Clemens every time," he lamented in that same July letter to Rogers, "and there is not much left of her for a day or two afterward. Every three weeks it comes. It will break her down yet." His sympathy was wholly for Livy. Little more than a month later, he announced the collapse he had predicted to Rogers, blaming "Mrs. Clemens's five years of constant anxiety and periodical shocks and frights on Jean's account."[51]

––––––––

On August 12, 1902, Livy became desperately ill, with sensations of suffocation so intense that her husband thought she was dying. She survived the attack, but a hoped-for full recovery never materialized. On September 23, still in York Harbor, the family again thought Livy was close to death. But Clemens wrote the next day that a Boston specialist had cheered everyone up—even the patient. The doctor banished family members from the sick room, and a professional nurse was installed with Livy's approval. Howells, repeating to a friend the diagnoses Clemens passed on to him, stated that Livy suffered from organic heart disease and nervous prostration. She often felt as if she was suffocating and had to sit up in bed, take oxygen, and sip brandy to revive herself. Despite the family's momentary cheer, her physical condition was deteriorating.[52]

After the family returned to Riverdale on October 16, the doctors continued to believe that Livy should be saved from all "dangerous emotions," in Sam's phrasing; only Clara, who had hurriedly returned from Europe, was trusted to be with her mother. Sam and Jean were barred from the sickroom—both undoubtedly taxed Livy's nerves. In Jean's case the tensions surrounding her epilepsy were undeniable. Sam's exile was shorter (he was back in the sickroom for brief rendezvous after an initial hiatus of three months), but the reasons for it were more complex.[53]

A loving husband but a demanding personality, Sam had a spirit of boyishness that Livy had captured in her pet name for him, "Youth." "The heart of a boy with the head of a sage; the heart of a good boy, or a bad boy, but always a wilful boy," was how Howells saw him. Aware of his shortcomings, Sam understood and accepted his own banishment with grace. Livy found some compensation for her sickroom seclusion, he told Howells, "in the reflection that now she should not hear so much about 'the damned human race.'" Actually the compensation she found was in the little notes that Sam sent to her sickroom several times a day. Clara called them "rainbows during the storm," noting that "the colors were never the same."[54]

"Don't know the date nor the day," Twain wrote his wife during his exile. "But anyway, it is a soft and pensive foggy morning, Livy darling, and the naked tree branches are tear-beaded, and Nature has the look of trying to keep from breaking down and sobbing, poor old thing. Good morning, dear heart, I love you dearly." Another note concerned a question about the lease on their house. "I will write Mr. Appleton what you say, Livy dear. My understanding was—was—was—oh, well dang it I don't know what it was—I don't reckon I had any. Often I have an understanding that I don't understand, and then I come to find out I didn't. Sleep well, Dearest."[55]

Livy asked him to write in her boudoir, so that she could hear him clear his throat. "[I]t would be such a joy to feel you near," she wrote. "I miss you sadly, sadly. Your note in the morning gave me support for the day, the one at night, peace for the night. With the deepest love of my heart." Sam hovered near his wife's room, sending in notes, and getting constant reports from Clara. To add to his woes, Jean developed a severe case of pneumonia two days before Christmas. Clara kept Jean's condition secret from their mother to protect her from any undue strain on her heart. During one conversation she told Livy that Jean was out coasting and then, after a few hours, forgot and reported that Jean would be back from town on the five o'clock train. Livy wanted to know how she could possibly do both, and Clara invented another train that she added to the route for this emergency. Sam would chuckle at Clara's inventions and enjoyed her close calls. In January Jean was sent to a Virginia rest home to recuperate until, as Sam wrote, she no longer "looked like the victim of a forest fire," while Clara continued to make up stories about Jean's daily actions and moods.[56]

Perhaps finding solace, or merely distraction, Twain was somehow able to continue working when Livy fell ill. Inspired by a five-day visit he had made to his boyhood home of Hannibal in May 1902, he spent time on a book about Huck Finn at age sixty, though he would destroy this manuscript some years later. He also returned to writings about Christian Science that he had begun in Europe, and he published a four-part satirical essay on Mary Baker Eddy, beginning in December 1902 in the *North American Review*. His attack on Christian Science has to be put in the frame of his family history. Twain believed that a man's imagination had the power to heal "imaginary ailments." Christian Science, he freely acknowledged, would save people from "imagination-manufactured diseases.... Meantime," he slyly added, "it will kill a man every now and then." Two of his children had died from the disastrous effects of real disease—and it was not lost on him that Susy had been a follower of a version of Christian Science. Added to that, the unremitting suffering of Jean and Livy must have fueled his interest as well as skepticism in the new religion. What he dubbed "its principal great offer: *to rid the Race of pain and disease*" was a desire he sympathized with but found thwarted in his own life. At his publisher's request he worked feverishly to expand the Christian Science articles into a book, finishing in the spring of 1903, only to have the manuscript gather dust at Harper's for several years before it was finally published.[57] This was the only long book that he saw from composition to print in the last twelve years of his life.

Twain also resumed work on the story he called "No. 44, The Mysterious Stranger." The first chapter in this tangle of intermittently composed manuscripts was actually salvaged from "The Chronicle of Young Satan," which he had abandoned when he sailed for America in 1900. Most of the rest of the dream-fantasy was written in three stages over the next several years. From late October 1902 through May 1903, in circumstances that were often defined by Livy's illness, he finished the first seven chapters.[58]

During these months he had some assistance from a new secretary. Isabel Lyon had been living with her mother in Farmington, Connecticut, in a house she had built next door to her sister and brother-in-law. Before her illness, Livy had planned to hire the Whitmore's former governess to be her private secretary. Isabel was eager for work, and so Sam took over her employment. "Slender, petite, comely, 38 years old by the almanac," was how Twain remembered her when she was hired, "& 17 in ways & carriage & dress. She was hired as a correspondence secretary but was gradually given more responsibilities, including a role as chaperone for Jean and Clara at various social functions. Lyon boarded out and apparently saw little of Mrs. Clemens.[59]

At the end of 1902, Clara wrote Mrs. Whitmore to thank her for recommending Lyon. "She not only is sweet and attractive, entirely lacking any disagreeable qualities," Clara observed, "but she is also a pleasure for she has a cheerful manner and way which are particularly welcome in a house at time of illness & consequent depression."[60]

———

By early July 1903, Sam and Livy had returned to Quarry Farm, where Clara and Jean joined them the first week of August. There Sam was able to enjoy something of his old companionship with Livy, devoting himself to her and spending little time on his own work. She seemed to improve slightly at the family retreat where they had spent twenty summers, but lying on the porch most days with her husband by her side, she stared at the hills and dreamed of another world of light and warmth. Happy memories of calm, serene days under clear skies drew Livy's thoughts back to Florence. Perhaps she hoped for a miracle in another clime—and on October 24, the family entourage, including Jean, Clara, Katy, Livy's nurse, Sam, and Miss Lyon and her mother, boarded the *Princess Irene* and set sail for Italy.[61]

The Villa de Quarto—a cavernous fifty-room mansion—was not ready when they arrived, for the owner had been unwilling to allow advance preparations. Countess Masiglia, the intransigent landlady, remained on the grounds and seemed bent on creating trouble for her tenants. The villa was approached down a long garden drive, bordered by poplars and cedar. The countess capriciously locked the gates, making it impossible at times for Livy's doctors to reach her. She turned off all the water to the mansion, which meant the family could not flush the toilets. The vicious woman even stopped the Clemenses' telephone service. According to Katy, "She was mad at having to rent her villa, 'cause she had to live in the stable herself." Sam was understandably livid and began backing lawsuits against her.[62]

The villa was nonetheless a beautiful place. Both Sam and Livy had rooms on the ground floor, which opened to a trellis-framed terrace edged by a lovely garden. Olive-pulp bricks burned bright in the palatial fireplaces, and the scent of roses, laurel, and orange blossoms floated from the garden through their open windows at night. While she and her sister occasionally went into the city to tour the museums and shops, with Lyon as their chaperone, Clara remembered that Sam would pace the terrace by the hour, loving the view of distant city roofs, ancient turrets, and church spires flashing in the sun.[63] Livy also loved the terrace but was soon confined to her bed, requiring round-the-clock care, with her nurse in attendance during the day and Katy at night. The mood inside the villa became increasingly somber.

Twain, evidently worried about the family's finances, wrote several pieces for publication while he was in Italy. His most effective was "The $30,000 Bequest"—a tale of greed and the obsessive dreams of riches gone sour. He also worked on a large chunk of "No. 44, The Mysterious Stranger." Apparently Jean typed the manuscript as her father finished sections of his composition. In Florence he wrote chapters 8 through 25, as well as his ending, which became chapter 34. "It is all a Dream," the mysterious stranger reveals in that chapter, "a grotesque and foolish dream. Nothing exists but You. And You are but a Thought—a vagrant Thought, a useless Thought, a homeless Thought, wandering forlorn among the empty eternities!"[64] Although this work was not published in Twain's lifetime, it is the most respected literary creation of his late years, perhaps because it resonates with doubts about life's meaningfulness.

Twain also spent some time doing autobiographical dictations. It was in Florence that he hit upon the method he would use for composing most of his memoirs—free association. Autobiography, he told Lyon, was "like narrative and should be spoken." When the mood struck, Sam would dictate to her in a little room that overlooked the terrace. He paced up and down while talking slowly, and she wrote rapidly in longhand. At the end of their sessions he would carry away a copy of his dictations.[65] Though unaffected by considerations of coherence or reader interest, these autobiographical outpourings became the most ambitious and, arguably, his most engaged writing of his late years.

Lyon stayed on the edge of the family circle, living in the servant's quarters on the grounds of the villa and taking occasional dictation; she saw very little of Mrs. Clemens. Her main preoccupation was the local priest, Don Raffaello Stiattisi. Their relationship had begun with an exchange of Italian lessons two nights a week for an equal number of English tutorials. "Yes, he is very lovely and is showing us a new world," she sighed after lesson number one. As time passed, Don Raffaello was coming regularly to visit "for a little or a long while," she wrote in her diary. "He grows more beautiful each day as priest and man." Lyon and Stiattisi had several romantic dinners in the hills above Florence. On one occasion they sat outdoors, listening to music and watching the city lights come out while the sun set on the Arno. "Best of all, always and forever was Don Raffaello with his beautiful face, his lovely buoyancy of manner, and his great sweetness of soul," she wrote devotedly. It did not seem to bother her that her mother made these encounters a threesome.[66]

———

Although she still managed to take voice lessons in Florence and even made her singing debut there on April 8, in a concert arranged by her teacher, Clara sat with her mother every afternoon during this time. She was the one family member who had complete access to the sufferer almost from the beginning of her illness. Sam kept a faithful vigil. Restricted to two brief visits a day at the villa, he broke the rules with regularity, slipping in to be near his beloved. Livy would put her arms around his neck, and he would hold her and kiss her tenderly. He refused to believe his wife would die, yet he knew that Livy would never get out of her bed again. Livy's suffering made his heart bleed. She had to sit up in bed for six months—day and night—and could sleep only by resting her forehead against a support. Five times in four months, he wrote Joseph Twichell, the old family friend and minister, she "went through that choking horror for an hour & more, & came out of it white, haggard, exhausted, and quivering with fright."[67] Cursing failed him in those hours.

One night, he came downstairs after he had seen her, sat at the piano in the parlor, and began to play and sing the old African spirituals they both loved. The music brought her joy, Katy observed—but not peace. "She so dreaded death, poor timid little prisoner," Sam revealed to Twichell, "for it promised to be by strangulation."[68]

In the end, Olivia Clemens was spared her worst nightmare. On June 5, 1904, she died in Katy's arms—one short breath and she was gone. Her husband rushed to her side, took her in his arms, and held her for the longest time. "How beautiful she is—" he said, crying, "how young and sweet—and look, she's smiling!" Both daughters put their arms around his neck and wept, Katy remembered, "as though their hearts would break." Later that night Katy found Clara curled up in a little heap under the casket. Sam stayed awake but paced like a sleepwalker between his bedroom and his wife's room all night. Jean had her first grand mal seizure in thirteen months soon after.[69]

"Well, we got to America somehow," Katy summarized the interim. The funeral was held on July 14, in the same house in Elmira, New York, where Livy and Sam were married; and the service was conducted by the same preacher, Joseph Twichell. After the coffin was lowered in the grave, "Clara gave a great cry," Katy recalled, "and threw up her hands and her father caught her in his arms and held her." Her cry pierced the heart of every mourner. Clara had turned thirty just three days after her mother's death. With her own life still so unformed, this must have given her loss a special import. Jean's loss would prove less immediate. Denied her mother's presence for so long, she had grown gradually accustomed to her absence. She could have no idea then what her mother's death would mean to her life. Sam, watching Livy lowered into the clay, vowed that he would never allow himself to witness another loved one's descent into the grave. Lyon, still caught up in her flirtation with Don Raffaello, felt her keenest sorrow in their separation.[70]

If there is no better judge of a person's character than her servant, Katy Leary's observations about her mistress are unimpeachable. "She'd been so wonderful to everybody all her life, so kind and loving and with so much common sense—always wantin' to help everybody, and so generous, too, with everything she had," Katy observed. "There aren't so many people like that in the world, and it makes those that are left behind lonely—as if a great hole had come into your life that you'd fallen into, and never was going to get up again."[71]

Sam had certainly fallen into a great hole after his wife's death. Livy had managed everything, made every plan—looked after every domestic detail. Howells hoped Sam's daughters could pull him out of that hole and help to close it—but then he caught himself. No one, he realized, not even her children, could take Mrs. Clemens's place.[72]

Sam was not only bereft, but also wracked with guilt. "I try not to think of the hurts I gave her," he agonized to his sister-in-law, Susan Crane, "but oh, there are so many, so many!" "And so, a part of each day Livy is a dream & has never existed," he confessed to Twichell. "The rest of it she is real, & is gone. Then comes the ache, & continues. Then comes the long procession of remorses, & goes filing by—uncountable." Her father had a habit of torturing himself, according to Clara, "with self-accusations of imaginary shortcomings and selfishness." The devastating loss may account for much of his free-floating guilt, but it is likely, as Clara speculated, that a more specific hurt was preying on his mind: Livy, he believed, had never gotten over Susy's death, and it was because of his willingness to gamble large sums on wildly speculative investments that they had been separated and Susy had died without her mother. However realistic and grievous his remorse, his sorrow was even more painful. "[S]he was our life, and now we are nothing," he told his friend Richard Gilder, the editor-in-chief of *The Century*.[73]

"She was just like the foundation to a house," Katy wisely explained, "and now that one of the great props was gone, we had to turn around and fill it up somehow." Turning around, the bereaved family, including Katy and Lyon, retreated to an extra cottage on the Gilders' farm in Tyringham, Massachusetts. But Sam was restless there and made frequent trips to New York, where the family had decided to rent a house in the fall. Clara was planning to run the household after they found a suitable New York residence. Abruptly, she decided she could not stay on at the farm, and on July 22 she left for New York, taking Katy with her. Describing herself as "completely broken down under the strain of Mother's long illness and the shock of her death," Clara consulted a doctor, who ordered her to remain in seclusion and avoid all forms of excitement or worry.[74]

Jean, however, always found country life restorative and especially welcomed the opportunity to go riding. She was out on a moonlight ride on July 31 with the Gilders' son Rodman when a trolley car spooked her horse. Trolley, horse, and girl collided. The horse was killed, and Jean was flung fifty feet and knocked unconscious. Though badly bruised, her only serious injury was a broken ankle that kept her in bed for a fortnight.[75] Sam called Clara's doctor, warning her to keep the newspapers' lurid accounts of Jean's accident away from his daughter. He told the doctor he would break the news gently in person. What really happened was a little different.

"He entered my room," Clara remembered, "and, after a brief greeting, handed me a newspaper with the headlines: 'It is hoped that Mark Twain's youngest daughter, Jean, may live. Her horse fell on her and crushed her.'" He then began to tell Jean's story in his most agitated and dramatic style. Shocked and horrified, Clara later wondered why "his actions were so at variance with his intentions." She never asked him. But she roused herself to return to Tyringham to check on Jean for herself.[76]

When the family finally moved in November to their New York address, 21 Fifth Avenue, Clara had already busied herself with its decoration. This "kind of got her mind off herself and her troubles," observed Katy, who was especially taken with the lavender wallpaper Clara had chosen for her music room. Sam also fussed with the interior, and Katy helped unpack and arrange the old Hartford furniture, likely looking its age in design if not in wear.[77] The Hartford House had been sold in 1903.

The winter of 1904–5 was hard. Uncharacteristically reclusive even when not indisposed, Sam caught bronchitis and spent more than a month in bed in the dead of winter. But he also began a period of productivity, turning to writing as a form of both refuge and recovery. Fired up at the end of January by a bloody massacre of Russian strikers gunned down by the czar's guards in St. Petersburg, he wrote "The

Czar's Soliloquy." By the time it was published in March, he had already begun a piece on the atrocities perpetrated by King Leopold of Belgium on the 20 million Africans under his rule in the Congo.[78] Rejected by the *North American Review*, this polemic was finally published as a pamphlet by the Congo Reform Association in the fall of 1905. During the winter he also wrote "The War Prayer," a compact, yet blistering satire on man's lack of empathy and the inhumane and cruel application of religion to wholly selfish ends; it remained unpublished during his lifetime.

If Twain used his writing as a form of recovery, his daughters had no such refuge to fall back on. Clara retreated again to the isolation of a rest cure in a private New York sanitarium, and when she did not improve, her doctor sent her to another sanitarium in Norfolk, Connecticut, where she accepted no correspondence from her family for almost six months. Jean lived a friendless and solitary life; another old family physician and friend, Dr. Edward Quintard, was in charge of her malady. Perhaps as both compensation and solace, Sam bought Jean an Aeolian Orchestrelle, a full-sized player reed organ that filled the house with Beethoven sonatas and symphonies, Chopin nocturnes, and Scottish airs.[79] Managing the household by default, Katy grieved over the loss of Livy's generalship. Isabel Lyon was now permanently living in: taking care of Sam's correspondence, playing cards with him and Jean by the hour, and perhaps beginning to dream of the family generalship for herself. She was undoubtedly the cheeriest member of the household.

CHAPTER 3

Rearranging
the Household

LOOKING FOR A PLACE to spend the summer of 1905—and perhaps, as
well, for a place to heal—Sam settled on an artist colony in Dublin,
New Hampshire. Dublin was the permanent home of the American
landscape painter Abbott Thayer, who had once touted the New
Hampshire highlands to his writer friend. If it was a good place for an
artist in paint, Sam reasoned, it would also be good for an artist in
"morals and ink."[1] When he heard that the house of the writer Henry
Copley Greene would be available that summer, Sam insisted that Katy
give it the "once over" before he committed to rent it. Jean volunteered
to go along, and so the two trooped off to New Hampshire in the dead
of winter. A summer resort, Dublin had no winter accommodations,
but the Thayers volunteered to serve as hostelry and sent a sleigh to
meet the scouts. After nearly freezing en route, Jean and Katy were delighted by the big roaring fire and piles of blankets that greeted them.[2]

While the pair was chatting with their hostess, Katy noticed that the
house had become quite still and the rest of the family had disappeared.
When she inquired, Mrs. Thayer told her that they had all gone outside
to sleep. "Just stuck themselves down in the snow and covered themselves up good with their blankets! Well—when I heard that!" Katy exclaimed, "I thought they must all be crazy! It made me actually shiver—
right there in that warm room."[3] The Thayers, who believed that an
unheated house was what kept them healthy, probably moved outdoors
so that their visitors could enjoy the comforts of a heated interior.

Poor Katy had an even greater surprise in the morning. The only access to the Copley Greene house was on cross-country skis, which Katy

called snowshoes. Ever the athletic type, Jean volunteered to go alone.

"No, *I've* got to see that house," Katy insisted. "Your father wants me to."

"Oh, Katy! *You'll* never be able to walk on those snowshoes."

"Well . . . , maybe not, but I'll try it anyway."

"So one of the boys mounted me on them snowshoes," Katy recounted, "and he tied them snowshoes on me good and hard; and Jean got hers on, and we started for that old house. I was beginning to hate it by that time! Oh, I had a terrible time! I fell down twice! And then one of my snowshoes bust off."[4] But the indomitable Katy persevered and returned to New York from her mission with a favorable report. Despite this inauspicious start, Dublin would prove a balm for at least two members of the family. Clara, however, decided to stay in Norfolk, Connecticut, where she had been in seclusion in a sanitarium since November. She rented a cottage there, and in June she began to practice her singing again.[5]

On May 1, 1905, Katy and Jean left for Dublin. Miss Lyon joined them a few days later, and Sam planned to follow shortly. Lyon and Jean found agreeable company in each other that summer. "Dear child that she is—," Lyon sympathetically observed, "Such a complex nature and yet so entirely simple—Consistent—yet so inconsistent—There is a power in that young nature." Sensitive to Jean's mood of sadness the day following an especially severe series of attacks, Lyon suggested an outing into the woods complete with a blanket and books. In turn, Jean enjoyed reading aloud to Lyon in the evenings. The older woman also took pleasure in the beautiful view of the local mountain, Monadnock, and the quiet, restful atmosphere of Dublin—the nearest railway station was an hour's drive, and from there, it was another three hours to Boston, six hours to New York.[6]

Jean was wildly enthusiastic about her summer home, delighted as always to be in the outdoors. She also had the chance to practice her woodcarving, which had become both hobby and lifelong avocation since her first lessons in London in 1897. Her studio that summer featured a big fireplace and two large windows that opened into the pine and hemlock woods, as "wild and beautiful as Nature herself made them." With her carving table nailed to the floor, she was ready to work on making "bookracks."[7]

If walking, birding, and carving were joys for Jean, her perfect joy was still riding, despite her broken ankle the year before. Patrick McAleer, who had served as the family coachman in Hartford for twenty years, had been hired in March to be her groom. A skilled rider and her constant companion on horseback, Patrick had one drawback—he spit constantly. "[I]t is too unpleasant to put up with," Jean confessed to her diary, "& yet he is such a dear that I hate to say anything which could hurt his feelings." Early that summer Patrick helped her buy a horse, a Kentucky bay she named Scott—"sweet and friendly in the stable, so obedient & willing on the road & such a beauty."[8]

Though she wrote more of plants and animals than people that first summer in Dublin, Jean's most important gift was being welcomed into the little community as one of their own. For the first time in many years, she began to socialize with her peers: the Thayers' children Gerald (Gra) and Galla, the brother and sister Gerome and Nancy Brush, Raphael Pumpelly, Barry Faulkner, and Tom McKittrick.[9] Although she was as much as eight or ten years older than her new friends, Jean's athleticism, the social effects of her illness, and the years she spent largely with her family may have made her seem younger than her age.

Sam's arrival was delayed until May 18. In early May, Clara had become ill with what proved to be appendicitis, and on May 10 she had surgery. Once he was assured she was on the way to recovery, Sam made the journey to Dublin—and proceeded to write for thirty-five straight days without a break, a personal record of 31,500 words in five weeks. He claimed he "got the disposition out of the atmosphere." Twain had fun with "Three Thousand Years Among the Microbes," the tale of a scientist who was magically turned into a cholera germ in the body of a tramp named Blitzowksi. He entertained his little household by reading from the microbe manuscript on multiple occasions.[10]

Twain also continued work on "No. 44, The Mysterious Stranger." He had No. 44 (an alias for Satan) travel the vast expanses of the universe at will, bring technological wonders back from the future, and even transform himself into a slave who sang minstrel songs. Twain's famous whimsy was specially engaged when No. 44 turned the lady's maid into a cat who could talk. He wrote chapters 26 through 32 in the first two weeks of July, thus completing all but one chapter of the unfinished manuscript he left behind at his death. In addition, he finished

"Eve's Diary," a charmingly sentimental tribute to his wife, which was published in the Christmas 1905 issue of *Harper's*. Twain imagines Eve's reaction to the newly created moon, stars, plants, animals; and to Adam, whom she first identifies as "the other Experiment." The Fall, Twain says, was worthwhile because of Eve's love for Adam: "The Garden is lost," Eve acknowledges, "but I have found him, and am content." The essay ends at Eve's grave, paying homage to Livy through Adam's simple eulogy: "Wheresoever she was, *there* was Eden."[11]

Perhaps encouraged by his daughters' long-standing commitment to animal rights, Twain also agreed to write a protest against bullfighting. "A Horse's Tale," about an old horse that is eventually killed in the bullring, was published in *Harper's Magazine* in two installments the following year. He read the tale aloud to Jean and her young friends in early October, toward the end of their stay. When Jean asked him how he could drop one story and work on another, he replied that while he was working on one story, "the tank is filling up for the one just stopped."[12]

Apparently the scenery was restorative. Sam loved the view from the house he occupied: the "soaring double hump" of Monadnock with the spreading valley at its base, the frame of hills, and beyond the frame the "billowy sweep of remote great ranges" rising to view. But it was the New England fall, he told a reporter, that stirred "his blood like military music." "In my bedroom dear heart, in my bedroom & drunk again with autumn foliage," he wrote to Clara in October. "The fact is, I am drunk with it all the time; it began weeks ago, & I have never drawn a sober breath since." He called it a "landslide of hellfire toned down for Sunday consumption."[13]

At least one member of the Clemens household "couldn't stand the place," however, and cleared out as soon as she could. "The country was pretty enough," Katy Leary admitted, "but you can't live on country!" There might have been amusement enough for the literati but not for someone doing a different kind of work. "If there had only been a dance hall or something lively like that—or maybe even a little bit of moonshine to stir them up! But, oh! that whole country was so quiet! Everybody was always working—I mean writing or painting. It was dull, I tell you, dull!" Little wonder that Katy was the first to leave Dublin, joining Clara, who returned to New York on September 19. After a month together, Katy wrote Clemens that his middle daughter seemed like her old self again, both physically and mentally. The two of them had been happily fixing up the house at 21 Fifth Avenue. On November 1, six weeks after Katy left Dublin, Jean and her father, with Lyon in tow, returned to New York.[14]

———

If Clara was her old self again, as Katy believed, this also included her strong need for an independent identity. She seemed unable to remain long within her father's orbit, returning to Norfolk, Connecticut, with Katy on January 6. Having set her sights on a professional singing career, Clara began to rehearse with an accompanist and to sing at informal musicals around New York; she also retained a manager. She came home to sing at the end of February and then seesawed between Atlantic City and her New York home three times in the next twenty-one days. While in New York on March 24, Clara looked in on her father in the living room as she was passing out of the house. "[T]hen a blast of cold and bedeviled loneliness swept over him," Lyon reported, "and made him hate his life."[15]

If Sam generously supported Clara's free-wheeling lifestyle even as he craved more attention than she was willing to give, he seemed often simply to ignore Jean. Unlike his wife, he made no attempt to integrate her into his busy social world of speeches and engagements. "I'll have to excuse Jean," he wrote in reply to an invitation from their old family friend Lilian Aldrich, "she would be too much responsibility for me."[16]

The winter of 1905–6 was a cruel one for Jean, isolated in New York and suffering again from grand mal seizures—including an unusual cluster of six in late November, according to Lyon's records. "I have been wretchedly ill & run down in every possible way," she confided in a letter to her Dublin friend Nancy Brush, "& everyone believes the country as early as possible will be the best cure." To Nancy, Jean lamented that she felt "obliged to do nothing at all" because of her health. Her mood was not helped by news that Patrick McAleer was dying of stomach cancer. Besides correspondence, only New York visits by Dublin friends afforded her pleasure. Lyon diagnosed Jean's condition early in the New Year: "Not only has her malady increased, but her whole physical condition is at a low ebb, and the child calls for great waves of love from those of us who care."[17] "The child" was twenty-five, but that made the need for love, especially from her father, no less urgent.

Sam's attitude toward his daughter and her epilepsy was not permanently fixed, but he never changed his feelings about its devastating effect upon his wife. "Her disease," he wrote earnestly before his death, "and its accompanying awful convulsions, wore out her gentle mother's strength with grief & watching & anxiety, & caused her death, poor Livy!" He moved from despair over Jean's lack of progress in Europe, to rage at the strain his daughter's illness was placing on his wife's health and well-being, to deep resentment after Livy became seriously ill, to blame after she died. This deep-seated blame surely cast a pall over their relationship. But if her father faulted Jean, his attitude toward her affliction also softened after his wife's death, perhaps because there was no one to buffer him against the full force of her malady. Calling it an "unearned, undeserved & hellish disease," he told Clara that he wished to learn to make a just allowance for Jean's condition. She is "not strictly responsible for her disposition & her acts when she is under its influence," he reminded himself, adding "(if there is ever a time when she is really free from its influence—which is doubtful)."[18]

Sam's disparagement of Jean's disposition was likely based upon the then widely accepted concept of an "epileptic personality or temperament." Persons with epilepsy were considered to be unpleasant, "careless in speech, prone to exaggeration, illogical in conversation, irritable in controversy, and erratic in ideas." A late-nineteenth-century medical text issued a common warning that "epileptics are self-willed, obstinate as a rule, easily angered."[19] In retrospect, Sam blamed epilepsy for Jean's rotten disposition from the age of twelve—fully three years before the onset of her disease. Perhaps forgetting the determination he had himself noted in the four-year-old who had countermanded him, in German, he described her as a lovely, joyous, affectionate, gentle, cooperative child who had transformed into a monster at twelve: "wilful, stubborn, rude, conceited, insolent, offensive." He was encouraged to project the traits of a so-called "epileptic temperament" backward in time by a physician who told him Jean "had long been possessed by this hideous disease."[20]

The mood changes he observed, however, might easily be found in many healthy adolescents. Moreover, Jean's tumbleweed existence, starting at age eleven, did nothing to improve her disposition. After her attacks began, the disease itself took a heavy toll on her psyche, but the negative emotional effects she suffered were probably induced as much by the era's culture of prejudice around epilepsy. A common fear of and repugnance at the loss of bodily control meant "that people liable to this loss are subjected to rejection and hostility" in many cultures. This potential for rejection weighed heavily upon Jean.[21]

Whatever his feelings, Sam was certainly willing to take responsibility for her medical treatment. "Poor child, she is turning her hopes again toward a surgical examination and possible operation," he had informed Clara in late October 1905, before their return from Dublin. "She wants an X ray examination, & we must see Dr. Hartley about it when I come."[22] But for all his sympathy Sam did not really know his youngest child. He had never been close to Jean before his wife died, and he seemed, as a single parent, not to know how to bridge the gap between them. That distance helped sustain his belief in her "epileptic temperament."

———

In the winter of 1906, Sam's attention may have been increasingly drawn to a relationship that seemed to present no such difficulties. When she entered employment in his household Isabel Lyon was single. In Florence she had had her flirtation with a priest. And just before they had all departed for Florence she had set her sights on a widower. "How I kept on a strange sympathy with that man when he lost his wife—" she confided to her diary eighteen months later, "but it didn't find a footing, he didn't need the sympathetic wave for he married his typewriter ever so soon." Seeing the couple out driving on Easter Sunday, 1905, she reflected on matrimony: "I've known several men who have married several times—they couldn't live without the companionship and sympathy of a woman—And I like the thought of it—."[23]

In the wake of Livy's death, Lyon had observed a respectful distance from her employer, seeming almost worshipful of both the living and the dead. "All my days I go the softlier because of his influence—" she observed. "His influence and the influence of the holy dead."[24] Slowly, however, she began to uncouple both herself and Sam from the past. By the time she sighted the "typewriter" in a carriage, the "thought" she enjoyed may have been of Sam.

I think a very great deal of Miss Lyon," Twain wrote with emphasis to Clara in June 1905. His high opinion of Miss Lyon continued to grow throughout that year, but he maintained certain family boundaries, excluding her, for example, from any responsibility for Jean's medical treatment. Lyon was nonetheless pervasive. "She sat at table & in the drawing-room when there was company & when there wasn't," Sam observed; "our intimates became her intimates; they visited her & she visited them; of her own motion & by her own desire she became housekeeper." The secretary had begun to "evolute," he explained several years later. "Not swiftly. No, quite slowly, & by stages: one affectation, one sham, one artificiality at a time." By his own admission, he had few defenses against flattery, and his secretary regularly buttered him up, not with a knife but a trowel.[25]

Lyon, of course, did not see it that way. "Oh, the richness of his nature, and his brain and his soul," she rhapsodized in her journal in January 1906. "He sounds the awfulest depths of the tragedies of earth and heaven and hell—he bubbles over with gaity—he melts with grief into silent sobs—he slays with satire your beliefs—he boils over into profanities that make you feel the terrors of the thunderbolts that must come—and he is the gentlest, most considerate, most lovable creature in all the earth—yet how he covers his true self away from most!" And in February: "What a glorious creature he is! It is his greatness—his genius—his magnetism—his strong humanness—and his great sweet soul."[26]

By that winter her relationship to Sam had clearly begun to expand. "Mr. Clemens and I were in the northbound subway train," she wrote in her diary, "he had been acutely aware of a beautiful girl who sat on 'the port side of the car.'" At dinner he asked Lyon if she had noticed the woman.

"No—I hadn't seen her—"

"Didn't see her! Why her beauty filled the car!" Clemens expostulated.

"When I reached C.C.'s [Clara's] room after dinner," Lyon continued, "I confessed to her that I hadn't seen that beautiful girl because I had been trying not to look at a glorious young God of a man. The little rascal told on me at tea this afternoon, to the delight of Mr. Clemens and Bynner," a writer and friend of the family. "In great glee, Mr. Clemens called us 'a pair of old flirts.'"[27]

———

As Lyon's attitude toward her employer evolved during the winter of 1906, so too did her feelings toward his youngest daughter. "This was a tragic day—," she stated ominously in her diary on January 27, 1906. "I came in from a shopping expedition for Jean and others—and when I went into her room for tea, she told me that a terrible thing had happened." According to Lyon's report, Jean said that "[i]n a burst of unreasoning rage she struck Katie a terrible blow in the face—."

"The significance of it is what is so terrible—," Lyon continued, openly signaling her intent to interpret the blow. "[F]or now she has done what I have seen in her [unreadable] and feared she would do— (She is distressed poor child)—She described the wave of passion that swept over her as being that of an insane person—" Lyon wrote dramatically. "She knew she couldn't stop—she had to strike—and she said that she wanted to kill." Thus ends the passage as originally written.[28]

That Jean hit Katy in the face seems possible, though Jean herself never mentioned the incident in her diary or letters. But if that fact seems simple, its meaning is ambiguous. If Jean did hit Katy, the blow clearly brought remorse—and perhaps a need to confess—as Lyon acknowledged in her important parenthetical phrase "(She is distressed poor child)." The incident may have been accidental, occurring during one of Jean's grand mal seizures, characterized as they are by involuntary movements of the arms and legs. Or perhaps the blow was intended, as Lyon seemed so ready to believe ("she has done what I have . . . feared she would do"). Jean had a temper, and her father had more than once called her disagreeable. But no one had ever suggested that temper led to violence, and Lyon's own indication of Jean's remorse further reinforces this judgment.

Katy offers no clues about this incident. Certainly, the housekeeper did not publicly signal any fear about Jean. Of course, she may have been masking her distrust for the sake of Jean's father and sister—and Jean herself—all of whom she loved. Whatever the case, she continued to care for Jean in a motherly fashion. And she continued to occupy the room next to Jean's. Many years later she remarked that "Jean was always interested in any kind of suffering, whether it was animals or humans," and her historical sweep was inclusive, "from the time she was a little bit of a girl, all her life." "You see," Katy added, "Jean had a very tender heart for any one she thought warn't treated right."[29] If Katy had any notion that Jean had tried to kill her in 1906, the down-to-earth housekeeper proved mighty charitable in her later portrayal.

Lyon's interpretation was strikingly negative, visibly framing the event as an expression of homicidal passion. "She knew she couldn't stop," Lyon wrote, "she had to strike—and she said that she wanted to kill." It is difficult to sort out what Jean might actually have said from Lyon's telling. And if this was indeed what Lyon had "feared she would do," if she had anticipated that Jean could turn violent, then this expectation would almost certainly have affected her ability to interpret the incident without bias. Just three weeks earlier, however, she had sympathized with Jean's loneliness and need for love from the entire family—in which Lyon included herself.

This would seem to signal that an important shift was taking place in Lyon's attitude toward Jean. With Sam in Washington from January 25 to January 30, Lyon apparently seized the initiative and decided to have a talk with Dr. Quintard, the family's general practitioner, about Jean's state of mind. This private chat was the first of many consultations she had with Jean's doctors—a practice Sam acquiesced in and ultimately encouraged.[30]

That people with epilepsy exhibited violent behavior was not only a popular prejudice of the era but was also held as a scientific belief. The Italian physician Cesare Lombroso convinced many of his peers that epilepsy was the cause of criminality. The *American Journal of Insanity* warned in 1890: "the history of epilepsy is the history of violence, of crime, of homicide." And *The Journal of Nervous and Mental Disease* later listed "aggressive violence without cause" and "an irresistible impulse, leading to suicide and murder" among the dominant characteristics of the condition.[31] Thus Lyon's assumption that Jean was prone to vicious criminality and violence mirrored the thinking of her period.[32] Nonetheless, there was something unusual about it.

On the basis of hundreds of patient case files, letters to doctors, and family questionnaires filled out in the early decades of the twentieth century, one expert concluded that "Those most hostile toward epileptics were also the most distant.... Families, by contrast, showed the least fear of epileptics and the greatest tendency to see seizures as but one manifestation of complex personal identities."[33] Another study of parental reactions to children with epilepsy concluded that mothers often held onto an empathetic knowledge of their children despite contradictory "scientific" judgments. The negative labels surrounding epilepsy were "sharply limited" in their influence on maternal feelings and knowledge.[34] Certainly this seemed to have been true of Jean's mother. And Lyon herself had showed no fear in Dublin the previous summer, sharing intimacies and a sympathetic companionship with Jean. Although families may have feared the disease itself and felt some of its stigma, their intimate experience practically always inoculated them against fear of the family member who had epilepsy.

Lyon became an intimate in the Clemens family, yet she maintained—or returned to—the attitudes of a stranger toward Jean. Certainly Sam saw no halo around his youngest daughter's head, but he never detected any proclivity to violence. Yet as Lyon became more entwined in the family, her apprehension and prejudice toward Jean seemed to grow.

––––––

Yet another shift in the configuration of the household took place in the winter of 1906. On January 3, Twain went to dinner at The Players, a private men's club from which he had resigned three years earlier. According to Lyon, a bookkeeper had posted "S. L. Clemens for non-payment of dues," which had triggered his angry resignation. After Livy's death, however, the club's members coaxed him to return. That evening, Twain apparently told David Munro, one of the Players, that he had found Albert Bigelow Paine's biography of Thomas Nast "damn good." Munro passed the compliment to Paine.[35]

Paine, who was then forty-four and twice married, had been staff editor for the children's magazine *St. Nicholas* and had written a number of other books for both adults and children. Hearing the secondhand compliment, he mustered his courage and quickly called on Twain with an audacious proposal to write his official biography. After some preliminaries, Twain looked at the younger man with one of his piercing stares and asked: "When would you like to begin?"

"Whenever you like. I can begin now," Paine replied.[36]

Paine did offer one suggestion: that he bring a stenographer who could take notes as Twain recalled incidents and episodes for the book. Twain, who had enjoyed using dictation in Florence, immediately took to the idea—with Paine to prod his memory and act as audience. But he altered a few features. He would pay for the stenographer, he told Paine, and he would own the results, which Paine could consult at any time. Twain decided to use the occasion to continue his autobiographical musings, again letting free association determine his pathway through the past.[37]

The first dictation, on January 9, 1906, set a pattern for many of the rest. Twain was in bed, propped against "great snowy pillows," and "clad in a handsome silk dressing-gown" with his pipes, cigars, and papers on his bedside table. Paine remembered that the bedside lamp cast a glow on his mane of white hair and chiseled face. Smoking constantly, Twain began with the history of the Comstock mines, then drifted back to recollections of his childhood, only to reconnect with current affairs near the end of his musings. "We were watching one of the great literary creators of his time in the very process of his architecture," Paine reported. He and the newly hired stenographer, Josephine Hobby, were so totally absorbed in the play of Twain's mind that they were amazed to find that over two hours had passed. Lyon kept notes, sitting in an easy chair and watching Twain talk. "He was magical this morning," she observed.[38]

Twain was elated. "Narrative writing is always disappointing," he explained. "The moment you pick up a pen you begin to lose the spontaneity of the personal relation, which contains the very essence of interest. With shorthand dictation one can talk as if he were at his own dinner-table—always a most inspiring place." Twain devoted himself to these dictations for the rest of the year, racking up a record 134 in spite of his hectic schedule of banquets, speeches, and public gatherings.[39]

In the winter of 1905–6 alone, Twain made no less than a dozen formal speeches in addition to his constant stream of informal remarks. He was always being called upon for commentary or entertainment, and he simply stopped preparing his talks. Paine believes that his daily dictations had given him the confidence that he needed to trust the inspiration of the moment. But his confidence drew from other sources as well. The press lionized him: reporters pestered him constantly for quotes, and his activities were zealously tracked. The public clamored for him.

At the Majestic Theater, where he spoke to members of the Young Men's Christian Association, one newspaper reported that ten thousand well-dressed men and women had stampeded the hall before his talk. A letter of Mark Twain's sold at auction for forty-three dollars, said to be the highest amount ever paid for a letter by a living author.[40] America's love affair with Mark Twain continued to flourish.

————

Immediately accepted into the family's inner circle, Paine was soon sharing long chats with Lyon on their favorite topic—Mark Twain. "This morning Mr. Paine said such a beautiful thing about Mr. Clemens," Lyon sighed, and then repeated Paine's words: "Oh, he's the *King*—he's the *King* and it's so glorious to know he is crowned."[41] They were full of rhapsodic praises for the man they called "King": "yes—he was far and away the King above all the others."[42]

They were not the only ones. William Dean Howells used this grand appellation in a public birthday salute to the man he privately called "old scratch-gravel."[43] Twain's publisher at Harper's, Colonel George Harvey, threw him a lavish seventieth birthday party at Delmonico's in December 1905. The guest list was a veritable who's who of American literati. Toastmaster Howells read a sonnet he had composed for the occasion, ending with: "Joke of a people great, gay, bold, and free, / I type their master-mood. Mark Twain made me." Then, raising his glass, Howells began the official toast: "Now, ladies and gentlemen, and Colonel Harvey, I will try not to be greedy on your behalf in wishing the health of our honored and in view of his great age, our revered guest. I will not say, 'Oh, King, live forever,' but 'Oh, King, live as long as you like!' "[44]

Howells, however, consciously refused to treat his friend like royalty. Though they both lived in New York, Howells remarked that they did not see each other often now. Various ailments as well as their advancing age were partially to blame, but not completely. "He expected me to come to him," Howells noted, "and I would not without some return of my visits, but we never ceased to be friends."[45] For Howells, affection and admiration were not the same as worship.

Lyon was incapable of making that distinction. Acolyte and high priestess, she worshipped the king with increasing fervency. More than half a year before he appeared in Howell's toast or Paine's conversations, the king had made his royal entrance in her diary. "Yes, I am near a throne," she wrote in June 1905. (Decades later, living well into her nineties, Lyon kept a shrine to Clemens in her New York apartment, featuring the artifacts of her days at court.)[46]

Keeping a diary seemed a crucial part of her worship. "Never, never on sea or shore of spiritual or terrestrial being could there be a man to equal Mr. Clemens," she wrote in March 1905. "The subtlety of his magic and he doesn't know it." Other entries echoed this reverential tone.[47] "These pages are full of repetitious adoration of the King," she self-consciously glossed her own diary the following year, "but that's how they should be, for each day brings its wave of recognition of his greatness and my spirit sings and claps its silent hands over the wonder and the beauty of him. He is the saint and the shrine before the saint— the God behind it all."[48] The awed Miss Lyon of these entries is humbly sacerdotal in Clemens's presence, almost simple in her praise of him. Yet an entry recorded the day after Clemens arrived in Dublin in May 1905 warns that appearances can be deceiving.

"Chiefs can read everybody—but who can rightly read chiefs—" Lyon asked innocently.

And she replied: "That makes me think of a little story I once read about a king—a mighty King whose life was governed by the words of an ignorant body servant—There was no greater *wisdom* in the land than the King's—and yet, by a sinister word the man servant could blast the better judgment of the King—could cause the King to condemn as worthless—as self seeking—the service and homage of those who would gladly place their hands between those of the King—in token of eternal obedience—and the King never saw that it was only jealousy in the man servant."[49]

Some time after the original entry, an addition, actually a comment on the original, was added in a lighter ink. Following "a mighty King whose life was governed by the words of an ignorant body servant," Lyon inserted: "No one suspected it."[50]

CHAPTER 4

Looking for Love

THE IMAGE WE HAVE of Mark Twain in his later years, as portrayed by both scholarly and popular writers, embodies a consistent theme of pessimism and despair, beginning from the time of Susy's death in 1896.[1] "The last two decades of Mark Twain's life veered into a dead-end despair," one critic wrote, describing him as "a man poisoned with self-loathing" and a "bitter and neurotic cynic." Another characteristically remarked, "Mark Twain lived the last fifteen years of his life a bitter pessimist." "Crippled," "brittle," "dulled," and possessed by a "rage at the obscenity of life" was another influential critic's characterization of the aging Twain.[2]

There are a few dissenting voices.[3] "[T]his notion of a sustained despair is beginning to look like a disposable myth of Mark Twain criticism," one commentator has hopefully observed.[4] But even as several scholars have challenged this myth, it continues to thrive. Perhaps the image of Mark Twain laid low reflects a nagging cultural apprehension of tragedy lurking behind success; or perhaps it satisfies an inclination to denigrate men of distinction. How better to undercut the great humorist than to show him lost in a cloud of impenetrable gloom and despair at the end?

One literary scholar, after examining Twain's entire published and unpublished output for the thirteen years before his death, concluded that the author was not so much despairing as inconsistent. Twain's purposes vacillated continually among contradictory goals—to write a popular novel; to write for his own amusement; to write serious philosophy; to write influential polemics; to write broadly appealing comedy or daringly irreverent and risky satire—and he appeared to be constantly changing his mind about which audience he wanted to please.[5]

As he aged, Twain seemed eager to express his ideas more freely and directly than in the past, which is probably why his enthusiasm for lengthy fiction waned and autobiography became his great love. Nonetheless, many of his short pieces, especially those with political intent, are brilliant; some of his fragmentary writing is memorable; and his autobiographical work carries out a courageous purpose that is consistent with most of his late composition: to make human pride, including his own, look ridiculous.[6]

Furthermore, to compare his writing of twenty years earlier to the later works is to recognize the fallacy of attributing unique despair to the elder Twain. In his early fifties, he was no less skeptical and pessimistic than in his seventies. *A Connecticut Yankee in King Arthur's Court,* published in 1889, with its vision of mass annihilation resulting from technological "progress," is as bleak and blistering an indictment of humanity's meanness as the much later *No. 44, The Mysterious Stranger.* Even *Huckleberry Finn,* though it is sometimes regarded as hopeful and affirming for its idyllic descriptions of nature and its sympathetic portrayals of Huck and Jim, takes an exceptionally dark view of both individual capacities and institutional values. The reenslavement of Jim at the end can be read as an uncompromising indictment of the failure of Reconstruction and the negative aftermath of the Civil War. Mark Twain, then, was always a person of many moods, in and out of print—gloomy and pessimistic but also cheerful, energetic, and loving. To the end he retained a degree of optimism at least equal to his vaunted despair.[7]

The truth is that after Livy died, Sam began to indulge himself. He went through a year of deep grieving for his wife, but the first summer spent in Dublin was a healing experience, and he returned to New York with a zest for life that would have been noteworthy in a man much younger than his seventy years. He worked only when it suited him. And when he did, he spent huge amounts of time on his autobiography. He played billiards to the point of satiety—and was unapologetic. He sought diversion and fun in his own home and in society. He indulged the freedom to travel when and where he fancied. He wrote letters to little girls he met and innocently pestered them in person. He acted on his whims and unabashedly enjoyed life and the fruits of his celebrity. In England, for example, he made the papers by walking across the street in his bathrobe and slippers. In New York, he would stroll up Fifth Avenue on a pleasant Sunday morning, timing his return to maximize attention from the crowds that thronged the avenue after church.[8] He also had great fun living under the same roof as an attractive, vivacious, seductive woman more than twenty-five years his junior, who adored him and constantly flattered his vanity, telling him that he had "the buoyancy belonging to a man of 45."[9]

———

After a stimulating winter in New York, Sam and Lyon returned to Dublin in mid-May for a second summer, full of positive anticipation. But for Sam the experience was disappointing.[10] This time he had rented the Upton house, which stood at the edge of a beautiful beech forest, some two or three miles from the town. Though the views of lake, forest, hills, and distant mountains were like a painting, the location sometimes seemed remote and austere. Apparently even the servants found it depressing. And once again, Clara spent no time in Dublin, preferring to spend another summer in Norfolk, Connecticut, where she was near her doctor. Only Jean was athletic enough to enjoy prowling around the countryside. She had arrived earliest, on April 30, with Katy and three servants to help her get settled in the new house.[11]

Twain planned to continue his autobiographical dictations in Dublin, so Alfred Bigelow Paine and the stenographer, Josephine Hobby both rented lodgings in the village and drove out to the house each morning. Twain began dictating on May 21, soon after he arrived. He skipped his dictation on June 5, the second anniversary of Livy's death, and did not resume till June 7, when he talked for more than two hours about his wife's last days in Florence. He had a personality that did not stay long in the shadows, however, and he soon resumed livelier reminiscences. When the weather cooperated, he would pace up and down the long veranda of the house, pausing now and then to soak in the vistas of the imposing blue mountain, Monadnock, and even bluer horizon. As the days got warmer, he would sometimes sit in a large rocking chair on the veranda, smoking and gazing at the hills, while he spoke slowly and deliberately of his past associations with Ulysses S.

Grant or Mrs. Clemens's final days or the foolishness of orthodox religion. Beyond his dictations in the morning, Twain did very little literary work, although he had brought his "manuscript trunk" with him.[12] Perhaps as a consequence, he was sometimes more bored than relaxed.

"We are living in solitude, but it is a pleasant one," Sam wrote to Clara in a contented mood. A few days earlier, however, he had been reduced to browsing through old copies of the weekly magazine *Littell's Living Age*. He quipped that he felt as if he were "looking at an asphalt pavement," and one morning in his dictation he commented, "I feel for Adam and Eve now, for I know how it was with them.... The Garden of Eden I now know was an unendurable solitude. I know that the advent of the serpent was a welcome change—anything for society." But even if he dubbed his summer home "the Lodge of Sorrow" and more ironically "The House of Mirth," it did offer some diversions. He never lost his ability to get large enjoyment from absolute simplicity. The antics of cats, for example, never failed to amuse him. Watching kittens he had named Sackcloth and Ashes chase insects gave him unequivocal pleasure. "He laughed extravagantly," Paine observed after one performance, "and evidently cared more for that moment's entertainment than for many philosophies."[13]

And one diversion in particular reveals the oversimplification of the myth of Twain's sustained geriatric despair. The Dubliners regularly amused themselves on summer evenings by playing charades, with two teams that mixed adults and children. Generally Twain and the artist George de Forest Brush were team captains, and Lyon and Jean played on opposite sides. One night Mr. Brush's side chose to act out "Monadnock." The first syllable, "moan," was dramatized as an Irish wake, "add" as a school scene, and "knock" as a satire of a spiritualist's meeting. Finally, as was their custom, the whole word was presented as a group of hikers camping overnight who were frightened by unrecognizable animal noises. Then Twain's team did "cocktail": first a scene with roosters and hens, then another school scene in which Twain was the teacher and "gave a talk on the art of telling a story," Jean recalled. "He explained that it wasn't necessary to have a point but to tell the thing well."

Brush's team next did "multiply," followed by Twain's "champagne." "Sham" was dramatized as a kitten imitating a lion and scaring a brave warrior. In the next scene, the curtain opened, Jean remembered, "exposing Father lying on the bench in a baby-cap and long white robe with a bottle in his mouth, asleep." Jean described how two nurses entered and began inspecting the sleeping baby, saying they were afraid to take his bottle away for fear he would start to cry. As if on cue, Twain began to howl. A doctor was called to the scene and he examined the "still violently yelling" patient. He ordered a warm bath, Jean remembered, and after a tiny foot-bath was brought in Twain dutifully rolled off the bench onto it. Jean reported that everyone was "nearly sick" from laughing so hard.[14]

That summer Twain also played, with delight and gusto, an emperor with a tiny top hat secured with a scarf around his chin, an archer shooting the apple off of William Tell's head, a telegraph operator, a doctor pumping a baby's stomach with a pair of fire bellows, a roaring Irish drunk, a guide to the Statue of Liberty (played by the visiting Colonel Harvey), an oculist advising a woman who had mislaid her glass eye on the prices for a speckled replacement, a veterinarian, a prosecuting attorney, and even a lover trying to coax his desperately shy fiancée into a kiss.[15]

When Dublin's diversions paled, Sam left to spend a month playing billiards and junketing on Henry Rogers's yacht, *Kanawha*.[16] Besides the occasional cruise, he enjoyed a regular routine in New York of nights on the water and days on land. After sleeping on the yacht, Sam was dropped off at 21 Fifth Avenue around eleven, where Katy, who had returned to New York on May 16 after getting Jean settled, was ready to offer her own version of indulgence. Sam did not usually take lunch, but Katy, wanting to entice him with something special, arranged with a local bakery to make a fresh huckleberry pie every forenoon. "I try to think of all the things you like—to try to make you happy," she told him proudly.[17] He would devour half the pie and a quart of ice-cold milk each day, much to their mutual delight.

"I have worked pretty steadily for 65 years," he wrote to his friend Thomas Bailey Aldrich, a well-known writer, "and don't care what I do with the 2 or 3 that remain to me so that I get pleasure out of them."[18] If Twain is to be characterized in this period by single words, vain, self-indulgent, and fun-loving would seem at least as accurate as gloomy, despairing, and bitter.

Jean, meanwhile, had returned to Dublin like a shipwrecked sailor grasping for a life raft. Her winter had been difficult and isolating, and her spirits soared at the prospect of the physical activities of country life and of seeing her friends. Energetic, fun-loving, and playful, Jean relished the rambunctious companionship of youth and continued to feel more at home with "children" than adults in Dublin. "I was very much surprised," Jean wrote in the middle of the summer, "when Mrs. Cheney said that she wanted me to see her daughter Ruth..., although she was a good deal older than I am. I asked Ruth's age and found it to be twenty-one. And this occurred on my twenty-sixth birthday!" Jean sometimes joined friends eight to ten years her junior in children's games such as stillpond or duck-on-the-rock, both frenetic variations on the game of tag.[19]

On one memorable night at the Thayers', supper was interrupted by a spontaneous food fight. Jean had "a desperate fight with both Robert and Gerry," she reported gleefully. "The latter nearly squashed me and if someone didn't come to my assistance he would certainly have won and carried off our grapes." The evening continued with word games including "twenty questions." She had a "beautiful time"—but the attack that followed the next day greatly dampened her spirits. The seizure had come sooner than her usual pattern, and she attributed the bad outcome to her "excitement" the previous evening. "This wretched, miserable disease," she wrote. "If I have any fun, the suffering at once follows."[20]

Nonetheless, she relished being outdoors. Climbing Monadnock was a favorite activity for all ages. Jean climbed with children and adults, going up the mountain with her best friend, Nancy Brush, who was ten years her junior, and Hildegaarde Henderson. She made another ascent with Albert Bigelow Paine, Lyon, and Nancy's eighteen-year-old brother, Gerry Brush. The foursome had a grand time, and even Lyon enjoyed the company, commenting that Jean was in a "wonderfully sweet mood."[21]

Jean's first climb in the middle of July, however, had raised red flags in the family circle. Both Sam and Clara, who weighed in by mail, objected to the lack of a chaperone in her hike up Monadnock with Tom McKittrick. "It wasn't about my health then but about the propriety of it," Jean decided, probably erroneously. "If those two can't leave me *any* freedom at all there will be trouble," she threatened "if not absolute refusal."[22] Her frustration was understandable. Clara went out alone with "young gentlemen," and her own mother had been responsible for two children at a younger age. That summer Jean began to rebel against this overprotective style of parenting, which she no longer recognized as legitimate. The urge to chaperone Jean, to protect and guard her was as understandable as her rebellion. But the threat of sexual impropriety during a seizure seems extreme. Earlier that spring, for example, Sam had forbidden a trip to the dentist without a female chaperone; George O'Conners, Jean's new groom, was deemed unsuitable. Sam had reason to be upset, however, by George's absence on a horse and buggy drive Jean took with her friend Nancy. Any seizure, however brief, would have had serious consequences with Jean at the reins. "Miss Lyon agreed to that," Jean observed, "so I have had my last drive alone with Nancy—for this year, anyway."[23]

As Jean's comment reveals, Lyon's influence in the household was increasing. It was also decisive and one-sided. "She invariably disagrees with anything I suggest that doesn't absolutely agree with Father," Jean observed. Sam and Lyon did not allow Jean to go anywhere alone, even to an amateur theatrical production in the local village.[24] These restrictions seemed excessive to her.

In fact, Jean yearned for independence and the autonomy that would follow if she had an income of her own. "For some time I have been hoping that I can earn a little something from my carving," she admitted, "but unfortunately carving is very slow work & fairly hard work besides." Vowing to apply herself with greater diligence to what had been merely a hobby, she finished three bookracks to sell by the end of the summer.[25] Jean hired carpenters to prepare and assemble her wood, but she did the drawing, carving, and staining herself, tiring work for a person whose strength was sometimes sapped by illness. Jean concluded that unless she was very well, the work was likely to "develop absent-mindedness," her term for petit mal, "and that is to be avoided."[26]

Carving was not only physically demanding work, it was time-consuming as well. She calculated that it took her slightly over fifteen hours to apply the design and to finish carving one bookrack. If sales outlets were scarce and she could sell no object for more than $10, as she believed, the commercial viability of her carving was doubtful. Nonetheless, near the end of her stay in Dublin she was still hoping to "put aside as cash whatever profit I make on my wood-carving" to help buy "a small plot of ground."[27]

————

If she was no healthier in Dublin, Jean's ability to cope with the psychological dimensions of her disease improved dramatically there. She decided to break with the familial strategy of concealment. Whether as a response to her mother's death, to the acquisition of friends, or to her own maturation, she became more open and adopted a less secretive stance in her summer home. Still fearful of prejudicial behavior, however, she remained reluctant about naming her condition. "I told them that I am given to having fainting turns which are very troublesome," she wrote in May 1906 about a conversation she had had the previous summer with Mr. Brush and his son, Gerry. "I felt as though I really ought to tell them what my disease is and yet I had a feeling that restrained me. It occurred to me," she revealed, "that with all his small children, if he knew, Mr. Brush might be afraid to have me about as much as I hope to be, because even when they have been told that there is always ample warning, people often are afraid & don't quite believe that that is so."[28]

Jean's reaction is a poignant example of "felt stigma"—avoidance of full disclosure of some condition in anticipation of a damaging or hurtful response.[29] Although within weeks of this anxious entry, Jean had confided in her four closest Dublin friends—Nancy and Gerry Brush and Gra (Gerald) and Galla Thayer—without any negative consequences, she still avoided using the word "epilepsy."[30] Nevertheless she began to gain more confidence after confiding in her mates. As she told more people about her condition, she also spoke more freely in her diary. Where previously she had referred only sporadically and euphemistically to her symptoms, by the summer of 1906 she began to use the term "petit-mal," noting that "some of them were very long."[31]

Jean suffered mild petit mal on a regular basis, experiencing "short touches of absentmindedness" that came in the morning and toward evening. One morning she reported a "remarkable" occurrence: she did not vomit after breakfast.[32] "Again I feel well," she wrote on another day. "Nobody not having my disease would be able to appreciate what it means to me to waken on a bright, beautiful morning and realize as soon as I am awake that my head is clear." But of a bad day, she wrote, "I was wretchedly ill all day long. Of course there were short moments in between the absent-minded turns, when I was clear-headed, but they were very short and often, all during the entire day, the turns were very long. After supper I was desperately tired and exhausted, so much so, in fact, that I preferred not to see Father." In May she made a telling contrast between sickness and health. "To one whose head is always clear, my delight over the days when I do not have to spend half of the time wondering what the person speaking has said, or whether some lovely bird has flown by during that moment of unconsciousness," she recognized, "that delight would be incomprehensible and to many an affectation."[33]

But she could cope with these brief lapses of consciousness. What she dreaded were the grand mal seizures—"hideous attacks" as she called them. During her stay in Dublin, Jean braved major attacks on three to five days each month.[34] She often received warnings of an impending grand mal, lamenting that "they are never false arrivals. I have learned to believe their statements and not to love them in consequence." As if to confirm her warning signs, she reported two major attacks the following day. The onset of menstruation was one signal; others included extreme restlessness and irritability.[35]

Servants cared for Jean during her attacks, trying to prevent her from injuring herself. "I fell off the bed and onto my face on the floor," Jean recorded early in the summer. "I struck my cheek bone and made it sore but without bruising it." Usually her caretakers had more success. "Anna said she had never seen me so violent before," Jean revealed about another episode, "and that it had been difficult to keep me on the bed." (Though Anna calls her "violent" here, neither she nor Jean gives the word any significance beyond the physical manifestations of her seizure.) As a result her eyes ached and her back and sides were lame. Aftereffects of a major seizure included weakness, exhaustion, and depression. She described herself as "limp and lifeless" and "blue."[36]

Jean constantly worried about her mental capacities. Afraid of embarrassing herself by what she forgot, she was particularly anxious about her "bad memory." A conversation with one girlfriend was revealing.

"She didn't think that people felt those lacks that I spoke of, in me," Jean recorded, skeptical nonetheless that close friends were not cognizant of what she called "those fearful conditions of my brain." But she was hungry for reassurance and eager to be convinced. "However, she seemed to be speaking as she felt and I really feel better." Predictably her deep fear of inferiority was only temporarily subdued by her girlfriend's support. "[J]ust now I am beginning to believe myself very stupid and utterly incompetent of judging books or plays," she wrote two months later.[37]

At that time Jean was under the care of Dr. Frederick Peterson, having switched specialists in the winter after Lyon's consultation with Dr. Quintard, the family physician who probably made the referral.[38] Peterson had been an assistant physician at Hudson River State Hospital for the Insane before successfully lobbying for a state-sponsored institution exclusively devoted to the care and treatment of persons with epilepsy in New York State. As a result, in 1896 the Craig Colony for Epileptics was established in southwestern New York on an isolated 1,800-acre property that was formerly the site of a Shaker colony. Peterson was its first president. Though sensitive to the social prejudice faced by epileptics, Peterson believed it was best to isolate them in order to prevent the spread of epilepsy to future generations. His attitude was far from unusual. Studies completed as late as 1983 show physicians' attitudes toward patients with epilepsy were often negative; three-quarters of a century earlier the situation was far worse. Unable to control the symptoms, much less effect a cure, physicians experienced continual frustration. Combined with stereotypes of menacing corruption brought on by neurological degeneration, medical views of epilepsy during this period were intensely hostile.[39]

There was no evident hostility, however, in Peterson's treatment of Jean during that second Dublin summer. He employed the standard regimens that included diet, drugs, and other physical restrictions. Jean was taking "prevention pills," perhaps in the family of bromides, commonly prescribed at the time. The doctor believed that delaying an attack, even if only for a day, was a step toward gradual improvement. Following the theory of an "exciting cause," he had Jean on a strict diet of cooked eggs at dinner. He also wished her to eliminate any overexertion, undue stress, and excitable entertainment. After a seizure, she was required to take a "regulation nap."[40]

Jean chafed at the restrictions. "Oh! this horrible disease," she cried, "how many things it interferes with, and, roughly speaking spoils utterly," referring to an invitation to stay with friends which she had to turn down. It also spoiled another pleasure. "It isn't enough to have this fiendish disease, but in the endeavor to improve it, riding has to be declared the most injurious occupation for me!" "Will I ever get rid of it?" she asked herself. "And if I do will it be before I am so much older than these friends that they won't want me around any more? I can't really have any hope."[41] But the truth is that both Jean and her father did hope for a cure.

Sam—and his secretary—may have been overzealous in their efforts to shield Jean from physical harm, but they offered meager help for her acute emotional vulnerability. Her father made allowances for her moods and reacted with pity to her suffering, but his patronizing forbearance was actually a high barrier to their intimacy. Nevertheless, his capacity to enjoy life could transcend even his own psychological barriers, and he responded charitably to his daughter's fun-loving side. "Father is almost invariably indescribably sweet and sympathetic about all my interests," Jean wrote under the spell of Dublin. "No one could possibly be as lovely as he always has been about my romping young friends. Some of these he has liked but he is always lovely to *all* of them." For her part Lyon sometimes denigrated Jean in her presence, reinforcing her fears that she was stupid and unattractive, yet they could still have their moments of tenderness. Lying on the grass one early September evening with Lyon's rubber cape spread beneath them, they watched the stars and giggled together like sisters.[42]

Jean also gained a rare sense of being admired by a few men, mostly middle-aged, who expressed appreciation. For its scarcity alone, any shred of praise was hoarded. When she was dressed as the Empress of India for a charade one evening in early September, with colorful scarves and silver necklace, George Brush "was tremendously enthusiastic." He told her, Jean recalled, that "he had always loved me but that he was dead in love with me now! Costumes and looking well," she dryly moralized, "seem capable of accomplishing a good deal." And Jean returned the compliment: "There are precious few people that I am as fond of as I am of Mr. Brush and of late I haven't seen him nearly as frequently as I love to."[43]

Another middle-aged man, Albert Bigelow Paine, admired Jean's looks, photographed her extensively, and sometimes teased her gently. "She dressed always in white," he remembered, "and she was tall and pale and classically beautiful, and she was often silent, like a spirit." By the time of his departure from Dublin, Jean confessed, "I felt almost like weeping—he has always been so sweet to me." Months earlier in New York, Paine had remarked presciently to Lyon that Jean "had the tragic beauty of a young queen doomed to the block."[44]

―――――

What Jean ached for, however, was not the appreciation tinged with tragedy of middle-aged men but romance, and, at twenty-six, she threw herself at one young man with all the finesse of a sixteen-year-old in the throes of her first crush. "[T]o my unspeakable happiness," Gerry Brush called the day after she arrived in Dublin. As "sweet, gentle, courteous and attractive a boy as I ever hope to see" was how Jean described him. "I realize more than ever how really fond I am of him," she confessed, "consequently, I can't help wishing our homes weren't so far apart." This was the moment when her crush began in earnest.[45]

In less than a month she discovered a rival: Gerry was taking frequent walks with Anna Cabot. "He is much Anna's superior," was Jean's initial response. She fervently searched for signs that Gerry's relationship with Anna was nothing "more serious than friendship" and that her own had romantic possibilities. Gerry spoke of Anna in a "perfectly commonplace way," she reported, "so that I have begun to think that he hasn't started any foolishness yet." Yearning for her own foolishness, she was much encouraged at the end of June when she had two dances and an hour's tête-à-tête with him.[46]

"The desire to have Gerry feel a real affection for me is so strong, that I am going to try and see if I can make it develop," Jean vowed. "It may be," she worried, "that I show too much pleasure in his company, too much affection and admiration for him." Deciding to show less enthusiasm without being unfriendly, she reasoned that "when a girl does show those things openly, it usually follows that the man quietly takes it all for granted ... and thinks very little or almost not at all, of the girl." But her resolution quickly crumbled. "No, that won't do, Gerry," she responded after he turned down a dinner invitation. She pushed to see him the following evening.[47] Jean realized that all her intentions to re-strain herself had gone "to smash." But she was willing to throw off her restraint to feel what she evocatively described as her "internals surg[ing] with joy."

Her joyful surge was soon quashed by gnawing uncertainty over Gerry's feelings for her. A shuttlecock for Cupid, one day she was over-joyed, feeling confident that he truly liked her. But the next day she saw Gerry and Anna in the village together and decided that "his friendship for Anna is so much greater than it is for me." She calculated in mid-August that he had only come to see her once without a direct invitation and that all the walks or drives were at her instigation. Crestfallen, she re-solved not to show her sorrow or to force herself upon him again.[48]

Jean's hunger for affection was riddled with self-doubt, and she pon-dered her life experience in a series of painful questions: "Why must I live on aimlessly, with nothing to do, utterly useless, all my life? I who long so for the love and companionship that only a man can give, and that man a husband. . . . Am I never to know what love means, because I am an epileptic and shouldn't marry if I had the chance?"

And she lamented, "I seem never to be attractive to men. Is that also entirely due to my disease? . . . And if a man that I could love loved me would it really be an actual wrong for me to marry him because of the possibility of the children inheriting my malady?"[49]

At that time, many physicians and psychologists shared the thinking of Dr. Peterson and would have answered affirmatively. The idea of transmitting so-called "degenerate" heredity was of great concern to sci-entists and social scientific professionals, who urged a variety of reme-dies including institutionalization and sterilization.[50] Jean was obvi-ously influenced by this climate of opinion, but her fear was also intensely personal.

"Will I have to go on indefinitely leading this empty, cheerless life without aim or real interest? Oh! it does not seem as though I could. This hunger, this passionate desire is so constant, that every time I see a young man that I like I begin to hope that he may before long do more than like me. Even when they are younger, as is generally the case, than I am, I cannot help wishing, wishing, wishing, that some day they may overlook my age my stupidities and especially my disease." Hers was a heartbreaking lament. "If only my memory could be good when I am with Gerry!!" she brooded self-consciously. "I wonder if he regards me as a terribly lacking specimen & is bored to death by being obliged to be with me? Good heavens, I hope not!"[51]

Despite her efforts that summer to be more open about her disease, Jean's "felt stigma" was a powerful discouragement and only deepened her lack of confidence. She found little to counter her sense of inferiority from her immediate family. Sam treated her like a child, in one instance correcting her grammar and reproving her use of slang in front of company. Jean resented her father's scolding and yearned for freedom. "That is a good deal why I can't get away from the feeling that I really would like to marry," she confessed. Lyon was generally no help either, praising Clara extravagantly, talking endlessly of the sister's "marvelous grace, subtlety, and wonderful powers—genius—." Jean herself saw Clara as talented and charming—and observed with some consternation that Clara had "the sort of charm and loveliness that make numberless people love her and yet she has decided not to marry. What an uneven mystery Life is!" Still Jean had no patience for Lyon's effusions. "I have known for a very long time," Jean commented astutely, "that to Miss L. Clara is heaven & earth, but I never get sufficiently used to her gushings for them not to bore, and as a rule, even annoy me."[52]

Lyon illustrates Jean's point by waxing poetic in her journal over "Santissima"—one of her pet names for Clara: "You who make a shrine of any house you inhabit—you who are a gift to every one who falls under your sweet thrall." At a later date Lyon cooed, "The very air must love to caress her as she passes through it." By comparison she found little to gush over, much less appreciate, in the youngest daughter. "The evening went well," Jean remarked after a dinner with Gerry Brush, "even though when Miss Lyon is about I am always more painfully conscious of my ignorance and stupidity."[53]

Jean did find some comfort in praise from a peer, Gra Thayer. "We were perfectly agreed in the heartiest affectionate approval of Jean as we now (then) knew her," she quoted from a letter he had written. "This we said, among other things that though Clara was charming, of course, yet we failed to understand how folks could be drawn from you to her, inasmuch as the 'higher criticism' must inevitably and instantaneously reverse the verdict!" The "we" included Gerry, and Jean was "thankful" to hear the verdict and reassured that Gerry "didn't dislike being with me."

With feelings toward Gra like a "very dearly beloved brother," she also admitted to herself that "I never feel really ashamed with Gra & I often do with Gerry."[54] When she desired a more intimate relationship, Jean felt a profound sense of inferiority, a tragic consequence of her seizures.

———

That summer Isabel Lyon also yearned for grand passion. "So wonderful is he—" she crooned about Twain, "that all others are bleak—So full of surprises of thought and action that there is no monotony where he is."[55] Starving for physical affection and inclined toward self-dramatization, she was continually frustrated by what seems to have been an elaborate tease on Sam's part. While he was in Dublin, he was in the habit of reading poetry to Jean and Lyon in the evening. "Such reading it is," the secretary sighed. "There never was any one to read so beautifully before—and to charm you so—and hurt you so—." One summer evening, with Jean at the Brushes, Lyon listened alone to selections from *The Rubaiyat.* One thinks, of course, of its most familiar passage:

> A book of Verses underneath the Bough,
> A Jug of Wine, a Loaf of Bread—and Thou
> Beside me singing in the Wilderness—
> Oh, Wilderness were Paradise enow!   (quatrain 12)

"Oh what a gifted man he is—what a marvel," she swooned. "[H]e is overflowing with a buoyancy belonging to a man of 45."[56]

For Lyon the "wilderness" of Dublin failed to transform into paradise, and she was dosing herself with Bromidia, a sedative, to help her sleep at night. She attributed her insomnia to loneliness, adding tellingly "not because one is alone, either—."[57] When Sam fled Dublin, Albert Bigelow Paine helped take up the slack. But when he left too, to be with his family, her mood dramatically worsened. "I cast my thoughts toward the ones with whom I would willingly be—but I am Prometheus—and am chained to the rock and daily my soul is torn out of me—no—*not* my soul—*not* my soul."[58]

Clearly the rock Lyon saw herself chained to was Jean. Sam expected his secretary to remain with Jean and act as her guardian when he was away, for they both believed his youngest daughter could never be left unsupervised, even in a house full of servants. Lyon's past experience as a governess clearly complicated her relationship to Jean. "[V]ery good and obedient" was the parenthetical phrase she inserted one day between notations of Jean's seizures. Procuring obedience from a twenty-six-year-old woman had to be an awkward task. "She is not my governess," Jean wrote after an especially infuriating lecture by Lyon, "and has no right whatsoever to dictate to me in the way she does."[59]

Stuck in Dublin trying to manage Jean while Twain and Paine were free to roam, Lyon became irritable and unpleasant. But her nervousness grew beyond irritability. On the way to celebrate July 4 at their club, the two women stopped at the post office and George, the groom, was dispatched on an errand. "[W]hen the horse jumped a little at the sound of firecrackers, Miss Lyon screamed," Jean reported, "and then screamed at each firecracker thereafter, even though Scott [the horse] was stoical. With George back in the wagon, she continued to scream at any strange sound."[60]

A few days later, on a day in which Lyon described herself in her diary as sad and moody, she and Jean quarreled over the contents of a letter to Twain. Hoping to fool her father into mistaking her handwriting for the secretary's, Jean wrote a few silly lines in a note that Lyon had already begun. According to Jean, the governess was determined to spoil the innocuous little joke; when Jean playfully tapped her on both cheeks to interrupt her tattling, Lyon indignantly tore the letter in half, snapping that "she wouldn't stand such treatment," Jean reported, "& that she wouldn't write Father at all, now."[61]

Strangely enough, Lyon completely ignored this incident in her diary, writing instead about her walk to Thorndyke Pond, her sad mood, and her desire to read Nietzsche.[62] Her silence is puzzling given the fears she had earlier expressed about Jean's violent proclivities. Jean herself was rather surprised that there was no "atmosphere" between them as a result. Lyon seemed lost in her own world.

———————

Romance was not the only longing affecting Lyon that summer. Soon after he had become almost a part of Twain's household in New York, Albert Paine spoke to her about a farmhouse on a seventy-five-acre piece of land for sale near his home in Redding, Connecticut, where he lived with his wife and children. Paine's rhapsodies about this site were infectious. She was drawn to his images of bucolic beauty and twenty-mile vistas. "With an aching heart I reached out for that farm," Lyon wrote, "for I don't ever want to go back to Farmington again—" and the house there where her mother still lived. "Life is such a tiny bubble," she mused; "why we reach out for material things I don't know; but we do it—and that old beamed farmhouse on top of the hill held out its arms to me."[63]

Interestingly, she visualized the farmhouse as her accepting lover, in contrast to the recalcitrant Sam. "I didn't think he would want it," she wrote, seeming to imply an emotional rejection as much as a judgment about a building. "I couldn't think he would want anything that I want—."[64] Petulant and wounded capture her attitude on that March day in 1906.

For Lyon, the farmhouse translated into the willing lover she would embrace at any cost. No obstacle was insurmountable, and she worked with an exhausting diligence to satisfy her longing. Persuading Clemens, with his usual reckless faith in good investments, to buy the property proved easy. Prodded by both Lyon and Paine, he purchased land in Redding less than two months after Paine joined the inner circle and continued to add to his holdings in May and September 1906.[65] Owning the property would be moot, though, if he could not be persuaded to build a permanent residence in the Connecticut countryside—a more difficult proposition.

Lyon had several key players to win over. Jean was delighted with the prospect of escaping New York in the winter but worried that with a country home in Connecticut her father would not want to summer in Dublin.[66] Reassured that Dublin would not be abandoned, she became an enthusiastic ally. But Clara, absent from his household as frequently as possible, remained to be convinced. She held sway as the eldest, and Lyon, intuitive and shrewd about social power, had long ago understood Clara's influence in Twain's entourage. Admiring her beauty and her beaux, Lyon constantly flattered Clara, thereby winning her affection and even her trust. "Nana" was Clara's pet name for the secretary, and "Santa Clara" or "Santissima" were Lyon's affectionate rejoinders.[67] Apparently Clara was sufficiently interested in the project to meet her in New York in mid-August to sketch plans for the Redding house with the architect John Howells, son of William Dean Howells. The trio made an on-site visit that left Lyon "overwhelmed with enthusiasm." The spot they chose on the top of a hill resembled an Italian garden, she reported to Jean, with twenty-three cedar trees and an abundance of bay-bushes. "It is very beautiful," Lyon commented succinctly in her diary, but back in Dublin her "gushings" nearly drove Jean to distraction.[68]

Paine was already more than an ally, having planted the idea in Lyon's mind to begin with. He cultivated her enthusiasm with a mix of altruism and blatant self-interest: he would be a neighbor and a readily available billiard partner for Sam, and, of course, it would be highly advantageous to him if the subject of his newest research project were to live next door. After Paine and Lyon surveyed the property together, he even offered her a strip of his own land on which to build a little house. But there was a condition attached. "[I]f I am good, very good," she reported as if some concrete promise had been extracted by Paine, and she vowed "Oh, I must be good—monotonously good—."[69]

Good about what is never made clear, but perhaps the shrewd contractor and jack-of-all-trades, Harry Lounsbury, had the answer. He saw her fall off his "sleeping couch onto the floor" the first night she ever spent in Redding. According to Lounsbury, she had requested whiskey for a sick headache and then drank the entire quart in two hours.[70]

Lyon seemed as susceptible to masculine flattery as she was to whiskey, and during that second summer in Dublin, Paine showered her with attention. They walked together; they philosophized under a hemlock tree in the rain; they sat on the sunset rock and talked about their obsession—Twain. They frequently walked to an isolated cottage, where Paine once comforted her "weeping mood. He is a rare good man," she noted, "and how I have needed him this year."[71] Paine's motive for befriending Lyon no doubt originated from his interest in Twain, whom they both revered. But their intimacy seemed to grow beyond mutual admiration of the King during the summer.

In late June Lyon traveled to Boston with Sam, who was bound for New York to escape his boredom with Dublin. Leaving him at the train station, she "went to shop and shop—with a foolishly miserable heart in my breast." But she surprised herself upon her return to Dublin, finding peace for the "first time—this year." Paine was chiefly responsible. They walked to the upper pasture and "the talk was steady and full of the interest of life—." "I am giving birth to something—" she confided to her diary immediately after Paine's departure for Redding. "The parturition pains are great, and the birth is a slow one—weeks and weeks." She described herself as being drawn away from the influence of Twain's mind by a "counter force of mind or personality, and our malleability is wonderful and beautiful." That "counter force," which she described as bringing balance to her life, was Paine. "He stands for a great amount of my strength just now," she concluded, "and I wish he might always—for he is a rare creature, and strong."[72]

When Paine returned from his trip to Redding, he and Lyon walked to the isolated cottage where they talked—"How we did talk!" Reviewing this scenario the following day, she asked, "What will this day bring?" "The grass is down!" she answered curiously. And then, in a highly charged and highly suggestive passage: "It was so ripe, so ready and willing, to be slain. (3 men have been working at it all the morning.) It began to be so tired; and when the scythe swept through it, it lay so still, as if glad and full of rest—like other deaths."[73]

"These are such beautiful days. The mountain has brought life to me," she wrote several days later, after climbing Monadnock with Paine. "Who could have thought that within the month there could be an awakening such as mine—an awakening out of black poisoned misery into the meaning of the mountain and the meaning and sacredness of life, whether in solitude or not." If it was the scenery that "awakened" her, she had a memorable day with nature because one year later she honored the anniversary of "The Monadnock Day" in her journal. Whether a partner in flirtation only or in actual embrace, she seemed a woman ripe for lovemaking.[74]

———

The summer's end brought unsettling developments. On a brief visit to New York in mid-September, Lyon must have had a discouraging talk with Clara and the architect, for the combined news of cost and logistics was gloomy. "Lioness told me that the idea of building at Redding, Conn., has been given up for the present," Jean confided, applying the nickname she had been using since midsummer.[75] John Howells calculated that the house would cost a minimum of $47,000; not prohibitive in itself but daunting when two other houses had to be rented and maintained. The New York house could not be given up, Jean reasoned, "because Clara and Father will both of them need it frequently during the winter." This "need" was most likely expressed by Clara. And Jean had her own demands. "Of course I am disappointed at the idea of entirely discarding the country-house idea and very likely selling the Redding property, but, I would rather give up all that than give up Dublin, which would mean giving up the one place in the world where I have real friends."[76] Both daughters were now roadblocks to Lyon's dream of a Connecticut farmhouse.

The day after Lyon returned with news that the Redding project looked doomed, Sam left Dublin for New York to attend Clara's North American solo debut in Norfolk on September 23. One critic praised her beauty and her voice, admitting she had yet to gain complete control of a song but predicting that she would be "one of the few good contraltos of America." Sam proudly wrote Jean that "It was a clean straight *triumph*." Paine too was gone and so could offer no immediate support. And Jean suffered her first major seizure of the month. Lyon called it "a dreadful kind of day—for Jean would not let me out of her sight." Trying to cheer Jean up, she put on a clown costume, but apparently the results were disappointing. "It was a dreadful kind of a day," the Lioness repeated, "for she couldn't keep it up." "The seriousness of Jean's disease is increasing and I am very anxious about her—" Lyon wrote on September 20 after the second attack that month. Yet Jean had been suffering as many as five grand mal seizures a month that summer.[77] Lyon's judgment that Jean's condition was worsening had no objective base. But it is a subtle clue.

Lyon herself suffered an emotional collapse on the evening of September 23. She took to her bed and, three days later, Jean noted that "Lioness is better but she has really been having a slight nervous breakdown." Lyon "went to pieces"—self-described, "and stayed in a dark room all day—suffering." "She is in terrible pain," Jean commiserated, "and her being very nervous is a natural enough result, but even though I recognize that it doesn't make it any less irritating to be told, on going in to inquire after her condition, not to speak to her and to go out."[78] Jean's sympathy was not welcomed.

Lyon displayed a set of behaviors in this pivotal crisis that she was to repeat many times while living in Twain's household. These strange interludes, characterized by sleeplessness, nervous hysteria, anxiety, emotional outbursts, and sick headaches, included the self-reported use of sleeping pills and the observation by others of alcohol abuse. The most important aspect of these episodes is that they were usually situated either immediately before or after some mysterious "birth." Lyon seemed to gather courage to plan and pursue her goals through retreats from the world around her. Her crises were turning points that followed a pattern of personal collapse and renewal.[79] And after Livy's death, they almost always involved some attempt to manipulate Twain. Between September 14, when she saw her hopes crumbling, and September 23, when she took to her bed, the Lioness had put in motion a plan to realign the Clemens household.

CHAPTER 5

A Pact with the Devil

ON SEPTEMBER 25 Jean paid a visit to the Thayer family in Dublin. "It seems curious," she wrote the next day, "that after the Thayers had asked if I had ever been in a sanitarium, yesterday, Dr. Sarah Stowell should have spoken most emphatically in favor of it, this morning."[1] Curious indeed, for Jean had never mentioned the subject to either party. It would seem as if someone had talked to the Thayers and Dr. Stowell, Jean's gynecologist, behind the scenes. Yet Jean's sister had never set foot in Dublin. Her father had left on September 15. Paine would certainly not have been privy to intimacies with Jean's gynecologist. And Dr. Peterson was in Europe (though Jean reports that he had always emphasized the need for a strict regime). There was no one in Dublin but the Lioness to plant the idea of a sanitarium—virtually simultaneously—with Jean's gynecologist and her family friends. No one but Jean, that is—who expressed her surprise at the coincidence.

It seems more than coincidence that on September 27—while Lyon was still in the midst of her "episode"—Jean should report, again with innocent surprise, that the secretary "had already spoken of it to Father and that he agreed to it absolutely, provided it was considered at all desirable."[2] The Thayers, Dr. Stowell, and Sam himself had been lobbied about a sanitarium for Jean without her knowledge. Lyon had procured her father's approval before Jean had even opened her mouth.

But skillful ventriloquists do not move their lips. "I have talked a good deal with Lioness about it," Jean wrote of a conversation she had with Lyon on September 26, "and she agrees wholly with me." Quickly it had become "[m]y sanitarium idea." Though she did not suppose that she would be very happy "in such a place with a lot of other epileptics," Jean was willing "to go into a sanitarium next winter," she revealed, with the "hope of wearing this disease out." Her hope was based on a belief, derived from past conversations with Dr. Peterson, that she might regain her health by "an absolutely regular and quiet, unexcited life" preferably "out in the country."[3]

Lyon played on Jean's fervent desire to find a cure. She also countered Jean's doubts by painting the sanitarium experience in colors that would appeal to her. Told that Anna, their young maid could accompany her, Jean noted, "That would make it ever so much less lonely." Although she had no actual knowledge of the medical regimen, Lyon also soothingly assured her she would be able to correspond with friends and could be out-of-doors, to go driving and walking. "I would not be a regular invalid," Jean echoed, "merely a person needing a fixed and unchanged mode of life."[4]

———

On September 28 Lyon wrote a long letter to Dr. Peterson. Given his belief that epileptics should be segregated and his work in the funding of public sanitariums as well as the founding of private ones, Peterson was predisposed to agree to the advisability of treating Jean in a sanitarium, even without guidance from the laity.[5] Sam had been effectively lobbied and was, as Jean had noted, awaiting Peterson's advice. Lyon was in command—the Janus-headed mediator among daughter, physician, and father.

At this time a new note enters Lyon's comments in her diaries. "She subconsciously feels my weakness," Lyon wrote on September 28, a day when Jean suffered two grand mal seizures, "and all her venomous points are to the fore; for it is absolutely essentially [sic] that a person who is mentally strong should be with her and should fearlessly direct her." Fiercely critical of Jean's demeanor, she also implied for the first time that she was no longer capable of supervising Sam's daughter. While this may be an unselfconscious reflection of her genuine anxieties, it also dovetailed with her plan to convince Sam that Jean belonged in a sanitarium. Jean's illness did make her cranky and occasionally angry. But more often her responses to life were good-natured, thoughtful, and empathetic. "Lioness is feeling badly, today, too," she observed on the same day her venomous points were supposedly to the fore, "and naturally, it didn't improve her nervous state any to have me in such a condition."[6] Despite her seizures and the fact that she felt ill for the remainder of the day, Jean was sympathetic to the secretary's suffering and critical of her own "condition." Lyon was simultaneously declaring Jean ungovernable.

Jean had decided on her own not to make a planned climb of Monadnock with Gerry Brush the next day, but to go for a walk instead. While chatting with Lyon quite early that Saturday morning, Jean had a series of petit mal, actually a routine occurrence. But Lyon became agitated, dressed hurriedly, and when Gerry arrived "she came right down stairs," Jean recalled, "and told him that when Father was away she was in supreme control over everything here and that she forbade him to go out walking with me before luncheon. I was rabid, of course, but I don't believe Gerry minded much." They spent the morning in her study and walked in the afternoon, mindful of the secretary's dictum. According to Jean's lights, they had a "perfectly delightful day, even with Miss Lyon's meddling."[7]

Lyon's version was different in tone and detail. "I have had to ask Mr. Clemens to come back on Monday," she wrote on that Saturday. "Today a climax with Jean—In the King's name I had to forbid Gerry Brush going with her for a long walk—then I collapsed—Jean would not listen to reason. She was far too ill to go."[8] Lyon depicted Jean as uncooperative, childish, irrational, and too ill to leave the house. By contrast, Jean portrayed herself as discerning and energetic and described the enjoyable walk she had with Gerry in the afternoon, demonstrating that she was apparently able to "listen to reason"—even from someone as antagonistic as Miss Lyon.

In her original diary entry, Lyon linked the construction of Jean as an out-of-control menace with her own portrayal as a victim. Clearly the two conditions were paired in her mind. Yet if she did indeed "collapse" in the morning, crushed by the burden of Jean's care, it was a short-lived prostration. "They all came up to my room after tea…and had such a gay time," she confided, naming Gerry, Jean, and Paine as participants. "Gerry recited nonsense verse," she recalled with pleasure, repeating a few lines to underline the hilarity of the gathering in her room. People can, of course, bounce back quickly from adversity. But such a dramatic turnaround contained contradictions that seem to have troubled Lyon, for at some point she inserted lines in the margin about Jean's propensity to violence that she apparently hoped would justify her behavior. "Because in Jean's present condition it isn't safe for me to be alone with her," she wrote. "She could easily lapse into the violence the doctors fear may come in time."[9] Apparently she had forgotten the claim she made eight months earlier—that Jean had already tried to kill Katy.

———

"The King has come back" was how the Lioness heralded Sam's return to Dublin at her urgent request, and he brought "joy and restfulness" in his wake. "I almost cry with happiness and with relief," she sighed.[10] Jean, however, was having second thoughts about the sanitarium idea. Discovering that Gerry Brush might settle in New York City for the winter, she decided that she would "actually be glad to live in New York"—meaning at home. Lyon's heart must have fluttered as she listened to Jean's waffling. "But, as Lioness was saying," Jean recounted innocently, "it would be better to be entirely away from Gerry and unable to see him because of the distance, than to be living within a few blocks of him and be constantly so ill that I could almost never be with him."[11] Lyon mounted her arguments with ingenuity and bold élan. Her work was less arduous after Dr. Peterson weighed in, not only approving the plan but specifying that Jean go to his own private sanitarium in Katonah, New York, a little southeast of Peekskill in Westchester County.

"The news is just as I hoped it would be and yet," Jean reflected, "now that it has come, I can't help having crawly feelings inside. To go away from the family is a thing I haven't done since 1895." Her hope was that she would be able to see her family, "at least occasionally." But wherever she landed for the winter, Jean had one overarching goal: to return to Dublin the following summer. Anxious about leaving, she sought her father's reassurance, confessing her fear that he would suddenly decide not to come back. "I have good friends here and nowhere else," she said simply. Her father's eyes, she wrote, filled with tears. Her plan was to "get into a pretty good physical state while I am in the sanitarium" so that through the sale of her woodcarving, plus gifts and her regular allowance, she could buy a small plot of ground in Dublin. She intended to build a house when she was able, and live in New Hampshire every summer.[12]

Her last full day in Dublin Jean yearned to have a conversation with Gerry Brush, and she "felt a painful gnawing on my inside." "Is there any possibility of my seeing him inside of six and a half months?" she asked rhetorically. "If he doesn't care enough about me to think of coming to say good-bye, then he is very unlikely to want to take over an hour's train-ride to come and call on me." Not expecting to see him until she returned to Dublin, she was unable to stop her tears. The clouds that encircled Monadnock that final morning looked to her as though the mountain, too, was weeping at her departure. But when they lifted, Jean was not reassured. "Oh! I do so hate to go!!!" was her regretful farewell.[13]

Arriving in New York on October 17, Jean found that Clara was considerably upset by the unexpected news that her sister was to go to Katonah. She had taken to her bed for three days, almost as if she were in mourning. The Lioness, however, was in high gear and hustled Jean off to buy dresses, silk blouses, and a Parisienne hat—all to be packed in her newly purchased trunk. She also arranged for a consultation with Dr. Frederick Hunt, who would be in charge of her case at the Katonah sanitarium.[14] During that first consultation, the doctor revealed Lyon's plans for Jean. "Dr. Hunt said he had gotten the idea from what Lioness wrote that I wished Anna to sleep with me!" Jean noted without suspicion. "Considering how I loathe having anyone in the room with me that really seemed laughable," she continued. "Dr. Hunt doesn't care at all about having anyone sleep with me; so that unpleasant suggestion is settled." Although he was perfectly indifferent to her sleeping arrangements, he had instructed in his earlier letter "that someone ought to sleep in the same room with me—," Jean reported.[15] Hunt, it seems, had passed on Lyon's instructions as if they were the "doctor's orders." This was interpreted by Jean as an innocent misunderstanding but in reality the secretary had assumed command, giving orders in the name of the King.

"Today Jean went out to Katonah," Lyon wrote on October 25, 1906. "It was heart stretching to have her go and to see her go."[16] Given her efforts toward Jean's removal, her "heart stretching" likely included a portion of jubilation and relief. Sam unquestionably felt genuine sorrow but shared some of his secretary's sense of release. "There's been a cloud-lift today," Twain had written his friend Mary Rogers on the day

Dr. Peterson's cable arrived blessing the sanitarium for Jean, "and I've got to jubilate with somebody or expire with satisfaction."[17] The day before Jean's departure, though, he wrote Mary's mother-in-law, Emilie Rogers, that he was struck with "a disease I am not much subject to—depression of spirits." Clara wept bitterly when Jean left and, after a visit to Katonah two days later, returned more depressed than her father and deeply touched by the pathos of her sister's situation.[18]

Jean had not been separated from her family for ten years. "It was desperately hard to leave Father and Clara in order to come out to a totally strange place," she acknowledged. "I tried my hardest not to cry before them, but as the time of departure began to approach I found it growing more and more difficult to restrain myself, especially when Clara began to cry, too, then it was really hopeless. Poor little Father seemed to feel badly, too, and the whole business was perfectly *horrible* to me."[19]

———

Jean's departure from 21 Fifth Avenue signaled several new opportunities in the Clemens household. To begin with, plans for the Redding house were now on again. The cause of the sudden turnabout is hard to prove but easy to guess. Jean was in exile, and her wishes no longer needed to be taken into account. Plans for the house were also probably scaled back—temporarily—to match Sam's cost ceiling. He had been up to see Jean in Katonah and saw the Redding project, surprisingly, as a way to meet his youngest daughter's needs. "I must have a country home for her," he wrote, in spite of her own wishes to summer in Dublin.[20]

Sam also had ideas of his own, independent of his aide-de-camp. After Jean left home, he immediately began preparations for a journey to Egypt. Lyon was "stunned" by the news that he planned to make the trip without her; Clemens insisted that she was still needed in the States.[21] Her dismay was short-lived, however, for on October 31 he gave up his Egyptian plan, ostensibly because of a severe cold and bronchial infection.[22] He may also have been influenced by something more frivolous. Since 1891, when he left Hartford, he had been without a billiard table. That changed when he was given a new state-of-the-art table by Emilie Rogers, intended for Christmas 1906, but purchased and installed in the late fall. On November 2, 1906, he played his first game on that table with Paine. "I'm not going to Egypt," he announced after the game had ended. "There was a man here yesterday afternoon who said it was bad for bronchitis, and, besides, it's too far away from this billiard-table." More significant than a change in travel plans was the billiard table's effect on the amount of time Twain spent writing. "After that the morning dictations became a secondary interest," Paine noted dryly.[23]

Though billiards once again became his favorite pastime, Sam did not give up travel altogether. He spent a week in Bermuda with Lyon and Joseph Twichell in early January 1907 and vacationed there again for five days with Lyon in March.[24] With Jean in Katonah and Clara off in her own world of music and men, the Lioness was now the only woman in Twain's life who was a constant presence—except for Katy, whose role had been significantly undercut by Lyon.

————

Miss Lyon now believed that she alone understood how to manage Twain's affairs. "I know that the King must be kept calm, where I know how to do it," she insisted. "He mustn't be harassed, he mustn't have unnecessary matters brought to him to fret over, he must be saved in all ways that he can be saved from anxiety."[25] Soon after Jean's "heart-stretching" departure, the secretary concocted a plan to save her employer from all anxiety and worry about his youngest daughter. Her plan, she told him, would be beneficial to both father and daughter. She would read Jean's letters and summarize their contents for him. His daughter's letters, she unctuously advised him, contained "complaints which were unreasonable & mere fictions of Jean's imagination." He believed her. She reminded him that Jean would ask for things "which it would be impossible to grant." His headstrong daughter, she cautioned sympathetically, would suggest "projects which it would not be possible to entertain." Why not let her read Jean's letters and save him the pain and sorrow of denying his daughter's requests?[26]

Twain agreed. Her false solicitude sounded reasonable at the time, and he was tortured by his inability to relieve his daughter of her difficult affliction. But if his motives were not entirely heartless, they were appallingly selfish. Shunning Jean's actual letters himself, he would listen to Lyon's version and then write a "few empty lines to Jean"—his later characterization of what happened. Relinquishing even more control, he would hand his draft to the secretary who edited the result, eliminating "such suggestions of feeling and affection as might have intruded into it under impulse," he admitted. Then he would rewrite "the vacuum," and return it to his secretary for mailing.[27]

Each time a letter arrived, Twain reenacted this ritual of betrayal, not only of his daughter but of himself, abdicating his role as parent and protector to save himself anxiety and distress. Though he could and did claim ignorance of his secretary's machinations, he was her conscious co-conspirator in agreeing not to read Jean's letters, placing his comfort, convenience, and undisturbed lifestyle above his daughter's happiness.[28] Lyon's vow to release her employer from any unnecessary anxiety and vexation of spirit reflected a high-minded rationale for an underhanded ploy. Her scheme cut Jean off almost completely from her own father and strengthened the secretary's dominion by closing an important channel of communication. Whether conscious or intuitive, she had embarked on a campaign to isolate him from intimates.

And at this juncture, Twain made what may be a very revealing decision. It is a well-known fact that in the winter of 1906 he began wearing white suits year round. "The King is filled with the idea of defying conventionalities, and wearing his suitable white clothes all winter," Lyon wrote before Twain left Dublin, "so he has bidden me order 5 new suits from his tailor; the suits to be ready against the time we arrive in N.Y." He wore his white serge in Washington, D.C., at a joint Congressional hearing on December 6, 1906, where he lobbied for an extension of the copyright law, and he loved the dramatic effect so much that he never stopped. He called the conceit "my don'tcareadam suit."[29]

"His white suits, which focused on him such attention—love, really—" one of his biographers observes, "were the fetish of what had become an obsession with guilt, with forbidden and therefore unclean thoughts."[30] According to this biographer, Twain's posthumous writings, everything he never intended to publish in his lifetime, were one manifestation of this guilt. Twain began wearing white suits soon after Jean had been packed off to the sanitarium and he had arranged not to read her letters. There is no way of proving an unconscious motivation, but can it be a total coincidence that his decision to clothe himself permanently in white came on top of his pitiable compact? He did have something to feel guilty about that winter, and the white suits may indeed have been more than an appealing sartorial invention.

CHAPTER 6

Life in the Sanitarium

JEAN HAD AGREED to the sanitarium at Katonah sight unseen. But the seven cemeteries on the train ride from New York to her new home were a distressing omen, even to her practical mind. Determined to "get accustomed to it in time," she threw herself into the sanitarium's play regime with gusto, going fishing, bowling, walking, and playing hours of croquet within the first week. Always an athletic woman, Jean loved outdoor exercise, and the four to five hours per day prescribed by Dr. Hunt were not unwelcome.[1]

His dietary rules were less salutary, however. Jean loved salty food, but salt was forbidden. Worse, she complained one night, was her starvation dinner of two eggs and part of a bad grapefruit. She was given soup and vegetables the next evening, a more satisfying but hardly sumptuous repast. In addition to once finding hair in her food, she complained fitfully of watered-down milk and tough meat. Meals at Katonah were consistently sparse and sometimes inedible.[2] "The less I eat, the better 'tis for me—queer idea, isn't it? but not a difficult one to live up to here." She was regularly ordering four to six pounds of chocolate to supplement her meager diet.[3]

Jean soon tired of the endless evenings of Parcheesi. In the beginning of her stay, her letter writing was restricted on doctor's orders, and other distractions were few.[4] She was allowed to continue her woodcarving, and she eventually sent a few pieces to the Society of Craftsmen, an artist's cooperative in New York that sold her work. This gave her some pride and a moderate purpose. Besides her woodcarving, she was also thankful for the chance to give individual language lessons in German and Italian, especially when her students were attractive men.[5]

Her maid, Anna, was even more bored and lonely than her mistress and threatened to quit before the end of her first month. With nothing to occupy her time, Anna fussed obsessively at Jean, pulling and poking at her clothes, talking incessantly, and watching Jean's every move. With characteristic solicitude, Jean recognized that her own impatience had contributed to Anna's dissatisfaction, and she apologized to her maid. "I hated to see her go," she admitted when Anna left six months later, "& really wanted to cry."[6]

An underdog herself, Jean often expressed sympathy for the downtrodden during her time at Katonah. She argued with friends—and even wrote a letter to the *New York Times*—about the "rank dishonor & injustice" of America's treatment of the Indians, especially its disregard for Indian treaties. (Katy Leary recalled that this had long been a cause of Jean's. "She used to be always talking about what a cruel thing it was the way the Americans treated the Indians in the early days. She felt terrible about that, and used to talk about it to her father.") Jean also thought President Theodore Roosevelt's dishonorable discharge of 167 African-American infantrymen without trial in November 1906 was a national disgrace.[7]

Despite her kind heart and generous nature, Jean was nonetheless committed to social hierarchy and certain forms of politesse, retaining a class-consciousness bred by her affluent upbringing, her father's fame, and her mother's attention to form. She protested to Dr. Sharp, the director of the sanitarium, about the presence of a valet at her lunch table, stating that having a servant "in the dining-room with the patients was an insult." And in an example directly influenced by her sensitivity to the stereotypes surrounding epilepsy, she wanted her father to use his influence to stop a millionaire patient from playing tennis barefooted with his trousers rolled up to his knees and a sleeveless jersey. The man shrieked constantly, she complained, and cursed everyone on the tennis court and "makes the whole place appear like an insane asylum." "Father dear," she pleaded, "please do write to Dr. Sharp yourself, because you surely must see that ladies should not be obliged to see such goings-on."[8]

Jean could take little solace from her father. "Father seemed very well indeed," Jean remarked, "but the visit was again disgustingly short." Only a trip her father made to Katonah without the Lioness in May 1907 was a "real visit." And his visits were infrequent, even though he could have made the round trip from New York to her sanitarium in an afternoon. Since he had agreed not to read her letters and almost never talked to her doctors, he received little direct information from or about Jean.[9]

His absence made the sting from his shaming advice all the more painful. One memorable example was written in early January 1907. "Bear with the situation as well as you can dear Jean, & call back the gentle spirit you were born with, & believe that all those people mean you well, for it is indeed so." Clemens only later understood the irony of his assertion. "It is your disease that makes you see ill intentions in them—they mean well by you," he continued. "When you are moved to think otherwise, call back your winning & kindly earlier nature, and drive away the thought. Think the *best* of people, do not dwell upon their faults, but try not to see them. You will be the happier for it."[10] Such pious advice would have made the satirical Mark Twain blush.

Jean's response was predictably self-demeaning. "As a whole the letter was sweet, but the statement of my having been born with a sweet nature surprised me," Jean wrote. "I had always supposed that as a small child, I had been regarded as a young devil."[11]

Surprisingly, Clara took an active interest in her sister at this time and lived up to her pledge to visit once a week.[12] For a while she even moved into a nearby sanitarium for her own rest cure. Jean visited Clara at Miss Mullhall's on Thanksgiving Day 1906 and compared their establishments. Clara's gained points for its lovely view on a hill overlooking the valley and its nicer appointments. The quiet dignity of Miss Mullhall's was also winning—the system of bells there meant that the staff and residents were not constantly bellowing in the halls. Still, Jean preferred her own situation because of the entertainment and what was for her the pièce de résistance at Katonah: its hill for coasting.[13] That winter Clara's proximity and the arrival of snow were both welcome diversions.

———

Life at the sanitarium perked up even more for Jean after she became acquainted with Dr. Hibbard, one of the staff physicians, who shared her love of sledding and downhill skiing. She even compared skiing with him to her best dances with Gerry Brush. Hibbard seemed to return her interest and asked her to accompany him on his rounds in the local village. One day, while Hibbard ministered to the sick, Jean talked to the families, who were Italian immigrants, living in tar-paper shanties with little or no heat in the dead of winter. Her heart was touched by their plight, though she also felt uncomfortable at times with their standard of cleanliness.[14] On one of their many long drives to make his rounds, Hibbard and Jean engaged in a discussion of sex, unusual less for its content than for how briefly they had known each other. Dr. Hibbard argued that girls were naive if they believed that the male sex drive was overpowering. Most men, he insisted, were simply "weak, dirty brutes," but they were not the chief culprits. Women were to blame because they tolerated men's loose sexual activities.[15]

Whatever Hibbard's motives in raising this topic, Jean was attracted to him "more than ever before" after this intimate discussion. Naturally athletic and under doctor's orders to exercise outdoors, Jean was grateful for his companionship, and wistful about his rumored engagement to a girl in Buffalo. Recognizing that her life was "empty" and "useless," especially in the sanitarium, she longed, as always, for someone to love and ached with unrequited affection for Dr. Hibbard. "I wonder if he does consider me a fearful burden?" she worried. "He always seems mighty nice & cordial & friendly, & I think he likes me but I must try & not force myself onto him too much."[16]

The day after, she wrote that it was rainy, and the roads were too muddy to drive. Jean, desperate for distraction, begged Dr. Hibbard to play squash. Vulnerable as she was, his response that she would have to wait brought on an immediate feeling of rejection. Later they did play three vigorous games, with Hibbard winning the rubber. In an apparent gesture of frustration after one of his good plays, Jean "forgot myself so completely" that she hit him on the back with her racket. She berated herself but also admitted that Hibbard was unconcerned. "It was a dreadful lawless thing to have done and I feel terribly about it."[17]

This incident is illuminating. Jean had a quick temper and was also prone to flagellate herself for the least fault.[18] Even she recognized, however, that in this instance her apology was "over-done" relative to her behavior. Although Isabel Lyon would have wholeheartedly endorsed the notion, Jean's hot-tempered reaction to Hibbard was not driven by "uncontrollable" epilepsy. But Jean's disease, especially because of the cultural understanding of her time, resulted in a powerful anticipation of disapproval and rejection. This in turn created something that was uncontrollable: a fierce need for love. Apparently Jean was not alone. Dr. Sharp's wife told a patient that her husband had had "much trouble with love affairs among the patients."[19]

Clear-sighted about her circumstances, Jean was afraid of ending her life alone and isolated. She recognized that her father would not live forever and that she and Clara were not "especially sympathetic." "The hard part of it is that the older I grow," she mused, "—the nearer and nearer to old-maidhood—I get more and more anxious to marry." Otherwise, she feared, she would spend all her "older years practically by myself." Constantly searching for a man who would love her, she saw that she "should almost at once fall in love with him," if he were "at all nice, were to propose to me and seem to be in love."[20] Though Dr. Hibbard met only the first of her three criteria, after just a few months she had grown completely dependent on him. "If it weren't for him this place would be absolute Hades to me," she reflected. "I should have nothing to do outdoors & no really attractive people to be with." She feared that Dr. Hibbard would leave Katonah "before I am considered well enough to live at home."[21] As it turned out, her anxiety was warranted, though she was completely unaware of the real reason.

On Saturday, December 14, 1906, Clara brought devastating news during her visit. "Dr. Hunt wants me to be here next summer," the messenger reported, and "all thought of Dublin has been abolished!" The doctor had resolved—fully six months in advance—that Jean would not be well enough to leave, and it seems all but certain that the doctor's prognosis was not made without assistance. In hopes of softening the blow, Clara, who herself planned to be abroad for the summer, passed along the suggestion that her father could spend the season in Katonah. "If he was lonely up in Dublin, where there are at least some very nice & interesting people, what under heaven would he be in this mud-hole containing not a soul?" Jean countered shrewdly. "I told Clara that I thought that if I must stay in Katonah I had better stay right in this establishment while Father had best go near some friends." Two days after this surprise announcement Lyon came to Katonah on a scouting trip to look for a summer rental for Clemens and stopped for lunch with Jean. Predictably, the secretary could find nothing suitable. She and Jean agreed, for different reasons, that Katonah was no place for him.[22]

Jean also spent that Christmas apart from her family, but so long as Dr. Hibbard was attentive, even that was tolerable. Clara did visit Christmas Day, as promised, but she stayed less than an hour. Jean felt only minor irritation at this slight and no pain at all from Gerry Brush's neglect. Even his failure to respond to her Christmas letter was swept aside. Hibbard had usurped Gerry's place in her heart. "I believe he likes me," she confided to her diary, "but I shall be loving him or very close to it before long. Povera me!"[23]

———

Jean's medical treatment at the sanitarium was ineffectual but earnest. Early on in her stay, Dr. Sharp diagnosed the source of her illness as "some difficulty in the circulation and he wants to try a certain kind of hyperdermic on me," she wrote. Trying to ward off an attack that was signaled by a long series of petit mal at breakfast, Sharp gave her three injections over the course of the day but the seizure came anyway, around suppertime. In early January 1907, she observed, "My head isn't quite so clear. I usually have two or three petit mal per day which delays my carving."[24] Dr. Hunt was briefly worried about Jean's consumption of hickory nuts and thought her eating two donuts might have helped to bring on an attack because they were fried in lard. Food was seen as an "excitable" cause, and Jean was subjected to a dizzying array of dietary regulations.[25] In the fruitless search for control of the disease, any out-of-the-ordinary food that preceded an attack might be blamed.

In fact almost any action the doctors wished to finger might be forbidden, simply by labeling it an "unhealthy, nervous effect." Jean's attack on February 1 was blamed not only on the doughnuts but also on a visit she made to a Miss Roberts, a former client of the sanitarium whom Dr. Sharp disliked and, with Hunt's approval, had asked to leave. The Sharps thought Miss Roberts a troublemaker who had fomented dissatisfaction in several patients, including Jean. As quickly as "abracadabra," all visits to Roberts were outlawed. Jean's response was docile: "If her influence on me is unsettling, then, of course, I shall have to give up seeing her, but I shall be rather sorry if that is necessary."[26]

The sincere, if futile, hope was that following a tightly controlled regimen of diet and exercise might actually cure a patient's epilepsy. But this physical regimen expanded, in this sanitarium at least, into an authoritarian set of rules that covered all aspects of a patient's life and often seemed arbitrary, created more out of a combination of staff personality and convenience than any medical reason. For example, tables at Katonah were normally set for two. But three female patients, including Jean, who sat together for their Christmas meal at a big table normally reserved for the Sharps and brought into the dining room on the special occasion, asked for permission to continue eating together. Dr. Sharp was at first agreeable but later reneged on his promise. "I wish to arrange the seating of the patients myself," he told the other women. "Three patients have never sat together & I don't think it's healthy. It is liable to make you more nervous & excitable." When Jean politely objected to his turnabout, he lied and told her that her friends were relieved "to be out of it." And then he offered her the ultimate bribe: she could sit with Dr. Hibbard.[27]

The unanimous conclusion of the patient establishment was that Mrs. Sharp, whom Jean depicted as a loud, shrewish woman, was behind her husband's change of heart. Three patients who were enjoying each other's company were barred from eating together for completely specious "health" reasons. This action was transparent, even to the pliant clientele.[28] In fact, Katonah treated most adult patients like children. Poker games in female rooms were forbidden, for no other reason than the rule against mixed gatherings. Yet with an abundance of same-sex chaperones whenever there were large groups of players, the point was largely a formality. The medical staff perpetuated the infantile treatment Jean had received at home, quite probably with the active support of Lyon and Clara. For example, Dr. Sharp forbade Jean to go the local club on New Year's Eve to play squash unless her maid accompanied her, even though the group of squash players included another female patient and a woman was in charge of closing the club.[29]

Jean also recognized how her economic dependence on her father deprived her of much of her liberty and yearned for an independent income and a home of her own. "I would give a good deal to live in the country & feel that I was of some use—if only to myself." And she saw herself caught in a double standard since Clara exercised ample personal freedom on her father's income. That double standard was not limited to money, however; it also extended to Jean's continual wish for companionship and love. Clara objected to Jean's frequent drives with Dr. Hibbard on rounds to visit patients, because, she said, it was the kind of thing a fiancée would do and might arouse gossip in the city. "Her attitude made me feel cold," Jean acknowledged, "& that her one idea was to stick to all rules & not regard—where it concerned me—my comfort or pleasure," adding "she feels, as mother did, that I must never marry."[30] In the minds of her closest relatives, Jean's epilepsy apparently not only barred her from having children, but also disqualified her from attractive male companionship. A damningly accurate assessment of the entire family.

Though resisting Clara's order to cease her drives with Hibbard, Jean did succumb to pressure from her sister to tell him that her room was off-limits. Dr. Hibbard's sudden withdrawal soon after this conversation puzzled Jean. At first she attributed his coldness to their talk, but she was not entirely satisfied by her own explanation.[31] What she discovered was that Clara had spoken to Dr. Sharp. "Her action was *low*, I think, & I don't feel that she had any right to do as she did. And I told her too, that she wasn't my mother."[32]

Though she tried to revive their easy camaraderie, good soldier Hibbard never returned to his old intimacy. "I wept bitterly and uncontrollably for some time," Jean admitted after getting another cold shoulder from Dr. Hibbard and spending the day alone. She felt as though she had lost a friend due to Clara's meddling. Not willing to buck the chain of command, Hibbard began giving his attentions to Mrs. Logan, whom Jean roundly, and not too objectively, abhorred. Her rationale that Mrs. Logan was loud, common, and coarse seems less likely than simple jealousy.[33]

————

Jean recognized that her family—Clara and her father—were glad to have her out of the way "& therefore relieved of the presence of an ill person, I am sure that they must feel so," she observed with remarkable objectivity. "That is in no way against them, it is only absolutely human. Also, the idea that they miss me is absurd," she continued. "Clara's & my interests are too absolutely different for us to be necessary to one another even if we are fond of each other & Father can't possibly find any entertainment or interest in me."[34] This was sadly true. Jean had the sensitivity to recognize her situation; the courage to face the fact that neither her father nor her sister were greatly distressed by her absence; and the low self-esteem to blame herself. This was her most tragic circumstance.

"I am sure he is fond of me," she reflected on her father's feelings, "but I don't believe that he any more than Clara, really misses me." Jean did not fight harder to go home because she understood that she was not wanted there. "I don't really miss either of them," she wrote defiantly, but the deeper truth was more painful. "I far more often feel a desire to see Father, than I do to see Clara which is only right & natural. I do often have a sort of hunger to get hold of him & hug him." That hunger persisted, despite all her efforts. "Father telephoned me!" she exclaimed after she had been at Katonah some months. "It was fearfully upsetting. Oh, I do so want to get to him. The tears would come, I couldn't keep them back & Father's voice broke, too."[35]

In early January, accompanying Sam on one of his rare visits to Katonah, Lyon informed Jean that she would have to wait to return home, even after her petit mal stopped completely. When Jean questioned Dr. Hunt, he responded honestly "that he still didn't believe that [the waiting] would be necessary." Obviously orders from headquarters had not yet reached Hunt, for he soon modified his position. "Lioness talked with Dr. Hunt on Wednesday, for Father," Jean noted a few weeks later. "He was hopeful but said this was barely the beginning & that I mustn't expect any real improvement inside of a year."[36]

With an intuitive grasp of behavioral psychology, however, Lyon understood the necessity for both the carrot and the stick. Visiting Jean on February 4, "Lioness spoke as though I would probably have to be here during the summer," clearly a bitter disappointment for Jean. But the secretary also came with plans for the Redding house, where Jean had hopes to rejoin her family in a healthy country environment. Pointing out with a flourish that Jean's room was very small in the original drawings, Lyon also noted that the maid's room had no separate access. The secretary then accepted Jean's gratitude for her intervention to correct these design flaws.[37]

The Lioness provided other compensations as well. Scott, Jean's beloved horse, was shipped from Dublin to Katonah, and George

O'Conners was hired again as driver and groom. Since Jean was now forbidden all horseback riding, a light carriage was purchased for the long drives that were supposed to improve her health. Being outdoors even in subzero weather was thought to be beneficial, and Jean spent many hours each day being carted around the countryside by Scott. Luckily, she was also able to enjoy winter sports, especially skiing, ice skating, and tobogganing.[38]

Given her condition and the many restrictions placed on her, Jean displayed amazing stamina and an admirable ability to have a good time with friends, no matter what the shared activities. She had experienced and enjoyed sophisticated culture but was probably even happier in the midst of a simple snow fight. And within a short time, she also once again attracted a male companion. Fun-loving Mr. Brooks soon took Dr. Hibbard's place in her heart. A Southerner, boyish, undisciplined, but athletic and musically inclined, Brooks never wearied Jean. Playing squash and coasting together were joyful for Jean, and she took pleasure in listening to him play his violin and the pianola. They began to spend whole days together.[39]

One rather surprising gaiety at the sanitarium was an evening of cross-dressing involving Hibbard and Brooks. After having dinner with the men, Jean and another female patient exchanged attire with them. Dr. Hibbard wore Miss Farrish's pink dress and jewelry while Mr. Brooks wore Jean's white dress, silver hairband, and pearl necklace. The men rouged and powdered themselves, though they retained their trousers underneath the feminine attire. The women wore the men's tuxedos and stiff shirts, high collars, and waistcoats over their skirts. The cross-dressing "gentlemen" received the "ladies" with great formality as they came down the stairs. An audience gathered and the dance began. The dancing couples were supposed to act out their drag roles on the dance floor. (That even the starchy Dr. Sharp, who joined the audience for the drag dance, approved indicates how uncontroversial playful gender inversion was in the early twentieth century.) When "Miss Clemens" refused a dance with "Mr. Brooks," the cross-dressing Jean retired to the opposite side of the room, telling Mrs. Benjamin that "he" had been offended. At Mrs. Benjamin's urging, "Mr. Brooks" made one more try, and "his" offer was finally accepted. "It really was deliciously funny," Jean concluded. "The poor men could hardly breathe and our collars nearly drove us crazy."[40]

Almost as soon as their friendship began, however, Jean discovered that Brooks planned to leave Katonah. "But that is about the way things seem to work themselves out with me," she observed mournfully. "I meet some one, grow very much attached & then something comes in to separate us." After his departure, the social scene shifted to the despised Mrs. Logan's circle, and Jean retreated to her room at night, isolated and depressed.[41] A visit from Galla Thayer on April 13, cheered her considerably, but her Dublin friend's departure brought nagging questions. "When shall I see her again? And Dublin?" Jean asked. "Dear Dublin, it has brought it & all its joys back again, fresh & sad. Oh! I do feel so sad & lonely!"[42]

Without a male companion or a congenial clique, Jean turned to birds and flowers in the spring. She proudly logged in her diary that she had eighteen vases of fresh flowers in her room, displaying marsh marigolds, hepaticas, dog-tooth violets, and rue anemones. She also watched birds—one day in May she identified twenty-seven varieties, and bird-watching brought continued solace throughout the summer.[43]

———

But that solace was not enough. As the days warmed, Jean wrote her father that she was "desperately homesick for Dublin and of course first & foremost for the several lovely friends I had there." She recognized that her father might not understand her clinging attitude. Disease and lack of opportunity, presumably a reference to her nomadic life, had delayed her social development, she explained. This accounted for the fact that almost all her intimate friends were younger. Campaigning with her father once again, she hoped that "if I get better I can make visits to Dublin even if we never again spend a whole summer there."[44]

But Jean did not leave Katonah. She welcomed a visit from Katy in early July and found companionship with Mr. Hosford, a kind, cheerful, middle-aged man who walked, played tennis, and took meals with her. She was appreciative of his "fatherly way" and especially his ability to make her laugh when she was blue. But Mr. Hosford could never take the place of her real father. "You can't imagine what I felt when I heard your voice yesterday," she wrote to Sam after he phoned in July upon his return from a trip to England. "My voice refused [to] come and my thoughts all fled—it was too beautiful to know you were really back again & yet so *horrible* too, when I couldn't actually get to you."[45]

Jean missed her father with growing desperation, and she expressed her loneliness in letters he did not read. "I don't want you to tire your-self, dear little Herr Doktar, but when you do feel up to a hard trip, *please* come out here & give me a squeeze. I sometimes feel as though I could not endure it much longer to stay away from you." Yet she found it difficult to express her feelings when she heard his voice on the phone. "I said 'Oh don't!' yesterday dearest, when you said you were sending me kisses & hugs. I didn't mean it that way," she explained, "I didn't know what I said I was so upset & so wild to get hold of you, not merely your darling voice."[46]

As 1907 turned into the dog days of summer, she seemed to have been abandoned by her family. Sam spent much of the summer in the exclusive enclave of Tuxedo Park, about thirty miles northwest of New York, but he did not come to Katonah. And Clara, who was initially so attentive, no longer made regular visits. Receiving a check for ten dol-lars from her sister for her birthday, Jean was crushed by the coldness of the gesture. "I think she tho't she'd save herself some trouble because she's studying." "As my 27th year draws near its close I grow more & more hurt at Clara's gift," she reflected three days later. "What in heaven's name does she expect me to get here?" She returned her sister's check, whereupon Clara sent another. But after Jean explained her feel-ings, Clara responded with "more sympathy for my troubles than I tho't." And Jean was delighted by the gift that replaced her outcast check: a string of carnelian beads—in a lovely pinkish-red hue.[47]

"Dr. Hunt says," she wrote on August 2, 1907, "he doesn't think he knows of any case that made the progress I have in the time." For what-ever reason, Jean had had no grand mal attacks since April 10, and under other circumstances the doctor's prognosis might have been a signal that her time at the sanitarium was drawing to a close. But Hunt worked under constraints that outweighed his medical opinion. In the same month, Jean had a dream about her epilepsy that obliquely summarized her quandary: in the dream she was expected to have an attack on her birthday and was followed about all day, never once allowed to be alone. In her dream, as in reality, she felt herself "rabid" but helpless.[48]

CHAPTER 7

Someone to Love Him
and Pet Him

ONCE SHE HAD JEAN placed in the vise of the sanitarium and the Redding house resurrected, the Lioness was able to move in on her most treasured goal: to walk down the aisle with America's greatest literary celebrity. Her machinations were endless but never lacked imagination—and had in fact begun well before Jean left for Katonah. An undeniably charming and pretty woman, the Lioness was always finding excuses to touch the King. "[A]rch girly-girly pats on the back of my hand" and "playful little spats on my cheek with her fan" was how he described the small moves designed to encourage his affection. But beyond these constant love taps were her "come-hither" poses. She "would get herself up in sensuous oriental silken flimseys of dainty dyes, & stretch herself out on her bepillowed lounge in her bedroom, in studied enticing attitudes," Twain remembered, "with an arm under her head & a cigarette between her lips." Recalling her stretched out on the chaise lounge in her harem gear—for he often visited her bedroom—he pictured her as "waiting for the eunuchs to fetch the Sultan; & there she would lie by the hour enjoying the imaginary probabilities." "I know all those machine-made enchantments of hers," he wrote in a moment of supreme disenchantment, "& that bewitching die-away light that she turns on, at the climaxes, from her handsome black eyes."[1]

Lyon also mounted public campaigns to win the Sultan's heart. The first was a defensive operation against an attractive young woman, Charlotte Teller Johnson, who was a neighbor in New York, living just down the street at 3 Fifth Avenue. She had caught Twain's eye at a meeting they both attended early in 1906 in support of Russian revolutionaries.[2] Johnson, a novelist and playwright, had written a play about Joan of Arc that Twain volunteered to read, and they became frequent companions. In October a rumor suddenly materialized that there was something "more" between the seventy-year-old and young Charlotte.[3] In response, Twain asked her to move out of the neighborhood. Considering that he was old enough to be her grandfather, she found the rumors ludicrous and refused.[4] But the damage to their friendship proved irreparable.

Circumstantial evidence points to Lyon as the source of the rumors surrounding Twain's relationship to Charlotte Teller Johnson. Ever on the lookout for intelligent partners in flirtation, he was most likely seeing Charlotte a little too often for the Lioness's taste.[5] Deeply enthralled and obsessively attached to her employer, she jealously tracked his every move. Just when she had succeeded in banishing Jean from the family circle, she was confronted with a new problem. In order to vanquish her imagined rival without getting caught, she may have invented the rumor.

If this was her solution, it was ingenious, but it was also stressful, and likely precipitated one of her episodes.[6] Redolent of fictional melodrama, her breakdowns often coincided with some embroilment resulting from her backstage manipulation of the family. As if on cue—and only two months after she had collapsed during the orchestration of Jean's removal to Katonah— she had another of her "strange interludes" in mid-November 1906 and retreated to Hartford from November 24 until December 10. "[M]y heart [is] torn into sobbing shreds by my homesickness for the King—," she moaned during her absence.[7]

By the time she returned from Hartford, her attachment had become a permanent ache. He "can go away from me," she vowed, "but I shall not go away from him again unless he sends me." In fact, Twain had gone to Washington with Paine to lobby Congress for a new copyright law. "Strength is flowing back into my veins," she wrote the day after he returned to New York, "and I am glad to be alive."[8]

———

By the beginning of 1907 Lyon was happily providing intimate little services for her King. "There is nothing I love so much in all the world as I love to wait upon him," she wrote on January 4; "to order his cigars,

to clean his pipes, his dear old cracked Peterson pipes; to fill his pen, to tie his necktie; to order his clothes & to brush him off when he is ready to start for somewhere." This was while she was on vacation in Bermuda with Clemens and his old ministerial friend, Joseph Twichell. Twichell warned her that she was making Clemens too lazy, but Lyon was undeterred. "I'm glad I can spoil the King," she concluded, "that is all my meat and drink and life in these days."[9]

In late January she deliberately waited on the stairs until he came out of the bathroom and then "rubbed his head dry." In early March, after he complained of a touch of gout, she "painted his right foot with iodine." She was also privy to his intimate spaces. "This morning I sat in the King's dressing room while he shaved and went over the batch of mail there," she wrote unselfconsciously. "Now at 1:30 I slipped down to his room to see him lying asleep with his glasses on and his hands clasped over his breast and over a volume of 'Plutarch's Lives,'" she admitted less than a week later. Rather than discreetly retreating, she studied him adoringly. "His body is so sweet, so gentle in these days," she observed, "but from the flash of his eye you can see the strong active crusader-like life he is living in his mind."[10]

She frequented Twain's bedroom. She loved to sit there, finding excuses to make conversation while she watched him smoke his calabash pipe. "It is always so peaceful in the King's room," she said, "there is something so soothing in his smoking." Back from Bermuda, she asked Clemens if she might also smoke a pipe. "The secretary can do anything she wants to, provided its proper," was his coy reply. Miss Lyon saw her employer in several states of undress. On one occasion she took pleasure in observing Sam standing in a hall "in his underdrawers." She described herself as wearing a "long thin black silk gown that made a little swish" which was just enough, in her words, to "make him look up at me with his eyes singing with delight."[11] Watching him watching her watching him was just one of the many little games they played.

For the summer of 1907, Sam took a home in Tuxedo Park, about thirty miles northwest of Manhattan, near Henry Rogers's son, Harry, and daughter-in-law, Mary, with whom he was especially close. There he found the society he had missed in the New Hampshire hills and told Lyon, in a burst of enthusiasm, that he had never seen such a beautiful place. He was probably inspired as much by the society as the scenery. The period of productivity he had experienced after his wife's death had come to an end, and he was now more involved in his social life than in his work. Though he continued his autobiographical dictations, even in that his pace had slackened. Where in 1906 he had completed 134 dictations, his output for 1907 was only about half that number.[12] Lyon, by contrast, was uninspired by Tuxedo's cozy coterie. "I'm beginning to feel a hankering, a great quiet longing for Dublin," she mused. Never the most athletic woman, Lyon looked backward with nostalgia. "There I was almost-a-free creature of the hills. Here I am a gloved and card-cased thing."[13]

Whatever her reservations about Tuxedo, however, she felt no uncertainty about her boss, and she remained his full-time, adoring audience. Even a description of the logs in his fireplace could set her heart to palpitating: "Every morning the King tells me his adventures, or lack of them, of the night before. It's a dear trait," she affirmed, "and he takes you so into his confidence when he explains that 3 times his logs broke into a gaudy fire and 3 times he drenched them." In late May she called Twain "the most wonderful creature in the world." "He is my most complete delight," she swooned four days later. "Evenings he sits in the living room under the great electric light," she observed, "and he seems to be all the colors of soap bubbles." "Such a beautiful man he is," she sighed, after he slipped into her room "with just his silk underclothes on." She was agog over his body as much as his mind and pronounced him "beautiful to look upon."[14] He was seventy-one; she was forty-three, but age presented no barrier to Miss Lyon.

When Twain sailed for England on June 8, 1907, to receive an honorary doctorate from Oxford, she was in a state. "I'm not sleeping any of these nights along here," she wrote on June 20. "I'm groping along to Something, with an indescribable loneliness. It's the terrible loneliness that always comes over me with the King so far away." Intensely romantic and full of fantasies about the possibility of becoming Mrs. Clemens, she yearned for the happily-ever-after ending. "I have been dreaming a wonderful love story in these days," she confessed. "A story all of beautiful colors—and it makes me so very lonely—and so sad."[15]

Sometime in late June or early July she appears to have launched a daring offensive to bring her dream in line with reality. Twain had hired Ralph Ashcroft, whom he knew through business dealings, to accompany him to Oxford, and Ashcroft and Lyon had immediately recognized a certain kinship in each other. When a rumor began in England that Isabel Lyon and Mark Twain were engaged, "Ashcroft brought it to me eagerly," Twain remembered and then speculated on its source. "I had introduced him to a few dozen London reporters, & suspected that the report was his work & had been done by Miss Lyon's request. I think so yet."[16]

The report of the engagement was cabled to America and began to circulate closer to home. On July 25, 1907, after he had returned to Tuxedo, a Hartford paper published the story that Miss Lyon was marrying Mark Twain. Clemens took the unusual step of addressing his private life in public. He not only denied the report publicly but also began to take chaperones on his drives with Lyon. "The King likes the 'protection' of it," she wrote dryly.[17] In an interview she gave over forty years later, Isabel Lyon claimed that Charlotte Johnson had threatened revenge and had kept her word by starting the rumor about the "innocent" secretary marrying her boss. She also claimed in her diary that Twain concurred in fingering Johnson.[18] But if we can believe Twain that he always suspected Lyon was the source, this is a textbook case of projection. The Lioness never approached Clemens directly about marriage, nor did she ever openly confess her matrimonial goals in her diary. She worked by indirection.

After planting the rumor of an engagement failed to produce results, the determined woman mounted a private offensive. "Miss Lyon threw out a feeler," Twain remembered, "she came, looking ever so arch, & girly-girly & engaging, & gave me one of those little love-pats, & said—

" 'What do you reckon they say?'

" 'Well, what do they say?'

" 'That we are going to get married!' [Burst of girly-girly stage-laughter to indicate how killingly funny & wildly absurd an idea it was.]

" 'Who say it?'

" 'Everybody. It's all over the town!'

" 'Oh, well, it isn't any matter. It wasn't started for fun, it was started for a purpose. We don't know what the purpose was, we only know that the person that started it is going to get left, as the slang phrase goes.' "[19]

Clara and Jean feared that Lyon's campaign to push their father to the altar would succeed. Both daughters recognized her hold upon their father and were afraid he would submit "—in fact, we *expected* you to submit," Clara later told him. Some of his friends agreed.[20]

Sam thought otherwise. "Was I unaware that before the middle of 1906 she had made up her mind to marry me? No—I was aware of it," he answered his own rhetorical question. "I am uncommonly lacking in insight, uncommonly unobservant, but I was able to see that. . . . But I didn't bite." The first, last, and most compelling reason was Livy. "I wonder if you are able to believe," Sam asked his friend Howells in a letter he never sent, "I could ever find a person who would seem to me to be her match, & thus be moved to marry again? Would it occur to you that if I found such a person it might, would or could be Miss Lyon?" he repeated rhetorically. "In all my (nearly) seventy-four years I have seen only the one person whom I would marry, & I have lost her."[21]

Whatever his secret musings, however, it is clear from his attitude and behavior that he enjoyed watching his secretary try to maneuver him down the aisle. He delighted, even reveled, in their flirtation and the ever-tantalizing possibilities that their relationship implied. Moreover, he made her his constant companion, taking her virtually everywhere he would a wife. Her pursuit of him was a spectacle he encouraged. The fun and excitement of their relationship was a mutual availability—and this meant that an erotic expectation existed, if only as a tease. Slipping into her room "with just his silk underclothes on," as he did on June 3, was hardly the act of a man who shrank uncomfortably from his companion's flirtatious attentions. "My paths have never been pleasanter," he admitted, "than they were during her reign."[22] Nonetheless, his age, his adoration of his dead wife, and the fun he was having without marrying his attractive pursuer make his denial of any matrimonial inclination believable.

————

If Sam would not submit, in Clara's word, to marriage, what he did submit to was total financial control. Given his obsession with making money, he had a peculiar disinterest in managing it. Lyon had informal control of the checkbook by summer 1906. Perhaps as a result, her attitude became increasingly imperious, particularly toward his daughters. "[T]he children must begin to realize that if they [the family as a whole] have only $25,000 a year to live on—they must manage to live on that."[23] Whatever she said about the "children" collectively, however, she did not treat them equally. She doted on Clara, who did not bear the stigma of epilepsy and who held more power in the household than her sister. Nonetheless Jean was treated with a certain amount of deference until early June 1907. Just before he left for England and Oxford, Clemens gave Lyon a farmhouse on his Redding property, plus twenty acres for services rendered. He also gave her legal authority to write checks on his behalf through a power of attorney. After that she began to display more open contempt for Jean's feelings and needs.[24]

For all her eagerness to control Sam's money, Lyon was always rather vague about any final reckoning of debits and credits. This constant uncertainty probably contributed to her impulse to hoard his money for her pet project—the house in Redding. One of her more stingy acts during the summer was to deny Jean a summer lap robe for outings with her horse. "Father doesn't want to buy me another robe, which means that Miss L. has told him I had one that was good enough," Jean wrote in her diary, now cognizant of Lyon's total power over her father's purse strings.[25] His refusal was the work of Miss Lyon, whose parsimony, he recognized later, was brutally petty.

"Miss Lyon kept Jean scrimped in the matter of money; & Clara, also; but I could not perceive that she scrimped herself," Twain comprehended belatedly.[26] And Clara was still in a privileged position the summer of 1907. While Sam was in England for his honorary degree, Lyon and Clara went on a vacation together to Newfoundland, departing June 29 and returning July 11. "That's nice economy!" Jean exclaimed. "I don't doubt that when Lioness gets my letter asking that the remaining $16.00 for Prosper [her dog] be paid to Mrs. Holmes that she will think it too much & that for economy's sake it shouldn't be done." As if on cue, her father objected to the "great extravagance" of $16.00 for Prosper's board, an expense not to be "countenanced." In fact, he insisted that her dog should be put down and the money for his board should be given to the poor. He relented after Jean reminded him that Prosper was the last gift she ever received from her mother, but his attitude remained uncharacteristically small-minded. "I wish I weren't dependent on anybody," Jean exclaimed in frustration.[27]

Lyon's meanness toward Jean became habitual. She refused to sanction a magazine subscription for the poor shipwrecked patient, promising to send magazines from the house after her father had finished them. "They haven't come & won't but it's an unnecessary & foolish expense to send them right to me," Jean wrote mockingly. "Kind peo-

ple!"[28] Early in 1907, Sam had written to her, "I could not help thinking all the time how grieved your mother would have been to see you
long for a thing—anything—& have to be denied it." Livy would certainly have been in deep mourning that year for all that her youngest
child was denied. "We shall do all permissible things we can that can
give you comfort & pleasure," he continued in the same letter, evidently
trusting that Miss Lyon would carry out his pledge.[29] But his decision
not to read Jean's letters made that promise a sad hypocrisy, however innocent he was of Lyon's conniving.

By the end of the summer, Jean was thoroughly sick of Katonah. "My
voice trembled," she reported after her discussion with Dr. Hunt, "and I
nearly broke down several times. The visit was unsatisfactory however, as
he was in such a rush."[30] Jean felt that Hunt occasionally sympathized
with her situation, so perhaps he was embarrassed by his role in her
predicament. "He said no arrangements had been made," Jean noted,
"that he hadn't talked to Miss Lyon about it—I know what that means:
it is taken for granted that I shall stay here—& that he supposed we were
waiting for Dr. Peterson." All she could do was dream. "My head is
full of castles regarding a farm of my own—living as I like." "Oh,
I can't stay here!" she burst out after a rare visit outside Katonah to see
Mrs. Thayer, her dear friend from Dublin, who was staying in the Peeks-
kills. "It nearly killed me to go to a real home once more. It seemed so
queer!"[31]

Now desperate, Jean spoke to Dr. Hunt and the Lioness; she also
wrote to her father, begging to leave Katonah. "Until the doctors have
discussed, it is useless for him to mention the matter," Jean summarized
his mechanical reply. "No word of regret about my unhappyness—
nothing." Of course, she could never imagine the reason. "Then a lot of
stuff about the maids & a child—all three absolute strangers to me! A
truly sympathetic Father."[32]

"I have seen Peterson," she reported on October 2, "& while I had little hope before, I have practically none, now. He said he believed in letting well enough alone & that as I had done so well here he tho't it a pity
to change but that he'd talk with Miss Lyon tomorrow." Jean knew what
this meant. "Within a few days I will get a note from father saying that it's
too bad but that as Dr. P didn't seem to wholly approve of my going, he
didn't feel like saying any thing. A note of few words & much meaning."
Despite Jean's belief that her father did not want her to leave, the next day

she was surprised by a "very sweet note from Father... & in it he doesn't show the feeling I tho't he would against my leaving."[33] After almost a year's absence, Sam may have been prepared to welcome his daughter home, with the blessing of her doctor. But his secretary had other ideas.

According to Lyon, Dr. Peterson "doesn't want Jean to leave her sanitarium where she is improving but hating the sanitarium viciously. I didn't tell the King how he said that the epileptic temperament rarely improved, but that it grew worse, and that Jean must never live with her father again, because her affection might easily turn into a violent and insane hatred and she could slay, just by the sudden and terrible and ungovernable revulsion of feeling. The one bounding out of the other & the person never knowing that he is passing from one condition to the other."[34]

In their meeting, Peterson and Lyon probably did discuss the connection between violence and epilepsy, a conviction then shared by both physicians and the laity. But she is almost certainly inventing dialogue and disguising her personal bias as a medical dictum when she has Peterson declare authoritatively: "Jean must never live with her father again." It was the secretary, not the doctor, who wished to keep Jean and her father separated. Because of epilepsy, so her story went, Jean might murder her father in a moment of "ungovernable revulsion of feeling." But the Lioness was explicit: "I didn't tell the King." Sam only heard that Peterson wanted Jean to remain in the sanitarium because she was improving. Apparently Lyon did not believe that he would swallow the categorizing of his daughter as a killer.[35]

Thus Sam retained his nearly invincible faith that all his secretary's impulses were good and fine—a state he later characterized as "peacefully asleep"—while his secretary nurtured hopes of matrimony. Hearing him walk up and down the porch singing a spiritual, she sighed, "[O]h, he does need some one to love him and pet him."[36]

———

Though Clara, too, recognized her father's need for love, she was not about to volunteer for the job of companionable daughter. She spent the late summer in Newport, Connecticut, and Sam lamented to Lyon that he never saw "anything of her," even in New York.[37] Perhaps he was trying to make his daughter jealous, and he certainly was trying to fill a void in his life, for in August he wrote rhapsodically of a visit by

Dorothy Quick, a ten-year-old whom he had recently befriended. "I am sorry that that child has gone away if you miss her so much," Clara replied. "It makes me feel that I ought to drop my career & trot right home," she admitted, "except that I am not [like Dorothy] a sun or a moon or perhaps even a firefly." Comparing herself to the young visitor, she expressed guilt, jealousy, and a nagging sense of inferiority. Clara feared her father's expectations. Tenderness, love, and devotion, however genuine, were easier in letters. "Are you as gay as ever Marcus dear and just as holy?" she teased in a later letter, adding:

> Here's a rumple to your curly locks
> A plea to Daily wear your socks
> A message of good luck to Sam
> Whose morning prayer is always *Damn!*

"Much much love Padre Mio," she signed off her affectionate missive, "from the prima donna."[38]

Indeed Clara shielded herself against paternal needs by taking the role of aspiring diva, pleading the demands of her career and its physical requirements, including that summer problems with her throat. "I am disappointed and a good deal irritated," she told her father in September, "not to be on my way to Tuxedo this moment." Dr. Halsey spoke against her going, she informed him, and both Lyon and Will Wark, her accompanist, also "joined heads to keep me here." Her throat was not yet healed. Health, career, and the advice of friends and professionals conspired to keep her away, she wanted him to believe. She believed it herself. But more to the point Clara was fighting for an identity outside the orbit of her celebrity father. "I am going to church, and since I haven't the honor to lunch with the great Mark Twain (Do you realize that you are as great as Shakespeare?) I'll listen to an apostle." Flattery preceded a flash of self-awareness. "I am beginning to feel quite queer to be related to you," she told him.[39] Being the daughter of Mark Twain was never easy for Clara. Nurturing her independence and the dream of a singing career with his money, she caught glimpses of her father's loneliness but often could not bring herself closer than letters. Free to occupy her father's house, unlike her sister, Clara often preferred to live elsewhere.

CHAPTER 8

A Viper to Her Bosom

As she approached the anniversary of her arrival at Katonah, Jean was desperately unhappy. When she had first agreed to leave home, she had anticipated that it would be for a few months and that she would spend the next summer in Dublin with her father. Now jaded and angry, she was not the naive young woman who had entered the sanitarium with high hopes of complete recovery. Even the absence of any grand mal seizures since April 10—almost six months—did not bring her joy.[1]

Jean recognized her own impotence. She had some hardheaded comprehension of her specific woes and was also aware, in a general sense, of Miss Lyon's power over her fate. Ever direct, Jean fired off a volley of complaints in the direction of the home front. "Oh, terrible—Terrible that his children cannot come under the spell of his glories, his subtleties, his sweetnesses," Lyon exclaimed with no trace of guilt or irony. "For this morning there was a cruel letter from Jean damning me—finding fault with him—with *him*." In response to this blast from Jean, Lyon rushed to Katonah to talk with Dr. Peterson. Jean foolishly believed that after the secretary consulted with Peterson she might be able to leave her sanitarium. Waiting in suspense for several days, she received the predictable answer: "Dr. Peterson insists on my staying here, for a while at least! And I feel as tho' I could not *endure* the place another week. It is ghastly."[2]

If Jean's critical letter to her father produced no immediate change in her circumstances, it did elicit a stalwart defense of his secretary. "I give Miss Lyon instructions—she does nothing of her own initiative," her father responded. "When you blame her you are merely blaming me—

she is not open to criticism in the matter." Sam still fervently believed in Lyon's loyalty and honesty. "She has failed to secure your confidence and esteem and I am sorry. I wish it were otherwise, but it is no argument since she has not failed in any other person's case. One failure to fifteen hundred successes means that the fault is not with her."[3]

Mark Twain would live to regret his exculpation of Miss Lyon at his daughter's expense. What he never understood, however, was the role his own attitude toward epilepsy played in giving her the upper hand. "God Almighty alone is responsible for your temperament, your malady and all your troubles and sorrows. I cannot blame you for them and I do not," he wrote his daughter. By reducing Jean's personality to a disease, he routinely discounted her feelings (when he was informed of them), blaming her "temperament" which he linked inextricably to her "malady." His problems in understanding his daughter were compounded by a conventional view of sex roles that remained curiously untouched by his iconoclastic response to other aspects of American culture. His rigid sense of masculinity, for example, actually encouraged—and, in a sense, condoned—his abdication of responsibility for his daughter's treatment. "Jean dear, if your mother were here she would know how to think for you and plan for you and take care of you better than I do; but we have lost her, and a man has no competency in these matters."[4]

Twain's self-ascribed lack of competency may be more accurately assessed as sheer complacency. Mr. Brush, Jean's artist friend and the father of several teenage children, consulted with two doctors about her disease in 1908. One, a surgeon, arranged to examine Jean, but Dr. Peterson intervened. He insisted that the examination take place in his office with another doctor because, he said, he was afraid Jean would have an operation "on the spot." The surgeon Peterson brought in for a consultation rejected Jean's theory that a fall on a bone at the back of her neck was the cause of her illness.[5] If a fatherly friend could take such an initiative out of loving concern, Twain's attitude of helpless passivity toward his daughter's illness cannot be explained as a result of gender alone. His inertia was also encouraged by his sense of determinism, as stiff as any Calvinist's. In *What Is Man?*, the philosophical dialogue Twain privately published in the fall of 1906, he reiterated his favorite ideas about "man as a selfish creature, life as an unbroken chain of events, and the mind as a machine."[6]

"Always he says that she is not to blame," Lyon summarized Sam's attitude toward his youngest daughter's affliction. He blamed a God who could "create such natures, such maladies as hers," Lyon explained, "and in the creating, run them into a mould as inflexible as bronze."[7] But his sex-role ideology and scientific determinism pale in comparison to the influence of Isabel Lyon on his treatment of Jean. Mired in a web of lies, the great anti-romantic of American literature had fallen prey to a soap opera queen in his own life, a confidante who constantly reinforced his very worst ideas about the "epileptic temperament." "I am anxious that Dr. Peterson shall place you to your satisfaction," Sam wrote Jean in early October 1907, "and I have not a doubt that he will find such a place if it exists."[8] "If it exists" is a telling qualifier, for Sam's belief in the "epileptic temperament," reinforced by Lyon's prejudice, may help to explain his cavalier attitude toward Jean's living arrangements. He seemed to doubt that his daughter could be happy anywhere, believing that her epilepsy condemned her to continuous dissatisfaction and discontent.

———

Certainly Jean was dissatisfied. "I feel myself a subject deserving sympathy because I am desperately unhappy," she unburdened herself to her Dublin friend, Nancy Brush. "I hate, no, I despise the heads of this establishment & one of the chief patients. All three are liars & wholly despicable." The heads of the establishment, the Sharps, were indeed petty tyrants who treated Jean like a hostage, albeit on orders from headquarters. The problem, however, was more personal as well. After devoting herself to birds and flowers in the spring, Jean had made three good women friends. Now, just as the weather grew cold, all three were departing. Clearly Jean was staying longer than most patients at Katonah, and she felt the friends she made there were continually abandoning her. "I am still in Katonah & shall be all winter & until when next year I can't pretend to know," Jean informed Nancy at the end of October. "*Dr. Peterson said I must be in some sort of a sanitarium* & that the only other one, near New York, he could think was in Greenwich, Conn. I had heard from a friend that it was not as comfortable as this one & as my desire had been, not to be in a sanitarium but to live by myself in the country, I decided to remain here & stick it out."[9]

Lyon apparently recognized that the prisoner was desperate enough to attempt a break-out, for her subalterns swung into action. Dr. Peterson suddenly announced that he would try to find a new place for Jean to live, and Dr. Hibbard was authorized to accompany her to the club to roast chestnuts and dance. Cheered by Hibbard's attentions and determined to endure her misery without further complaint, Jean was nonetheless chagrined to find a letter from her father commending her on her happy and contented spirit. "I only meant that while I *had* to stay I was trying to make the best of things, but never did I mean to convey that I was content, happy! in such a place," she exclaimed. "That shows how little he appreciates how I feel or he *could* not write in such a way."[10]

Jean concluded that her father was extraordinarily obtuse. "His empty letters, telling me to have a good time are silly when he won't really try to rectify bad conditions," she wrote shrewdly. Yet she distinguished letters of genuine feeling from her father's more artificial mouthings. After sending him a Christmas gift of an ashtray with a frog smoking a pipe, her own creation, she received a letter "wild with appreciation" and, she noted, "the letter had a true ring."[11] She had learned to expect wildly inconsistent letters from her father, who vacillated between expressions of mechanical indifference and genuine concern, but she remained unaware of the Faustian bargain that could have explained them. "Father's letter of tonight made me tired," she reacted to another missive. "He spoke wholly of playing billiards for hours & *said* not one word regarding the business troubles. Nor one about my letter—that he was supposed to have been touched by." It is impossible to be touched by a letter you have never read, but Jean had no thought of that cowardly possibility. She resorted to a benign, all-purpose explanation. "I should be used to his peculiarities, by now, I suppose, but I can never wholly reconcile myself to some of them." Through it all, Jean held an unquenchable faith that her father would never deliberately hurt her.[12]

Her demands to leave Katonah continued to bring expanded freedoms in an effort to placate her without actually changing her situation. On the theory that an urban environment was detrimental to her health, Jean had been forbidden to travel to New York City and was thus denied all access to her home. Suddenly the theory metamorphosed, and she was given permission to go to New York to shop and to see friends. She even once made a visit to the family home at 21 Fifth Avenue. But the limits of her expanded freedom are illustrated in what happened after that. Dr. Peterson refused permission for a subsequent visit to New York City until he learned that Jean did not plan to see her father. Then the doctor acquiesced immediately.[13] Apparently what was now held to be detrimental to her health was going home.

If her demands to leave her sanitarium brought more freedom to travel, little changed on the financial front. After the Knickerbocker Trust Co., where Twain had $51,000, suspended payment to depositors in October, Clara told Jean that while there was money for the sanitarium and her regular allowance, she would have to pay all other expenses herself.[14] Writing several days later, Sam himself said he stood to lose little or nothing, and would be only temporarily cramped.[15] Obviously he expected that depositors would eventually be reimbursed. Nonetheless Jean was made to feel impoverished. Lioness wrote her a note saying that she "must save every penny." Reduced to writing on notepads rather than more expensive stationery in order to economize, Jean began to believe she might not be able to receive her regular allowance for some time. Even though, over the next month, it became increasingly certain that most of the money would be recovered, Lyon's tightfisted rule was now supreme.[16]

"I don't quite know what our condition is," Jean confided in Nancy, "but this sample will show something. Last winter I paid one dollar a day for the use of a cutter in which to drive Scott (who came early in Feb.)." Since this year she would be driving Scott all winter, Jean calculated that buying a cutter for thirty or forty dollars would be a real saving. "So I wrote to Miss Lyon on the Subject. She seemed to misunderstand my reason for making the request & stated that Father could not possibly afford that much of an output on a not absolutely necessary object. Of course her thinking I was unreasonable in asking for gifts under the existing conditions but the fact that, say, $35 couldn't be spent does show pretty well how things lie."[17] In fact, Clemens projected that his income for 1907 would be somewhere between $70,000 to $80,000.[18] To deny his daughter's request for thirty-five dollars was an act of petty tyranny.

For the first time, however, Clara too was made to feel a financial squeeze. She told Jean that she was now forced to pay her own bills on the installment plan. Always given preferential treatment in money matters in the past, she was in no mood to support Jean's request for a cutter. Nevertheless, Jean rationally assumed that her cost-cutting motive would be respected. But Clara berated Jean for even suggesting the idea. "I've had as much as I can stand of their treatment," Jean exclaimed in response. On December 15, she wrote Dr. Peterson that she could not stand the sanitarium any longer, and one week later she mentioned for the first time that she had some hope of getting out.[19]

Feeling the full weight of her alienation, however, she decided not to go home for Christmas. Jean was desperately hurt by the callous indifference she felt from 21 Fifth Avenue and described herself in the days before Christmas as "tearlessly eating my heart out." Even in her sorrow she was sensitive to her father's feelings. "I didn't want to hurt Father by deliberately refusing," she wrote. "He never hurts anyone knowingly & his part of this trouble must be due to some extraordinary noncomprehension." Instead, she spent the holiday with friends whom she had met in the sanitarium and who now lived in Bronxville, near Yonkers. On Christmas Eve, they brought a package to a poor family in Mount Vernon, New York, decorated a tree, and hung stockings. On Christmas Jean exchanged gifts with her friends and delighted in their company. But she especially missed one absent member of her family. "I am racked by the thought & the realization of how different all would be if Mother's sweet heart were only here to understand all."[20] Perhaps reflecting his pique at Jean's absence, Twain gave his daughter-in-exile a paltry ten dollars for Christmas. Since he was not by nature a stingy man, one suspects another hand helped him close the wallet. Nevertheless, it was the Lioness who telephoned on Christmas Day with news that was more valuable than any gift: Jean would soon have an opportunity to leave Katonah.[21]

———

As a widower, Clemens relied upon many hands. He would have expected Katy Leary, devoted as she had been to Mrs. Clemens, to take a motherly interest in his surviving daughters. But while Katy expressed affection for Jean, she was much closer to Clara. During the tragedy of Susy's death, Katy had helped Clara cope with her mother's heartbreak. Katy and Clara were also constantly together in Mrs. Clemens's sickroom. As a consequence, they seem to have developed a close bond.

Katy had accompanied Clara when she fled from the Gilders' cottage in Massachusetts to New York in the summer following her mother's death. She often helped Clara settle into a new place, and sometimes traveled with her on her concert tours.[22] Katy was supportive of Clara's musical career, not only because she had transferred some of her feelings for Mrs. Clemens to her middle daughter, but also because she identified with unmarried women, and Clara was still single.

So was the Lioness, who also received some of Katy's sympathy. Stumbling across Miss Lyon smoking a pipe, Katy gave her benediction—after recovering from the shock. " 'Oh go ahead do anything you can to have a good time,' " she told Lyon, " '—we've both of us missed so much.' "[23] Displaying a keen sense of Lyon's emotional neediness, Katy passed judgment on the deprivation of single life. Observing the growing number of intimacies Lyon shared with Clemens, she must have seen that her boss's loneliness was lightened by the attentions of his secretary. And she probably approved of their mutual enjoyment. "Oh go ahead do anything you can to have a good time—" was likely a common blessing she bestowed upon the unattached in Clemens's extended household.

But Katy's sympathy for single women could not have kept her from seeing the incongruity between Lyon's role as Clemens's employee and her behavior as his equal. Katy watched Lyon make 172 pincushions to augment her income during the summer of 1905 and then stop altogether the next year.[24] Perhaps she noticed that this coincided with Miss Lyon's check-signing privileges. At about the same time, she observed Miss Lyon assume a place at Clemens's table and drawing room alongside his friends and family.[25]

The contrast between the two women's sense of status was palpable, readily explained by their differing backgrounds, education, and expectations. Born into a working-class Irish family, Katy had a sense of class boundaries that translated into an almost prideful embrace of her role as servant. "As for doing things that I wanted to do," Katy reflected in her old age, "if it interfered in any way with them, I wouldn't ever do it—they came first." She clearly understood her own motives: "Because where the Clemens was seemed just like my home, and I spent all my time thinking of what was best for them." The child of a college professor, Isabel Lyon had a middle-class pedigree that did not translate comfortably into a servant's role, however much she worked to please her employer. According to Clemens, she treated his servants badly, bragging to him about her verbal violence at their expense. "I told her more than once," he remembered later, "that it was not a thing to boast of, but to be ashamed of; but it had no effect." He concluded that "she despised servants & did not know how to treat them." But Katy was an exception. She held a special place in the Clemens household, and Lyon trod lightly in her direction. In return, Katy was outwardly supportive. "Little Katie has been a motherly angel to me," Lyon noted appreciatively at the end of August 1907, "and tried to rub the pain [in the back of her head] away."[26] As long as Clara, Twain, and Lyon were in a mutual admiration society, Katy would remain an honorary member.

———

Starting in June 1907 the atmosphere—financial and otherwise—of Clemens's household began to shift. Ground was broken for the Redding house, and Clemens made his gift of land, with its rundown farmhouse, to his secretary. But the most significant change was the entrance of Ralph Ashcroft into Twain's entourage.[27] Ashcroft was a social climber, inventing and reinventing himself as he rose. Twain later described him as "obsequious, watchful, attentive, and looking as if he wanted to lick somebody's boots" and surmised that he had been either a bedroom steward or a valet in his native England, observing "he knows the latter trade to perfection." But it was his divestiture of personal history that was most intriguing. "In the 5 years that I have intimately known Ashcroft I have never heard him utter a single word about his past history except that his birthplace was Liverpool, that he retains his English subjectship, & that his father was a dissenting minister," Twain explained. "He is absolutely corked-up & sealed, concerning himself. I have encountered nothing resembling this before."[28]

Twain's first association with Ashcroft came, predictably, with a company that ultimately went bankrupt. Started in London but relocated to New York, its doors closed in 1905 while Ashcroft was its secretary-treasurer.[29] Twain believed the dietary supplement called Plasmon, which the company produced, would prove to be the fountain of youth. As was all too typical of his investments, he began by hoping for a financial geyser but settled for a trickle and then a drought, finally losing the entire $25,000 he had invested in the original Plasmon stock. Ever the optimist, Twain had also sunk $4,500 in hairpins and locking safety pins after being solicited by Ashcroft on behalf of his uncle in September 1904. Miraculously, he resisted Ashcroft's advice the following year to buy stock in a company that made insoles for shoes.[30] Fifteen months later, on October 30, 1906, the enterprising Englishman was hired to be Twain's traveling secretary on his trip to Egypt, but was soon out of a job when Twain canceled the trip.[31] Within weeks, however, Ashcroft was advising Twain to invest $30,000 in the American Mechanical Cashier Company. (Apparently he resisted at the time, though at his death he owned 400 stock shares and 32 bonds in the American Mechanical Cashier Company, all worthless after the triumph of the rival National Cash Register Company.)[32]

Ashcroft, who lived in Brooklyn with his sisters, kept up the connection through business correspondence until Twain again needed a companion in June 1907, for his trip to Oxford. Though Lyon was initially miffed that Ashcroft had usurped her rightful place by Twain's side, after their return she slowly accepted the Englishman into the King's inner circle.[33] Ashcroft began writing letters for Twain, who had been impressed with his abilities while they were in England. Inching closer to the throne, Ashcroft almost immediately began scheming on behalf of a boss who could never resist rolling the financial dice. Suggesting trademarks in Mark Twain cigars, tobacco, and whiskey, Ashcroft had registered patents on whiskey and tobacco in Twain's name by November. He also later suggested incorporation in the form of the Mark Twain Company to protect copyrights that were about to expire.[34]

It was probably Twain himself who tutored Ashcroft in the marketability of his name. Twain was quite vain about his ability to command large royalties and was ever vigilant concerning the monetary value of his moniker. One of his angriest later complaints about Lyon was that she failed to appreciate the amount of money (his estimate was $15,000–$20,000) she could have made by co-editing, at his invitation, a collection of his letters.[35] Ashcroft was a quicker study—as his idea for the trademark patent demonstrated.

By early fall 1907, the Englishman had been invited to join the King as a guest at his summer home in Tuxedo. "Little Ashcroft came out and spent the night," Lyon noted on October 1, "and we had a very sweet, cosy and gay time"—the first indication of her affection for Ralph. Two weeks later he turned up again for an all-day game of hearts. "Ashcroft makes a pleasant, bright, considerate and properly appreciative third hand," Lyon calculated approvingly.[36] (It should be noted that Ashcroft was never formally employed by Clemens; although he received many perks through his association with Mark Twain, a salary was not one of them.) Ever alert to fill a social need in the Clemens household, Ashcroft's willingness to accommodate to Twain's schedule was winning. But at the beginning of 1908 it became clear he did lack one essential skill. "It is dreadful to have such a dearth of amusement for the King," Lyon lamented in early January. And at 21 Fifth Avenue amusement meant billiards. "My life is so empty," her boss complained at dinner, "it seems a pity that I cannot have a game of billiards when I want it." Twain remained obsessed with the game, playing six or seven hours at a stretch when he could. But his billiard pals, especially Albert Paine, were all "submerged" in work, and on January 10 he had to settle for dinner and cards with Ashcroft.[37]

Since Twain had lost interest in his autobiographical dictations, Paine had begun to focus on other projects. On January 11, however, he returned to New York from his country home in Redding to attend a Lotos Club dinner in Twain's honor, and the two played billiards until 3:30 in the morning. "[T]he King said that they stopped playing," Lyon recalled, "only because he 'was weak from loss of profanity.'" But Paine's preoccupation with work continued, and it was Ashcroft who was recruited to prowl around Bermuda with Twain at the end of January.[38]

If Paine's absence put a dent in Twain's chief pleasure, the nonstop billiard game, it created a more serious vacuum in the life of his secretary. Lyon had relied heavily upon Paine's companionship, conversation, emotional support, and practical help since the summer of 1906 in Dublin.[39] He was still coming to her rescue in late February 1908, packing the King's trunk for another trip to Bermuda and then "soothing my spine"—presumably giving her a back rub.[40] But sometime in the early part of that year, this began to change. The astute Ashcroft needed very little time to figure out that the woman who controlled the purse strings was vague about the totals at the bottom of Twain's debit and credit columns, as were the boss and his daughters. Of the inner circle, only Paine was capable of financial oversight and close enough to Lyon and her boss to interfere. Well-established in the Clemens household, the biographer never suspected that his entire project would be jeopardized by Ashcroft's maneuvers to ingratiate himself with Twain and Lyon.

————

"Today I telephoned out to Redding telling AB [Paine] that the King is going to Bermuda and that he needn't come down," Lyon commented on January 23, 1908, two days before Twain's planned departure with Ashcroft. "Somehow all my confidence is gone, and I do not greatly want to see him [Paine]. My anxiety over the Howells letters incident seems almost to be making me ill. My philosophy is gone."[41]

Paine had been gathering materials for his biography of Mark Twain, with his subject's full approval. This included tracking down letters that the famous author had written to friends and relatives, but somehow Lyon had become persuaded that Paine's routine request to borrow the correspondence in Howells's possession was treacherous. "I slipped away to talk with Ashcroft about the letters episode," she reported, "and he approved of my method of procedure with Mr. Howells for I wrote him of the fact that the King is quite unaware that Paine sent for the letters." Her behind-the-scenes consultation with Ashcroft ushered in a new era of tension with Paine. "When the King spoke of the Howells letters, my heart stood still," the secretary revealed, "for my anxiety had projected itself into his mind; and he said the thing he should have said." Mental telepathy aside, Lyon began to chip away at Paine's credibility with her boss. "The King said last night that the next thing Paine would be getting letters from Howells," Lyon confided to her journal, "and he proceeded to write to Mr. Howells asking him not to comply."[42]

But Twain's request was too late. It never occurred to Howells that his friend would have the slightest objection. "I saw Paine on such intimate terms with you," Howells wrote Twain, "that I should not have hesitated to offer him all your letters." This was indeed an accurate assessment of the author's relationship with his biographer before Ashcroft became Lyon's collaborator. Howells's reaction was telling. "I don't think Paine could abuse the confidence put in him, or would make an indiscreet use of them," he stated flatly. "Of course Paine will do exactly what you say about them; he spoke to me with entire judgment and good sense." In fact, Howells had sent Paine only ten or twelve letters because the "vast bulk" of his correspondence with Twain was at his vacation home in Maine.[43]

"Nowhere is a man's life and nature so revealed as in his letters," Paine wrote to Lyon at the end of January, in the midst of the struggle over Howells's letters. Fighting against the suspicions and opposition he had suddenly encountered, Paine sought to allay the secretary's fears about his work. Twain's letters would only be used as necessary evidence in his biography and would not lessen the market for a future volume of letters by her or Clara, he reassured her. No, he did not intend to embarrass the King or "parade the things he would wish forgotten." To the contrary, he argued, full access to his subject's letters would allow him to construct "a personality so impregnable" that Twain's critics would not be able to discredit or belittle him. Paine was himself an artful manipulator and understood the necessity of flattering both the Lioness and the King. Thus he closed his appeal with a strong overture of friendship to her.[44]

But Paine eventually had to confront his loss of face in the Twain household. Deciding not to pull out of the project altogether, he confessed later that he deliberately removed some biographical materials "fully within my province as his biographer" without Lyon's knowledge or consent, and stored them for safekeeping in a safe deposit box. Paine believed that he acted to protect a project that had been unfairly jeopardized by the jealousy of Twain's secretary.[45] As if to underscore that belief, in early July, Howells shipped off "a huge mass" of letters to Clemens from his summer home, "because I am vague as to their going direct to him [Paine], after your doubts of last winter," he explained. Writing to Paine, Howells tactfully excused his action, saying that he was giving Twain the chance to "look them over first. He probably won't," Howells added, "but it is best for all that he should have the chance."[46]

Perhaps coincidentally, one of the clearest demonstrations of Ashcroft's behind-the-scenes bid to discredit Paine also occurred in July, soon after Twain received the letters from Howells. "Ashcroft came to my room with me," Lyon wrote, "and told me—after questioning me about Paine's friendship for me—that coming up in the train [from Redding] on Friday Paine sat with him and talked against me. Said that I am ruining my mentality, etc. with drugs, fenascetine—Why I can't even spell the word."[47] Paine was no doubt concerned about and critical of her use of alcohol and drugs. But Ashcroft cleverly turned this conversation with Paine into evidence of his rival's double-dealing. Broaching the subject to her as a confidant, he convinced her that Paine "talked against me."

Choosing Ashcroft over Paine was a fateful pairing—especially so for Lyon. Her emotional retreats and intuitive efforts to placate even those she disliked were a protective device that Ashcroft's more aggressive style would blunt. His psychological skills were inferior to hers, but he had a knack for numbers and some financial expertise. He was also single. As Ashcroft wormed his way into her trust, he became her financial advisor and aide-de-camp. "I could not do it alone," she wrote of her heavy load, "but I am unafraid, for always there is Benares [her nickname for Ashcroft] to be near me, and to help me. And not merely to help me, but to *do* the many things I cannot do."[48]

Left to her own devices, Lyon had been muddling along with great success. She was gregarious and charming, in fact a grand hostess. She also had real talent and skill in the decorative arts. And she worked hard at tasks she enjoyed. If she was disorganized when it came to matters of business, it was mostly because she avoided tasks she found distasteful, like paying bills. But her scattered financial stewardship really made no difference in a household with plenty of money. She may not have known the bottom line, but she instinctively knew how to cater to Sam and Clara. Thus it is very significant that Ashcroft's ascension to the right hand of the woman-who-signed-the-checks coincided with the first reduction in the flow of money to the eldest surviving daughter. This appears to be an act of Ashcroftian rationality for which the normally discerning Lyon would pay heavily. Late in life Lyon told a private detective that she "soon discovered that she had taken a viper unto her bosom."[49]

CHAPTER 9

Innocence at Home

As THE NEW YEAR of 1908 approached, Jean received much-hoped-for news—the prisoner of Katonah was being sprung to a house in Greenwich, Connecticut, twenty miles away. An old friend of Lyon's from Farmington, a woman named Mildred Cowles, had turned up as a patient at the sanitarium in early November, with her sister Edith along as helper and nurse, and the secretary seized the opportunity to set up a "little household" for Jean with the two women.[1] These were no ordinary companions, however. Mildred told Jean in early December that she was at Katonah because she had attempted suicide several times and "at one time always kept poison on hand." But when Lyon learned that Mildred might be released to her sister's care, such dubious qualifications were outweighed by the chance to employ a pair of loyal retainers and reliable spies.[2] "When the dear Cowles girls came here on Christmas day to see if Mr. Clemens would be willing to have Jean change from Katonah to Greenwich (& fearing to come)," Lyon wrote to a Dublin friend of Jean's, "the King could not speak for a moment, & with his dear voice shaking he said 'Anything, anything you can do to make that dear child happy first, & then comfortable, you are privileged to do. I am a man. I can do so little for her.'"[3]

Presumably Lyon had arranged the meeting with Sam, who, if she accurately described the scene, was excessively grateful. No doubt he was under the impression that the sisters were sacrificing other opportunities to minister to his "child." Financially strapped and emotionally precarious, the Cowleses were, in truth, anxious to secure this situation. Although Jean assumed that Dr. Peterson had first suggested a cottage in

Greenwich to the Cowles sisters and that she needed his permission to join them, in fact the sisters would probably have not been able to pay the rent without Clemens's financial support. Peterson, however, was quite agreeable to the change that Lyon probably engineered and told Edith to get ready in three days. On January 9, 1908, Edith, Mildred, Jean, and Peterson's former governess, a French immigrant named Marguerite Schmitt, now employed as a companion for Jean, moved into the Greenwich cottage.[4]

The sisters were not the best of roommates. Mildred attempted suicide several times in Greenwich; apparently Edith was afraid to let her out of her sight, which only drove Mildred to ever more frenzied expressions of rage. She regularly refused to eat or go to bed, and she threw a constant stream of temper tantrums. This led Jean to observe slyly: "Mildred is ill. That is she is really ill through love of *herself*." Her sister Edith "slaves for her, thinks for, works for, wastes even money for her, forgets everyone else's needs for her, as though Mildred were the sun & she the miserable little earth following her around." Apparently Mildred had a tantrum whenever her wishes were thwarted, and Edith always capitulated. Thus Jean suspected, since the Cowleses were short of money, that the trinkets Edith bought for her sister were given at the expense of food for herself and the servants. The evidence was obvious enough. While Edith was in charge of the household budget, the servants never had enough to eat and Jean was denied more expensive food such as vegetables in winter. Jean did not unburden herself to her family, however, since she had been well tutored to their indifference in the past.[5] She was also grateful to flee the confines of her sanitarium under any pretext.

Thus liberated, she began to have hopes again for her future, and these hopes were given a great boost by a visit from her friend Mr. Brush, who was in the Greenwich area before departing on a trip to Italy. Brush's generosity and kindness in inviting her to join his friends for a day makes it a strong possibility that he had deliberately arranged to see Jean. "You can't imagine what it meant to me to see him and that darling household," she confided to his daughter Nancy. "I have been so long without the sort of home life that you have that when I catch a glimpse of it—especially one containing some one I love—it is very hard for me to control my feelings, which give way extremely easily at such times."[6]

She caught up on all her old Dublin friends on two more "glorious" visits Mr. Brush made to see her. It was at this time that he sought medical opinions on Jean's condition, only to have his efforts cut short by Dr. Peterson. And on the way to the train station after his last visit, Brush asked if he could make a small drawing of Jean before leaving for Italy. Modest, even to the point of self-effacement, she was dumbstruck that Brush admired her looks enough to want to paint her, though both he and Albert Paine had complimented her on her appearance in Dublin. "I don't suppose you can understand how I felt," she wrote Nancy. "But the utmost I have ever been told was that I looked quite pretty or somewhat so in an evening dress or something of the sort, & those compliments were almost all from the Lioness, I believe." Never dreaming that Mr. Brush favored her appearance, she had noticed him staring but simply assumed he was trying to assess her health.[7] Though a handsome woman, she thought of her physical self primarily in terms of her stigmatized condition.

Brush's visits stimulated her desire to return to Dublin, especially after he offered her his house there while he and his family were abroad. After a consultation with Dr. Peterson on March 2, Jean gleefully told Nancy Brush that the doctor "fully believes in Dublin."[8] However crazed, the Cowleses were a movable feast (or rather famine), and a summer in Dublin beckoned furiously. But Peterson subsequently changed his mind.

What could have possibly made Dublin objectionable? Jean had a house and chaperones already in tow—however dubious their worth. She had friends who would welcome and protect her; moreover, she wanted with all her heart to return to the one place where she had been happy. She always exercised strenuously in Dublin, but her vigorous physical activity in other locations raised no medical objections.[9] Twain provides the clue when he wrote that he hoped Jean's summer residence would be close to New York in order for her to see him and her doctor. Certainly Jean accepted the first part of this rationale, hoping to see more of her father if she remained close by. But Dr. Peterson ordered her father's visits to be restricted that summer literally "to hours," and Sam had followed this advice to the letter when he and Ashcroft visited her in Greenwich in late April. Moreover, with only a few exceptions Jean's visits home had been proscribed from the moment she entered

Katonah; thus her father's proximity was hardly the key, much as they both may have thought so.[10]

It would seem it was rather the doctor's proximity that was essential. "I have persuaded the little family at Greenwich to give up the Dublin idea," Peterson wrote conspiratorially to Lyon. Instead, he suggested Gloucester, Massachusetts, because he frequently summered there, in his father-in-law's house. Not only did he expect to visit once or twice, he knew a doctor in the area whom he could supervise, and he had found that his epilepsy cases were "greatly benefited" by the climate in the summer.[11] His ability to supervise Jean's treatment in Gloucester, then, provided the main rationale to scotch Dublin. But the rationale for whom?

Initially, access to his patient for the summer did not concern the good doctor. Not only had he told Jean that he fully believed in Dublin, but he also held Twain's proxy. "[S]ubmit it to Dr. Peterson," Twain wrote Jean, referring to her summer home, "& if it satisfies him it will satisfy me." Peterson had also written to Lyon, "The vicinity of New York is very hot, as you know, in the summer, and a change of this kind would be, I believe, most satisfactory provided it meets with Mr. Clemens' approval."[12] Obviously, Dublin fit these criteria as readily as Gloucester. Uppermost in Peterson's calculations was a famous father's preference. Uppermost in Clemens's calculations was the advice of a medical expert. In the end someone else was pulling the strings.

Most likely Lyon scratched Dublin in favor of Gloucester, and her motive was control. In Gloucester she could maintain her authority through the kowtowing doctor and his deputy. In Dublin, surrounded by friends and treated by an independent physician, the patient she surreptitiously managed would be dangerously unencumbered.

Jean herself felt only her own lack of autonomy. "I have been very much troubled lately and perfectly furious at my helplessness caused by my inability to earn my own living," she wrote. "You can't imagine how enraged I get, at times, at my stupidity & uselessness. It does seem as though I had the right to some means of doing *something* even with my illness, that doesn't need to prevent my working between times, especially now."[13] Jean felt unable to insist upon Dublin because she was living on her father's money. Therefore she once again acquiesced to what she thought were his wishes.

"Jean dear, welcome to your new home & happiness therein!" Sam wrote enthusiastically. Unfortunately, "therein" was not an environment conducive to happiness. "It is hideous and I'm not staying here," Mildred Cowles announced halfway through a tour of the new house in Gloucester. Locking herself in her room, she refused to come out and paced the floor like an unhappy cat. After Jean threatened to have a deliveryman break down the door, Mildred emerged in her hat and coat, insisting that she was returning to Boston. The local doctor was called, and he immediately ordered her to bed. The suicidal Mildred, who remained disruptive throughout the summer, was hardly the ideal roommate. Yet Sam was still writing about Jean's "epileptic temperament" as if her real environment were irrelevant to her happiness. "In earlier days I would not have expected you to be otherwise than unhappy in a new & strange home," he pontificated, "but your spirit & your philosophy have undergone great & beneficent improvement in these latter days, along with your improved physical health. I am aware that you are sweet, & forgiving, and helpful, now & not fretful & not given to complaining, & fault-finding."[14] The assumption that any fault-finding on Jean's part was not connected to her real environment but rather to her inner character, which improved or declined in relation to her "physical health," by which he meant her epilepsy, set up a classic psychological double bind for his daughter. He compliments her for finding no fault with her unbalanced roommates.

"Dear heart," Jean began her response, "your last letter both delighted & pained me. Of course I am infinitely glad that you consider my character better and less disagreeable than of recent years," she wrote honestly, "but I am equally sorry that I should ever have seemed complaining. That quality is one I detest, & always have." Nonetheless, Jean did not back down on her criticisms of Katonah. "I know, perfectly, that I hadn't much good to say of Katonah," she admitted, "& it may be that I filled my letters with tales of woe instead of ignoring the inevitable. I can say but little good of the place even today." She conceded only that Peterson's treatment was beneficial and that she had made three good friends there. But she had few defenses against her father's attack on her character. Surprised that he saw her as a "fault-finder" at home, she vowed to become more self-aware. "I thank you for writing as you did," she responded humbly, "because it has opened my eyes and if there has involuntarily been some improvement, then perhaps by trying I can regain what you apparently consider that I had once, but lost."[15]

Her father's smugness had reached new heights, however. "The best sign I have heard of is, that you are not absorbed in yourself, now, so much as you are in those about you, & in contributing to their lives whatever of comfort & peace & sunshine you can. I wish I was like this, myself, but it has long ago been petted out of me if it was ever in me & I am too old & 'set,' now, to learn to interest myself in anybody's welfare but my own," he wrote on May 20. In ways he could not yet imagine, this assessment was ironically accurate. "Evidently there is something that has been kept from me—but that is right, & as it should be, unless it is something that I could remedy," Sam complacently assured Jean in a letter written the following day. Admitting that he wanted "all sorts of distresses" kept from him, he praised Miss Lyon (as well as Clara and Mr. Paine) for keeping him in the dark. "They know I desire this; for I am taking my holiday, now after 60 years of work & struggle & worry & vexation, & am willing to know nothing, ever any more, of what Susy used to call 'the wars (woes) of life.' "[16]

He was so unaware of Jean's victimization that he boasted openly to her of his willing ignorance while sending her "ever & ever & ever so much love, dear child." His complicity in her predicament, however, is conditional. "But whenever there is anything that depends upon *me* and *my* help," he added, "I want to know all about it."[17] Sam's distinction between his own desire for ignorance and knowledge is redeeming in principle, though hardly a definition that mattered to his secretary.

————

In mid-June, Sam wrote to Jean, "Indeed I should like to tarry with you a considerable spell, but Dr. Peterson will not allow that. For your good he will restrict me to hours, not days." So much for refusing Jean's request to summer in Dublin on the basis of her father's accessibility. A few days later, he sounded even more cheerfully obedient. "Certainly it *is* a pity that I can't stay all night in your house, but your health is *the* important thing, & I must *help* Dr. Peterson in his good work, & not mar it & hinder it by going counter to his judgment & commands."[18]

Sam had hardly seen his daughter since the fall of 1906, yet he accepted this lengthy separation as a medical necessity. He even invoked the sacred ghost of Livy: "I am very grateful to him [Peterson] for the wonderful work he has done for you, & I feel that you & I ought to testify our thankfulness by honoring his lightest desire. Your mother would say this too, out of her grateful heart."[19] Sam had been barred from his wife's sickroom for months at a time, which may well have conditioned his acquiescence to separation from his daughter for her health. But the fact that Mr. Brush could stay overnight in Jean's house while Sam was restricted to hours stirred not a breath of protest from his rebel heart.

In August, George de Forest Brush's youngest daughter died, and Twain wrote a moving sympathy note to the painter. In the midst of his grief, Brush responded with a letter that expressed concern for the welfare of Twain's youngest daughter. "I believe Jean can get well," he tenderly reassured his friend, "her long illness and separation from you is a great trial to you both. We take it to heart very much all of us," the painter continued to push gently, "& every move which is made for her good interests us deeply."[20]

Jean's younger friends were less subtle. They not only charged Sam with indifference, but attempted to intervene, writing to Isabel Lyon in early February 1908. (They seemed to know where the power lay in the Clemens household.) Sixteen months of unhappy exile were so extreme that, with trepidation, her young Dublin friends pled her case. "We have been sore, though, at your king, for what has looked from outside like indifference about lonesome and afflicted & often misunderstood brave pitiable beautiful Jean," Gra Thayer wrote on their behalf. "That is butting in where sacred satyrs fear to butt; yet you know that Jean is fond of us & we of her, & that she doesn't grant us quite the position of outsiders."[21] Lyon copied this brief extract from the accusing letter into her stenographic notebook—alongside her lengthy defense.

Her first parry was that Jean never understood her father's "great wealth of love" for her. Predictably, the secretary blamed Jean's epilepsy. "The doctors know that she cannot help misrepresenting things," Lyon explained. She sought to assure these Dublin friends that Jean's criticisms were uncontrollable distortions of reality resulting from her epilepsy. Lyon may have believed this symptomatology. But even she must have recognized the breathtaking dishonesty of her next remark. "Jean has said to me and to Clara many times," she wrote, "that she doesn't want her father to go & see her."[22]

Jean's diaries and letters consistently reveal her yearning to see her father and her aching sense of deprivation. It was the secretary who constantly objected to Clemens's visits, on the grounds that he would disturb his daughter by reminding her of home. Even as she acknowledged his daughter's painful longings, she persuaded him that he would be doing Jean a kindness if he stayed away, for his visits would only provoke and exacerbate her desperate homesickness.[23] Repeatedly, and ever more ingeniously, she talked him into keeping his daughter at arm's length.

———

One of Lyon's tactics seems to have been to support his relationships with what he styled as his "grandchildren." Clemens began his quest for these surrogate children in the spring of 1907, explaining that he had reached the "grandpapa stage of life" and needed grandchildren. "What is a home without a child?" he asked revealingly. "It isn't a home at all, it's merely a wreck." He even bragged that while other grandfathers had no choice, he had the freedom of making his own selection.[24]

Lyon became an eager facilitator of her boss's propensity to strike up friendships with young girls. She wrote sweet, encouraging letters to one of his young friends. She sometimes met his stand-in children at the train station in New York and delivered them back into their parents' arms. She took photographs of him and the children and sent the girls copies as souvenirs. She stayed home to give one mother tea while Clemens went out with his young visitor. "I was glad too, to do it," she wrote, cognizant of her helpfulness.[25]

"The darlingest thing I know is the way the King exerts himself to entertain little Dorothy," she noted approvingly of his relationship with the ten-year-old Miss Quick. "Reading foolish-like tales to her, going through great picture books, posing anyway and everyway for her to photograph him, and really wearing himself out in his anxiety to make her happy and to make her comfortable." Lyon also exerted herself to make Clemens's fictive children happy. When she and Dorothy Quick spied a turtle in the train station, she helped the child capture the animal and found a box to house it. To show her gratitude, Dorothy named the turtle Lyon. Lyon gave several of Clemens's schoolgirls such lavish attention that they regularly sent her love and kisses in letters to him.[26]

If Clemens had remained satisfied with a few substitute grandchildren to delight and entertain him, he would probably have garnered tolerant approval from future generations. But in early 1908 he began a more troubling phase. "Off he goes with a flash," Lyon observed in early April in Bermuda, "when he sees a new pair of slim little legs appear and if the little girl wears butterfly bows of ribbon on the back of her head then his delirium is complete." On his two vacations to Bermuda in the first half of 1908, he began to "collect" schoolgirls. By June he had constituted an "Aquarium Club," which numbered a dozen surrogate grandchildren whom he called his Angelfish, a name that occurred to him after visiting an aquarium on the island where he was fascinated by the colorful angelfish. "As for me, I collect pets:—young girls—girls from ten to sixteen years old," Twain declared serenely, "girls who are pretty and sweet and naïve and innocent—dear young creatures to whom life is a perfect joy and to whom it has brought no wounds, no bitterness, and few tears. My collection consists of gems of the first water."[27] In sheer numbers alone, his craving for the company of children had shifted in 1908 to something of an obsession. And numbers aside, his willingness to pursue little girls as if they were collectibles is troubling.

The debate over his friendships with young girls has centered, predictably, on sexuality. One biographer charged that Clemens was motivated by a "latent sexuality."[28] The assertion seems pointless, for which adult, after Freud's introduction of the unconscious, could ever be said to be free of latent sexuality? Numerous photographs of Clemens with his surrogate children generally suggest an avuncular relationship.[29] That Albert Paine, who was still closely connected to Twain, had no qualms about his daughter Louise being among the Angelfish also indicates a filial relationship. Moreover, there is little erotic content in the letters traded between him and his girls; the letters are playful, but not libidinous, exchanges. Finally, Lyon kept a hawk-like watch over his behavior. She would never have encouraged these girls, especially the adolescents, if they had posed any sexual or romantic threat to her relationship with the King.

Nonetheless, this was no ordinary hobby. Sexually innocent though it almost certainly was, treating children as collectibles is neither charming nor benign. Collecting Angelfish was part of his habit of self-indulgence after Livy died. Playing endless games of billiards, staying in bedclothes until late in the afternoon, walking up and down Fifth Avenue to attract attention and turn heads—these were only a few of his many indulgences. Twain even collected adult women admirers, whom he assembled for his enjoyment in so-called "doe luncheons."[30] The Angelfish must be understood as part of this pattern. They amused him, therefore he must have them to play with.

But the Angelfish also served a compensatory function. These young girls may have reminded him of Susy, his favorite, whom he could further idealize in her early death. They may have recalled his own lost youth or fed some lifelong nostalgia for the honesty and simplicity of childhood, especially as it had appeared in the Hartford years when his three daughters were young.[31] But their most immediate context concerned his late-life relationships with Clara, who was home only sporadically, and with Jean, who had disappeared into the exile of her illness. Clemens appears to have tried to fill a deep emotional hole with fictive kin: Lyon as surrogate wife and the Angelfish as surrogate children. In many ways, his strategy was both ingenious and workable.

He was delightfully playful with these children and they with him. On his first trip to Bermuda in 1908 he met a little girl named Margaret Blackmer, and they became, in his words, "close comrades." He went for long cart rides with her, pulled by a donkey named Maude and accompanied by a keeper named Reginald. Margaret drove, with Clemens riding beside her. On their first excursion to the beach on Spanish Point, Clemens found a whole shell that was easily parted at its hinge. He gave one half to Margaret and kept the other, instructing her that they should use the matching pair as secret identification whenever they met. Next morning when he approached her at breakfast, he said: " 'No, I am mistaken; she looks like my Margaret, but she isn't, and I am sorry. I will go away and cry, now.' Her eyes danced triumphantly, and she cried out, 'No, you don't have to. There!' And she fetched out the identifying shell." Each time they met, either Margaret or Sam played this game, much to their mutual delight.[32]

Clemens obviously gave affection and received it in return from his substitute granddaughters. But, with the exception of Dorothy Quick, he took only superficial interest in their lives and welfare beyond the hours spent with him. His Angelfish were entertaining diversions—

toys, if you will, and trophies for his ego. Indeed, he eventually hung their framed pictures in the billiard room of the new house in Redding, which he initially named "Innocence at Home"—in honor of the twelve Angelfish, who, he quipped, would "furnish the innocence."[33]

With Livy in the grave, and Clara flitting hither and yon, Sam had no family around to rein in his worst instincts.[34] Lyon had the power to modulate his behavior, but instead she cheerfully supported his Angelfish obsession. Though she cannot be blamed for his excesses, the secretary must have been aware that these little girls served her interests, in diverting his attention from Jean.

Little girls who were virtual strangers were welcomed, even coaxed to visit, while Jean was barred from her father's house. Dorothy Sturgis, Dorothy Quick, Frances Nunnally, Irene Gerken, and Margaret Blackmer were welcomed to 21 Fifth Avenue in 1908, each for at least a day. Dorothy Quick, Dorothy Harvey, Louise Paine, Marjorie Breckenridge, Dorothy Sturgis, Frances Nunnally, and Margaret Blackmer romped around "Innocence at Home" in Connecticut.[35] By contrast, Jean, blocked by Isabel Lyon's collusion with Dr. Peterson, appears to have spent at most two hours under her father's roof that entire year.[36] Sam was also a more faithful correspondent with his surrogate children than with Jean. While he joyfully composed letters to his bevy of little friends, he often wrote drivel, heavily censored by Lyon, to his own child.[37] And he once begged his youngest Angelfish, Dorothy Quick, to visit him, reassuring her that Miss Lyon "would take the best care of you." Yet even as she admonished Dorothy Quick about keeping to a promised visit—"Please do not disappoint Mr. Clemens"—Lyon was busy deflecting Jean's fervent longing to see her father.[38]

One day in early February 1908, Sam paced up and down his New York house in anxious anticipation of a visit from Dorothy Quick. He bolted for the front door whenever the bell rang, and after several disappointments, he finally exclaimed, "a watched Dorothy never boils."[39] Had he ever looked forward to seeing Jean with such eagerness, her life after her mother died might have been different—but her father wanted only the uncomplicated refuge of young girls to whom life had brought "no wounds, no bitterness, and few tears."

CHAPTER 10

Stormfield

Isabel Lyon had hatched the dream of building a little cottage for herself in Redding, Connecticut, during the summer of 1906. At the time, she was much taken with Albert Paine, who had cultivated her dream in the hopes of persuading Clemens to buy property next to his own home in Redding. Under their influence, Clemens had bought his first parcel of land there on March 24, 1906, and added to his holdings in May and September.[1] He had authorized his best friend's son, John Howells, to draw up plans for the house. Clara also wholeheartedly supported the project, even though she never intended to make it her permanent home. With Clara and Lyon conspiring, the plans became increasingly elaborate. In 1907, even though Clemens had signed a contract to build, the project almost folded—both because of cost and because of the isolation of Redding. Construction had already begun when Clemens changed his mind again and tried to stop the building in August. But John Howells's hard-headed reckoning of the financial losses that would result now that construction had begun squelched the last noises about pulling out.[2] In an unusual groundbreaking ritual, Lyon and an entourage of men, including the architect and Paine, "dug each a tiny shovel of earth on the appointed spot...and then they poured in some whiskey." "I wonder why?" she added with mock-innocence.[3]

Clara's rather grandiose ideas continued to affect the architect's plans after the groundbreaking. She envisioned a suite for herself, and the blueprints were changed at the last minute to assuage Howells's and Lyon's fears of her displeasure. Or so it appears.[4] Clemens refused, much to the chagrin of his friends, to discuss the Redding house or be consulted about any aspect of the project once the contract was signed, and wanted only to see his new dwelling after it was finished. "And he said he wouldn't move in," Katy recalled, "till the cats had had their breakfasts and was purrin' on the hearth. When they was doin' that, he said, he'd know everything was settled and he'd be ready to come, too."[5]

Six weeks before Sam's move-in date of June 18, 1908, trouble over the Redding house erupted between Clara and Lyon. The overt cause was Clara's sense that she was being ignored in the choice of new furnishings.[6] The Lioness's decorating skills may have threatened Clara's pride in her own taste and discernment, or Clara's vision for the house in the planning stages may have involved a greater investment in the interior design than Lyon had calculated. A deeper miscalculation was at work, however.

Over the past year there had been a gradual shift in the once close and affectionate relationship between the two women. In June 1907, Lyon had gushed that "Santa [a pet name for Clara] was bursting with glee tonight and called me Nan-Pan-Pete-Pan and snuggled her darling head in my neck."[7] And she continued—at least for a while—her practice of signing checks for Clara without hesitation. As late as January 1908 Lyon was blowing flattery in Clara's direction like a windmill in a hurricane: "The very air must love to caress her as she passes through it" and "The King and C.C. are perfect companions for me."[8] But sometime during the spring their love feast ended. In the late fall of 1907, after the Knickerbocker Trust scare, Clara had been put on a budget. Since Twain lost no money in the bank failure, the financial rationale for this squeeze was hazy to her—and many others. Obviously, by spring the Redding house was draining money from Twain's coffers; even so, he should easily have been able to afford Clara's extravagances. But this was the time when Lyon's loyalties were shifting from Paine to Ashcroft, who was now her chief confidant and advisor. He also became Clemens's "self-appointed" business manager.[9]

"There was hardly anything for him to do," Clemens sniffed later, "except errands & small matters." Again in the hairpin business, Clemens entrusted Ashcroft with "ten or twelve thousand dollars" for a new company that never held a stockholders' meeting, made no official reports or accounting, and returned not a penny—while Clara found herself strapped for cash.[10] In March and April 1908, in fact, Clara suffered a serious financial crisis and was reduced to borrowing $300 from Ashcroft and an additional $500 from Dr. Quintard while Lyon and her father romped about Bermuda on a six-week holiday.[11]

"Headache. So ill all day, for I wept without control for hours last night, because I was exhausted," Lyon disclosed on May 2, 1908, "—and the fact that Santa misunderstood all my efforts in working over the house—My anxiety over the finishings, my interest in my search for the right thing for the King's house has all been misinterpreted, and the child says I am trying to ignore her." The tone is placating. "All my effort has been to please her, to keep her from the dreary search of hours and hours to find the right thing, or shape or color," she pleaded. "I am only trying to save *his* money and Santa's strength—Oh, so ill I am." Unfortunately, the secretary misunderstood the source of her trouble with Clara. "Somebody has put all these sickening ideas into Santa's head—and I feel that my interest in the house is dead forever," she concluded two days later.[12]

The real source is apparent in a letter to Lyon written from England six weeks later by Will Wark, Clara's accompanist and a key member of her touring entourage. Clara had left for one of her many recuperating periods in Europe, with travel companions in tow, including Katy Leary. Wark listed a few expenses, so Lyon would "understand just how the money is being used," barely pausing before he blurted out, "I shall probably have to send for more [money] in a few days—It is really something fierce." Defensively noting "We really haven't wasted any money," he ticked off his plans to save money—concerts near London next year "on shares so that Clara won't be under any expense" and an upcoming stay at a cheap country place in France—and nervously begged for reassurance, using the family's pet name for Lyon: "Now Nana please tell me frankly if you think Clara is spending too much." Hopeful that Nana would be sending another cash transfusion, he wrote that they both "would give anything to have you here," and he closed with the ironic but sincere "We need you."[13]

In a letter sent by the same post Clara asked, "Why don't you feel as if everything were all right?" and answered her own question with no hint of trouble: "Probably because you are tired out." "Dear little Nana we often speak of you & wonder how you are. I am *sorry, sorry* that you have been depressed—depression is too awful and so unreachable sometimes," she sympathized, underlining the second "sorry" twice. "How soon shall you move into the house? You certainly have too much on your shoulders.—You poor dear good sweet kind courageous faithful Nana!" If this warm, embracing letter is sincere and not some cynical attempt to manipulate the check-signer at home, it indicates that Clara held no grudge over their disagreement about furnishing the Redding house. In a postscript she added: "Dearest Nana here is a huge big enveloping velvet hug for you & a million good wishes. We love you very deeply & I have missed *you many* times. Devotedly C."[14] But if this reflected a restored confidence, that confidence was short-lived. Clara would not long be devoted to anyone who forced her to economize on a lifestyle that she believed was her entitlement as the daughter of Mark Twain.

Ashcroft, however, was taking a hard line toward Clara. "Clara Clemens traveled about like a prima donna," he sneered in a later financial report, "with a violinist, accompanist and maid in her train." This attitude was infectious—and ultimately disastrous for Lyon. During the more than three months that she was abroad, Lyon practiced some industrious cost-cutting on Clara's side of the ledger. "I must do Miss Lyon this justice: she was faithful & diligent in persuading me (when Clara was on the other side of the water)," Twain testified, "to send her only two or three hundred dollars whenever she asked for five hundred." According to him, his secretary argued that "the more money she had on hand the more careless & squanderous she would be with it."[15]

Both Ashcroft and Lyon had started to act as if Twain's money was their own. They became convinced that they were putting the brakes on a careless daughter's endless demands for *their* money. Clara was not a thrifty soul; nevertheless Lyon was foolish to scrimp on her pet and thus earn her enmity. As long as Twain's secretary was depriving Jean, she was safe. But when she began tightening the other daughter's purse strings, she was courting danger.

Twain moved into the Redding house on June 18, 1908, and initially christened his Italian-style villa "Innocence at Home," a title brimming with irony. His youngest daughter was barred from crossing the threshold on the contrived orders of her doctor. His other surviving daughter was beginning to fume quietly from across the Atlantic. Meanwhile the woman who signed their father's checks spent freely—and drank cocktails in the same style. When her own supplies ran short, according to Katy Leary, the secretary furtively downed liquor reserves in the new guest rooms.[16] Meanwhile Twain's financial adviser and man Friday was scheming to manage the old man's money, with or without his consent. Only the King, it seems, was an innocent at home, completely unaware of the forces that threatened to undo him.

With preternatural vision, Clara insisted on renaming the Redding house "Stormfield" when she returned from Europe in September. Her father readily acquiesced. Clara's choice appealed to him because the loggia end of the house was built with money he received for his magazine piece "Extract from Captain Stormfield's Visit to Heaven." Twain had finally published his burlesque of a conventional afterlife, written and revised over nearly forty years, in the December 1907 and January 1908 issues of *Harper's Monthly*.

Twain's heaven was a busy place where work was essential to combat boredom. With typical Twainian insight and irony, it also included pain and suffering. "You see," explained Captain Stormfield's celestial guide, "happiness ain't a *thing in itself*—it's only a *contrast* with something that ain't pleasant." The guide concluded that the pain and suffering in heaven, because it was temporary, created "plenty of contrasts, and just no end of happiness." Happiness in Twain's heaven had another unexpected feature. Almost everyone wished himself young again, but only a fool was inclined to remain young. As a person gained knowledge and experience in paradise, his guide informed Stormfield, "he lets his body go on taking the look of age, according as he progresses, and by and by he will be bald and wrinkled outside and wise and deep within."[17] Qualities of mind defined enjoyment in heaven if not on earth.

Twain had a second reason for thinking Stormfield an appropriate name—the Redding house was set on a hilltop and would be a magnet for storms. He little knew what storms were brewing.[18]

———

Lyon had dedicated herself to separating Jean from her natal home since the summer of 1906. She privately renewed her resolve the following summer: Jean was never to live with her father again, she announced in her diary. She also declared her intentions to others in Twain's entourage. "Jean Clemens and I can never live under the same roof, which means that she can never come home," she confided to Clara's nurse, Miss Gordon. At least three other friends were privy to this confidence, according to Twain, but they all remained mute in his presence. After moving into Stormfield, Lyon even told the neighboring farmers that Jean would never be coming home because she was "crazy."[19] The move to Redding posed new challenges for Lyon, however, principally that Stormfield was a "healthy environment" as defined by the doctors, who believed that country living was beneficial to those who suffered from epilepsy. Jean happily anticipated rejoining her father in Redding.

Certainly Clemens himself was enthusiastic about the "healthy environment," describing his villa as regally perched above richly wooded hills, with only half a dozen houses in sight, cool breezes in the summer, and no sounds but the singing of birds. He wrote one of his Angelfish that "the stillness and serenity bring peace to the soul." And he and his guests spent much of their time in the arched loggia, which opened out from the living room to Connecticut vistas and the country air. But even as he welcomed schools of Angelfish to "Innocence at Home," Sam made no objection when his youngest daughter was barred from moving into his new house. "Yes-indeedy, it was just *too* bad that there wasn't a solitary junior member of the family here to help me christen the house," he chirped. "But you know the adage: Man proposes, but God blocks the game."[20]

In fact, Clemens had planned to visit Jean in Gloucester for an unprecedented two days before he moved to Redding, but he soon abandoned that notion. Jean may not have been able to locate suitable housing for her father, after Dr. Peterson barred him from staying overnight in her house. It was at this time that Clemens told an obviously disappointed Jean to be thankful for Peterson's good work and "to testify our thankfulness by honoring his lightest desire. Your mother would say this too," he piously intoned, "out of her grateful heart."[21]

In spite of the best efforts of Peterson and Lyon to keep father and daughter apart, for once God threatened to block their game. Learning of the death of his old friend Thomas Bailey Aldrich, Clemens made plans to attend the memorial service in Portsmouth, New Hampshire, at the end of June. He was accompanied by Paine, in whom he had a supportive sidekick to back his spontaneous impulse to visit Jean on the way home. Expecting the worst on the basis of information supplied by Lyon, both men discovered, to their shock, that she was healthy and vigorous in both mind and body. After a nine-month hiatus, Jean had suffered five seizures on January 10 (significantly, the day after she arrived in Greenwich), but it appears she had few, if any, grand mal after that, in either Greenwich or Gloucester.[22] Clemens returned to Stormfield bursting with enthusiasm and "said Dr. Peterson must cancel her exile and let her come home at once." The local contractor who built the Redding house later told Clemens that he carried a telegram from Miss Lyon to Dr. Peterson that day. Lounsbury had read the message: Lyon's instructions were to refuse consent to Jean's return home. That evening Paine also overheard Lyon say to Ashcroft, "This is the *last time*! He shall never leave this place again without one of us *with* him!"[23] Neither Lounsbury nor Paine said a word to Clemens at the time; they knew he would not believe them.

Though her father's visit to Gloucester did not end Jean's exile, it resulted in a scheme whereby Jean would buy a farmhouse near Stormfield. The place Sam had in mind turned out to be "a poor trifling thing," he informed his daughter, "like the rest of the ancient farm houses in this region, it has no room in it." Paine had confirmed that the house was uninhabitable, at which point Sam threw up his hands. "I am so sorry," he wrote Jean. "I wish I could situate you exactly to your liking, dear child, how gladly I would do it. And I wish I could take your malady, & rid you of it for always. I wish your mother were here; she could help us. I will not try to write any more. I love you dear, dear, dearly, & I am so sorry, so sorry. What can I do?"[24]

Clemens's uncharacteristic effort must have triggered alarm bells in his secretary, but Jean's own scheming apparently sent her into full alert. "Miss Lyon has a house near ours—which father gave her—and she is going to sell her Farmington home," Jean told Nancy Brush sometime in July. "My hope is that Dr. Peterson will let me live in her house—if Miss Lyon is willing, next winter." Initially Jean had reasoned that her father and Miss Lyon would be back in New York City for the winter, and Lyon's cottage on the Redding property would be vacant. But when she learned that her father intended to stay in Redding all year—and that therefore Lyon would be in residence at Stormfield—she reported to Nancy, "Now Father thinks it would be a good place, anyway, be-cause by being out of our house, I should have no difficulty in avoiding late entertainments & unhealthy goings-on & yet I could be near enough to see Father as often as permitted & have a healthy country life such as I need and want to have."[25] Jean's letter exposes the "medical rea-sons" being used to keep her from sharing her father's domicile. Though the country location was healthy, nightly "entertainments" and "un-healthy goings-on" in the Clemens household were still held out as in-surmountable barriers. Although both father and daughter accepted this rationale, they were also taking steps to advance their reunion—an unusual initiative for Sam.

If Lyon panicked at the news that Jean hoped to live in her cottage, she did not lose her strategic poise. Jean's name was placed on the pas-senger list of an ocean liner—with Berlin as her ultimate destination. Jean loved Germany and had once even considered trading off a sum-mer in her beloved Dublin for one in Germany. But this news came to her in late July "like thunderbolt from a clear sky," as she wrote her friend Nancy, and she was initially resistant to trading her father for Germany. "I have just had a note from Jean expostulating against going to Germany," Peterson confided to Lyon, "but I will write her that she must do so for the sake of her future." "As I wrote Father," Jean confided to Lyon herself, "I am delighted and distressed, both. I had hoped to be with him this winter. No one was ever more astonished than I when I read the decision." Determined to be reunited with her father, Jean wound up derailed by the one alternative that was genuinely inviting. Even though she felt "rather badly about going," she admitted to Nancy, "[o]f course I am wildly excited at the idea of going abroad again & of seeing Berlin—I saw it last when I was only eleven years old."[26]

Four months with the Cowles sisters in Gloucester obviously en-hanced the prospect of Berlin. "I don't want to be unkind," Jean insisted to her friend, "but I am so deadly sick of those two girls (women) that I can hardly bear to look at them." Although, predictably, Jean could feel pity for them—"I am no longer fond of them but their lot is a ter-ribly hard one," she wrote to Lyon—she was nonetheless eager to be rid of them. Mildred had been threatening to throw herself off the rocks of Gloucester all summer, and Jean "quaked at the mere idea" of prolong-ing her contact with either sister. At the same time she remained conflicted over going to Germany. "Is it positively settled that I must go to Berlin?" she queried Lyon. "I have a dread of it. I did *so* want to be in Redding."[27]

Jean's powerlessness was reinforced in the firing of George O'Conners—for two years her groom and driver on land, first mate at sea, and all around boon companion—whom she had hoped to keep on Twain's payroll while she was in Berlin. "He has been restful & almost invariably helped calm me when I was overwrought," she explained to Lyon, "& he has often pulled me out of myself & the unhappy life at Katonah, here & at times, in Greenwich." Lyon preferred to keep the newly hired Harry Iles. "To me, it is the most horrible injustice," Jean argued. "We haven't ever treated our servants so before & surely Father would consider it right to let Harry go in order to keep George if he appreciated what a help he had been to me." Softening, she pleaded, "You are the planner & arranger & you can do what I beg & can make Father see the justice of it if you only will."[28] George was laid off, while Harry remained on the payroll.

Routinely treated as if she were eighteen rather than twenty-eight, Jean allowed herself to be ordered about and relied upon higher authority for direction. Her problems were not just the lack of an independent income (which was a huge barrier in itself) but a lack of self-confidence bred by the stigma of her disease. For Twain fitfully and for Lyon fully, Jean became her disease. Most tragically, Jean too let her identity wrap itself around her epilepsy. With massive outside pressure to collapse herself into her illness, she most often identified herself as a patient in search of a cure, an all-consuming role that put her fate in the hands of others.

It would seem obvious, then, that Jean was being sent to Berlin as a patient in search of a cure, to consult with a world-renowned German specialist. "I am going to see a physician of whom Dr. Peterson highly approves," Jean informed her friend Nancy on August 1. Yet a few days later, Dr. Peterson told Jean that he had never heard of Dr. Hofrath von Renvers, the physician she was being referred to for treatment. His name had come to Lyon through some old family friends, the Stanchfields, who were enthusiastic about his treatment of their daughter. Peterson had in fact written to another doctor, whom *he* considered the best in Germany, and was waiting for a reply to his query. Lyon, however, preferred to make her own arrangements for Jean, although, despite Peterson's impression that all had been settled by mid-August, she did not request Dr. von Renvers's services until September 4. And he did not mail his confirmation until September 16, only ten days before Jean's scheduled departure.[29]

————

Initially, in a burst of enthusiasm, Lyon had included herself in the trip abroad. "The plan was for me to take Jean to Germany, but I must not go away from the King, ever—He is too wonderful." Wonderful he may have been, but the immediate reason she declined to leave his side was that she was worried about his health. On August 6, Sam had what everyone thought was a violent bilious attack, akin to what is called "stomach flu" in the early twenty-first century. He thought it was brought on by the intense heat during a journey to New York City to attend the funeral of his nephew, Samuel E. Moffett, who had drowned while on a family vacation. Lyon also discovered that ten days earlier Sam had become dizzy and disoriented during a billiard game with Paine. "I have lost my memory. I don't know which is my ball. I don't know what game we are playing," he told Paine. The condition passed in an instant, and neither man thought much of it at the time. But Lyon told her old friend and employer, Mrs. Whitmore, that the doctors and Colonel Harvey, Twain's publisher, "have vested me with the high moral obligation of never leaving the King alone again." Describing herself as "moving through this house with my spirit hands folded in prayer that I may be the right woman in the right place," she vowed not to leave Clemens's side, unless she could entrust him to the care of Ralph Ashcroft.[30]

Clemens recovered rapidly, but by then the secretary had another source of anxiety. She and Ashcroft were worried about the influence Paine might have in her absence. Twain's biographer had remarkable staying power, in spite of Lyon's best efforts to discredit him with her boss, and he remained determined not to be driven from the inner circle. With Clara returning home just as Jean was about to be shunted off to Europe, Paine insisted on joining the welcoming party, even though he knew his presence was unwelcome to some. "We met Santa today at the Cunard pier," Lyon recorded on September 9. "Paine came in pale, and I begged him not to quarrel there. He had no intention of that though."[31]

Working relentlessly behind the scenes, Ashcroft continued to egg Lyon on in an attempt to cut Paine off from his sources, and thus disable his biography of Twain. The secretary described one revealing instance in which she phoned Paine to demand that he return some letters, with Ashcroft "standing beside me to courage me up." In another, she gave her sidekick two letters Paine wrote to her and noted that Ashcroft kept her from reading another "that must have been terrible."[32] But the shrewd biographer was surprisingly difficult to detach. For nine months the campaign had been waged against him but he had not decamped from the battleground. Paine lost several key skirmishes, however, and the outcome of this literary war did not appear favorable to him after Twain moved to Redding in the summer of 1908. At their apex of power, Lyon and Ashcroft wrested considerable literary control away from Paine.

"She persuaded me that Paine had dark & evil designs," Twain wrote a year later. Those designs included "clandestinely reading letters he hadn't any business to read; always dishonorably slipping away with important letters & papers, & leaving behind him no list of them & no receipt." In fact Paine did, by his own admission, take important biographical materials and place them in a safety deposit box, fearing that Lyon would block his access to them. He undoubtedly left no list or receipts for his holdings. But his motivation was not "dishonorable," as he demonstrated with the biography he eventually published. Lyon also led her boss to believe that Paine would use so many letters in his biography that the proposed volume of Twain's correspondence to be edited by Clara and Lyon would be commercially damaged. As a result of her influence, in August Colonel Harvey was given the official biographer's role, with final editorial power over Paine's work. More significantly Twain placed severe limitations on Paine's use of quotations. At Lyon's behest, Twain even added a codicil to his will that restricted Paine's use of letters to only "such as she approved."[33]

"In a word, she never missed an opportunity for poisoning his mind against me," Paine recognized. Defenseless and disheartened, the biographer found his position "so distasteful and distressing," he confessed later, "that more than once I was on the point of laying down my work with him, altogether."[34] As it turned out, his role as affable neighbor was his strongest weapon. The easy access he had hoped to gain in having Twain build a home near his own in Redding was ultimately guaranteed through his willingness to play billiards. Clemens's fanatic devotion to the game had not flagged. "I was comparatively a young man, and by no means an invalid;" Paine recalled, "but many a time, far in the night, when I was ready to drop with exhaustion, he was still as fresh and buoyant and eager for the game as at the moment of beginning." Paine remembered that Clemens would smoke incessantly and endlessly circle the billiard table, always "with the light step of youth" and without the least motion of fatigue.[35]

Paine's mistakes at the game merely gave the famous author another opportunity for amusement. Twain always enjoyed his opponent's "perplexities." In return Paine loved to watch Twain lose his temper when he himself was playing badly. But Paine was there for more than his own entertainment. He devoted a number of hours each day to being beaten at billiards because, he explained, "the association was invaluable" for his research. Paine became Twain's intimate while playing billiards; and because he was always willing to play what Twain called "the best game on earth," he held onto a crucial advantage: access to the King.[36]

CHAPTER 11

An American Lear

In the summer of 1908, while the King was preoccupied with billiards and Angelfish, his lady-in-waiting was busy running the kingdom—and beginning to worry about household expenditures. "Last night I couldn't sleep, so the morning broke with no strength in it," Lyon admitted. "But I dismissed Hobby, paid her in full—so that expense is closed up." Miss Hobby, Twain's longtime stenographer, told him later that she was sacked because she helped Lyon write checks and knew too much. However much she knew, the stenographer's salary of $25 per week made her Twain's highest paid employee. By contrast, Katy Leary earned $35 per month and Lyon $50 per month. Hobby's replacement cost $8 per week, and was quickly followed by another stenographer who ultimately charged $15. Whatever her other motives, Lyon indeed saved money.[1]

The Lioness was feeling the pinch of her spendthrift ways. While Stormfield was being built, she was fixing up her own Summerfield—also called the Lobster Pot—the farmhouse on twenty acres Clemens had given her in 1907. He had no idea that she was renovating her own property while Stormfield was being built until she hinted—well into the process—that she wanted to borrow money from him to repair the place. "She named the sum she would need ('about $1500')," soon after Clemens moved into Stormfield, "& I said borrow it of me," he remembered later. Just before Christmas 1908 she told him her house was done and that the cost of all the remodeling was just pennies under $1,500. He forgave $500 of her loan as a Christmas gift. In a burst of generosity on Christmas Day, Clemens told Ashcroft he planned on forgiving the remaining debt "$500 at a time." Within twenty-four hours Ashcroft came to him with a bold suggestion: Why not cancel Miss Lyon's entire loan balance today? This Clemens declined to do, though the piggish request merely seemed ill-mannered to him at the time.[2]

In fact the secretary was in a quandary. Somewhere along the way she had stopped making a distinction between her money and Twain's. She had no clue as to how much she was spending on herself. Her loan request, for example, did not cover the actual costs of repairing her farmhouse. (Clemens acknowledged later that he would not have balked at a higher figure.) Lounsbury, who was the general contractor for both Stormfield and Summerfield, could have enlightened her, but Lyon remained vague about her own expenditures—and she was equally uncertain about the boss's money. Seemingly panicked at times about the balance in his bankbook, she would flail about in haphazard cost-cutting efforts that had one thing in common: they were never aimed at her. "In fact," Twain wrote with caustic precision, "she scrimped everybody but herself. Herself & Stormfield."[3]

She probably meant to cut her own expenses, but Clemens's checkbook was an irresistible temptation. Clothes, furniture, and flashy accessories called to her like a siren song. She especially loved clothes and bought lavishly. "Mrs. Freeman told me," she divulged while vacationing in Bermuda with the boss, "that living as I am with the greatest human being, there can be no danger of my ever over dressing the part, the danger will be in my failure to dress up to it." There would be no danger of her dressing down for her role as long as she could play "blind man's bluff" with his checkbook. "The King would love to have me in rich soft clinging silks and splendid or delicate colors," she recorded, "and when I told him what Mrs. Freeman had advised me to do, he said that she was a wise woman."[4]

What was a girl to do? Suits, jackets, gowns, piles of lingerie, shawls, scarves, silks, and beads: they just made her take them, cut the price to nearly nothing, and told her they were meant for her. She told anyone within earshot that the shopkeepers just begged her to buy their finery. If she resisted, they threatened to give her the clothes anyway. "I couldn't resist any longer, could I?" she would ask her boss, "with a bird-like upward cant of the innocent face." Her remarks "became the joke of the house," because she made them so often, Twain said, "& even the servants got to mimicking those airs & speeches."[5]

At one time, after Lyon had refused several offers of a raise, Clara had told her to buy some clothes at her father's expense. She could never have imagined that her father's employee would need the largest closet at Stormfield. "Katy maintains," Twain wrote later, "that Miss Lyon had more clothes than Clara." He saw the local seamstress arrive every day at the new house in Redding. Lyon bragged to Paine and her boss that she would need her "practically the whole winter." She also frequently boasted that "she spent little or nothing on herself, but spent all of her $50 salary on her mother's support." Clemens knew that the seamstress charged two dollars per day. Yet he did not put "two and two together," as he wryly acknowledged later.[6] For two years, Lyon spent Clemens's money on herself under his nose and he as much as condoned her behavior by his silence.

She "unloaded some New York shops of their overplus of rugs, & brass pots, & copper pots, & general jimcrackery of a luxurious & tasteful sort," Twain recalled about shopping sprees that may have merged her employer's decorating needs with her own. Twain described her as a master in "shopping for bricabrac of a quality she couldn't afford." She loved antique Russian coppers and brasses that she bought by the armload. She described her favorite haunt, Boyagians, as "my outlet for superfluous emotions" and delighted in what she called the "something junk" that she found there. She bought old tea jars, candlesticks, mugs, porringers, and rugs—each one an irresistible "bargain."[7]

Clemens never objected, though Lyon always ostentatiously admired her purchases in his presence. She would bring home a bolt of silk, for example, and "spread it over a chair, & arrange its sweep & its folds effectively," he remembered; "then stand off & worship it critically a minute, cocking her head first one side then t'other, then step forward & give it another artistic touch-up with her practised hand, then step back & worship again." He observed the bounty of her many shopping trips and said nothing. He put his money at her disposal, never looked at a single bill, and treated her like one of the family.[8] Thus, he was in part responsible for her grave blurring of boundaries. But her boundary confusion extended only so far. While she was spending his money rather freely on herself, she deprived his youngest daughter of a summer lap robe and magazine subscriptions.

Jean sailed for Germany on September 26, 1908, with her maid Anna, and her paid companion Marguerite Schmitt, nicknamed Bébé, who had become a friend as well after nine months living under the same roof with the Cowleses. (According to Jean, Marguerite still had nightmares in Berlin about the sisters.) Even before she left the country, Jean worried about spending her father's money. "I have felt before that I have been too much of an expense," she confessed to Lyon, "therefore I shall try above everything to keep our expenses down." True to her word, Jean contemplated moving to a smaller room to save fifty cents a day after she arrived. Her modest allowance—fifty dollars a month— did not allow her to meet even her circumscribed expenses. She was deprived of the cash to splurge on an opera and even felt constrained not to buy a cup of tea. The daughter of one of the most commercially successful authors of the era was reduced to making her own tea, without milk, to save seventy-five cents a day.[9]

Though financially strapped, Jean was happy in Berlin. This contentment, at least at first, extended to Dr. von Renvers, who did not simply order her about arbitrarily. Dr. Peterson, she observed in a letter to Lyon, "used to irritate me by invariably stating that such & such a thing was better for me or not feasible but without ever giving a definite explanation. In that respect I like this doctor better."[10] Dr. von Renvers, it appears, did not have to shape his medical decisions to meet the dictates of Miss Lyon.

After a slow start, which included a two-week moratorium on all reading and writing imposed by her new doctor, Jean's social life began to accelerate. In December, much to her delight, she successfully narrated Twain's "The Golden Arm" for a charity performance and attended both a concert and a dance. Scrimped but resourceful, she decided to use some of her own money to enhance her life in Berlin. Modest dividends from some small stock holdings she had inherited probably allowed her to purchase Christmas gifts for her family: little spiders for Clara, cats and frogs for her father, which she asked Lyon to place on their napkins at Christmas breakfast or lunch. She even sent a sketch of how she wanted them arranged to the Lioness, who also received a present.[11]

Jean's happiness was short-lived. On December 17, 1908, she was shocked to receive peremptory orders to return home. "You sail January ninth steamer Pennsylvania passage prepaid. Send Marguerite home. Don't cable. Father." According to Sam, Jean had become "doubtful of the Berlin doctor" and had sent one of Dr. von Renvers's prescriptions home for inspection. Dr. Peterson, disapproving of the medication, told them to "order her home at once." Sam did not know that Jean disregarded his order and sent a return cable begging to stay in Berlin at her own expense, which she could manage by teaching English. Her request was denied by his secretary "on account of financial stringency," a specious excuse.[12] Since Lyon had a large stake in keeping Jean in Berlin, it seems likely that Peterson, in a rare show of independence, asserted his professional authority. Peterson later bragged, Jean told her friend Marguerite, that he was the one who had brought her back from Germany. Lyon likely acquiesced in the doctor's decision because she needed his future cooperation.[13]

She consulted with Peterson on a new residence for Jean that, predictably, was a safe distance from Stormfield.[14] The town of Babylon, on Long Island, thus met Lyon's needs, but stunned Jean by the contrast with her life in Berlin. The residence she was placed in contained a "crazy woman," her two nurses, and a tedious married couple who quarreled incessantly. The environment outside was not a bit more inviting. "The country was as flat as a pan-cake," Jean observed, "and contained nothing but a few bushes and small ponds used as ice-ponds. After Berlin and the varied life and broad interests that one sees over there, it was too much of a comedown." Jean was so discouraged and disheartened that she did not write her father for two months. "I really couldn't write you from Babylon," she explained, "because, as I have already said, I didn't want to start complaining as soon as I had gotten back and I was so anxious to get away and leading such an utterly empty life that I couldn't find a thing to write about."[15] She was quite aware that her past complaints had often elicited lectures from her father on improving her attitude and doing for others. Not writing was an act of self-assertion, a modest but potentially efficacious protest to a literary father.

She did, however, appeal to Clara the moment she returned from Germany, and the exile was finally relocated to a small private care facility in Montclair, New Jersey, a happier situation if no closer to Stormfield. "You don't know how glad I am to be here!" she wrote her father, breaking her chilly silence. The country was beautiful and the mosquitoes were not hungry yet, she reported. Her nurses were lovely, and one had been helping her care for a puppy she acquired in Germany.[16]

———

If Jean's unexpected return was inopportune for Lyon, this paled in comparison to the rising current of tension between her and Clara throughout the fall of 1908. Redding was not large enough for the two of them, especially with Lyon at the apex of her power and Clara increasingly unhappy about her lack of funds. As Clemens mused later, "Clara was not in a good-natured mood."[17] The minor trouble that had erupted between the two women before Clara left for Europe could have been repaired with adequate funds, and on the surface, it appears that Lyon was applying the necessary remedy. Clara received a budgeted allowance of $200 per month. But the aspiring singer and her entourage in fact spent $22,903.25 over a two-year period ending in February 1909, according to an independent audit. Moreover the figures indicate Clara actually went through roughly $400 more in 1908 than in 1907. A closer examination of the auditor's report, however, indicates that cash "claimed to have been paid" to Clara Clemens in the year ending February 26, 1908, was $1,890, while the next year the total plummeted to $350.[18] A decline of $1,500 in cash allotments from 1907 to 1908 was one important reason why the aspiring singer had become disgruntled with the secretary. Most of Clara's expenses were paid directly to her creditors, so these cash allotments were the only source of disposable income directly under her control, other than her allowance. Thus the reduction was probably a special irritant because of the loss of freedom it entailed. The reduction largely occurred "when Clara was on the other side of the water," according to Twain, so that Clara arrived at Stormfield in September more dissatisfied than ever and determined to discover why her wealthy father had so "little" to spend on her.[19]

Lyon observed in late October that her soul was "over its ears in mud—the mud of criticism—no, misunderstandings fired by C.C. [Clara], and I'm a coward to not know that mud can clarify things in time, and can build a foundation from which I'll be the better able to see the King." Her entry, though a bit cryptic, probably signals her belief that she would be able to weather Clara's "mud"—her criticism—and build a "foundation"—that is a relationship to Clemens—that would withstand Clara's attacks. "Benares [Ashcroft] went hurtling away today, glad to get clear of the mud," Lyon wrote in the same entry. "[B]ut breathing at me his sweet philosophy that we must pay for what we have. And to hold so great a treasure as the King means that the price one must pay can never be too high a one."[20]

"He is strong," she had described Ashcroft earlier that fall, "and by his calm judgment he carries me through difficulties, he gives me a support and a knowledge of the value of things." But in relying on Ashcroft's knowledge of the value of things, Lyon lost her intuitive touch in handling the King's daughter. The secretary felt Clara's resentment but never understood its source, much less granted it legitimacy. She now saw her former pet in Ashcroftian terms—as the demanding prima donna who needed discipline and harsher limits. "But to know that you know the King" she philosophized, "is to send big roots down to support your tree."[21]

––––––––

Though Clara was technically mistress of the Clemens household, she functioned more like an absentee owner whose frequent travels left day-to-day decisions in the hands of a professional manager. The manager, in this case the secretary, had free reign except when the owner was on the premises. But rather than defer to Clara after she returned to the new family manse, Lyon made a serious misjudgment in provoking a power struggle over who was in charge of the household staff.

Clara rang up a servant and gave an order that was then countermanded by Miss Lyon, who, according to Twain, "added that all orders must pass thro' *her*."[22] Given the certainty that sooner or later Clara would depart, Lyon's confrontational style at Stormfield was foolishly miscalculated. Since her mother's death, Clara had lived apart from her father more than she lived with him. She spent most of the year after her mother died in a sanitarium. She never stepped foot in Dublin nor was she long in Tuxedo, which accounts for the summers from 1905 through 1907. She took refuge in a sanitarium near Jean before her western concert tour, scheduled to begin at the end of January 1907. She was in Europe on another concert tour in 1908 when her father moved into Stormfield. And less than a month after she returned, Clara had rented an apartment in New York where she actually spent much of her time.[23]

With all her check-signing power still intact, Lyon had the advantage. But her actions were nonetheless irrational. Why go toe-to-toe with Clara over an order to a servant when she could easily have flattered and placated Clara into submission? Why rile her unnecessarily? Twain believed it was Miss Lyon's "passion for power, & she wanted *all* of it—no division. She couldn't bear anybody near her throne—even on the bottom step of it. Not even Clara," he said later.[24]

Her drinking probably played a significant role. Claude, the butler, and Katy Leary watched one September day in 1908 while Lyon drank an entire bottle of Scotch. Katy told Twain that the secretary consumed more than whiskey, keeping a "bottle of cocktails" in her bedroom cupboard, which usually lasted about a day. Not only did Clemens's staff think Lyon was an alcoholic, but many of the guests who frequented Stormfield held the same opinion. "[T]hey speak rather frankly of my dulness in not perceiving that she was a drunkard," he noted wryly; "and when they don't speak of my dulness in this connection, they doubt that I am telling the strict truth when I say that I did not know that she was a heavy drinker." Even though she was constantly raiding the whiskey supply in his own room, excusing herself by saying she was not feeling well, Clemens never suspected her behavior.[25]

Soon after Clemens arrived in Redding, Isabel had "an attack of hysteria," in Paine's words, over a minor disagreement with the butler. Paine reported later that he helped her gain a grip on herself. "[S]he was relying more upon bromides than she should," he told Twain privately, and "in her unstrung, nervous condition she was not qualified to cope with the servant problem."[26] If Lyon was indeed mixing bromides, a sedative, with heavy use of alcohol, that could have seriously affected her judgment and weakened her ability to control her feelings. Predictably, Paine's warning had no effect on Twain.

On October 1 Claude, the butler, quit, and all the maids went with him. Though Lyon told everyone the servants left because they were frightened after burglars broke into Stormfield on September 18, the truth is that Claude could no longer stand to work for her. And dealing with the passel of new servants only brought greater tension to the household. Lyon blamed the problem on "a *certain* derangement" in another part of the house. "The servants do not want more than one head," she complained, assuming that she was rightfully that head, "hence the wearying, wearying confusion."[27]

Certainly the secretary's unbroken record of success in manipulating Twain nurtured her mounting arrogance. There was also the influence of Ralph Ashcroft, whose rise to power in the inner circle had marked the onset of the hard line toward Clara and her attitude of privileged entitlement. (The irony is that Clemens could have easily afforded to indulge both his daughters and his secretary.)[28] Unfortunately for the pair of schemers, Ashcroft drastically underestimated Clara's power and the strength of father-daughter ties. Clemens believed in retrospect that they were both "feeling absolutely sure they could turn me against Clara, drive her off the place & reign over Stormfield & me in autocratic sovereignty." Actually Lyon, when left to her own reckoning, was more uncertain. "The burden of this house is heavily upon my shoulders—Being on my shoulders it is an alien weight and has all the chances of being shifted to other props—," she mused six days before Clara's return, "I keep it there rather than in my heart *too* securely for if it were, or when it is taken from me, all the bleeding heart of me would be torn out with it."[29]

This musing suggests why, beyond her use of bromides and alcohol, her behavior seemed so at odds with her earlier pampering of Clara—Lyon's intense identification with Stormfield. She had nurtured the house from its casual beginnings in a conversation with Paine through design, placement, and construction, down to the bric-a-brac she so lovingly chose and arranged inside. In Twain's insightful quip, "She and Stormfield were one—& she was the one." She saw herself as mistress of Stormfield even when Clara was in residence. Before she built Stormfield, Lyon would never have attacked the one servant whom Clara would always defend. "Miss Lyon told me," Twain recalled, "Katy had been angering the servants by refusing to eat at their table—'wouldn't eat with Italians.'" Clemens reprimanded Katy, who was incredulous and denied even thinking such a thing. Clara stood by her, insisting vehemently that "Katy's denial of the charge was sufficient, & made the charge a falsehood."[30]

This incident reveals several crucial aspects of power in Twaindom. First, Lyon's control of Twain was so complete that he believed her charge against a servant who, as he himself admitted, "had served us 27 years & had not been accused of putting on airs before." Clara's influence, however, remained strong enough to counter the charges and restore Katy to his confidence. Clara's effectiveness in this turnabout can be measured by Lyon's clever response. She denied ever bringing the charge to him. "I wish to be damned," he wrote, "if I didn't *believe* her!"[31] Clara may have won the battle over Katy's character, but Lyon's sway over Twain's mind was so great that she persuaded him she was never one of the combatants.

Control was always central in her relationship to Clemens, but it had been transmuted from the power of seduction to the exercises of a doting mother by the beginning of 1908. She watched that he did not get into drafts "when he stands at the leaky loose windows to watch the snow and the children and dogs." In fact she was constantly standing guard. "I stayed with him while he finished his dressing and seeing that he hadn't fastened his trousers, told him so. Darlingly he cocked his head at me and said, 'I don't always; but since you are so particular I'll do it this time.'" She was always anxious when he left her immediate orbit, fearing his independence more than her own inability to protect him.[32]

But once Clemens occupied Stormfield, control edged into tyranny. "She commanded one of the maids to never answer *my* ring at all!" he recalled incredulously. "Miss Lyon informed me that when I wanted anything I could ring for Horace the butler." At the time Sam accepted her injunctions meekly. His only form of protest was through sarcasm. Sparked by her claims that she was trying to save him from the scandal of having the maids serve him in his room, he told her that he thought she and Ralph could furnish "scandal enough for *one* countryside without help from me." "[I]n honor of their efforts," he offered to change the house's name to Scandal Hall, for the pair spent long hours together in her room on weekends and sometimes burned the midnight oil with her door shut.[33]

It seems likely that the door was closed only after Clemens was safely at rest, for he observed that Lyon was a "born spy" and always kept her door open so that she could watch him and, he quipped, "the rest of her subjects." She attempted to create her own internal spy network at Stormfield, extending her tentacles throughout the household staff. "Whenever a bell rang," Twain remembered, "she would summon the servant whose bell it was, & inquire who had rung it & what was wanted."[34]

Two incidents clearly demonstrate her incessant snooping. Clara was visiting her father in his room and rang for Teresa, a maid, to order her five o'clock tea. Teresa was then immediately called into Lyon's room and asked for the details. "Don't you ever answer Miss Clemens's bell again without first reporting to me," she decreed. "Then I'll tell you whether to answer it or not." The second incident is more chilling. Normally Clemens wrote his letters to Jean under Miss Lyon's nose, giving her a draft to edit, which he recopied and returned to her for the post. But he veered out of his normal routine and wrote a long spontaneous letter without his secretary's guidance, even flagging down Lounsbury to put it in the mail. Miss Lyon was spying in the "telephone closet," according to Lounsbury, and she intercepted him on his way out. Mr. Clemens wants that letter back to add something that he has forgotten, she told the skeptical courier. Odds are the master of the house never saw his letter again. At such moments Lyon probably let herself believe that she was clever enough to secure her position next to the throne.[35]

———

Isabel Lyon's power stemmed, in large part, from her willingness to work and to take responsibility. She looked after all the details of running Twain's house, his social life, and his children. By the middle of 1907 she had accepted "all the housekeeping" into her hands, down to such details as supervising the table decoration. And no task was too small when it came to Clemens's personal effects. She gladly cleaned her boss's closets and organized his bureau drawers. At his occasionally imperious bidding, she made his telephone calls and wrote many of his business letters. Of course, she acted as his interior decorator for the Redding house, which required arduous shopping for upholstery, wallpaper, and light fixtures. She cleared out his New York house—"packing and clearing out the dreadful rubbish of many years' accumulating," in her words. She was also a superb hostess who was capably entertaining twenty guests per month after they moved to Stormfield. She was often, though not always, as busy as she portrayed herself.[36]

There were some essential tasks, like paying bills, that she shirked.[37] But she was never lazy where it counted—in the work to gain more household power. Ironically, if she had been lazier, Twain's family would have suffered less. Certainly Jean would have suffered less if Lyon had not taken over consulting with Jean's doctors and diligently making all her living arrangements. If she had not assumed full responsibility for managing the large household staff at Stormfield, relieving Sam of almost all domestic burdens while minutely supervising his social life and travel, he might have seen through her artifice. She always volunteered to accompany her boss on any excursion and took care of all the little details of his trips, including packing. She was his gatekeeper and screened all visitors; she even gave interviews to reporters. And she simply doted on him, seeking to please him in every possible way. As she once remarked on a very busy day, "I gave the King all of my presence that he required. I played Hearts for an hour, just as I was going up to lie down for that hour."[38] Her motives were far from pure but the effort she took was also far from minimal.

———

As Twain's unofficial business manager, Ralph Ashcroft was also making more than minimal effort. He took care of preparing many papers for Clemens to sign. And he was often in a hurry, giving his boss just a brief overview of their import. He also routinely presented papers for signature without duplicates. If the old man wanted to see what he had been signing, the business manager brought him an unsigned copy—"at least what purported to be a copy," Clemens realized later.[39]

In the flurry of paper shuffling that fall and early winter of 1908, two signatures requested by Ashcroft stuck in Clemens's mind. In the first instance the business manager asked Clemens to sign a duplicate deed to the property he had given Miss Lyon in 1907. This was required, Ashcroft told his boss, because she had failed to record the original deed. Clemens remembered that after he had perused the document, Ashcroft turned away, carried it to the table, rearranged the papers on the table, and called him to sign, which he did without reexamining the document.[40] He discovered later that the original deed had, in fact, been recorded and was completely legal. Did Samuel Clemens simply sign a superfluous property deed that day or was a switch made at the last minute?

The second occasion that Clemens recalled was a typewritten charter for the Mark Twain Company that his business manager presented to him as routine boilerplate copy. No need to read the legalese, Ashcroft reassured him. Clemens simply glanced down the page before he signed but remembered afterward that he had spied the phrase "real estate" and wondered to himself what a copyright corporation would have to do with land or housing.[41] What kind of document did Mark Twain actually sign that day?

Ralph Ashcroft was busy around the middle of November 1908. John Nickerson, the local Redding notary, routinely certified Clemens's signature on documents without requiring the famous author to appear in person. After visiting the notary with Clemens's papers, Ashcroft went to the Fairfield county clerk's office in Connecticut and had the notary's authority reconfirmed, even though such action was completely unnecessary. Traveling to New York City to house the legal document in Twain's safety deposit box, Ashcroft stopped off to have the paper officially recorded again in New York. Twain's business manager seems to have been remarkably anxious about this document's legitimacy and possible standing in a court of law.[42]

Around this same time, Lyon had another of her "episodes," writing in her diary that she had gone "to pieces." Noting that her "forces are very much scattered," she took to her bed for several days, including the day the notary affixed his seal to Ashcroft's carefully tended document. She attributed her collapse to the testimony she was required to give at the trial of the two men who had burglarized Stormfield.[43] But it clearly fits her pattern of breakdown when she was plotting against her boss or his family.

Samuel Clemens swears he never knowingly signed away his financial lifeblood.[44] Nonetheless, as of November 14, 1908, his signature was affixed to a power of attorney that gave Isabel Lyon and Ralph Ashcroft the legal right to supervise all his affairs, including his real property, his stocks and bonds, and his investments. His two employees could draw checks or drafts upon any financial institution in which he had money on deposit as well as receive, collect, and dispose of all dividends, interest, and royalties due him. By the end of November a piece of paper was sitting in Twain's safety deposit box in New York City that gave Lyon and Ashcroft the power to buy and sell his fortune out from under him and his children. His two employees now had a reason to believe "that all in good time they would be indisputably supreme here," Twain wrote later, "& I another stripped & forlorn King Lear."[45] But, at the time, like his fictional counterpart, this American Lear remained almost willfully unaware of his peril.

CHAPTER 12

Illusions of Love

MARK TWAIN SENT OUT photographic postcards to mark the Christmas season of 1908. In the image he duplicated for his friends, Twain sits squarely in a window at Stormfield, with a petite Lyon standing in profile on his left outside the window and a goateed Ashcroft hovering just behind him on his right. As the photograph plainly displays, Isabel and Ralph had become Mark Twain's family. He did not make a move without them, and anyone who stood in the way of their dominion was at risk. Lyon, who had already told the entire countryside around Redding that Jean was to be exiled for life "because she was 'crazy,'" was also busy spreading a rumor that Clara was "insane" and simultaneously subverting the daughter's authority at Stormfield. Lyon could dismiss a servant at will. Only Katy was protected by her past tenure, but even the faithful family retainer was under attack. Paine was holding onto his biographer's role by a thread. The pair of manipulators had so effectively insulated the old man that his relatives were afraid to approach him.[1]

Even his own daughters did not have access to their father except through his two pets. Jean remained in exile in New Jersey, and Clara was chafing furiously under the budgetary restrictions placed upon her by the woman who signed her father's checks. Try as she might, however, Clara got nowhere when it came to criticism of Lyon. "I wouldn't listen to any attack upon her character or conduct," Twain later confirmed, "no matter who or what they might be."[2] Clara's frustration grew as she repeatedly saw what everybody close to him knew: her father was a captive of Lyon's persuasions.

Both Ashcroft and Lyon had become convinced that they owned Mark Twain, that, as Twain so cogently observed, "I couldn't help myself." In fact his two employees campaigned to create a relationship of total dependence. And it was almost natural that he became as persuaded as the pair of manipulators that they were indispensable. "[T]here was no menial service which he omitted," Clemens remarked about Ashcroft, whose daily ministrations, down to stripping him at night and putting on his nightshirt, fooled all three of them into believing that Clemens could never do without them. The effectiveness of Benares and the appropriately dubbed Nana was not simply that they served his physical needs. They combined exquisitely detailed service with something else even more potent: the illusion of love. "There isn't anything that Benares wouldn't fix for you in your own way, if he could; for you stand first in his heart as in mine," Lyon crooned in a note written to Clemens in February. "And our dearest wish is to try to fulfill your slightest wish."[3] It was heady stuff to have two intelligent, witty, sophisticated adults vying to fulfill your "slightest" wish and flattering your every conceit.

Other less susceptible folks were also fooled. Dr. Quintard, the family doctor, remarked that "for three years she deceived him completely. All through that period he regarded her word as gold, her spirit as beautiful, her ideals lofty." Exactly what tipped the scales against Lyon in Quintard's mind is unclear, but it started with Clara, who had borrowed $500 from him in the spring of 1908. Eventually, Clara told her father, Dr. Quintard called her to a consultation and insisted that Twain's secretary and man Friday were crooked and should be investigated immediately.[4] The doctor apparently perceived the incongruence of Clara's pinched (by her measure, at least) financial circumstances in the midst of her father's plenty. Though Clara probably exaggerated his role as instigator, Quintard played a crucial part in solidifying her angry frustration, sullen discontent, and suspicions into a plan of action.

"Ask for an audit" was the doctor's advice—but it was to prove harder than it sounded. Twice, with her father's permission, Clara arranged with a lawyer named Jackson for an investigation of Lyon and Ashcroft, and twice Clemens then nixed her plans. Twice Clara resolved to see Mr. Rogers with Clemens's knowledge, and twice her father opposed the errand.[5]

Twain meanwhile was absorbed in dictating a long rumination titled *Is Shakespeare Dead?* One critic has accurately labeled the piece, which was published as a little book by Harper's in April 1909, "one of his least well received and most misunderstood works."[6] Though it is commonly assumed to be nothing more than a stale and embarrassing rehash of the Shakespeare-Bacon controversy, Twain was up to something more than flimsy literary criticism. He was using the debate over Shakespeare's real identity to satirize prejudice, intolerance, and self-importance—in himself as well as others.

He first engages the debate by vigorously attacking the "Stratfordolators and Shakesperiods"—those who uncritically believe that Shakespeare was actually a farmer turned actor from Stratford. He also defends the then popular theory that Francis Bacon wrote the plays. But after his passionate diatribe against the "Stratfordolators" and his vigorous support of the Baconians, he cheerfully admits that both sides are built on inference. Leaving no doubt about his satirical intent, Twain then gleefully subverts his entire argument. After seeming to be a serious, even angry, combatant, he denies that he intended to convince anyone that Shakespeare was not the real author of his works. "It would grieve me to know that any one could think so injuriously of me, so uncomplimentarily, so unadmiringly of me," he writes mockingly. "Would I be so soft as that, after having known the human race familiarly for nearly seventy-four years?" We get our beliefs at second hand, he explains, "we reason none of them out for ourselves. It is the way we are made." Twain has set a trap—an elaborate joke at the expense of what he scornfully refers to as the "Reasoning Race." He is satirizing the need to win an argument when it is virtually impossible to convince anyone to change sides in almost any debate. His excessive rhetoric of attack is obviously absurd—calling the other side "thugs," for example—yet it has been taken at face value.[7]

As the essay's subtitle, "From My Autobiography," clearly signals, Twain is also examining his own life, especially his place in history.[8] Punning on his family name, he considers the success of various "claimants," that is, those who make large assertions about the meaning of their life, including Mary Baker Eddy, and of course Samuel Clemens. Shakespeare was not a claimant in his lifetime, Twain notes, dying in obscurity in his own village. He savors the irony of the factual void surrounding the most famous writer the world has ever known. And he ponders how long his own fame will last. He had already piled up close to 450,000 words in autobiographical dictations. By contrast Shakespeare left almost no life record. But what counted for Shakespeare was "the Works," which Twain acknowledges "will endure until the last sun goes down."[9] At seventy-three, he knew he had reached the pinnacle of celebrity. What he could not fathom was if his own works "will endure." This was Twain's highly personal and idiosyncratic meditation—full of self-doubt—on the fate of his own writing after he died.

———

As the chill of a Connecticut winter surrounded Stormfield, a different sort of frost was withering all sentiment between Clara and her father's pets. Despite the setbacks, Clara was stubbornly determined to audit Lyon's accounts and would not be deterred. (Interestingly Lyon would later blame Paine for instigating the audit, even though he sailed for the Mediterranean in mid-February, to retrace Twain's steps in *The Innocents Abroad,* and was not a participant in the early battles of the audit war.) Getting wind of Clara's intentions, Ashcroft called her on the telephone. He was willing to be examined, but did *she* really want to risk an investigation, he asked with mock innocence. Puzzled, Clara demanded an explanation. Well, he responded, was she willing to risk exposing how much of her father's money she had been spending these past months? Ashcroft produced a figure—$860 for a recent month—that Clara vehemently denied.[10]

Ashcroft's ploy is instructive—both clever and self-defeating. He not only disapproved of Clara's lifestyle but believed her father would be similarly disturbed. He also apparently thought Clara would be ashamed or at least embarrassed. Clearly her spending habits bothered him. And his censorious attitude was a crucial ingredient in the pattern of denial in 1908 that had sparked Clara's investigative zeal. He failed to grasp that his adversary was not especially guilty about spending money. The spoiled, pretty daughter of a father who communicated his sense of intellectual superiority and of a mother who imbued her with a sense of genteel privilege, Clara was not a woman to be intimidated about money. Self-centered and confident, she possessed a strong sense of her entitlement. Clara Clemens backed off not an inch from her audit plan.

Though the idea of an audit frightened Ashcroft, he did not show it. Outwardly charming and pleasant, he was his normal self, according to Clemens. Lyon, however, could not disguise her distress. She was the one who had check-signing privileges, paid the bills, and was responsible for the family budget. As the pressure mounted, she began to drink heavily. Ashcroft referred to her outbursts as "hysterics," and attributed them to overwork. Cocktails, whiskey, and bromides might be a more accurate list of causes. Clemens said later that he never suspected whiskey was the main culprit.[11] But if he failed to grasp that his secretary was an alcoholic, he apparently was finding her increasingly difficult to live with. Although he still staunchly defended her to others, he claimed he was "beginning to cast an eye around for somebody to take her place."[12]

Unwell much of the month of February, Lyon reported she was perilously close to a nervous breakdown and received daily visits from the local doctor. Her spells and the three-day headaches that sent her to bed were nothing new. Even her retreat to Hartford to be near her mother the last week of February was not unprecedented. Here again was an "episode" that followed the usual pattern of collapse and renewal, usually accompanied by substance abuse but always closely associated with a fresh strategy to benefit herself. It was while she was in Hartford that Ashcroft presented her new plan to the boss. Awkwardly, sheepishly, hesitantly, he told Clemens that he and Isabel were getting married.[13]

"It was as amazing as if he had said they had concluded to hang themselves," Clemens confessed. He was dumbfounded, he told Ashcroft, at this "unbelievable" and "insane" idea.[14]

'We'll put it aside,' Ashcroft quickly assured him.

'No,' he insisted, 'you must go your own way and take the responsibities yourselves.'

'We'll postpone the marriage, as long as you wish.'

Clemens told him that he was not willing to participate in this decision in any way.

'We'll marry secretly then,' Ashcroft promised, struggling for middle ground.

'Don't think of such a thing,' Clemens replied. "[I]t could get us all into hot water presently."

Ashcroft repeatedly assured Clemens that nothing in his household would be changed by the marriage, that it would be just like old times.

But Clemens was both skeptical and assertive. 'I won't have any married people in the house, nor any babies,' he flatly told Ashcroft.

'There will be no babies,' Ashcroft said coolly and authoritatively; 'it is not that kind of a marriage.'

"Why, how you talk! Don't you love her?"

"Not in that way."

"Then what in the world are you marrying her for? What is your reason?"

'Because she needs my care and protection and I sympathize with her vulnerability and want to nurse her back to health,' Ashcroft replied dispassionately.

"Marriage without love," Twain responded, "is foolish and perishable."

'It is not a marriage wholly without love,' he parried, 'because she loves me and I have a great respect for her character and qualities.'

Ashcroft returned to the subject of babies and flatly asserted there would be none because there was nothing animal in his relationship to Lyon. At that point Clemens bet him ten dollars to one that they would have children—probably responding to Lyon's youthful style more than her chronological age of forty-five. He again reiterated that he would not have married people in his house. As he recognized later, neither one believed him.[15]

Explanations for Ashcroft and Lyon's motives for this marriage multiply depending on the interpreter. Perhaps it was meant to assuage Clara by eliminating any possibility that the secretary would marry her father, thus reducing (they hoped) her feelings of distrust. Forestalling an audit was certainly one of their major goals, as is reinforced by the fact that in the first week of March Clara's monthly allowance was raised to four hundred dollars. This one-two punch was meant to take Clara out of the match: give her more money and reduce her fears that her father's estate was vulnerable through marriage—though of course Lyon did not articulate such a motive publicly. Perhaps the secretary also thought tying the knot would allay any local gossip about her relationship with her employer.[16]

Both Ashcroft and Lyon skillfully presented the reasons they gave for marrying. Ashcroft portrayed himself to Clemens as a self-sacrificing bridegroom, marrying only to give Isabel protection and nurse her back to health. This was hard to swallow, even for a still-trusting boss, who thought at the time that Ashcroft was being hypocritical. Unclear as to the real motives for the marriage, Clemens suspected there was some-thing sexual—a compulsion was his word—in their haste to get married. "I took it for a marriage of fools," he commented, "I didn't know it was a marriage of sharpers." Lyon's thinking was more credible to Clemens at the time. Her reasons, confided to Mrs. Lounsbury, were that she needed support and protection, "somebody to lean upon," if she were suddenly ousted from Stormfield. Clemens could see that this rationale had wisdom. Lending her motive credence, Ashcroft told him that it was Isabel, eleven years his senior, who proposed to him and urged the marriage.[17]

Thirty years later Lyon told a dramatically different story as she reminisced with an undercover detective posing as a literary agent. "She stated that her marriage was part of a deal whereby she would thus legitimize her standing in the household in consideration of the breaking off of all relations between C.C. [Clara] and 'Will,'" the detective reported. She told him that this deal was "originated by Mr. C. [Mr. Clemens], who objected strongly to 'Will,' and was honorably carried out by both women."[18] Will Wark was Clara's accompanist.

By February, when the Ashcroft-Lyon marriage was hatched, Clara and Lyon were barely on civil terms. "Frost on the vine" was how Twain described it; sentiment between them had been "withered, rotted, squashed" and "discarded," in Twain's inimitable words, "[f]or all time." Clara was intent on a full investigation of Lyon, whom she, by then, considered an enemy. Moreover, Clemens was not a man to propose human trades with the people he loved. Believing as he did that marriage without love was "foolish and perishable," he would not have conceived this kind of human swap—whatever his feelings toward Will Wark.[19]

"I can't go on alone carrying the dear weight of wonderful Stormfield," Lyon wrote Clemens, somewhat more convincingly. "And you won't ever know anything different from the present plan," she reassured him, "except that I will have one with the right to watch me, & keep me from breaking down." Striving to convince her boss that the impending marriage would change nothing for him, she described her feelings for Ashcroft in unusual terms. "[W]e have grown very close together in our love for you," she told him, "& we couldn't be happy away from you."[20]

In fact, marrying Ashcroft was a serious miscalculation on the secretary's part. It did nothing to placate Clara, and it distanced Clemens in ways that began to break her death grip on his mind. His furious and, in part, no doubt jealous reaction to her engagement suggests that his possessiveness was more than paternal. It was a major jolt to discover that the woman who had been acting as his surrogate wife for several years was about to become someone else's real wife.

————

Several days after Ashcroft announced their prospective marriage, Clemens told him directly that Clara wanted an audit. The timing hardly seems coincidental. Presumably Clara had been pressing her father all winter and suddenly, at the beginning of March, he decided to get behind the audit idea. Ashcroft's response was predictably chilly, though Clemens claimed he expected lighthearted compliance. That his man Friday was not overjoyed at the prospect seemed suspicious to him. He declared that this was his first warning that something was amiss. "The frost touched me then;" he wrote, "but it was only a touch, it did not invade my bones right away."[21]

Aware of the sudden shift in her fortunes, Clara raced to see Mr. Rogers, who said he would talk with Ashcroft and have him bring the checkbooks and vouchers to the Standard Oil offices, where they would be examined by an expert. Clara, by now a veteran in the audit wars, knew enough not to celebrate yet, but she did pounce upon her unexpected advantage. Knowing that the secretary and business manager held the keys to her father's safety deposit box, Clara persuaded him to revoke their authority to use the keys and to ask for their return. She also persuaded her father to obtain an independent inventory of the contents of the box. It agreed with a previous list made by Ashcroft. Nothing was stolen or missing in the box, according to the report from Twain's emissary, Mr. Duneka, who was the general manager for Harper's, Twain's publisher.[22]

Still Clara had the sense that something was awry. About this time she went on a shopping expedition with Katy. Admiring an especially delicate piece of underwear, Clara longingly laid it aside. When Katy asked her why she didn't buy it, Clara responded that she couldn't afford it.

"Why, Miss Clara, Miss Lyon's got lots of those things," Katy exclaimed. "Miss Lyon affords it, & so I don't see why you can't." Clara's new allowance—four hundred dollars a month—was eight times Miss Lyon's salary.

"Because she can sign checks for my father. I can't," Clara snapped peevishly.[23]

Katy's questions took deadly aim at the heart of Clara's anger. In this instance, and perhaps others that went unrecorded, the loyal servant reminded Clara of Lyon's free-spending ways and reinforced her determination to reign them in. Despite that determination, however, her father foiled her once again. If, as he later claimed, "relations were now strained—strained all around," including himself, the strain was either short-lived or very slight.[24] Ashcroft had refused to turn over the various pieces of bookkeeping evidence to Henry Rogers, and, on the evening of March 10, he succeeded in talking Clemens out of the independent audit Clara and Rogers had arranged.

At half past two in the morning of March 11, Clemens, who was unable to sleep, took pen in hand to explain this decision to his daughter. It was Clara's worst nightmare come true, for Ashcroft had talked his boss into letting *him* do all the accounting. The checkbooks were not to leave his house, Clemens insisted, under the influence of his business manager's persuasions. Friends could read Ashcroft's reports and discreetly compare his numbers with the checkbooks and bank deposits. Unless you can furnish concrete evidence of their wrongdoing, he firmly instructed his daughter, we will wait for Ashcroft's report. Dismiss your lawyer, he advised Clara, for you will find that his services are unnecessary.[25]

Clemens went on to lavishly praise Miss Lyon as a housekeeper, house-builder, decorator, and hostess. "These services of hers," he told Clara proudly, "have been very valuable; but she has charged nothing for them." This was a crucial point to him. "She has not been dishonest, even to a penny's worth," he loyally declared. "All her impulses are good & fine." "She has served me with a tireless devotion," he continued to insist, "& I owe her gratitude for it—& I not only owe it but feel it. I have the highest regard for her character."[26]

He also lavished praise on his business manager. "He has served me in no end of ways & with astonishing competency—brilliancy, I may say." He mentioned Ashcroft's fight to save the Plasmon venture, his invention of the Mark Twain Company as a way to preserve copyright, and his constant daily service. "I am quite without suspicion," he concluded, "of either their honesty or their honorableness."[27] Clara's suspicions had hardly made a dent in her father's devotion. Whatever he thought of Ashcroft and Lyon's prospective marriage, it had not damaged his high estimation of their character.

———

Ashcroft and Lyon had just won a decisive battle in the audit wars—only if untrained friends found discrepancies in Ashcroft's financial report would Clemens agree to bring in professional accountants. They should have declared victory and gone home. But the conspirators, now anxious and uncertain, could not contain themselves. Ashcroft, who was a less talented schemer than his soon-to-be wife, must have convinced her that they needed more protection. On March 13, with the ink barely dry on Clemens's impassioned defense, Ashcroft brought four formal contracts, a memorandum of agreement, and four promissory notes to his boss. Twain later called the event "General Clean-Up Day."[28]

The first contract he read made Ashcroft his general business manager. This one Twain prized, he said later, because it would save him all the annoyance and trouble of managing his business affairs himself. He happily signed it. The second contract appointed Ashcroft the official manager of the Mark Twain Company for two years, with the job of collecting all Twain's royalties directly from his publisher, Harper's. Ashcroft was to charge a commission that Twain assumed was compensation for his general services as business manager. Twain was to put all his instructions to Ashcroft in writing and was not to expect a report more than once every three months. He signed again.[29]

The third contract raised Miss Lyon's salary to $100 a month, limited her duties to those of "social secretary" or hostess, and explicitly removed any housekeeping responsibilities or letter writing from her job description. This contract also stipulated that Lyon was to be housed and fed under Twain's roof. "This did seem to me to be immensely impudent," he noted, "after all I had said about not allowing married persons to live in the house." Because her contract could be dissolved with one month's notice by either party, Twain said he "gratefully signed it."[30]

The fourth contract was for an edited collection of the "Letters of Mark Twain" to be prepared "promptly" by Lyon. In this agreement she formally renounced all claims to any royalties from the volume. The man whose letters were being edited took immediate umbrage at this rather strange act of denial. She was throwing away more money per year than she would ever earn in her lifetime, he thought to himself, by renouncing her one-tenth interest in this letter volume, but he signed without comment.[31]

Then Ashcroft produced a typed memorandum detailing Miss Lyon's services and compensations, which the boss read and also signed. Finally, Ashcroft gave his boss four notes, "for $250 each—his notes," according to Clemens, "remarking that he wished to assume Miss Lyon's debt of a thousand dollars to me." Clemens did not sign the promissory notes. "I never meant to collect them," he said later. "I told Ashcroft to put them away & keep them for me. Which he probably did; I did not see them again."[32] Writing this recollection in late June, he was completely unaware that one note would surface again—with a coda he never endorsed and a signature he had never affixed.

Was Clean-Up Day a success? Sam had not yet mailed the March 11 letter to Clara that had all but bestowed a lifetime sinecure upon his pets. "Nothing is as it was," he wrote in a postscript on March 14. "Everything is changed. Sentiment has been wholly eliminated," he noted dryly. "All services rendered me are paid for, henceforth." "But there is no vestige of ugly feeling, no *hostility* on either side," he wrote. "The comradeship remains, but it is paid for: also the friendship. Stormfield was a home; it is a tavern, now, & I am the landlord."[33]

Sam Clemens said many things in retrospect about General Clean-Up Day but one thing is clear. It was a debacle for Ashcroft and Lyon. Before Clean-Up Day, he had said that Lyon could not have been replaced at any price, that he considered the pair "practically members of my family."[34] Before Clean-Up Day, they had been his fictive kin who satisfied his desperate yearning for emotional intimacy better than his own children. But by putting their relationship in legalese, defined as a business exchange of money for services, they stripped it of the love that Clemens needed to believe was its source. This was his second jolt, more severe even than the shock that Lyon would marry. As he told Clara, he did not want to run a tavern; he wanted a home.

———

Clemens began to cogitate on the contracts and the memorandum. The more he cogitated, the more agitated he became. His first mental stop was the memorandum. Why did he need a list of Miss Lyon's services and compensations? And if he had no need for such a list, who did? Clemens hit upon "the sensitive place in the memorandum" right away—the clothing. The memorandum read that he had agreed to allow "her to purchase, for my account, such items of clothing as were necessary or desirable for the proper maintenance of her position as hostess of my house."[35] The day after Clean-Up, March 14, Clemens instructed Lyon to telephone Ashcroft with the message that he wanted to reread the memorandum.

Ashcroft returned to Stormfield and nervously blurted out, before his boss had even touched the document, that Lyon had spent about three hundred dollars on clothing, which was an authorized expenditure.

"Who authorized her?" Twain asked.

"Miss Clemens," Ashcroft responded, explaining that Clara had given Lyon permission to buy clothing so that she was properly dressed to meet company.

"Ashcroft, Miss Lyon knew Miss Clemens's authorization was without value. You knew it, too."[36]

Twain locked the memorandum away, and Ashcroft made no comment. But in trying to fix everything, "to leave nothing indefinite between us," in Twain's words, Ashcroft had decisively cut the cords of trust and affection that had all but secured the pair a total victory just a few days before. In the coming days, these contractual agreements would be a source of growing irritation.[37]

March 14 became the equivalent of Twain's personal declaration of independence, for in addition to confiscating the memorandum, he orally revoked Lyon's check-signing power, which he had conferred in 1907 through a "power of attorney with the banks."[38] Though he did not put this instruction in writing until May 29, he nonetheless decided almost immediately that if she was not to be his secretary, as per Ashcroft's contract, then she would not have the privilege of signing his checks. He also asked Clara to assume the role of official housekeeper at Stormfield.[39]

Yet beyond revoking the check-signing privileges—no small matter—he was willing to resume the old comradeship. "The Ashcrofts & I were soon very friendly & sociable again," Twain admitted, "& I hoped & believed these conditions would continue."[40]

Olivia Langdon Clemens as a young wife, c. 1872.

A youthful family in Hartford, 1884.
(*left to right*) Livy, Clara, Jean, Sam, and Susy Clemens.
REPRINTED BY PERMISSION OF THE MARK TWAIN PAPERS,
BANCROFT LIBRARY, UNIVERSITY OF CALIFORNIA, BERKELEY (MTP).

A mature family in the Adirondacks, 1901.
(*left to right*) Jean, Clara, Livy, and Sam Clemens.
REPRINTED BY PERMISSION, MTP.

Katy Leary in Jean Clemens's study, January 1905.
REPRINTED BY PERMISSION, MTP.

Jean and her father in Dublin, New Hampshire, summer 1905.
REPRINTED BY PERMISSION, MTP.

Jean Clemens riding Scott in Dublin, New Hampshire, 1905.

A favorite pastime: Twain smoking in bed, 1906.

Clemens with Dorothy Quick, one of his favorite Angelfish, in August 1907.

Twain on the porch of the Upton house, Dublin, New Hampshire,
where he dictated several sections of his autobiography, summer 1906.

Twain and his best friend,
Henry Huttleston Rogers,
in Bermuda, 1908.

Quintessential Twain, 1908.

Sam and Clara Clemens playing cards, 1908.

Isabel Lyon (*left*) posing dramatically with a friend at Stormfield, 1908.

Albert Bigelow Paine and Mark Twain playing billiards, 1908.

Isabel Lyon and Ralph Ashcroft on the deck of her farmhouse near
Stormfield, in Redding, Connecticut, 1908.

Ashcroft and Twain at Stormfield, 1908–9.

Twain with William Dean Howells, his closest literary friend, at Stormfield,
March 1909. This house in Redding, Connecticut, was designed
by Howell's architect son for Twain.

Clara Clemens's wedding, October 1909. (*left to right*) Sam,
Jervis Langdon (a cousin), Jean, Ossip Gabrilowitsch (the bridegroom),
Clara, Joseph Twichell (the minister).

Jean Clemens reunited with her father, 1909.

Closing Words *

of my # Autobiography.

Stormfield, Christmas Eve,

11 a. m., 1909.

Jean is dead!

And so this Autobiography
closes here. I had a reason
for projecting it, three years ago:
that reason
it perishes with her.

The reason that moved me
was a desire to save my copyrights
from extinction, so that Jean &
Clara would always have a good
livelihood from my books after
my death. I meant that whenever
a book of mine should approach
its 42-year limit, it should at
once be newly issued, with about

The first manuscript page of Twain's "Closing Words of My Autobiography."

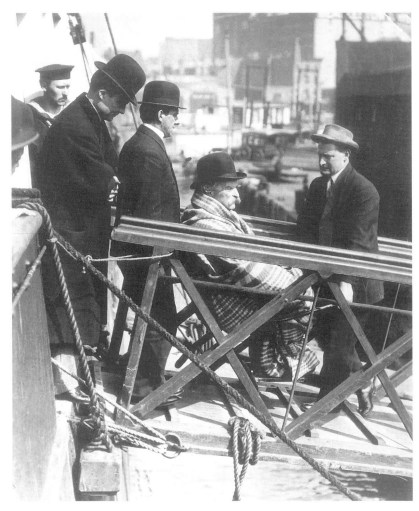

Going home to die, April 1910.
Twain is being carried off the ship from Bermuda to New York.

CHAPTER 13

Unraveling

WEDDING BELLS TOLLED ON March 18, 1909, for Isabel Lyon and Ralph Ashcroft. Nine people attended the traditional church ceremony in New York City, including Clemens, who said that Lyon acted the sweet, girlish, radiant bride to perfection. As was often the case in her life, presentation did not match substance. On the train ride back to Stormfield the bride "stayed apart" from her bridegroom, and the newlyweds continued their silence at dinner. Eyebrows arched and tongues wagged when they took separate rooms and continued to sleep apart for the ten or twelve nights that they remained under Clemens's roof. "They could not have been a colder pair" he quipped later, "if they had been on the ice a week."[1]

Whatever effect her marriage was having on the crowd at Stormfield, Lyon wanted to make a special impression on one absent member of the inner circle. She sent an announcement of her nuptials by telegram, costing almost one week's wages, to Paine in Egypt.[2]

Uncertainty was the new watchword at Stormfield. The Ashcrofts took up "night quarters" at Lyon's Lobster Pot and "day quarters" at Stormfield. Clara was now her father's housekeeper. The new Mrs. Ashcroft was his official hostess—with her duties contractually circumscribed. Secretarial tasks were to be farmed out to stenographers. Clemens had assumed control of the checkbook and the safety deposit box, and had arranged for Ashcroft to audit his books. He hoped the crisis was over and that Clara would be placated and the conflict under his own roof laid to rest.[3] But normality was only a mirage.

Sometime in the middle of March, Clemens received a private message sent by Frederick Duneka, at Harper's, who had checked the contents of his safety deposit box. Duneka, recognizing that his client's mail was being opened by both the secretary and the business manager, had taken the precaution of sending this message orally. "Do you think it safe," the messenger asked, "to sign the transfers on the back of your securities & trust an outsider with the key [to the box]?"[4] Twain realized immediately that it was an "insane thing to do," for the signature made the securities negotiable for whoever had them in hand. "I asked Ashcroft if I had done it. He said yes," Twain reported. Ashcroft explained that he had thought it unwise but that Twain had insisted—he "could not very well object," he told his boss.[5] Clemens's signatures on the securities were authentic, and he never disputed Ashcroft's claim. But his immediate response—"that was an insane thing to do"—is puzzling if he had independently pushed for the stock transfer signatures. One thing is clear. The only person who witnessed this folly—Ralph Ashcroft—still had a key to the safety deposit box and had told no one that Clemens had signed the transfers.

With Ashcroft in tow, Clemens visited his safety deposit box and scratched off the transfer signatures on his Mark Twain Company stock. But his mind was already elsewhere. Prodded by his memory that the phrase "real estate" had occurred somewhere in the incorporation papers of the Mark Twain Company, and disturbed that these papers were not among the inventoried contents of the box, Clemens personally searched every scrap of paper and came away empty-handed. He decided that his business manager had somehow stolen the incorporation paper "from under my nose, & had it upon his person."[6]

He went straight to his business lawyer, John Larkin, and pulled him aside. Does the Mark Twain Company have any authority over my real estate? No, was the lawyer's reply, "over nothing but the copyrights." Relieved and content, he immediately repented of his suspicions of Ashcroft.[7] But the fact remains that by the middle of March, Clemens was willing to believe that his business manager had stolen a key document for some nefarious purpose—which involved control of real property against his own wishes. Though he wanted a peaceful rapprochement with the Ashcrofts, Clemens's trust had been shaken.

———

Undaunted by the signs of growing skepticism in their boss, the Ashcrofts continued to fight on several fronts. Toppling Clara's housekeeping regime seemed to be their first priority. With Lyon again undergoing a crisis, which meant retreat accompanied by heavy drinking, implementation of the couple's battle plans fell to Ashcroft. Four days before his wedding Ashcroft had a heart-to-heart talk with the young butler Horace. "Miss Clara has hated you from the very first," he revealed. She tried to fire you but was restrained by Miss Lyon and Mr. Clemens, he whispered confidentially to the surprised butler. Horace told Clemens later that Ashcroft had advised "everyone of the help to leave before they got kicked out." Summoning the entire household staff, Ashcroft went so far as to deliver his warning in person.[8] He was never the most subtle manipulator. Hoping that Clara would prove incompetent to run her father's house, the Ashcrofts were giving the staff a little boost out the door. Bereft of servants, would not Clemens gratefully call Lyon back into service?

Having been promised by Lyon that his salary would advance until it reached $60, Horace went to the new housekeeper, Clara, and asked for a sizable salary increase and an extra afternoon and evening off. After consulting with her father, Clara raised the young butler's salary from $35 to $45 plus the extra evening. Horace claimed he was satisfied. Clemens and his daughter left the next morning—March 31—for New York; Sam planned to leave from there with Ashcroft for Norfolk, Virginia, to attend the dedication ceremony for a railroad built by Henry Rogers. During the drive to the station, Clara told her father that she and Horace had come to an agreement. In what might be termed a revolving train, Ashcroft returned from New York that afternoon and corralled Horace, telling him he was going to be fired—that Clara was planning to make a clean sweep of the servants.[9]

Bewildered and confused—and cajoled with the promise that he would get a month's wages—Horace succumbed to Ashcroft's counsel: write a letter to Clemens confirming that you were discharged. Returning to New York with the letter up his sleeve, Ashcroft waited for an opening. Accompanying Clemens to Norfolk, he continued to function as traveling companion and nursemaid—"just in the old-time way, the old charming way, the old happy way, and just as if nothing had ever happened to interrupt our heaven-born relations" was how Twain described their trip. The man Friday finally sprang his trap on April 3 in Norfolk, the evening Clemens was to attend a banquet to honor Henry Rogers. Coming to Clemens around dinnertime with Horace's letter in his hand and feigning complete innocence, he announced that Miss Clemens had discharged the butler. The master of Stormfield was completely shocked and immediately denied Ashcroft's claim.[10]

Horace was absolutely honest, the business manager insisted.

"He has lied this time, all the same," Clemens flatly asserted, "unless something has been happening since I left to cause his discharge."

"Well, he wasn't going to stay, anyway," Ashcroft countered.

"He wasn't? How do you know?" Clemens replied.

"He told me so himself. He said he would not serve under Miss Clemens for any wages in the world." And "He does not know *how* to lie," Ashcroft observed of the young butler's character.[11]

But Horace flatly denied ever uttering a word against Miss Clara, describing her as a perfect lady in all her dealings with him.[12] If Ashcroft's judgment of the young butler was essentially correct, then he himself was the liar—with the powerful motive to convince the boss that his daughter could not function as his housekeeper and that he could not run his house without the services of Mrs. Ashcroft. Unfortunately the new husband lacked the prevaricating skills of his wife. To make matters worse, Clemens and his daughter were now in close communication, and the proprietor of Stormfield was no longer sleepwalking through his domestic trials. He pounced on Ashcroft's story that Horace had disparaged his daughter's supervision.

"He said that [he would not serve under Miss Clemens] to you?"

"Yes."

"Did you recognise that he had insulted you?" "Did you try to knock him down?" "Were you skunk enough to take that?" Clemens fired one volley after another past Ashcroft, who stood in helpless silence.[13]

"When did he tell you these things?" Clemens asked probingly.

"The night before you left."

"Why didn't you repeat that conversation to me, so that we could secure a new butler in New York?'

Meekly, Ashcroft muttered that he had not really believed Horace meant what he said.[14]

Rallying his forces, Ashcroft then insisted that Clara had discharged Horace without proper notice and he was entitled to a full month's wages. Over Clemens's protests, he quickly interjected that the check was already in the mail. Clemens was furious. "Get that check back!" he ordered. "And don't lose any time about it."[15]

The schemers lost considerable ground in this exchange. Taking Ashcroft at his word, Clemens telegraphed Clara with the news that Horace had "pronounced himself discharged." Clara contacted their former butler, Claude, who agreed to return to the Clemens household on one condition—that he never serve under Miss Lyon, whom he despised. Clara had telephoned Katy at Stormfield with the news, and Katy telephoned back to report that Mrs. Ashcroft was "so scared she was white as a ghost."[16] Handling the manufactured crisis with aplomb, Clara was more firmly entrenched than ever as housekeeper. Ironically, Lyon's resignation from that position had forced father and daughter to work together, and, perhaps to their mutual surprise, their relationship was dramatically strengthened. In addition, the naïve farm boy would be replaced by a mature adversary—surely not the outcome the Ashcrofts had envisioned.

In the meantime Horace, whose guileless manner would later make him a credible witness, was still at Stormfield. Recognizing the danger, Ashcroft alerted his wife by telephone. She immediately called her favorite servant, Teresa, and ordered her to get Horace out of the house at once. "Mr. Clemens is coming, & is in a perfect rage," she shrieked. Horace fled in fear. Mrs. Ashcroft also warned Teresa that Clemens was going to discharge all the servants when he returned, and she urged her to get them out of the house. The servants packed their bags in anticipation of the impending storm.[17]

———

On April 7, before returning home on the afternoon train, Clemens dropped by Clara's New York apartment for a family council. Never doubting for an instant that his daughter's denial was the truth, he found himself "perplexed to a standstill" about Horace's claim that she had discharged him. "[T]hose Ashcroft's are in it somewhere," Clara suggested. While the two were chatting, Jean happened to telephone, and she sounded so strong and healthy that both her father and sister became convinced she was well enough to come home. Such conviction was not unprecedented, but Clara's next step was. She immediately called Dr. Peterson and made an appointment to see him herself.[18] Inspired by her father's confidence and driven by dissatisfaction with the status quo, Clara's newly minted authority spurred her to intervene with the doctor on her sister's behalf—for the first time.

April 7 was a red-letter day indeed. Urging her father to discharge Mrs. Ashcroft had become Clara's mantra, but this time, as she pressed her case, Clemens suddenly agreed. He would fire her on April 15, when the first month of her contract was complete. This timing lends credence to Clemens's claim that the contract he signed on Clean-up Day, March 13, settled his resolve to wait thirty days and then dismiss his secretary on the terms so conveniently provided: one month's written notice.[19] It is doubtful, however, that Clemens would have made good on his resolve if Clara had faltered in her new role. But one daughter's success as housekeeper, coupled with the prospect that the other might return home healthy, had reduced his perception of dependency on Lyon. Her marriage had also disturbed his feelings of attachment.

The Ashcrofts' campaign to stampede the servants into leaving en masse failed. Clemens arrived home on April 7, and the servants, quietly observing the boss's noncombustible mood, unpacked their bags. Lyon met him at the door full of hypocritical delight over the prospect of Claude's return. Her day, already spoiled, was about to get worse. Clemens announced proudly that he and Clara were certain that Jean could come home.[20] This time Dr. Peterson will consent, he exuberantly predicted.

"Miss Lyon flushed, her eyes spewed fire," Clemens wrote, "& she was hysterical in a moment."

"Indeed he will not! Jean come home? It isn't to be thought of for a moment; she is far worse than she looks; she has convulsions two & three times a month," Lyon responded intemperately. Clemens was surprised.

"How do you know?" he asked.

"From Anna. She keeps me posted all the time."

"How?"

"By letter."[21]

Twain did not know that Mrs. Ashcroft was lying and so immediately assumed that Clara's visit with Peterson would be a disappointment. It would be several months before he heard that Jean had suffered only three grand mal seizures total in the three months since her return from Germany or that, from all indications, she had had no seizures for nine months before that.[22] In large part, it was the deceit and manipulation of others that had kept his daughter out of his house. But it was Clemens himself who judged her health and fitness to return home by the unrealistic standard of a completely seizure-free life. This had led him to accept unquestioningly that several seizures a month would disqualify her from living with him.

On April 11 Clara went expectantly for a consultation with Dr. Peterson, full of the good news of her sister's health.[23] Predictably, Peterson refused to even consider the possibility that Jean might return to her father's house. Finding his unbending recalcitrance mystifying, Clara asked him why this option was unthinkable and was astonished to hear the good doctor's reason: her father would be "disturbed by Jean's presence." She told Peterson that his notion was "utterly groundless," but he refused to believe her. After years of manipulation by Miss Lyon, Peterson's attitude was set in concrete. Always headstrong and now on a mission, Clara called in Dr. Quintard to reason with him, but even a peer could not dissuade Peterson from his conviction that it was Clemens's own wish to keep his daughter away.[24] Clara would have to send in the chief.

Teetering on the brink of a break with Clemens, Lyon continued her zealous efforts to keep his daughter in exile. Anticipating his appointment with Peterson, she summoned the doctor to Stormfield for a consultation while Clemens went down to New York to attend Clara's concert on April 13. Both the Ashcrofts canceled their earlier plans to accompany their boss, and stayed in Connecticut to confer with Peterson. The next day, when Jean's father at last went to see her physician, Dr. Peterson was fresh from "listening to Miss Lyon's falsities all day," Twain wrote, and "wouldn't believe *me* at first." As a result, the astonished father reported, "All I could get out of Peterson was permission to allow Jean to come home for one week."[25] Even after his visit with Jean's doctor, however, Sam still did not recognize the machinations against his daughter. He had not yet connected the dots on the conspirators' chart.

Mindful of the terms of his wife's contract, which he had constructed, Ashcroft went to Twain after he returned to Stormfield, in anticipation of the falling guillotine. Since Mrs. Ashcroft had not yet moved her possessions out of Stormfield, Ashcroft confided her fear that Clara would have her trunks searched and would even go so far as to have her arrested. Nonsense, Twain replied. Clara would, if she felt it necessary, apply to a lawyer, who would not allow her to proceed upon a whim. In fact Clemens's daughter was itching to search Mrs. Ashcroft's trunks but, even in her most furious moments, she gave no hint that she also wanted to involve the police.[26]

On April 15 Twain did what only the previous Christmas seemed an absolute impossibility. He wrote a note to Mrs. Ashcroft in the morning giving her the requisite one-month notice. "With thanks inexpressable," she closed her short acknowledgment in the afternoon, "for the wonder & beauty you have brought into my life."[27]

CHAPTER 14

The Exile Returns

DESPITE THE TONE OF resignation in her note to Twain, Mrs. Ashcroft had not yet given up all hope of reconciliation. After she was fired, she returned to Stormfield each day, trying to wriggle her way back into her boss's good graces. She arrived at ten in the morning and fussed around until five, when she left for home. "Now & then she would sail into my room," Clemens remembered, "artificially radiant & girlish with something killingly funny to tell me, & would stand by my bed & detail it with all sorts of captivating airs & graces & bogus laughter—& get no response." She haunted Stormfield, hoping to reestablish the old magic.[1] She pretended her relations with him were pleasant, but she could no longer bewitch the master with her charms and flattery. He had lost his taste for flirtation.

Though he still believed in her essential honesty and good character, she irked him mightily. When she began a speech about how her marriage was a sacrifice for him, Clemens interrupted brusquely, saying he had "enough of that offensive nonsense already from Ashcroft, & didn't want any more of it. I said the pair had done a silly thing, with a purpose in view—'God knows what, I can't guess!'—& it couldn't be palmed off on me as having been done for *my* sake."[2] Her marriage to Ashcroft was a potent vexation.

The master of Stormfield was also irritated by Clean-Up Day. "[T]he insolences & impertinences of her contract of March 13th were rankling in me," he revealed, "& the sight of her exasperated me." One contract especially dropped acid on his heart: her casual rejection of the permanent one-tenth interest in the royalties of an edited collection of his letters. Ashcroft had told him she considered the royalties "petty," which stung the author's vanity. He thought she was throwing away fifteen or twenty thousand dollars a year—more than she would ever earn in her lifetime. The casual way she treated his manuscripts also rankled— "dumped helter-skelter into drawers" was his exasperated description.[3]

She must have been perplexed by Clemens's genuine indifference to her artful insinuations. Declaring her willingness to save him from a despairing old age, Mrs. Ashcroft was met with a coldness that contrasted sharply to the welcoming reception she had grown to expect as Miss Lyon. She who in early March had been his powerful queen, adored and pampered, was by late April a mere lackey, licking his boots and getting kicked for her trouble.[4]

Meanwhile, Clara finally had her father back. Confident now that she would not be the one who was rebuffed, Clara again called on Henry Rogers, who agreed to oversee a complete "overhaul" of Twain's financial affairs. Once more Rogers put himself at the service of his famous literary friend. "In the last two or three years," he wrote to Clemens, "I had my suspicions of things, which you in your good natured way have overlooked." Praising Clara's dignified, articulate, and in his words "convincing" story, Rogers said he would be glad "to assume such burden in the matter as was necessary."[5] Unfortunately for Clemens, his friend would not live to fulfill his promise.

As the time of Jean's return approached, the Lioness knew her grace period had run out. She left just before Jean arrived and never set foot in Stormfield again. But before her departure, she was busily packing up her trunks and spending considerable time in the attic. Just as Ashcroft had anticipated, Clara wanted those trunks inspected and demanded a key, which she got. But Clemens, uncomfortable with such a humiliating shakedown and still unaware of the extent of the Ashcrofts' scheming, blocked Clara's search. "It was a mistake," he later believed, because she had taken some now unstrung carnelian beads that had been worn by his wife.[6] After Lyon left Stormfield for good, however, she returned the beads through a third party to an open attic trunk, and instructed her favorite maid, Teresa, to tell Clara where they could be found.[7]

The whole incident is trivial and might be brushed aside except for the reactions of the family. Clara, in a confrontation with Lyon before she finished packing, demanded that she find the missing carnelian beads, described by Paine as "highly valued." Twain, in his own commentary, called them "hallowed keepsakes." But these so-called "hallowed keepsakes" had been gathering dust in the Clemens attic for years. No family member had shown any interest in Livy's unstrung beads until Clara surprised Lyon by her hawk-eyed inventory of attic memorabilia. Though Lyon returned the beads, Clemens called this incident the coup de grace to his faith in her honesty and good character. Yet his vehement reaction to this minor theft seems grossly out of proportion against Lyon's real theft of three years of his daughter's life—a much more painful fact to come to grips with and one he faced only by degrees.[8]

———

"Dear child," he wrote to Jean four days after he fired Mrs. Ashcroft, "you will be as welcome as if it were your mother herself calling you home from exile!" On April 26, 1909, Jean was joyfully restored to her father, and the week of grace that Peterson had granted turned in to a permanent stay. She was "eloquently glad and grateful" in Clemens's words, "to cross her father's threshold again." Having so yearned for that day, she must have devoured the moment. Both father and daughter were happy, but his feelings could not compare to hers. For as she crossed his threshold, she knew she loved her father while he could not yet anticipate how much he would grow to love her.[9]

One of Ashcroft's last acts as Twain's business manager had been to purchase a local farm for the boss. Clemens now gave this farm of about seventy acres to his daughter, who began immediately to turn it into a working unit. She repaired the house and barn and bought chickens and ducks from the surrounding farmers. As usual, she gloried in spending time outdoors, working on the farm and riding for pleasure. Jean also begged to take over the role of Twain's secretary, happily paying his bills and answering his letters. She soaked up the pleasures of being at home.[10]

Never a helpless invalid, Jean was now working like a day laborer and loving it. Finally allowed to live in her father's house, she rose before seven, ate a quick breakfast, and rode to get the mail at the post office. By nine she was giving her father his newspaper, exchanging pleasantries, and glancing at a few of his letters. Then she changed clothes and spent the rest of the morning at her farm, where her tasks included mixing chicken feed, feeding her brood, watering her hepatica plants, and doing some light carpentry. She usually returned to Stormfield around noon, where she worked on her father's bank books and other accounts. Eating a quick twenty-minute lunch around one, she went back to her farm, where she often worked until four. She returned to Stormfield for tea around half-past four and then worked in her room, writing checks and business letters, addressing envelopes, and going over accounts for her father. "At 7:00 we had dinner," she concluded a description of her day, "and after dinner I played billiards with my father until 9:00! Arrived in my room I was finally allowed to look at the newspaper, the first in four or five days and to read a little in a book, I went to sleep (I was already in bed) at 10:00."[11]

"Jean is a surprise & a wonder," Sam wrote to Clara three months later. A surprise because he had not really troubled himself to understand her before she was exiled. And having had almost no communication with his daughter for three years that was not heavily manipulated or totally censored by his secretary, he was shocked to discover Jean's "wisdom, courage, definiteness, decision; also goodness." Now Jean could talk to her father unmolested by conniving doctors, spying associates, and the lady-in-waiting—and the stereotype of the "epileptic personality" melted away. He discovered she had "a humane spirit, charity, kindliness, pity; industry, perseverance, intelligence, a clean mind, a clean soul, dignity, honesty, truthfulness, high ideals, loyalty, faithfulness to duty—she is everything Miss Lyon isn't."[12]

Her father found the great truth he had missed all along about his daughter—she was "like her mother." Maybe his judgment sprang from an upsurge of guilt at their reunion, but he was also influenced by fresh observation and experience. "Jean's—like her mother's—was a fine character; there is no finer," he concluded. And how could he not be swept off his feet by a child who played billiards? Now that Jean was home at last, her father was deeply involved in the process of getting reacquainted.[13] Conditioned to think of Jean only in negative terms, he was genuinely surprised by the happiness he felt. His enlightenment was a wonder of courage and cussedness—his hallmarks.

Jean was not the only refugee who reappeared at Stormfield soon after Lyon was fired. Horace Hazen came to pay his respects, probably timing his first visit to coincide with the news of Lyon's fall that traveled the local gossip circuit. Clemens jumped at the opportunity to ask his former butler why he had falsely claimed that Clara fired him. When Horace calmly responded that Ashcroft had "*made him do it!,*" Clemens was shocked and genuinely perplexed. "Ashcroft? How could Ashcroft make you do it, & he away down in Virginia?" Horace explained that Ashcroft had returned to Stormfield just after Clemens himself had departed and told him that he was going to be discharged. At Ashcroft's instruction Horace wrote a letter to his boss using the word "discharge," which, the business manager assured him, would be worth a month's salary. Ashcroft had then carried the letter away, practically before the ink was dry. Clemens was dumbfounded. Convinced by the young butler's version of events, he began to revise radically his estimate of his business manager.[14]

The only concrete action against the Ashcrofts was still pending: an independent audit to be supervised by Henry Rogers. After answering Rogers's summons to discuss the financial imbroglio, Ashcroft dashed off a letter to his boss. At first glance, his purposes seem innocent. The audit would soon prove, he wrote, that Clemens's affairs were conscientiously managed by both "Miss Lyon and me." But Ashcroft could not contain his contempt for Clara. Her charges, he claimed, "emanated from a brain diseased with envy, malice and jealousy, and it is only when one forgets this fact that one views them seriously." Nor could he contain his fury at the unjust treatment accorded his new wife. The business manager then painted a dramatic turnabout in Henry Rogers's attitude toward Lyon and Clara. "Mr. Rogers seems to be of the same opinion that many of your other friends are," he lectured Clemens; "that the ghastly treatment accorded to Miss Lyon during the past few weeks by a member of your family is a mightily poor return for the way in which she has, since Mrs. Clemens' death, looked after you, your daughters and your affairs."[15]

Did Henry Rogers, after voicing his "suspicion of things" and calling Clara's story "convincing" in a letter to her father, actually tell the business manager that Clara's treatment of his wife was "ghastly" and unfair? It is doubtful that Rogers betrayed his famous friend in defense of Mrs.

Ashcroft. Perhaps Mr. Ashcroft simply projected his own feelings of contempt for Mark Twain's daughters onto the man behind the desk at Standard Oil. "There is no reason on earth why the rest of your days should be spent in an atmosphere of artificiality, restraint and self-sacrifice," Ashcroft scolded his boss. Clearly, he thought Twain's daughters were irrelevancies, if not impediments, to the famous author's personal pleasure. "[A]nd while I don't suppose that the happiness that was your lot during the last six months of 1908 will recur in all its fulness and entirety," he sneered, "still I trust that you will, regardless of your philosophical theories, exercise your prerogatives of fatherhood and manhood in a way that will be productive of the greatest benefit to yourself."[16]

If Ashcroft was attempting to prod some chivalric defense of his wife from her ex-boss, his undisguised arrogance produced the opposite result. "I am nearly 74 & a figure in the world," Twain said, "yet he blandly puts himself on an equality with me, & insults me as freely & as frankly as if I were his fellow-bastard & born in the same sewer." But Ashcroft's disdain for the boss who he believed was not man enough to control his daughters misses the point. It was not his daughters—or the Ashcrofts—Clemens needed to control; it was himself. A virtual puppet of Lyon, who pulled his strings for years, he finally dislodged the pair of manipulators through self-rule. It never occurred to the business manager that the old man had a spine.[17]

———

Clemens discovered around the first of May that Rogers's second secretary, a Miss Watson, had been put in charge of the audit. This disturbed him, because he feared that a woman would be more susceptible to lies and flattery than a man and that she would become the Ashcrofts' friend and champion rather than their judge.[18] (His own gullibility and the disastrous effects this had upon his family entirely escaped his gender calculations.) Clemens calmed himself, however, with the thought that Rogers would be the final arbiter.

While he was awaiting the results of the audit, an unexpected and accidental revelation destroyed whatever credibility Mrs. Ashcroft still had with her former boss. On May 9 or 10 Clemens and Paine were being driven to the train station by Harry Lounsbury when one of them mentioned the cost of rehabilitating Lyon's cottage—$1,500.

"Lounsbury said, 'Fifteen hundred?'" Clemens remembered. "'Why, it cost thirty-five hundred!'"

Clemens argued with Lounsbury, telling him that Lyon had given him the exact figures a day or two before Christmas. But the general contractor did not budge from his numbers. Right then and there he produced "his deadly memorandum book" from which he furnished "the figures, the names, & the dates." Sam was stunned, but he had more surprises in store. "The dates showed that Miss Lyon had spent about $2,000 of my money on her house *before* I had offered to assist her with a loan," he wrote incredulously. Though he claimed this honor for the theft of the carnelian beads, it was Lounsbury's little memorandum book that actually fixed Miss Lyon's dishonesty in his mind.[19]

Clemens spoke the lethal words: "This was plain simple, stark-naked *theft.*" Up until that moment, he had believed that the numbers furnished by his ex-secretary were entirely trustworthy. Once he discovered the duplicity surrounding her cottage renovation, his attitude shifted abruptly. This was an important turning point. Before Lounsbury brought out the memorandum book, Clemens had only been conducting an "inquiry" meant to satisfy Clara. After the incident, he was pursuing a "case" with legal ramifications. He immediately put the matter in the hands of his lawyer, John Stanchfield. On May 25 Paine and Clemens went to see Stanchfield, who, perhaps in part because of the unexpected death of Henry Rogers on May 19, wanted the audit transferred to an independent accounting firm.[20] Clemens retrieved the checkbooks and vouchers from Miss Watson, whose coldness confirmed his earlier suspicions that her investigation was being influenced by the "injured-servant tears" of Mrs. Ashcroft. A professional accountant was now in charge of the inquiry.

The final auditor's report confirmed that "IVL" (for Isabel V. Lyon) was added at a later period to many check stubs with the original notation: "Work on the Redding House." Lyon had indeed merged the costs of Clemens's house construction with her own remodeling jobs. Afterwards she fiddled with the checkbook stubs in a crude attempt to cover up her theft, apparently hoping to convey the impression that she was keeping track of her own expenses. The ink being less darkened by age, however, meant that her revisionist impulse could not be disguised.[21]

Once the "deadly" memorandum book appeared, Paine urged Clemens to hunt for more evidence of her graft and thievery. After their visit to Standard Oil to reclaim the checkbooks, Paine took the boss to an Armenian rug dealer, remembering that Lyon had borrowed $45 from him to buy a rug that cost $90. They discovered that she had paid the balance with her boss's checkbook. Paine also trotted the boss to Strohmeyer's, where they found that she had purchased $115 worth of furniture for her newly refurbished cottage, probably paid for by means of Clemens's handy checkbook. Lyon loved objets d'art and had an eye for style, color, and design, which Clemens lauded. On a salary of $50 per month, which she stretched to support her aging mother, it is likely that while she shopped for his house in Redding, she was also decorating her own. It would have been effortless to combine the decorating expenses for both houses; she already had practice merging her construction costs with his.[22]

But she also had another source of revenue available to her that could not be traced. The Clemens household version of petty cash, referred to as "house money" within the family, was used "only for trifling expenses which could not be paid by check," Clemens explained. This untraceable source of cash—$5,500 for a two-year period—was a ready temptation. Lyon turned down several offers of a raise, perhaps based upon a less formal "arrangement." "House money" may have functioned in her mind as something akin to a personal expense account, which she no doubt justified as a well-deserved salary augmentation. "She was not an easy creature to understand," Twain admitted. Why would she turn down a raise, he wondered, and yet steal money from him? Why, if she were hard up for cash, would she refuse his checks to buy gowns?[23] The answer, of course, is that the secretary had stopped making a distinction between her money and his. In her own mind she had no need for a salary, much less a raise. She had no need for special checks to buy gowns, much less permission to use his cash. In her mind, she had ceased to be his employee; she had become his virtual "wife."

———

Another lightning bolt struck Stormfield at the end of May 1909. On a trip from the train station to the Ashcrofts' cottage, Harry Lounsbury's son, also named Harry, was discussing the local gossip about Clemens with Ralph. "He!" Ashcroft snorted. "I can sell his house, over his head, for a thousand dollars, whenever I want to!" Harry told his father, who told Paine, who, "greatly worried," approached Clemens with the dramatic news.[24]

The old man was sanguine, believing it was all brag, but Paine and Clara were not so certain. They decided to visit the local notary, Nickerson, who had routinely affixed his seal on documents brought to him by Twain's emissaries. He recalled certifying Clemens's signature on a general power of attorney in November or December; he thought both Ashcroft and Lyon were assignees. Clemens was convinced that Nickerson was wrong, but Paine insisted that they search the New York banks. With Clemens lounging at his hotel, Paine went on his hunt and, in the Liberty National Bank, found the pirated treasure: a comprehensive power of attorney. Clemens was astonished. "By it I transferred all my belongings, down to my last shirt, to the Ashcrofts, to do as they pleased with," he quipped sarcastically. Having gone through a painful bankruptcy that had left deep scars, he was not a man to be casual about his last shirt. "These people had not asked me for a power of attorney," he stated categorically and unequivocally, "and I had not conferred one upon them. The subject had never been mentioned."[25]

Those who believe in the innocence of Ashcroft and Lyon doubt Twain's memory or suspect he was getting dotty in his seventy-third year. "Self-incriminating" is what one biographer calls his indictment of the pair; he concludes that Twain was "a gullible and foolish man" who created the Ashcrofts' corruption "in his own mind."[26] Even Twain would agree that he was gullible and foolish. But the evidence of his activities in 1908—and of the 429 pages of detailed, forcefully argued criticisms of his newly discovered foes that he composed the following year—suggests that he was far from intellectually feeble. There is every reason to believe he was in full possession of his mental faculties in November 1908 when he signed—and supposedly forgot—a comprehensive power of attorney that gave his business manager and secretary virtually complete control of his estate while he was alive.

At the beginning of 1908 Twain gave a moving speech at the Lotos Club banquet in his honor, came home, and played billiards with Paine until quarter to four in the morning. In the spring he spoke at the Cartoonists' dinner, the Booksellers' banquet, the British Schools and University Club, and a dedication for the City College of New York. In late June he gave a spontaneous eulogy at a memorial for his friend Thomas

Bailey Aldrich that swayed his audience with ripples and then waves of laughter. During the fall of 1908 he could talk for long stretches on geology and time, the future of democracy, King Leopold's depredations in Africa, the history of Tacitus as compared with the biblical accounts of Rome, the unseen forces of creation, and the unity of nature. This display of mental agility and range came at the very time he was supposedly going senile.[27]

What is intriguing about Ashcroft's power of attorney, beyond its dubious origin, is that it included Lyon. One wonders why he included her and if she was in on the ruse beforehand. Twain pondered the question himself. "Ashcroft had conceived the ideal of robbing me on a comprehensive & exhaustive scale," he concluded, "& he did not feel safe to carry out this plan without first closing Miss Lyon's mouth."[28] In making her a confederate on the General Power of Attorney, Twain believed that her future husband effectively beguiled her or frightened her into fraud on a grand scale.

Ironically Twain's interpretation is very similar to the one Lyon offered some thirty years later, when she told the detective posing as a literary go-between that Ashcroft "proved to be a forger and all-around crook for whose actions she was equally blamed." But her protestations of innocence should always be viewed skeptically. Ever willing to revise history to suit her needs, she told the detective a string of lies.[29] The veracity of her charge that Ashcroft alone was to blame for unnamed fraud and theft—probably encompassing the power of attorney—is problematic at best. She was already "borrowing" money to renovate and furnish her Redding cottage. And as signer of the checks, she had long ago lost the distinction between Clemens's money and her own. It might have taken little to persuade her that with this power of attorney she would be able to protect her boss from everyone else: errant daughters, avaricious relatives, and benighted friends. She was treating him like a precocious child and she the doting, though occasionally stern, mother. She could easily have rationalized this additional power as one more self-sacrificing act to save him from himself.

The fact is, however, that the power of attorney was never used to rob Twain. There was no rush, he noted wisely: he was seventy-three, and "they could go on living upon me comfortably until I should some day get sick unto death, then they could sell my securities & my Mark Twain stock & decamp." Or, even more chilling, they could remain and "furnish death-bed approvals of their acts," he wrote, "worded in the first person, & with my signature forged to them." Or after he was dead, if his transfer signature had remained on all his stocks and bonds, they might have legally transferred ownership to themselves, and pocketed what he estimated at over a million dollars. "However," he mused in his classic deadpan, "I didn't die."[30]

Whether the pair intended to use the power of attorney for good or ill can never be established, but its fraudulent origins cast a pall on their motives. Moreover, by taking the unusual legal precautions he did to certify the document's legitimacy, Ashcroft was behaving as if he had some guilty knowledge. Curiously, he incriminated himself in a bizarre memo he sent to Clemens's lawyers, itemizing all the unpaid labor he had rendered his boss, with a mocking dollar value attached to each claim. The man Friday suggested, for example, that he was owed $880 for "accompanying Mr. Clemens to England," and $500 "for his services in checking over Miss Lyon's account." With daring nonchalance, he included an unpaid fee of $10 for drafting the power of attorney.[31]

Smarting from the calculated insult, Clemens reacted furiously to Ashcroft's mock charges. First, he sent his lawyer a counter list of charges for services that *he* had rendered Ashcroft. For example, he requested $500 compensation for introducing Ashcroft to the Lord Mayors of London and Liverpool, many London journalists, and members of Parliament. "But for me," he noted, "he could not have gotten access to these prominent and useful men." Still angry, he penned a point-by-point rebuttal to Ashcroft's cheeky inventory and vigorously denounced Ashcroft's insulting mock-fee of $10 for the power of attorney. He once again repudiated the legitimacy of this legal instrument and "all acts perpetrated by the Ashcrofts under its false authority." Ashcroft apparently used the power of attorney once to sell some Knickerbocker Bank stock five points under its market value without Clemens's knowledge. Clemens suggests that the $800 brokerage fee was split between the broker and Ashcroft. Even if this is true, he suffered relatively minor damage. In any event, on June 1 he formally revoked the legal power that he never knowingly gave away, thus ending a significant danger to his family.[32]

Clemens was now thoroughly disillusioned. By the end of May, he had moved from an almost unshakable faith in Lyon's integrity, honesty, and trustworthiness to the extreme opposite opinion. "The muscle in her chest that does duty for a heart," he wrote, "is nothing but a potato." Clemens suddenly wanted her out of his sight, out of his life— and he definitely did not want her to remain his neighbor. "[S]he cares for no one but herself," he recognized with a shudder. This was the same judgment he made of his business manager. "What I always admired about Ashcroft," he wrote ironically, "was his diligence & single-mindedness in looking out for Number One."[33]

CHAPTER 15

Confrontation

AT THE OUTSET OF his reunion with Jean, Sam was deeply impressed by her energy, pace, and strength, all of which contrasted with the "sick" image cultivated so assiduously by his former secretary. "Not a single symptom of her cruel malady has ever shown itself," he said proudly. His judgment of her health and fitness to rejoin him continued, however, to be grounded in a symptom-free standard. He never fully understood how this standard had contributed to Jean's exile. What he did comprehend was that his youngest daughter was a delight and that that "reptile Lyon" had been mistress of his house while Jean was "barred out of it."[1]

At the end of May, Sam encountered a fact so unsettling that he waffled about its accuracy. Most likely through tête-à-têtes with Jean, he discovered that his youngest daughter had been healthy enough to return home for two years—even by his own criteria. Jean had experienced few grand mal seizures since April 1907, and only three since her return from Germany in January 1909. He quickly backed away from this discovery. Finding it difficult to admit the enormity of his failure as a father, he returned to counting her exile in months rather than years in his autobiographical writing. Only sporadically could he bring himself to face the actual length of his daughter's banishment and with it the extent of his own complicity.[2]

Ashcroft had predicted that, surrounded by his children, Clemens would spend the rest of his days "in an atmosphere of artificiality, restraint and self-sacrifice."[3] Nothing could have been further from the truth. The athletic Jean delighted in her farm. And both father and daughter took pleasure in each other's company and in her new role as his secretary.

———

In early June, while the independent audit was in full swing, the Ashcrofts left Connecticut. In a letter written to Clemens on June 3, Ashcroft indicated that the couple would sail for England "in a few days to be gone about four weeks." Suspecting that their intention was to flee prosecution, one of Twain's lawyers, an associate of John Stanchfield named Charles Lark, asked Ashcroft to remain in the United States until the independent audit was finished. "[H]e had not engaged passage," Ashcroft told Lark on the telephone, "and had no idea whatever as to when he would sail." But Ashcroft and his wife boarded an obscure steamer bound for Holland on June 8.[4] Their deception created an especially dramatic impression of guilt and fear for Twain's lawyers.

Almost immediately, the lawyers retaliated by suggesting that their client attach Mrs. Ashcroft's Connecticut cottage to recover the money she had stolen for its renovation. Twain acquiesced, unprepared for the media circus that this action would trigger. The local sheriff conveyed the news to the papers, according to Twain, and it was cabled straight to London, where Ashcroft had chummy relations with reporters based on his earlier trip to Oxford with Twain. The Ashcrofts were jumped upon by the press as soon as they arrived in London, and, as Twain quipped, "the cable began to twang." And the telephone to ring. Alone in the house, Jean answered the phone and talked to a reporter, breaking a longstanding rule of the Clemens household. She guilelessly told the reporter that Lyon had stolen her father's money to renovate her farmhouse.[5]

Mrs. Ashcroft vowed to newspaper audiences around the world, in response to Jean's interview, that she would return immediately to vindicate herself. She declared her intention to clear all the false charges lodged against her by Miss Clemens. "[S]he must know," both Ashcrofts asserted, "that every step taken in the restoration of the farmhouse in Connecticut was with her father's knowledge and approval." Citing the loan of $1,000 signed by Mr. Ashcroft, the couple claimed that there had been "no request made by Mark Twain for repayment of any money spent," which was technically true, followed by a lie, "while Miss Lyon several times refused suggestions on his part to consider the cost of renovation as a present from him."[6]

Mrs. Ashcroft had just put an ocean between herself and Twain. Why return to America alone? What was the urgency?[7] Did she still think she could worm her way into Twain's good graces? She was coming back to vindicate herself, she said, and clear her name. A melodrama of reconciliation seems to have been playing in her head. Stepping onto the docks of New York on July 13, she was greeted by a bevy of reporters whom she was glad to oblige with an interview.[8] "Mr. Clemens is one of the most lovable of men," she crooned, "and no one has known him better than I." "I am confident," she revealed, "that this reported action on his part was not made voluntarily." There it is—the reason for her precipitous return. Clemens had not turned against her, she believed, but was forced against his will to take legal action by his daughter. But the newspapers offered different opinions about which daughter to blame: Jean or Clara.[9]

All the newspaper accounts agreed, however, that Mrs. Ashcroft intended to make haste to Redding and beard her lovable ex-boss in his den, clearing up their misunderstanding in the process. She, as usual, exhibited a talent for revisionist history. "Questioned as to whether she was financially indebted to Mr. Clemens," one newspaper reported, "Mrs. Ashcroft replied that at the time he gave her the house he had also advanced her $4,000 to rehabilitate it." Less than a year before, when she was practically able to convince him that black was white, this readjustment of the truth would not have been a serious problem. But in July 1909, Clemens had awakened fully from his sleepwalk. He had lent her $1,500 last Christmas, he reiterated privately, after she had already spent $2,000 on unreported renovations, a sum that was documented by the contractor himself.[10]

One part of her interview with the newspapers was accurate. She returned to her Redding cottage the next day accompanied by her mother. But she remained inside, seeking no contact with Clemens or his family. Still taking her at her word, Clemens summoned his lawyer to Stormfield, hoping they could arrange a settlement on the spot. For two days Clemens and Lark waited—and nothing happened. Finally, Mr. Lark suggested their side take the initiative, go to her cottage, and open negotiations. Of course, he would need a witness. But who?

"Paine?" Clemens asked. "Oh, *hell* no! Me? Oh, *hell* no! It wouldn't be a conference, it would be a riot, right at the start. And who would get the worst of it? Paine & me. That cat would scratch our eyes out."[11] The two brave men scurried for cover and eagerly pushed Jean out into the open field—asking her to confront the woman who had exiled her for three years.

———

After Jean was restored to her family, only a novelist would have imagined a face-to-face meeting between the exile and her nemesis. But occasionally, life imitates art. And in this case, a firsthand account of the event was recorded by one of the chief protagonists. At the bidding of her father, Jean agreed to make a call on Isabel Ashcroft, accompanied by Mr. Lark. "[T]ake sharp note of everything," her father admonished her, "for you might have to go into court some day as a witness."[12] At his bidding, she wrote a twenty-four-page narrative of her experience.

On Saturday, July 17, Jean and Mr. Lark drove down to Mrs. Ashcroft's cottage. Mrs. Ashcroft's mother, Mrs. Lyon, met Jean and Lark at the door around 11:00 A.M. and told them that her daughter was too ill to see them. Lark asked Mrs. Lyon to telephone him at Stormfield if her daughter was able to receive them later. The telephone rang almost as soon as they walked in the door at Stormfield, with the news that Mrs. Ashcroft would see Mr. Lark between 2:00 and 2:30 P.M. She requested an audience alone, which he refused, explaining that he had to have a witness in attendance.[13]

After lunch, Jean and Lark again drove down to the cottage. They were admitted by Mrs. Lyon, who was dressed as if in mourning. Before Jean was fully seated, Mrs. Ashcroft entered the room, clothed in white, with no ornamentation except her rings. Deliberately avoiding eye contact with Jean, she stared at Mr. Lark while bowing slightly during her entrance. Jean acknowledged her by quietly pronouncing her name. With Jean and Lark already seated on the sofa, Mrs. Lyon took the large armchair nearest the lawyer, and her daughter sat in a small chair nearest Jean. Thus Jean was positioned between Mr. Lark and Mrs. Ashcroft.[14]

Their seating launched an awkward silence, finally interrupted by Mr. Lark. The newspapers had reported Mrs. Ashcroft's return and her intention to settle her dispute with Mr. Clemens, he reminded the small assembly. Since she had not appeared at Stormfield, he explained, they had decided to approach her at home. Mrs. Lyon interrupted Lark at that point, pleading with the lawyer to treat her daughter as a lady. Mrs. Ashcroft curtly admonished her mother to keep still and not interfere. A more sympathetic Lark turned to Mrs. Lyon, telling her that he had every intention of treating her daughter as a lady. He suggested, however, that Mrs. Lyon might prefer to withdraw, as the conversation could be difficult for her. With no response from either daughter or mother, Lark plunged into the heart of the matter.[15]

At first Mrs. Ashcroft denied knowledge of any possible reason for the attachment on her house. She argued that she had not been allowed to see the checkbooks and had not been given the chance to make a statement based upon examination of her financial records. Lark responded that she and her husband had in fact made a "statement of the cost of putting her house in order" that was "absolutely incorrect." She countered that if she could have access to the bills, she could prove that her cost estimates were correct. Lark then shifted ground. Who had done most of the work on her house, he asked? The only people who had worked on both houses were Lounsbury, Adams, the carpenter, and Hull, the plumber, she replied, and their work had amounted to very little. "It was Hull's bill of over $400," Lark reminded her, "which she had put down as work done at 'Stormfield.'"[16]

Jean observed that Mrs. Ashcroft gave Lark "a long pathetic, absolutely unwinking gaze" meant to melt an iceberg. But Lark did not thaw. "She was very sorry," she said wearily, "if she had done wrong." Soon rallying for another round, she insisted that Clemens gave her permission to use his money for her own house repairs. Lark replied that she had drawn checks as far back as the summer of 1907 and that Clemens had not authorized use of his funds until the summer of 1908. After several attacks and parries, Lark put Clemens's offer on the table. If she would deed back the property, and repay the $1,500 mortgage she had just drawn on the cottage, Clemens would drop his lawsuit. Lark then added an incentive. A huge amount of house money—$4,000 cash was Lark's figure—had been drawn for which there was no explanation. Clemens would overlook that disparity if she would deed him back her cottage and leave the neighborhood.[17]

The detailed account of the costs of renovating Lyon's cottage that Lounsbury had kept in his little memorandum book may have been the sharpest thorn in her side, but the auditors had located another patch of bramble. They found that she had racked up over $5,500 in house money charges for a two-year period ending in February 1909.[18] Although Clemens was certain that his household "never needed more than $300 or $400 cash in a year," he woefully underestimated the cash demands of his domestic circle. Paine, a more practical man with a clearer grasp of the debit and credit line, roughly estimated that $1,500 was necessary to meet those demands. If one accepts Paine's estimate of legitimate expenses, simple arithmetic suggests that $2,500 in cash withdrawals made by Lyon are suspect. Larger figures were cited by Lark and Clemens, but this smaller amount seems to be the most responsible estimate. In fact there is no way to prove that any of the house money was stolen.[19] But Lark's suggestion that she filched some portion of the cash withdrawals charged to house money seems all but certain.

Mrs. Ashcroft was resistant. She claimed she bought most of the furnishings for Mr. Clemens's new house with cash, a feeble defense that was easily discredited.[20] She never had a large bank account, she offered next as proof of her innocence. Lark was unpersuaded.

'Did you support your mother during part of 1907 and 1908?' he asked.

'Yes,' she answered, 'beginning in the winter of 1907.'

'Do you realize that Mrs. Lyon's board would use up the greater part of your salary?' he pressed. Mother and daughter both protested that Mrs. Lyon's board was never more than $8.50 per week.

'That leaves Miss Lyon fifteen dollars to dress on,' the lawyer replied pointedly.

'Mr. Clemens gave me permission to buy clothing,' she countered, 'because I several times declined a higher salary.'

"I told Mr. Lark," Jean interjected for the first time, "that that permission had not been given in New York but here, last winter."

Lark circled back to the settlement offer, emphasizing that Clemens was being more than generous under the circumstances. Mr. Clemens would be taking her to court if she were a man, Lark reminded her; he was willing to settle out of court only because she was a woman.[21]

The lawyer then supplemented his presentation with a dose of intimidation. Clemens was growing impatient and angry. Since Mrs.

Ashcroft "felt unwilling to accept the proposition now made," Lark threatened, a "complaint had been made out by the Grand Juror of the district and would be handed in. When she didn't understand what that meant," Jean continued, "he explained that the complaint would be given to the prosecuting attorney of this county."[22] Mrs. Ashcroft remained calm or at least, as Jean noted, "controlled herself admirably." Mrs. Lyon asked if they intended to include furniture in the settlement. Lark responded negatively—only land, barn, and cottage.

"Mrs. Ashcroft said she *couldn't* give up her home," Jean had already noted, "that she would raise the money to pay everything back with, that she had borrowed from Father with the understanding that she was to pay when she was able to, that she was very sorry, must think a while, first, was unable to do so, must talk it over with her mother, must see her lawyer before deciding." She also wanted to go to New York to see Stanchfield, Clemens's chief lawyer, whom she knew and had entertained. Lark suggested that she would not be allowed to leave the jurisdiction of the state, alluding once again to possible criminal proceedings.[23]

"I'm very sorry," she kept muttering, on the verge of surrender.

"You know I wouldn't do such a thing, don't you, Mother?" she asked plaintively, alluding to the charges of embezzlement.

"No dear, of course you wouldn't," her mother responded.

"Mrs. Lyon," Lark replied sternly, "you were not a witness on those occasions, the checks are the witnesses of that fact."[24]

Twice Mrs. Ashcroft repeated that she would raise the money to pay everything back, and finally she told Lark "to do as he chose, that she and her mother 'had each other' and were satisfied with that." Lark said he would return with the deed for her signature on Monday morning and, as he and Jean were leaving, mother and daughter fell weeping into each other's arms.[25]

But the drama for the day was not yet over. Lark discovered that a deed could be obtained from the notary on the spot. So he hurried back to Summerfield with Nickerson, the notary, who read the deed aloud to Mrs. Ashcroft in the back parlor while Jean and Lark sat in the front parlor with Mrs. Lyon, who had her back to them all the while.

After the reading was finished, Mrs. Ashcroft signed the deed back to Clemens and drafted the mortgage check, albeit with a great deal of nervousness and some confusion as to the date and the correct procedure. Nickerson then handed her the dollar bill "necessary to make such a proceeding legal"; she tore the dollar in half and threw it on the floor, "screaming and exclaiming that she would not take it." Nickerson retrieved the two halves of the dollar and carefully tucked them into his wallet.[26]

Tearfully pointing out that they had no place to go, Mrs. Lyon asked if they could stay until September 15. Lark agreed, but after he stepped outside, Jean objected to the nearly two-month grace period and suggested that September 1 was sufficient time. Lark stepped back inside and informed them that they had six weeks to vacate the premises. Mrs. Lyon telephoned soon after they reached Stormfield and asked Lark if they had to "live in daily dread of further trouble." Lark responded carefully that he thought Clemens would bring no other suit against them, but that the final decision was his client's alone.[27]

Lark's skillful manipulation was probably all in a day's work. Jean, however, was in a unique position. Her witnessing of Mrs. Ashcroft's humiliation was a special sort of dispensation. She did not seek revenge, but it had been given her, if not by the gods then by her father's lawyer. Her job was to observe the woman who had kept her away from her father for three years. What was Jean thinking and feeling? She reveals little, interjecting only one comment in the conversation itself. Her mode of reportage is dispassionate, with an emphasis on description and externally observable behaviors. Only in denying Mrs. Lyon's request to remain until September 15 was there a telltale hint of hostility.

Her father revealed some of the complications in her private attitude when he remarked that she "despised" Miss Lyon, but did not hate her.[28] This would fit Jean's character: an essentially fair-minded person who was sensitive to misfortune. Jean had suffered greatly from her disease, and her heart was tender toward the pain of others—even an antagonist.

Twain's reaction is also telling. Writing the next day, he described Miss Lyon as being "stretched upon the rack." "God will punish Paine. I know it," he told Clara. "Because he is so intemperately glad over yesterday's tragedy." While Paine was gloating, Clemens felt pity for his lady-in-waiting and called the incident a "tragedy."[29] Whatever it was, the episode outdid the most improbable fiction.

CHAPTER 16

A Formidable Adversary

SUSPICIOUS AND PERHAPS UNEASY, Twain's lawyer decided to ask Mrs. Ashcroft to sign a lease for the six weeks she had permission to remain in her cottage.[1] By this action, Mr. Lark was aiming to protect his client's interests as much as the law would allow. More than Mrs. Ashcroft's regret and fickleness was at stake here—Lark may have been worried that she would refuse to vacate the cottage or try to invalidate the transfer deed that returned ownership to Clemens. He went back to the cottage on July 20, three days after the transfer deed had been procured. Again in need of a witness, Lark deputized Clara to accompany him on his errand. This time, however, the determined lawyer would confront a more formidable adversary than he expected: Mrs. Ashcroft's mother.

Clemens had always harbored a vague antipathy toward Mrs. Lyon, finding her meekness and lack of humor uninteresting and even mildly irritating. He recognized, however, that her current situation was pitiful and that she was suffering "most undeservedly." She had been in hell with the Ashcrofts for several months, he noted sympathetically. Nevertheless, he described the poor woman, as only he could, as "a humble, unassuming Christian doughnut."[2] But Mrs. Lyon was about to exhibit more spunk, intelligence, and courage than he thought possible.

Mrs. Lyon greeted Lark's entourage, which also included the elder Mr. Lounsbury, on the porch by the kitchen door in an agitated frame of mind. Her daughter was ill, she told them. "You took an unfair advantage of us last Saturday and did not keep your word," she exclaimed loudly to Mr. Lark, "for you promised us to go away and bring back the deed in two or three days but instead of that you came back with it the same day and therefore it is not *legal*. My daughter does not even *know* what she signed and we are both of us *crazy*," Mrs. Lyon continued, her voice getting louder and louder. "[Y]ou intimidated her into giving her signature by threatening to arrest her if she didn't—and you *never* would have *dared* to do such a thing if there had been a *man* in the house."[3]

Mrs. Lyon did not once look at Clara, who nevertheless charged into the fray. "Mrs. Lyon I don't see why it should ever have been necessary for us to *ask* your daughter to return this property, why wasn't she eager to do it of her own accord?"

"Do you think *I* want to stay here another day?" Mrs. Lyon burst out. "Do you think I want this horrible land or house or anything remotely connected with the Clemens family? No—No—No. We're packing to get out as fast as we can—"

"Very good then Mrs. Lyon," Clara interrupted, "that is all that your daughter signed last Saturday, she merely returned what you do not want yourselves & what we have no use for as property but what we do want because of the circumstances which make your daughter's presence so unpleasant."

"If you had any pity, any pity…," Mrs. Lyon sobbed.

"I have great pity for you Mrs. Lyon," Clara said, "but none whatever for your daughter."

"I have never had one happy day in this house, not *one*," Mrs. Lyon cried.

"I know how unhappy you must have been for your daughter treated you so horribly," the emotionally inept Lark sputtered.

"My daughter treated me horribly? How *dare* you say such a thing? She has always been good to me, how dare you, how *dare* you?" Mrs. Lyon screamed as she rushed toward Mr. Lark.

Taken aback, Lark and Clara tried to appease her and persuaded her to sit down on a bench on the porch. Still weeping, she spoke again. "How could you accuse her of such things after her seven years of devotion to your family?" she sobbed quietly. "[S]he *lived* for you all and worked so hard in your interest—"

"That was what we believed," Clara said, "and we appreciated it and for that reason my father gave her this place & lent her money for the repairs—"

"She worked so very hard, looking after the servants and the household."

"And Mrs. Lyon, that is why we offered to get a housekeeper which she refused," Clara agreed sympathetically, "or to raise her salary which she refused. We tried to make her feel that she was one of us and when she did not wish to accept a higher salary for her increased services, I told her to at least buy herself dresses now and then which she was willing to do. But I can't talk about all this with you, Mrs. Lyon," Clara gently sought closure, "there are so many things that are impossible to say to you about your own daughter."

"But what is it all anyway," asked Mrs. Lyon, still sobbing. "We haven't any money. We haven't a bit—"

"You haven't any—no," Clara agreed.

"Nor has Isabel."

"No I suppose not—"

"Well then," Mrs. Lyon asked perceptively, "who do you think has it, Mr. Ashcroft?"

"It does not matter who has it, Mrs. Lyon, for it is not the money we want," Clara reiterated, "it's merely this house and land and that you have relinquished."

Though Mrs. Lyon was, in Clara's words, "sobbing and moaning all the time she talked," she continued to ask the smart questions.

"Why did your father give power of attorney to my daughter and then deny it afterwards?"

"He denied having seen the extraordinary paper by which Miss Lyon could possess herself of everything and ruin us if she chose."

"But she didn't use it."

"No, Mrs. Lyon, she hadn't yet and I do not believe that your daughter did all these things by herself. Of course she was influenced but it was a terrible thing for her to *be* influenced when she held that powerful and trusted position."

"Yes—Yes," Mrs. Lyon muttered, "[S]he *lived* for you all and worked so hard in your interest—"[4]

"I used to think so until I heard from various sides in New York that she was telling lies about me and betraying my confidences—she changed very much in the past two years."

"Yes she has changed," Mrs. Lyon admitted, "but she has been very ill for some time; and then why did you not answer the letter she sent your father asking whether it would be all right for her to go to England instead of waiting 'till she got over there and then shaming her by attaching her property and letting it all come out in the newspapers."

"My father never received any such letter, and besides Mr. Stanchfield telephoned to Mr. Ashcroft in New York and told him not to go to England as he needed him & Mrs. Ashcroft here. The whole thing got into the papers through the Bridgeport notary and not through us for certainly we did not care for this newspaper talk—"

Clara, suddenly feeling like the accused, broke out vehemently— "Mrs. Lyon your daughter is guilty—*guilty.*"

"Guilty of what?" she asked, rising and rushing out to the grass beyond the porch where Mr. Lounsbury and another man were standing. "Do you hear what Miss Clemens says? She says my daughter has been guilty of stealing, of stealing, of stealing," she screamed uncontrollably. Lounsbury observed Mrs. Ashcroft peering out of an upstairs window while Clara and the men below tried to comfort and calm her distraught mother.[5]

"Why didn't you come and settle it all with us instead of going to the law about it and ruining our name for life?" Mrs. Lyon sobbed that she had never been in such a position before and could not live through the disgrace.

"I might have gone to *you* but what good would it have done to go to your daughter?" Clara asked sincerely. "There never would have been all this trouble anyway if she had simply left our vicinity instead of insisting upon staying here."

"But she had done nothing wrong, she *couldn't.* Yet think what we have got to face. All her friends ask her why she does not refute these accusations but of what use is it for *her* to refute them, your father is the only one who can do that. Oh! I have always believed in my God in Heaven. I had faith in my Redeemer, but what trouble I have had and still have."

Clara was so moved that she began to cry. Seeing her tears, Mrs. Lyon put one arm around Clara's neck and pleaded, "Please say in the paper that she never did anything that wasn't perfectly honorable and straight."

"Would you like us to say that she has made restitution and that her accounts had gotten mixed because of overwork?" Clara offered compassionately, first glancing at Lark.

Mrs. Lyon agreed but then thought it was probably better for them to say nothing. Suddenly her knees seemed to buckle, and she exclaimed, "I feel so sick, so sick." They helped her into the house and laid her on the living room sofa.

Clara leaned over to say good-bye. "You nearly killed her when you suspected her of taking things that time in the garret when Dorothea Gilder was there—" Mrs. Lyon whispered in a low voice, referring to the altercation over the missing carnelian beads. Clara defended herself against the accusation.

Sobbing again, Mrs. Lyon drew Clara down even closer and confided barely above a whisper in her ear. "If she ever did anything wrong it was because she was ill."[6]

No one benefited from this encounter. Mrs. Lyon was an emotional wreck when the Clemens entourage finally left. Ironically, it was not his legal maneuvers, but Lark's inept attempt at sympathy that pushed her into her emotional spinout. As a result, he did not get his lease. Mrs. Lyon informed the lawyer that her daughter would not sign a lease because she intended to take his client to court to annul the transfer deed. Lark told Clemens that he was untroubled. Mrs. Ashcroft's attorney would not approve an action to set the deed aside, he asserted. Though Lark's confidence was belied by his attempt to procure a lease, his prediction proved correct.[7]

Clara felt deep pity for Mrs. Lyon, but she was unable to assuage the poor woman's grief. Dignified and compassionate, Clara tried to defend the Twain side without further damaging Mrs. Lyon. This was an almost useless exercise, as Clara herself recognized. Almost, because Mrs. Lyon conceded the possibility that her daughter might have done something wrong. Mrs. Lyon had many opportunities to observe her child at close quarters. She could have been referring to her drinking in excusing her daughter "because she was ill."

What is remarkable is how quickly she put Clara on the defensive. Mrs. Lyon—a much shrewder woman than Twain imagined—succinctly summarized her daughter's side of the argument and sought a dialogue over what had happened. In her confrontation with Clara, she presented a multidimensional case against Twain. First, her daughter had served him devotedly for seven long years without adequate recompense, she argued. Attaching her house and forcing her to re-deed her property was the foulest, most ungrateful "repayment" imaginable. Second, mother and daughter were penniless. Where was all the money she had supposedly stolen? Third, why did Clemens deny the power of attorney he actually signed? And if there was any criminal intent, Mrs. Lyons asked pointedly, why was it that the power of attorney had never been used? Fourth, why did Clemens attach Isabel's property after she had left the country, when she had written him a letter asking permission to go abroad? Fifth, why did he not at least give her the courtesy of settling the dispute privately? Why bring in lawyers and involve her in the justice system, thus making her look like a criminal in front of her friends?

Mrs. Lyon's questions were poignant and incisive. She was caught up in her daughter's mixture of facts, lies, and half-truths. Sorting out one from the other is indeed difficult. Imagine Mrs. Lyon's quagmire, trying to decipher fact from fiction about her own child. The very questions she asked attest to the depth and honesty of her struggle. To her credit, she held out the possibility that her daughter was not totally innocent. Her vehement appeals are selflessly maternal: that her child be treated with respect, whatever her mistakes.

Though she was eager to enter the fray, Clara too acquitted herself with honor. She reacted with restraint and sympathy without abandoning her own position. Significantly, Clara's perception that Mrs. Ashcroft had changed over the past two years was shared by her mother. Mrs. Lyon blamed this change on "illness" while Clara blamed Ralph Ashcroft. Until he became her confidant, Isabel and Clara were practically sisters; without a doubt, Ralph came between the two women. It is tempting to blame him for most of her financial skullduggery as well. Twain himself hypothesized that Ashcroft taught his wife how to steal. And she told an undercover detective many years later that she was merely a pawn in Ashcroft's fraudulent financial schemes.[8]

A few inconvenient facts, however, mar this cultivated image of innocence. Lyon's animus against Jean predated Ashcroft's influence, as did her plot to keep Twain's daughter in exile. Clearly the Lioness was an accomplished manipulator before she ever met Ralph Ashcroft. Whether she was an accomplished thief is less certain. When she lived in Hartford, however, she managed the Hartford Woman's Exchange, an institution that sold crafts made by female members. According to the husband of a member who was sympathetic to Miss Lyon, she once faced a significant shortfall in her Exchange accounts and was rescued by the Whitmores and other friends, who got the money together to save her from a scandal.[9] Gossip is not proof, but there is at least the possibility that she was not a virgin to the temptations of easy money before she became the keeper of the Twain checkbook.

———

Twain eventually speculated that his former secretary was stealing money to support Ashcroft. It is possible but unlikely. To steal for Ashcroft would have required more unselfish inclination and planning than she gave to her thefts. Her embezzlement was more haphazard, spontaneous, and self-absorbed. Furthermore, she asked Ralph Ashcroft to marry her because she saw him as an anchor and refuge in the coming storm.[10] If she were stealing money to support him, he would not have appeared to be her future protector.

The question of where Ashcroft's money was coming from is an intriguing one, however. Even though Twain functioned as his boss, Ashcroft never drew a salary, except the commission he specified in one of his Clean-Up Day contracts.[11] Given the variety of services he performed as Sam's man Friday, including acting as his valet, the absence of a salary may seem strange. It is nevertheless consistent with Sam's desire to see Ralph and Isabel as his friends. He wanted to believe that their services were given as his intimates, not his employees. But if he did not provide Ashcroft with a salary, he was more than generous, even reckless, with his money in the investment arena, sinking $12,000 in Ashcroft's hairpin companies "upon his representation that it was a Good Thing." Clemens also persuaded John Stanchfield to invest $6,000 in hairpins.[12] Whether this was the result of malfeasance or just another in a long line of poor investment decisions on Twain's part, the stock was worthless at his death.

Twain's admission that one company "has never held a meeting, that I know of... has never made a report or an accounting to any one, so far as I know" indicts the author as much as the business manager. By requiring no accountability whatsoever, Twain gave Ashcroft a virtual $12,000 carte blanche—an amount of money that makes Miss Lyon's cottage renovations pale by comparison. "Hasn't Ashcroft been living on the stockholders' money?" Twain belatedly queried.[13] By his cavalier attitude toward money, he offered huge temptations and failed to provide his employees with any checks on their greed or their need.

Any claim regarding Ashcroft's fiscal dishonesty is mostly built on a mountain of circumstantial evidence. If he was an honest man, however, one conclusion is definite: he was a lousy financial adviser. Twain lost $12,000 in hairpins at Ashcroft's urging; $25,000 in a new version of Plasmon, which Ashcroft engineered; and $30,000 in the American Mechanical Cashier Company, the losing rival of the National Cash Register Company, another stock purchase that Ashcroft solicited.[14] What is most remarkable about these investments is that Twain recouped nary a penny. Admittedly the great humorist—and skeptic— was capable of squandering hundreds of thousands of dollars on his own steam, but the guidance of his business manager still stands out for its unerring folly.

CHAPTER 17

False Exoneration

RALPH ASHCROFT RETURNED TO America on July 27, 1909. Wasting no time, he met with Mr. Lark two days later and then sat down to write a summary of his position at the lawyer's request. Clearly, Ashcroft had come home prepared to mount a spirited defense of himself and his wife, which he undertook in his letter to the lawyers and in two carefully crafted statements he made to the *New York Times* in the course of the next weeks. Taken together, the letter and the statements yield important glimpses into the man. Revealing character, motives, and submerged feelings in his skillful assertions, the elusive individual who married Isabel Lyon comes into clearer focus.

Ashcroft's letter first demonstrates a strong loyalty to his wife. She did not seek power over Twain's family, he insisted. She acquired it through the default of his uncaring or inept daughters. Ashcroft's formulation of Lyon's motives is revealing in two ways. He indicts Clara and Jean for a lack of care and effective oversight of their father. And he extols his wife's high-minded purpose. Ashcroft blames the current dispute on "women's jealousy," referring to his bête noir, Clara Clemens. Twain had at first sided with Miss Lyon but drifted toward his daughters' camp, according to the business manager, after hearing only lopsided persuasions from his wife's enemies. In Ashcroft's mind, the old man was putty, never strong enough to resist the last person who had his ear. After observing Miss Lyon successfully manipulate her boss for years, he scoffed at Clemens's capacity to think and act independently. Energetically defending his new wife, Ashcroft invoked testimony from Henry Huttleston Rogers, now deceased and conveniently unavailable for corroboration. "[S]he came to the front," Twain's friend is supposed to have said, "and has stayed at the front all these years, and no one has any right to criticize her." Given Rogers's suspicion of the pair, the sentiment attributed to him is likely Ashcroft's own invention.[1]

Ashcroft also invented favorable audit results. "Miss Lyon courted a rigid investigation," he concluded, explaining that he spent two months preparing an account that was submitted to Rogers, whose secretary "reported that the account was correct." Since the lawyers reading the letter knew that the first examination of Twain's books by Rogers's secretary was incomplete and that the second audit had identified serious discrepancies, such lobbying efforts would seem to be wasted on them. They would not, however, be wasted on the Whitmores, the old Clemens family friends who had originally recommended their former governess for a job as Livy's secretary. In an obvious attempt to lobby the Hartford crowd, Ashcroft sent a copy of his letter to the Whitmores, at his wife's request, and invited them to show it to friends. Perhaps with those friends and acquaintances in mind, he reviewed his wife's many years of loyal service. "She loved Mr. Clemens as a daughter," he wrote the lawyers without a trace of irony, "anticipated his every wish and desire; labored day and night for seven years for him, and indulged in a sort of hero-worship; and the return that Mr. Clemens made her for these services and sacrifices has broken her down in health and spirit."[2]

His claim that she "indulged in a sort of hero-worship" is tinged with negativity. He described his own service to Clemens as motivated by "fondness and respect for him," but it was a respect that was strangely contemptuous. Displaying disdain for Clemens's nonliterary judgment and capacities, Ashcroft expressed neither admiration for nor veneration of his wife's employer. What he displayed in rich abundance, however, was an audacious sense of gamesmanship and a huge conceit. He demanded, as his condition for an amicable settlement, that Twain wholly and completely exonerate his former secretary of any financial improprieties. He also required that Clemens do penance by apologizing for his daughters' criticism, going so far as to compose a model letter of the kind he expected his boss to endorse. In doing so, he was likely taunting the great man of letters.[3]

On August 3, Ashcroft and Lark met again. In a dramatic shift from the tone and content of his previous letter, Ashcroft said he would "do anything in reason and was willing to put trifles aside and deal with essentials only." Lark called Stormfield and announced confidently that tomorrow "the long wrangle" would be over.[4] But Clemens opened his *New York Times* the next day, only to spy the headline "Ashcroft Accuses Miss Clara Clemens." Reading the article was another jolt for our famous author, his daughters, and their lawyers. A masterpiece of its kind, Ashcroft's August 4 bid to shape public opinion in the *New York Times* was snake-oil salesmanship of the highest order.[5]

He forcefully accused Miss Clara Clemens of jealousy, a charge that has stuck to this day. Ashcroft let loose a barrage of invective, true and false, in his newspaper interview. His charge that Clara "thought more of her musical career than of taking care of her old father and filling her mother's place" was essentially true, as she demonstrated by leaving her father with Lyon for long stretches. He made a true, albeit nasty, jibe that her "vocal ambitions" exceeded her "capabilities." But the conclusion he offered the *Times,* that this "bitter realization" caused her to strike back at Isabel Lyon, is doubtful. The man who was so skeptical of her musical talent influenced his wife to put the squeeze on Clara's free-spending ways, thus creating her real motive—one that Ashcroft never grasped. He could not see beyond his condemnation of her character and lifestyle to the aspiring singer's real concerns.

Although in his letter to Clemens's lawyers Ashcroft maintained that old cash withdrawals, with no expenditure notation other than "house money," were "extremely difficult, if not impossible" to trace, in his statement to the *Times,* he publicly blamed Clara for gobbling up the bulk of the unaccounted cash withdrawals charged to house money—money his wife had been accused of stealing. Twain's cash was used for the "delightful experience of paying for the hire of concert halls destined to be mainly filled with 'snow' or 'paper,'" he told the *Times,* "for the maintenance of her accompanist, Charles E. [Will] Wark, and to defray other cash expenditures."

Twain held to his policy of keeping his personal life out of the newspapers, but in a kind of tit-for-tat with Ashcroft, he privately countercharged that 90 percent of the large cash withdrawals that were credited to Clara or "C.C." were stolen. He later modified his position and hypothesized that Clara may have spent a portion of the cash outlay under her name. Nevertheless, he continued to maintain in private that the

Ashcrofts had helped themselves to some of the money charged to Clara.[6]

The final audit report suggests that where Clara's finances were concerned, both men were wrong. The accountant's statement clearly shows that the bulk of Clara's expenses were not paid in cash but were drawn as checks to specific payees.[7] Unverifiable cash accounted for only 5 percent of the money charged to Clara. If, contrary to Ashcroft's charges in print, her expenses were not paid in untraceable currency, then she could not be blamed for the mystery of the disappearing house money. But this also clears the Ashcrofts of Clemens's charge that they stole large chunks of money attributed to C.C.

Ashcroft was a clever publicist, however, and understood the importance of manipulating an image. In this vein, he shrewdly quoted from Clemens's passionate defense of Lyon in an October 1907 letter to Jean. The letter, now nearly two years old, praised Lyon's treatment of doctors, friends, servants, reporters, and even strangers. "She has failed to secure your confidence and esteem and I am sorry," Clemens wrote his exiled daughter, "I wish it were otherwise, but it is no argument since she has not failed in any other person's case. One failure to fifteen hundred successes means that the fault is not with her." Clemens wrote it and deserved to have it thrown back at him. But it conveyed feelings that he now vigorously recanted. All but the most careful reader, however, would conclude that his trust and respect for Mrs. Ashcroft were still current. Fuming privately, Clemens denounced Ralph's use of the letter as dishonest and dishonorable and remarked that Miss Lyon "puts the final stamp of treachery upon her character" by making available private correspondence she copied while his secretary.[8] Using the old letter was an effective counterattack in the press; it also rode the edge of duplicity.

But Ashcroft's forthright lies are what makes the *Times* article of August 4 most arresting. "Mr. Ashcroft declares that it was without the knowledge of the humorist's New York lawyers that the cottage at Redding, Conn., adjoining the Clemens estate, which he gave to Miss Lyon, was attached in his recent suit." This is a ludicrous falsehood that Ashcroft expands to include imaginary conversations with Lark and Stanchfield. "Mr. Clemens's New York lawyers now state that Mrs. Ashcroft's cottage was attached without their knowledge or advice."

Ashcroft had just talked to Lark the day before and knew the extent of the lawyer's involvement in the case.[9] His wife had had two confrontations with Lark—and Twain's daughters—in her home, which he knowledgeably referred to in his letter.

Ashcroft, however, was just warming up to tell a real whopper. "The only person, so far as I know, who has charged Mrs. Ashcroft with dishonesty is Clara Clemens. Mark Twain has not, and his lawyers have not." Less than a week before, Ashcroft had privately rebuked Clemens for attaching his wife's property, calling it a "bone of contention" between them. He also had blamed Twain directly for the accusations that broke his wife's health. And he had attacked Twain for unjustly questioning his wife's honesty. Clearly Ashcroft was able to deliver the big lie without compunction.

His next invention, however, is even more damning. Ashcroft offered the *Times,* as evidence of his wife's innocence, a promissory note that the newspaper reproduced. He claimed that it made Twain's suit against Mrs. Ashcroft for indebtedness "absolutely groundless and farcical." The promissory note included a clause, to wit, "this receipt being given on the understanding that said Ashcroft will pay in like manner any further amounts that the examination of my disbursements for the fiscal year ending Feb. 28, 1909, shows were advanced for like purpose." Certainly a clause worthy of someone who foresees the need to cover funds already spent but not yet "advanced." "I hope I may land in perdition before I finish this sentence," Clemens swore, "if I ever heard of that piece of writing until I saw it in that interview in the *Times.*"[10]

Remember Clean-Up Day, March 11? Clemens reported later that he signed all four of the contracts that Ashcroft put before him without comment, as well as a typed memorandum detailing Miss Lyon's services and compensations. But he did not sign Ashcroft's four promissory notes. He never touched them, he wrote in late June, more than a month before Ashcroft's rigged promissory note showed up in the *New York Times.* Twain speculated that either his signature was forged or writing was removed from, and then reinscribed on, a paper he had signed for another purpose.[11]

Ashcroft ended his interview in the August 4 *New York Times* with a half-truth. "The matter has been settled amicably as far as Mark Twain, Mrs. Ashcroft and I are concerned." Nothing had as yet been settled;

only anticipation of a settlement was in the air. Ashcroft had still demanded two conditions in his meeting with Lark and Paine the day before he dropped the *Times* bombshell. His first condition was already on the table: a note by her former boss exonerating his wife of any dishonesty and "regretting that by an unfortunate mistake she has been wrongly charged with it." The second demand was also familiar: a note regretting the loss of Ashcroft as director of the Mark Twain Company. Twain's lawyers rejected both conditions, and in fact no member of the family agreed to exoneration in any form—written or oral. By the close of the meeting, however, Ashcroft had dropped these demands, leading the lawyers to think an "amicable settlement" was in sight. Ashcroft even assured Lark as part of the proposed settlement that he would resign as manager of the Mark Twain Company but the next day the *Times* quoted him as saying he would "remain for the present. My contract has nearly two years to run." Lark and Stanchfield were surprised but not shocked, Twain noted wryly.[12] Other experiences had prepared them for this fiction.

"What I always admired about Ashcroft," Twain observed sarcastically, "was his diligence & single-mindedness in looking out for Number One."[13] Nonetheless, his impulse to defend his wife transcended mere self-aggrandizement. He fully conveyed his loathing of Clara Clemens as a talentless, petty spendthrift who was hounding Lyon because of a rivalry for Twain's affection. Expressing genuine anger over Clara's treatment of his wife, Ashcroft's defensive maneuvers on his spouse's behalf reveal a protective and chivalrous impulse. Still, he was no Don Quixote, defending his Dulcinea out of some pure, if exaggerated, sense of honor. He vindicated his wife because not to would have meant his own ruin.

He was sometimes too clever by half, however, spinning protective schemes for the pair that eventually backfired. His world divided into two halves: manipulator and manipulated. Lacking intuition about human behavior, he relied more on calculation than insight, often reading situations as a struggle between prey and predator. Ashcroft's arrogance was immense and clearly extended to his former boss. After Twain fired Lyon, her husband angrily laid bare his disrespect for the old man in letters and interviews. Twain returned the compliment. He had a list of grievances against Ashcroft, whose newly revealed contempt sorely rankled him. Taking deadly aim in private, Twain denounced his business manager for being shabby enough "to drag the dead out of the grave to give false evidence," referring to his friend Henry Rogers. "When it comes to lying," Twain quipped, "Ashcroft seems to have *no* reserves, no modesties."[14] His falsehoods, however, were not random or capricious but artfully crafted to explain his role and protect his reputation.

Ashcroft actually achieved by deliberate fabrication what he could never have gained directly. Since Clemens refused his request for letters of exoneration, Ashcroft exonerated himself and his wife of all wrongdoing in one of the country's leading newspapers. By his claims that neither Twain nor his lawyers had accused Lyon of any wrongdoing and that the lawyers had no knowledge that her house was being attached, Ashcroft expunged in two strokes the taint from his wife's reputation. It was only the jealous daughter of the beloved celebrity, he falsified strategically, who had complaints, the result of petty female infighting. Ashcroft even managed to get published a phony legal document that covered his wife's key problem: unauthorized Clemens money spent for renovation of her cottage. He also cleverly portrayed himself as the still trusted business manager, in charge of all of Mark Twain's business dealings and with two years left on his contract. Any questions in the future could be put to rest by pulling out a copy of the *New York Times,* which publicly absolved him and his wife.

Ashcroft used the newspaper articles that he so shrewdly constructed to "prove" his innocence (and his wife's) to family and probably to others. A sister-in-law remembered that he sent her newspaper clippings that she passed on to other members of the family. She was certain the clippings established his innocence.[15]

————

Once he discovered that Twain would not joust in print and that he could win almost any newspaper contest by default, Ashcroft must have smiled to himself. He understood that he could, with a little luck, invent the ending he wanted to the controversy with Twain, wrap the package, and tie a rhetorical ribbon to his best advantage. He did not waste his opportunity. In a magnificent *New York Times* finale on September 13, 1909, he marshaled a series of lies that completely exonerated him and his wife. And he managed to get the *Times* to ratify every one. "All criticism of the conduct of Mrs. Ashcroft has been withdrawn," the gullible *Times* reported in its article about the final settlement between Clemens and the Ashcrofts.[16] Endorsing another of his fabrications, the newspaper pronounced the cottage to be the crux of the dispute, "the gift of which to his former secretary on her marriage is understood to have been the beginning of the trouble." The trouble was late in coming, the *Times* narrative suggested. It insinuated that the jealousy within Twain's family began with this generous wedding gift to his secretary in March 1909.

Of course the cottage was not a wedding gift, but it played well. Although the property had been given to Lyon in 1907 and Mr. Lark had had to threaten criminal prosecution in order to procure the deed from Lyon, Ashcroft told the *Times,* and the *Times* told America, that the Ashcrofts magnanimously ratified the transfer of their property back to Twain to end the trouble between them.[17] "In addition, Mr. and Mrs. Ashcroft have agreed to withdraw the suits which they brought against Mark Twain and Miss Clemens for defamation of character," the *Times* reported. No such suits existed, but it sounded fine and gave substance to the Ashcrofts' defense. Ashcroft also invented another suit that Clemens supposedly filed against Mrs. Ashcroft for "an alleged loan of $3,050." Clemens never filed such a suit, but inventing one for a loan is another brilliant maneuver.[18] Having Clemens drop a nonexistent suit for a non-existent loan gave weight to their claim that they never stole a dime.

The next set of lies was the most astonishing. "Reparation has also been made for the hard things which the Ashcrofts alleged had been said of them by the author and Miss Clemens."[19] In a shift from his earlier strategy in the *Times* of denying Twain's involvement, the reparation idea allowed Ashcroft to "admit" that the famous author had made accusations against them, which he now regretted. The *Times* reported that Clara had retracted her criticisms "to the satisfaction of Mr. and Mrs. Ashcroft." In addition to unspecified reparations, the *Times* even had Twain sign a nonexistent document "acquitting Mrs. Ashcroft of all blame for her conduct of his affairs while she was in his employ as his secretary." After generously inventing fictions to exonerate his wife, Ashcroft saved the final paragraph of his newspaper finale for himself. "Meanwhile, Mr. Ashcroft continues to be Secretary and Treasurer of

the Mark Twain Company," the article intoned solemnly. "It is understood that on the exoneration of his wife he offered to resign his place
but Mark Twain requested him to continue to hold it." Ashcroft thus
pictured Twain groveling at his feet, while he and his wife were primp-
ing for sainthood, a fantasy fully endorsed by the *Times.*

Of course this fantasy ended the controversy on a much more satisfying note for the Ashcrofts than if the *Times* had reported the mundane facts of the case. In actuality, Clara never retracted a word. Twain
never signed any document acquitting Mrs. Ashcroft. No reparation
was ever made to the pair of manipulators by anyone inside or outside
the Clemens family. And Clemens and his new board of directors had
formally asked Ashcroft to resign on September 11, which he did.[20]

Ashcroft was more than a fabulous counterfeiter, reinventing himself
to launch a new life. He was a trickster who discarded facts as easily as
candy wrappers. Granted that his deception in the *Times* is crafty, ser-
viceable, and even rational in its aims, the magnitude of his dishonesty
is unnerving. Liars make a mockery of the truth, for they float above
their own experience, utilizing it in ways that are focused upon manipulating others. They are without limits, except for the plausibility of the
construction itself. Fabricating history to suit their needs, they wreak
havoc upon the common assumption that people will base claims, however flawed, on their actual experience.

In his famous 1968 biography of Twain, *Mr. Clemens and Mark Twain,*
Justin Kaplan suggested, in the only negative reference he makes to
Ralph Ashcroft, that Clemens had "grounds enough to charge them
[the Ashcrofts] with mismanagement and possibly larceny." Ashcroft's
sister-in-law and nephew took deep offense. They vehemently insisted
that the Ashcrofts were completely exonerated by Twain, offering Kaplan, his publisher, and the Mark Twain Papers the *New York Times* clipping of September 13, 1909, as proof.[21]

In his letter of protest to Kaplan's publisher, Ashcroft's nephew made
special mention of the totally bogus last paragraph. This indicated, he
innocently argued, that Clemens had repudiated all charges and, to
make amends, had asked his uncle to remain as business manager. His
nephew, like many upright newspaper readers, believed Mark Twain

had cleared his former employees of all charges because he read it in the *New York Times.* Given Twain's reluctance to joust in print, Ashcroft had had an open playing field in the newspapers. "Obscurity and insignificance," Twain cautioned the publisher of the *New York Times,* "possess certain privileges which are denied to prominence and distinction. The oiler of your steam presses can slander you & your family in print," he explained, "but you cannot undignify yourself with a reply." Twain was resolute: he could not defend himself in print against the invective of his former employees because this would only whet the public appetite and thus increase media coverage.[22]

It was nonetheless the responsibility of the *Times* to check the facts, especially those of a so-called "final settlement." According to Twain, his lawyers, who would have been known to the *Times,* were never contacted. Ashcroft took masterly advantage of his dominion but not without the full cooperation of gullible or vindictive *Times* reporters. Twain believed it was the latter, but whatever its editorial motives, the *Times* published an unverified account of the settlement of Twain's case against the Ashcrofts in the omniscient voice, giving the impression that it was a factual summary of a settlement that had been agreed to by all parties. All the news that was fit to print, the *Times* motto, was exclusively defined by Ralph Ashcroft. Such collusion between a private individual and a major newspaper is journalism at its worst. As Twain wryly observed, "At last...the Times speaks *for* them! tells their falsehoods *for* them, & personally (tacitly) vouches for their veracity!"[23]

———

Still, the Ashcrofts most significant deception remained hidden from the outside world. Clemens, however, brought it to the fore in reviewing the newspaper coverage of this controversy. Both Ashcroft and Miss Lyon "worked hard during three years," he at last admitted, "through lies told to Drs. Hunt and Peterson—to keep Jean exiled from her father's house." This was Clemens's longest, and most accurate, assessment of his former secretary's conspiracy against Jean. (Perhaps by now unable to separate the two, he missed the mark on his business manager's involvement in Jean's affairs, which was almost certainly less than half his three-year reckoning.)[24]

The Ashcrofts "told friends of ours," he reported incredulously, "that Jean would be a trouble at home & that they should keep her away the

rest of her life—for *my* sake!" Clemens had initially supported Jean's departure—although at least in part because he had hoped for a cure—
and more than eighteen months passed before he took any initiative to
bring her home again. (He began to look for a farmhouse for her near
his Redding mansion in late June 1908.) His avoidance strategy even extended to her letters. There is little reason to doubt that, before she left,
he found Jean a trouble at home. But he was astounded by the proposition that *therefore* she should be kept away from him for the rest of her
life. He shunned her letters, but he had no intention of barring her permanently from his house. If, because of his complacency and contentment with the status quo, he did not realize that she met his seizure-free
criterion to return home at the end of her first year, he always expected
to welcome her home eventually.[25]

Clemens was, if possible, even more appalled by his secretary's verbal
assaults on his daughter's sanity. Lyon told his Connecticut neighbors
that Jean was "crazy," he discovered, and would never be able to live
outside of sanitariums. Despite his belief that Jean's epileptic temperament made her "disagreeable," there is no hint anywhere in his writings
that he ever believed this extended to serious mental illness or violent or
homicidal urges. He condemned Lyon's pernicious portrayal of his
youngest daughter. Indeed, by the end of August he had completely re-
assessed the character of his former secretary. She was, he now insisted,
a "brute: just a plain, simple, heartless brute, & rotten to the spine."[26]
Such vehemence was not just about Miss Lyon's offense against Jean. It
was the judgment of a man who was deeply guilty about his own paternal failing.

CHAPTER 18

The Funniest Joke
in the World

GEORGE BERNARD SHAW REMARKED that it was Mark Twain who taught him that "telling the truth's the funniest joke in the world."[1] Shaw's line captures the genius of great humor: it is always trying to penetrate the façade of self-deceit and the conventions of respectability. Shaw recognized that the connection between humor and truth was central to Twain's writing. Twain continued to take aim at the truths of his life and society as he grew older, but—ever self-conscious about the cash value of his persona—he wrote increasingly for himself rather than his reading public. Consequently he composed, yet withheld from publication, certain controversial material, including an essay condemning lynching that he knew would depress book sales in the South.[2] He also deliberately withheld the 429-page autobiographical exposé commonly referred to as the Ashcroft-Lyon manuscript.

Twain began writing the manuscript—part history, part rumination, part diatribe—on May 2, 1909, a little less than three weeks after he fired his secretary, Isabel Lyon. She and her new husband, Ralph Ashcroft, are central protagonists in the unpublished work that bears their names. Twain struggled with his narrative for almost four months. He listened to his daughters, consulted his lawyers, and solicited the observations of his close friends and relatives about what had happened in his inner circle. And he observed the maneuvering of his former employees with fresh vigilance. He assimilated other evidence—his general contractor's little black book, newspaper interviews by Lyon and Ashcroft, an independent auditor's report, even memos and letters unflattering to himself that he had written in the Ashcrofts' defense. Twain included most of this raw evidence in the unrevised manuscript, often providing commentary alongside the documents that he hoped would stand as witness to his veracity. When he started the Ashcroft-Lyon manuscript, Twain grasped very little of his family drama. On his journey of self-discovery, he would be shaken to the core. By late August, however, he had achieved a fair measure of understanding. Though he sometimes gave way to erratic emotional tirades in his composition, he also candidly reviewed his life since Livy's death and reinterpreted its meaning.

This autobiographical quest for self-knowledge was loosely structured as a series of letters to William Dean Howells. Twain believed that by addressing Howells he could imitate a confidential conversation with his friend. He was hoping to "talk right out of my heart, without reserve."[3] A free-speaking Mark Twain is worth listening to at any age, but especially at the end of a long life when he is intent on turning himself inside out. Twain's series of intermittent conversations with himself is the most sustained and important writing of his final years. Yet—since its public unveiling in 1970—this manuscript has become the most maligned and misunderstood work in his entire oeuvre.

One influential biographer, giving the manuscript its first and most widely accepted interpretation, claimed that Twain and his daughters were "illogical and lacking in compassion." He charged Clara and Jean with harassing their father's "defenseless and high-strung secretary." The manuscript, he concluded in an attack on Twain himself, "is a geyser of bias, vindictiveness, and innuendo." He encapsulated an all-but-definitive stance toward the Ashcroft-Lyon manuscript when he concluded: "It condemns a gullible and foolish man for misplacing his trust for so long in such obviously corrupt antagonists as the Ashcrofts whom he created in his own mind."[4]

For telling the truth about himself, Twain has been accused of being deluded, demented, and worse. Through Lyon's guile, Ashcroft's wiles, and some scholarly gullibility, Twain's old age has been discredited. He has also been discredited through stereotypes of the aged and a willingness to believe in decline and venality, ingratitude, and superheated ego in a man of notorious celebrity and recognizable vanity.

———

"I'd like immensely to read your autobiography," Howells wrote to Clemens in a real letter. "I fancy you may tell the truth about yourself. But *all* of it?...Even you won't tell the black heart's-truth. The man who could do it would be famed to the last day the sun shone on."[5] But Mark Twain did tell the black heart's-truth in the Ashcroft-Lyon manuscript, and scarcely anyone has acknowledged it.

While it is undeniable that his manuscript is raw and uncrafted and contains several full-scale evasions, it also includes the most painful personal disclosure he ever committed to paper. The greatest act of courage in Twain's entire body of autobiographical writing is his confession—which he agreed to expose to the public fifty years after his death—that he abandoned his own daughter. Not many parents would voluntarily admit to the entire world "that I, who should have been her best friend, forsook her in her trouble to listen to this designing hypocrite whom I was coddling in the place which should have been occupied by my forsaken child."[6] Only in recognizing Twain's massive vanity about his public image can one gauge the force of this remarkable revelation.

Twain said he could never "strip myself naked before company," but that is what he did in this work. He spared himself very little, in an act of brutally frank self-examination that he knew would become public. If he indulged in petty diatribes, such as his fits over his secretary's erratic bill paying, or occasionally slipped in below-the-belt remarks, such as his gibe that Lyon was a three-week-old fetus, he also ruthlessly stripped away his illusions.[7] That he did not accomplish this task systematically is neither surprising nor worthy of condemnation.

The Ashcroft-Lyon manuscript was Twain's therapy, a literal form of recovery. He wrote it in dribs and drabs as events continued to unfold and as he had the time or inclination. On July 11, after a visit by the Twichells, he self-consciously told his future reader that he was in no hurry. "It is my only employment; also my only diversion, except billiards—daily from 5 to 7 p.m. with Paine." Even as he wrote this autobiography for his own edification and enlightenment, he also understood that it had a value beyond the personal. In an act that mixed pride and self-abasement, perhaps only possible for Twain in old age, he offered his "remarkable little tale" to the world. "Come," he invited his reader, "*isn't* it just like an old-time machine-made novel?"[8] Realizing that his real-life drama was as melodramatic, stagy, and racy as bad fiction, he occasionally stopped to reassure his reader that he was not spinning a yarn.

He composed the Ashcroft-Lyon manuscript like letters from the front. Writing in the wake of constant turmoil, Twain was rocked by one humiliating revelation after another during the summer of 1909. He worked in the chaos of immediate events, often grappling with the impact of an earlier revelation as the next experience exploded around him. The separation between his real experience and his writing about it varied from weeks to years. But even with the longer time lag, his responses were raw and impromptu. Whipped by the maelstrom of circumstance, his mind was neither tranquil nor organized. He was struggling, not to produce a lyrical prose masterpiece, but to overcome his personal demons by writing—the only way he knew how.

———

Mark Twain began his confession of folly and betrayal not long after what he must have hoped was the climax of his story, the firing of his secretary. He introduced Ashcroft and Lyon as the hero and heroine of his "sordid little romance." And he named a long list of friends who had been suspicious of his self-described pets, while "I remained peacefully asleep," as he sheepishly admitted. "I had the most absolute & uncompromising faith in the honesty, fidelity & truthfulness of that pair of rotten eggs all the while. Yes, & so had Clara." Twain accentuated his unwillingness to listen to any attack upon either their character or conduct by recalling the pattern of gullibility that had been a lifelong defect in his business dealings and outlining how much his blind loyalty in the past had cost him in actual dollars and cents. This time his loyalty was even more expensive, and not in terms of money lost. Poses of gullibility and obtuseness were major devices of his nonfiction writing as well as mainstays of his fictional humor.[9] Yet it was sometimes difficult to find humor in the unfolding events where the obtuseness was his own.

On May 27 he candidly owned up to his embarrassing defense of the Ashcrofts, recalling his letter of March 11 to Clara, where he poured out his admiration, his gratitude, and "esteem without stint."[10] Ashamed to have written such a slavish and worshipful defense of the pair, he nonetheless appended the whole letter to his manuscript. It is one of the many acts of unflinching honesty in this remarkable autobiography.

Though the manuscript includes some self-serving, conceited, and fatuous ideas, Twain was nonetheless engaged in serious self-examination, which included a detailed reassessment of Isabel Lyon. Remember that Twain had only begun to form a new perception of her character a few weeks before he began this writing. For many years he had held her in the highest esteem, believing her word to be above reproach. His revisionist thinking now led him to consider her arrogance, her thirst for power, and her attempt to dominate him and his household.

Writing at the end of May, he was struck by her erratic work habits, which probably reflected her binge drinking. Over the next three months, Clemens repeatedly circled back to Lyon's pattern of sickness, including her three-day headaches, recognizing at last that she was often drunk in his employ. He confessed that while he had always naively taken her inebriated state for "hysterics," everyone around him knew she was a lush. As he reviewed her history, her motives, and her character in early June, a touch of the Twain humor struggled to the fore. "[B]etween the Human Race & the Great Humorist she stood erect, impressive, & all alone, like Liberty Enlightening New Jersey, & none of that Race could get a chance to lay a prayer at his feet without her permission." He remembered that in complimenting her husband, she gushed, "Isn't he *dear?*...and so *honest!*" "Honest!" Twain retorted incredulously; "Howells, it is like one old prostitute praising another's chastity."[11]

Gathering strength, momentum, and perhaps reassurance from his humor, a determined Twain sat down to write again on June 14. After almost six weeks of reflection, he was ready to plumb Lyon's most vicious crime: keeping his daughter exiled in sanitariums when she was desperate to return to her father's home. He also found the strength to confront his own transgression—his pact with the Devil—exposing his secret collusion in the process that exiled Jean. "It cuts me to the heart, now, to know that Jean made many an imploring & beseeching appeal to me, her father, & could not get my ear," he confessed with hard-edged candor; "that I, who should have been her best friend, forsook her in her trouble to listen to this designing hypocrite whom I was coddling in the place which should have been occupied by my forsaken child."[12] No one need ever have known about Twain's compact with his secretary, yet he chose to admit to posterity that he conspired with her not to read his youngest daughter's letters.

Still, his next confession had to be almost as difficult. Hovering "like a pair of anxious and adoring nurses," the Ashcrofts would not let him out of their sight. They watched to see "that I didn't catch cold or get run over by a baby wagon," he quipped. "And I liked that nursing & petting & was vain of being a person who could call out such homage, such devotion." This confession of vanity was a humbling act of contrition. Joining self-deprecating humor and acumen in his phrasing, he called the Ashcrofts his "crutches," his "carbuncles," and "worshiped pets of mine." He drips acid on them, as his critics have noted disapprovingly, but they fail to see that he did not spare himself. "The pair were laughing at me all of the time, but I never suspected," Twain told the world. Though he exaggerated their mockery, in doing so he was frankly acknowledging his foolishness.[13]

On June 19 he returned to the more mundane history of the audit of his secretary's accounts. At this time he conveyed in detail his conversations with Ashcroft about the business manager's plans to marry Lyon. This is where he makes his self-conscious remark about King Lear. They thought they owned him body and soul, he wrote. They thought "I couldn't help myself; that all in good time they would be indisputably supreme here, & I another stripped & forlorn King Lear."[14] It is a powerful image of his folly, his weakness, and the vulnerability of old age.

On June 30, he gathered courage for another engagement with the painful treatment he had accorded his daughter Jean. He faced the fact that Jean could have returned home two years ago "but for the scheming of that pitiless pair & my own inexcusable stupidity!"[15] Dr. Peterson's conviction that Twain would be disturbed by Jean's presence in Redding was unshakable, he reported, even in the face of protestations by Clara and the family physician, Dr. Quintard. For three years, Lyon had been conducting a form of shuttle diplomacy between Jean's doctor and father, assuring Peterson that Twain did not want his daughter at home while telling Twain that the doctor thought Jean was too sick to return. Only through Twain's direct and forceful intervention on April 14, 1909, was a concession won for an experimental week at home. Jean returned—permanently—to her rightful place by her father's side on April 26, where they both embraced the chance to become a family again. Twain exulted briefly over his reunion with Jean in his writing but then almost compulsively returned to the narrative of his secretary's fall.

On July 11 he finally reached the point in his story when he fired Lyon. After that climactic moment, nearly three months behind him in real time, the narrative slackened, and Twain lost direction for a spell of several weeks. Jumping from subject to subject, he became apoplectic over her erratic bill-paying habits. Scarred by his previous bankruptcy and sensitive to his hard-earned reputation as a scrupulous debtor, he seemed to take the payment of a bill upon receipt as a matter of honor. "At my very laziest," he deadpanned about relative speeds during one of his diatribes on her bill paying, "I could hear myself whiz, when she was around." He vented more spleen over her lackadaisical pattern of paying bills—letting them lie for from six weeks to as much as four months—than almost any of her other sins.[16] Incorporating long-term statements from department stores is just one illustration of his focus on the inessential. Flailing in trivia, he almost drowned in misdirected fury.

His business manager's insulting letter of April 29 was another target of his wrath. In suggesting that his boss was too weak to stand up to his daughter Clara, Ashcroft revealed his contempt for Twain in this missive. Twain was furious and flung venomous insults back at Ashcroft through his pen. "It stands in a class by itself: it is *the* Literary Vomit of the Ages," he wrote intemperately. He also fulminated over Ashcroft's plot to drive the servants away and gave grand significance to the deceptions involving his young butler, Horace. But in late July and early August, Twain once again zeroed in on his central narrative, and here he observed that for all her wiles, for all her lust for power and her vicious plotting, Lyon was guiltless of the plan "to *rob* us, strip us naked, take the roof from over our heads." That was Ashcroft's department, he declared.[17] Reporting Ashcroft's brag to young Harry Lounsbury about selling Twain's house over his head, he showed how this led in late May to the discovery of the fraudulent power of attorney. Twain spent some time discussing possible ruses used by Ashcroft to obtain the power of attorney without his knowledge. By August 11 he was incisively probing why the Ashcrofts needed or wanted such control. He also owned up to the embarrassing act of signing the transfer signatures on all his Mark Twain Company stock, thus making them negotiable and giving anyone with access to his safety deposit box the chance to sell his literary rights out from under him.

He again recognized how close to being Lear he really was. "[T]hey were feeling absolutely sure they could turn me against Clara, drive her off the place, & reign over Stormfield & me in autocratic sovereignty"—a sovereignty that included exiling his youngest daughter forever. After coming so far in his narrative, however, Twain confessed a surprising feeling about his former secretary. "I think I pity her," he acknowledged, "but I hope to be damned if I *want* to."[18]

Sometime around the middle of August Twain shifted his focus once more. After a month of silently swallowing sensational press coverage about his suit against the Ashcrofts, he sought an outlet for his frustration in writing. The Ashcrofts had captured public attention in a series of lurid press conferences and newspaper interviews, but because he believed that any public statement on his part would only make his former employees more newsworthy, Twain vented his spleen in the Ashcroft-Lyon manuscript. Spending more than a week privately correcting falsehoods in the newspaper accounts, he also fantasized about what he would like to say to the press. "If it suits Mrs. A's ideas of propriety to wash her private linen in public, let her do it," he wrote in one sample news release that he set aside. "It is her privilege; I never wash mine at all." He even composed a letter to the Associated Press, which he never intended to have published. "It is the best way to quiet your indignant soul," Twain noted of a practice he had used for forty years—"putting on paper what I would have liked to say."[19]

Probably around the third week of August, he shifted back to narrating his life—about a month behind the events in real time. He picked up the story as Lyon returned in mid-July to her cottage in the Connecticut countryside, having declared to reporters that she intended to confront her former boss and settle their dispute. After waiting several days for her to appear at Stormfield, Twain's lawyer, Charles Lark, took the initiative. Under intense pressure from Lark—detailed in the narratives written by Jean and Clara, which are included in the manuscript—Lyon re-deeded her cottage back to her former boss. When Ashcroft returned from England in late July and entered negotiations with Twain's lawyers, Twain discovered that what his business manager could not achieve in an actual settlement, he could nonetheless claim as fact in the *New York Times*. Twain had charged Miss Lyon with dishonesty "everywhere except in print," he asserted privately—a telling qualifier that explained why the Ashcrofts had the newspapers in their pocket. Maintaining a stoical public silence, Twain offered an effective point-by-point rebuttal only in his manuscript. As he ticked off his list of correctives, what sparked his most vivid and intense rejoinder was Ashcroft's claim in the press that both daughters were "afraid that Mark Twain would marry her."[20]

———

On August 30, 1909, Twain composed one of the most important sections of this autobiographical narrative, in which he categorically denied that he had had any thought of marrying Lyon. "In all my (nearly) seventy-four years I have seen only the one person whom I would marry, & I have lost her." If he had secretly harbored even a flicker of marital interest, his lady-in-waiting would undoubtedly have waltzed him down the aisle. She used every wile she knew, and then some, but her boss never wavered.[21] Livy's ghost probably did save him from total surrender to the Lioness. "Miss Lyon compares with her as a buzzard compares with a dove," he wrote. "(I say this with apologies to the buzzard.)" Manipulatable in almost every conceivable corner of his life, persuaded to all sorts of uncharacteristic actions by his secretary, Clemens never wavered in the marriage department. His claim that she had no sexual attraction for him, however, is suspect. Calling her a "little old superannuated virgin," he wrote that "her caressing touch—and she was always finding excuses to apply it—arch girly-girly pats on the back of my hand & playful little spats on my cheek with her fan—& these affectionate attentions always made me shrivel uncomfortably—much as happens when a frog jumps down my bosom." One of the most revealing passages Mark Twain ever wrote about his sexuality is a denial. "Howells, I could not go to bed with Miss Lyon, I would rather have a waxwork."[22]

Clemens could not bear the thought of any physical attraction to the woman he now abhorred; the woman he now believed was rotten to the core; the woman he now recognized had pushed him to betray his daughter; the woman who almost took him over bodily. "[S]he was an old, old virgin, & juiceless," he wrote, "whereas my passion was for the other kind."[23] His after-the-fact revulsion at any hint of Lyon's allure is understandable at the end of August. But the evidence of his constant flirtation in the preceding years and his self-confessed enjoyment of her attentions and flattery surely signal that the enticement was not one-sided. While Clemens said that he "could not go to bed with Miss Lyon," which is probably true, his disavowal of any physical attraction is hypocritical. Her very power over him was connected to her allure. An extremely attractive woman twenty-five years his junior had an enormous crush on him, and he had been hugely flattered.

Does a man read romantic poetry to a woman whose very touch he recoils from in distaste? Does he take her along as his boon companion on frivolous vacations to Bermuda? Does he let her into his bedroom for daily tête-à-têtes? In calling her a "little old superannuated virgin," he demeaned her sexuality while maintaining his own persona as a virile lover. Yet his masculine vanity was clearly overwrought. It is doubtful that her affectionate attentions "always" made him "shrivel uncomfortably." If he had shriveled more, Lyon would have had much less power in their day-to-day transactions. Clemens's confession of abandoning his daughter is real, but his denial of sexual feelings for his former secretary is a sham. In his frank self-examination at age seventy-three, this was one blind spot he could not see around.

To his credit, in the midst of his denials, he paused to check the facts. "I have stopped the press," he wrote, "to call Clara in & ask her if she & Jean were ever afraid I would marry Miss Lyon."

Clara responded with a blast of candor. "No, we were not; but we were afraid she would marry *you.*"

"Really & truly afraid, Clara?"

"Yes, really & truly. . . . [S]he seemed to have gotten such a hold upon you," Clara told her father bluntly, "that she could make you do whatever she pleased. She was supreme. She had everything her own way in the house." Clara did not attempt to spare his feelings, perhaps because he had already faced a complete description of his own predicament. "She had stopped making requests," Clara continued, "she only gave orders. You never denied her anything." Clara hammered away, and he reported her criticism in exquisite detail, almost relishing his comeuppance. "You were putty in their hands, father," his daughter continued, "and they could mould you to any shape they pleased. That had not been your way, before; you had a will of your own—before the Ashcrofts came."[24]

Shaping the narrative, even though he was ostensibly quoting his daughter, Twain returned to his greatest humiliation and excoriated himself. "Once you wrote a letter to Jean—& it was probably a *real* letter," he had Clara say, "a letter from father to daughter—a letter with some feeling in it, some sympathy, not a page or two of empty & unexcitable commonplaces such as Miss Lyon was accustomed to dictate to you as replies to that poor friendless exile's appeals—"

The phrasing is pure Twain, as is the flagellation. "By God I can't stand it, Clara!" he had himself interrupt, in dialogue mode. "[I]t makes me feel like a dog—like the cur I was; if I could land Miss Lyon in hell this minute, I hope to be damned if I wouldn't do it—and it's where I belong, anyway. Go on."[25]

He himself went on, describing the time he had written a "real letter" to Jean, the letter he gave to Lounsbury to mail, only to have his courier intercepted by Lyon on the false pretext that Twain wanted to add something he had forgotten. Neither Lounsbury nor Twain saw that letter again. "Do you think that that letter ever reached Jean, father?" Clara asked him accusingly.

"No, I *don't* think it. I think that that misgotten gutter rat destroyed it," he replied.[26] But he saved his most biting sarcasm for himself.

"Well, that's all. I don't want Clara to come in here any more," Twain mockingly announced. "I like the truth sometimes, but I don't care enough for it to hanker after it. And besides, I have lived with liars so long that I have lost the tune, & a fact jars upon me like a discord."[27]

———

Why did the Ashcrofts attain so much power over me? Why did they gain such mastery over my life? Why did I become the Ashcrofts' mental slave? In the closing days of August, Twain directly tackled the questions that would haunt any reader of the Ashcroft-Lyon manuscript. How could a man of such intellect and insight, with a matchless ability to demolish pomposity and fakery, be taken in by such poseurs?

Twain's answer was hypnotism, first proposed to Clara by her close friend Mary Lawton. Clara passed on the theory to Clemens, who believed that it looked "reasonable" since no one could think of any other plausible way to account for his "enslaved condition."[28] At first glance, Twain's willingness to believe that he was hypnotized seems foolish and simpleminded. His acceptance of this theory looks like an evasion of responsibility—a face-saving sophistry. And indeed it was exculpatory, but it was not self-satisfied.

Twain's contemporary, Hippolyte Bernheim, perhaps the most important late-nineteenth-century proponent of the psychological approach to hypnotism, saw it "as the induction of a peculiar psychical condition which increases the susceptibility to suggestion." This "[s]usceptibility to suggestion occurs in the waking state," Bernheim insisted. Indeed, according to one historian of psychology, Bernheim believed that hypnosis was "a form of behavior continuous with normal waking behavior, capable of being produced in nearly everyone."[29] While Twain may not have read the work of Bernheim or his disciples, he closely perused an article by Dr. Frederik Van Eeden, "Curing by Suggestion," which utilized Bernheim's work. Van Eeden described the power of suggestion in very ordinary actions: persuasive dialogue, vivid images, strong assurances, and rising expectations.[30] As it happened, Twain stumbled upon this piece on the very day that he and Clara had their discussion of hypnosis.

Van Eeden insisted, citing Alfred Binet, that "the aptitude of taking and realizing suggestions—is a normal faculty of the human mind, but greatest in youth."[31] He added, however, that old people were sometimes as susceptible as children to suggestion. Twain knew that Van Ecden's unflattering description of the docile and childlike elder applied to his behavior. So impressed was he by this account that he cut and pasted an entire paragraph into the Ashcroft-Lyon manuscript. "Old people," the excerpt began, "though in all appearance still independent and responsible, are often entirely under the suggestive influence of some masterful or interested person." Reading that line before bedtime, Twain recognized himself. "I have seen cases," the article continued, "of rich old men apparently normal, who acted entirely against their original character, against their true inclinations, against their own interests, under the influence of some nurse or attendant who had succeeded in mastering the master's mind."[32]

Here Twain identified a controlling factor in his mental servitude. He was one of those wealthy old people whose money had made him vulnerable to takeover by his caretakers. "In such cases the intriguer knew how to apply his suggestions," the excerpt concluded, "so as to rule at last the whole household, cheating the legitimate heirs out of their rights or bringing about a marriage contract." Twain recognized that he had barely escaped complete domination. After 422 pages, he fully acknowledged his childlike dependence. He knew that Lyon and Ashcroft had, for a time, become the master's master.[33]

Hypnosis was the explanatory device he used to understand his condition. But another more recent concept, unavailable to Twain, probably more accurately describes his plight. Dubbed "learned helplessness syndrome" by modern behavioral psychologists studying animal conditioning, the term has been applied by less technically minded educators and social workers to children, the disabled, and the elderly who can be taught to think and act with total dependence upon their caretakers.[34] Twain indeed may have believed that he could not live comfortably without the ministrations of his caretakers. Certainly, he became a victim of their "care" for him. "I couldn't even go...to New York (an hour & a half distant), without one or both of them along to see that I didn't catch cold or get run over by a baby wagon," he wrote ironically. They kept "solicitous watch over me all the time," he remembered, "like a pair of anxious & adoring nurses." "I was never able to get to my room in time to take my clothes off unassisted— he was always at my heels," Twain wrote of Ashcroft's ministrations; "he always stripped me, he put my night-shirt upon me, he laid out my clothes for next day, & there was no menial service which he omitted."[35] Nobody but an infant or a king has his clothes taken off at night. Such a level of physical attention, when added to the psychic cocoon of ease and comfort the Ashcrofts provided, left Twain limp and docile.

His vulnerability to this condition of learned helplessness was not just accounted for by his age. The foundation was laid years before by Livy, who relieved her husband of almost every mundane task and assumed almost complete responsibility for his children. "Mrs. Clemens always had the management of everything in the old days," Katy observed. "She made every plan—looked after everything....Mr. Clemens never crossed her in any plan and never upset anything she did."[36] Thus, he had already been conditioned to rely on someone else for almost all his family's everyday needs. But several additional factors made him more vulnerable to takeover after his wife's death.

First, he decided that he had at last earned a rest and that he would please himself in his old age. He set his mind to divesting himself of responsibilities, onerous and otherwise. When she was well, Livy did not hesitate to demand a higher level of moral responsibility from her husband than he might have asked of himself—such as paying his creditors dollar for dollar after his bankruptcy or including Jean in every possible social occasion. His wife rarely let him escape his familial obligations and public trust.[37] But Isabel Lyon cultivated his irresponsibility, reinforcing his freedom from family duties and public service. She fed and nurtured his self-indulgence and constantly salved his conscience, thus dulling it. She would agree to almost anything to please him, doing more than he asked of her and more than she could possibly handle. In her zeal she became virtually a one-woman band that marched to his every whim.

If it is accurate to say that many of Lyon's moves to control him were instinctual, it is also true that she operated on a Machiavellian level of such complexity as to put to shame Twain himself. He became totally reliant upon her household management, her personal advice, and her familial services. These included making all the medical decisions, paying all the bills, doing all the shopping, and arranging all the details of his trips. The list is long. His every move was carefully orchestrated by Lyon, who was joined in the last two years of her vigilant tenure by Ralph Ashcroft.

Twain's other major blind spot was his refusal to recognize how much work this had entailed. By the beginning of the summer, his anger had slammed shut the door of validation. He unselfconsciously attacked Lyon with a remark that was both racist and sexist, claiming she was "much the laziest white person I have ever seen, except myself."[38] In applying this bigoted censure to her, he was showing contempt for the energy and time demands of the "woman's work" that his secretary constantly performed in place of his wife.

Neither Mr. or Mrs. Ashcroft was the source of Clemens's laziness, selfishness, or stupidity, but they are accountable for deliberately deceiving and deluding him. He trusted them and was not an ungenerous boss, giving them gifts and opportunities to make money, even if he did not reward them with an adequate salary. They responded to his trust by attempting to govern him completely—including his money. His scandalous passivity came from his own indolence but also from their sinister manipulation.

The Ashcroft-Lyon manuscript is not great art, but there is something grand about it nonetheless. For Twain confessed the most painful truth of his old age. In trying to tell the "black heart's-truth" about himself, he had to confess that he had almost lost himself—in his seventies. That he came very close to being taken over by another human being and close, very close to losing both his daughters. "She was master, & I was slave," he said bluntly. "She could make me do anything she pleased. In time—& no long time—she would have become permanently supreme here, & Clara would not have been able to stay in the house, nor Jean to enter it."[39]

Twain's autobiography is an admission of the folly of old age, not without a cushion of exculpation but yet with the force of a head-on collision with reality that was his greatness as a writer. And it is an affirmation of life—not an easy, mellow, peaceful lyrical prose poem but a raging, disorganized, frustrated, guilty struggle to understand what went awry. Consider it a manuscript written during the process of unraveling a mystery—the mystery of his capitulation to a seduction of the mind.

What Mark Twain grappled with at seventy-four was the problem of self-identity, which is not just a problem for the young. "It should haunt old age," observed another American author, "and when it no longer does it should tell you that you are dead."[40] Shakespeare's Lear asks: "Who is it that can tell me who I am?" Twain's quest for an answer to this question in the summer of 1909 makes the autobiography compelling. "Thou shouldst not have been old till thou hadst been wise," the Fool in Shakespeare's play tells Lear. Both Lear and Twain acted with supreme folly in old age. Neither could tell their loyal friends from their betrayers.

Critics have suggested that the Ashcroft-Lyon manuscript is an exercise in the senseless phantasms of dementia brought on by Clemens's despair and loneliness, thus extending the parallels between him and King Lear. But the living character does not suffer the same tragedy as his fictional counterpart. Writing the manuscript was Twain's journey toward wisdom. He examined in gritty if embarrassed episodes his susceptibility to the sycophantic lies that cost his daughter three years of often hellish exile. He owned up to his servile dependence on the

Ashcrofts, who so fed his ego that he barely stopped the indulgence in time to save himself and his daughters. In his last and perhaps greatest piece of autobiographical writing, Samuel Clemens discovered a "most humiliating truthfulness."[41] Telling the truth is the funniest joke in the world only if you can bear the pain.

CHAPTER 19

Melting Marble
with Ice

TWAIN ENDED THE Ashcroft-Lyon manuscript most peculiarly. After more than four months of sometimes gut-wrenching narrative about himself and his family, he closed with a memorandum on the controversy over who discovered the North Pole. This seemingly inexplicable non sequitur prompted the most influential critic of the Ashcroft-Lyon manuscript to conclude that "it ends with the quite irrelevant and almost irrational comment about Peary and Cook both discovering the North Pole."[1] And at first glance this criticism seems rather mild. Twain gave no context, offered no explanation or hint as to why he saw the discovery of the North Pole as a fitting way to end the autobiographical account of his late years. He simply plunked down a two-page memorandum in closing that appears to have no relation to his life. Yet Twain's odd North Pole memorandum was actually a slyly perverse and very timely joke.

Frederick Cook announced on September 1, 1909, that he had discovered the North Pole the previous year, on April 21, 1908. Five days later Commander Robert Peary announced the date of his own discovery on April 6, 1909. "Hurrah for Peary!" was Cook's response as he congratulated him on his achievement. Peary was less enthusiastic: he charged Cook with fraud in a dispatch to the Associated Press.[2] Each man had prominent defenders who attacked the credibility of the rival claimant, and the controversy ignited a fierce war of words. "Half the world believed Cook, the other half didn't," Twain wrote on September 7. "But the entire world believes Peary. I believe both are speaking the truth."[3] Initially, many people granted, as did Twain, that both men had reached the North Pole. They thought the only difference between the explorers was that Cook had accomplished this astounding feat a year before Peary.

Cook's delay in getting the news of his discovery to civilization was a major impediment to his success, according to Twain. "Apparently Dr. Cook sat down among the icebergs to waste a year—in writing about the discovery?"[4] Cook's explanation for his delay was that his failure to make base camp in time made another winter in the Arctic necessary. During his four-month stay in Greenland, Cook "went over all his notes and data" he explained, "and completed his book describing his trip to the pole." He wrote, he said, a hundred thousand words that he squeezed between the lines of previous entries in three small memorandum books.[5] Twain predicted that Peary's claim would win out because of Cook's "foolish" behavior. By "writing about the discovery" rather than publicizing it, said Twain, Cook allowed Peary to take first place, just as Urbain Leverrier bested John Couch Adams in the discovery of Neptune. (Both Adams and Leverrier predicted the existence and position of Neptune through mathematical calculations in the early nineteenth century, but Adams left his work unpublished and did not pursue the necessary proof in actual astronomical observations.)[6]

In closing his long narrative by discussing the scientific controversies over the discovery of the North Pole and Neptune, Twain was surely drawing parallels to his own situation. Twain, Cook, and Adams all had something important in common—failure to push their claims at the start. Twain must have seen himself in Cook and Adams, who were passive when they should have been aggressively pursuing validation in the world. The parallels to the North Pole and Neptune discoveries also extended to consequences. Adams came in second, and Twain predicted the same fate for Cook. By implication, Twain's leap to the North Pole, deemed irrelevant and irrational, was probably his sly way of predicting his own failure as well. His little parable suggests that the Ashcrofts, who aggressively pursued their story in the press, paralleled Peary and Leverrier, while he was like Cook, who foolishly sat around working on a manuscript for months in obscurity. At the end of 429 pages, Mark Twain was passing judgment on the efficacy of his own behavior. I will lose, he obliquely predicted; the Ashcrofts' version of reality will prevail.

The ironies of Twain's North Pole parable are many. Twain was in no position to know the outcome of the Cook-Peary controversy when he finished his manuscript in early September, only days after the story broke; certainly he had no way of telling he had compared himself to a poseur. But he was still alive when Cook presented his case to scientists at the University of Copenhagen. Their verdict, delivered on December 21, 1909, was that Cook had not supplied convincing astronomical observations or sufficient details regarding the expedition to support his claim. Many of Cook's former supporters eventually denounced him as a fraud, including Roald Amundsen, discoverer of the South Pole. Cook was officially expelled from the Arctic Club of America in early January 1911, the same year Congress declared Peary to be the legitimate discoverer of the North Pole.[7]

In fact, Frederick Cook was a flat-out imposter. Not only did he lie about reaching the North Pole, but he had deliberately faked his ascent to the summit of Mount McKinley three years earlier. The North Pole controversy led to a reexamination of his McKinley claim. In evidence that could have been inspired by a Twain satire, the men who left Cook's expedition before his "final" ascent testified that he had no climbing rope. In addition to many other discrepancies, Cook's photographs of the summit were shown to be twenty miles from the top of McKinley. Cook was expelled from the Explorer's Club on December 24, 1909. "Indignation is, however, swallowed up in pity," observed Hudson Stuck, a man who successfully ascended the summit, "when one…realizes that the immediate success of the imposition about the ascent of Denali (Mount McKinley) doubtless led to the more audacious imposition about the discovery of the North Pole and that to his discredit and downfall." His pity might be lessened knowing that Cook maintained he made $10,000 a year from lecturing on his accomplishments.[8]

In an ironic end to a narrative dedicated to exposing the deception in his own house, Twain was taken in by another fraud. This deception only adds to the self-mocking that Twain intended in concluding his autobiographical work with a commentary on who discovered the North Pole. He saw his own foolishness reflected in Frederick Cook—down among the icebergs—writing about his discovery. "It's the greatest joke of the ages," Clemens remarked to Paine.[9]

———

Twain added one more piece to his manuscript before he quit. That autumn, probably in mid-to-late September, he composed an introduction that he addressed "To the Unborn Reader." His cynical and cryptic North Pole finale contrasted vividly with this upbeat and accessible preface. Artful and sharply drawn, his introduction was his final word in chronological time. Attentive as he was to the skepticism that might greet his work, Clemens also exuded a fair amount of optimism in his preface. He began by dramatizing the act of reading his manuscript as an unveiling of much-sought-after knowledge. "This original Manuscript will be locked up & put away," Twain told the reader, "& no copy of it made. Your eye, after mine, will be the first to see it." He imagined a moment "one hundred years hence" when his reader would find unknown details of domestic life "in naked and comprehensive detail."[10]

He described himself as "the born ass" and the Ashcrofts as "a pair of degraded & sufficiently clumsy sharpers."[11] A highly self-conscious disclaimer followed this sketch. "These three characters have figured as clever inventions in many romances, but in this Manuscript we are not inventions," Twain insisted, "we are flesh & blood realities, & the silly & sordid things we have done & said are facts not fancies."[12] His artful effort to persuade his reader that he was a truth-teller signaled some hope of winning against his antagonists.

Lobbying hard for his side of the controversy, Clemens compared his autobiography to the Paston Letters, a collection of more than a thousand letters, memorandums, state papers, and legal documents written in the fifteenth century, across a span of almost ninety years, by husbands, wives, servants, stewards, friends, ecclesiastics, and business acquaintances of the Paston family of Norfolk, England. The education of these correspondents varied hugely, as did their purposes in writing—from business and politics to marital negotiations and household economy.[13] "[I]magine the value of it!" he exclaimed, "if the Paston Letters had been a free-spoken private communication to a Howells of four & a quarter centuries ago, imagine the light it would throw upon domestic life in England in that old day!"[14] Clemens surprisingly denigrated the historical value of the Paston Letters when compared with his own autobiographical manuscript. He exposed all the "silly and sordid things" in his life with utter frankness, he proudly declared, in contrast to the Paston Letters.

Twain's autobiographical writing, however frank, cannot compare to those multitudinous documents in scope or diversity or significance for social history. Nonetheless his affirmation of the long-range historical value of his autobiography speaks volumes about his own state of mind. The preface and conclusion were written within a span of days or weeks. The latter predicted the Ashcrofts' ascendancy and the former at least urged, if it did not forecast, Twain's eventual triumph. These opposing attitudes were undoubtedly products of the author's mood but also reflected more rational considerations.

He had decreed that no one would see the Ashcroft-Lyon manuscript for fifty years. In the short run, therefore, the Ashcrofts had the best chance of achieving narrative victory. But Twain was hopeful that when his autobiography came to light the manuscript's "large value" would be recognized. As usual, he saw dual possibilities. He was *both* an optimist and a pessimist, moving closer to one or the other at different moments but never hugging one pole for too long—even in old age.

———

"Time shall unfold what plighted cunning hides," the disinherited Cordelia predicts to her disingenuous sisters in *King Lear.* And time had indeed unfolded most of the hidden artifice in Twain's life. When he finished the Ashcroft-Lyon manuscript, most likely by the end of September, he was a knowing survivor of the last great crisis of his life and a man who more than ever wanted to enjoy the time there was left to him.

He found special joy in his daughter Jean, who was constantly by his side and full of love and delight in being home. She was simultaneously running her farm and Stormfield and was as happy to get her chickens to lay eggs as to write letters for her father. Jean rode her beloved Scott to the post office every morning, even though the old horse was getting stiff and unsteady. She had to ride cautiously, and as a result, she noted, "instead of my being in the seventh heaven of joy, I am in the fourth & a quarter." She continued to see Dr. Peterson, but his manner irritated her. She tolerated his boast that he had brought her back from Berlin, but balked when he took credit for bringing her to Stormfield. "I laughed," she told her friend Marguerite Schmitt, "saying but *you* haven't made me go home." He continued to insist until Jean reminded him of a few inconvenient facts and changed the subject. "But he has not dared speak of Miss Lyon," she added; "he knew enough to keep quiet on that subject."[15]

To her father's delight, Clara also returned to Stormfield in late summer, with Ossip Gabrilowitsch, the Russian pianist, in tow. He had come to the family's country estate in Redding to recuperate from an operation for appendicitis. Clara had met him in Vienna in 1898 when they were both students of the renowned piano teacher Theodore Leschetitzky. Gabrilowitsch, it seems, had made a lasting impression. Katy had carried notes between them in Vienna and also in New York. At Stormfield, she continued her shuttle diplomacy, delivering notes to their rooms at opposite ends of the house. "I certainly helped that courtship along," she chuckled, " 'cause I was always for him!"[16]

But unlike Jean, who stayed above the fray, Clara was fighting mad at the Ashcrofts' positive press, especially Ralph's magnificent settlement hoax published in the *New York Times*. She had been worried since July about the effect that the Ashcrofts' newspaper accounts would have on her own public image and her career. "I do wish," she implored her father, "... that you personally would make a simple statement for all the papers saying that you were grateful to me & my friends for discovering Miss Lyon's dishonesty etc." Clara feared that if her father said nothing, it would all seem "a mere difference between women."[17]

"[I]f I alone were concerned," Twain admitted, "I wouldn't take any notice of the rotten Ashcrofts." But goaded by Ralph's amazing hubris, Twain at last succumbed to Clara's pressure. He made no statement to the press but acted privately instead, sending Paine as his emissary to the *New York Times* for a summit meeting with its publisher, Adolph Ochs. His newspaper would "let Mr. Clemens alone, or at least to adhere to facts," Ochs promised Paine. The publisher kept his word for the rest of 1909. Nothing about Mark Twain or his personal affairs appeared in the *New York Times* until the newspaper reported on December 21 that the famous author had retired.[18]

A settlement was finally completed on September 26, and Mark Twain's connections to the Ashcrofts were legally severed. But he continued to be conflicted psychologically over Lyon's fate. On the one hand, he could fantasize about throwing her in jail for stealing money from him, as he said, "diligently" and "liberally—for more than a year." On the other hand, he understood that she had been "awfully punished": she had lost her home and married Ashcroft; she lived in Brooklyn and was out of society, which she coveted. His list was meant to be satiric but it was also a perceptive catalogue of her fall. Twain sat down on September 10 and toted up the debit and credit column—his version of taking stock. He concluded that he had lost about $30,000 through the pilfering of the Ashcrofts. But his "unforgiving heart" was not on fire over the lost money. What he could not forgive or forget was her treatment of Jean. He continued to rage over "the plots & lies and malignities of that unspeakable person."[19]

In the fall, Twain also took stock of his literary life. The occasion was a commission by *Harper's Bazaar* to write a piece on what became the title of his essay: "The Turning Point of My Life." The most important determinant of his career, Twain claimed, and the reason he became a writer was a severe bout of the measles at age twelve. "For when I got well my mother closed my school career and apprenticed me to a printer. She was tired of trying to keep me out of mischief," he wrote, "and the adventure of the measles decided her to put me into more masterful hands than hers." Twain linked his itinerant life as a printer with his apprenticeship as a pilot, his retreat to the Nevada silver mines during the Civil War, and thus to his career as a journalist, which led to his first book, *The Innocents Abroad*. He commented that as much as he tried to plan his life, "it came out some other way—some way I had not counted upon." "Circumstances do the planning for us all," he reiterated his longstanding conviction, "no doubt, by help of our temperaments."[20]

Isabel Lyon Ashcroft did a different sort of taking stock in August. "I miss the King so terribly, terribly," she wrote on a card that was wedged into one of her diaries. "[F]or there is no one in all my world now who can love a wonderful bit of English as he could, whose eyes grow shining over a phrase of Lafcadio Hearn or Kipling, as his did. There is no one now whose voice breaks into a sob over a sonorous line of prose or poetry; there is no one now," she bitterly lamented. "[T]here is no one to teach me those beauties; no one with the leisure or the wit to think literature."[21]

While she was mourning her loss, the Clemenses were celebrating their future. Recovered fully by the end of September, Ossip Gabrilowitsch agreed to give a benefit concert at Stormfield for the local library building fund. Twain had begun to raise money for a library in Redding the previous year by levying all male guests at Stormfield a fee of one dollar. He called this the "Mark Twain Library Building Tax" and printed up a mock broadside to give out as a receipt. Clara also sang at the benefit—and announced her engagement to Gabrilowitsch that evening at a private party. There was dancing, and Jean pranced down that great living room, Paine recalled, "as care-free as if there was no shadow upon her life."[22]

Two weeks later, on October 6, Clara married a man whom her father both liked and respected. "Only a few intimate friends were invited to the wedding, and everyone was in bright spirits," the bride remembered, "like the October day that blazed brilliant in resplendent autumn colors." Clara told Joseph Twichell, once again officiating at an important family ceremony, that she wanted the word "obey" deleted from the service. Jean was maid of honor and wore a new white silk dress, trimmed with lace. Twain, never one to be upstaged, wore his Oxford robes. For her part, Katy was agitated. All the preparations had fallen on her and Jean—with one week's notice. "I worked all the morning," Katy remembered about the wedding day, "and I was looking after everything and everybody was calling me this way and that. I didn't know who was there, hardly." She was too busy downstairs to help Clara dress, but she watched her descending the stairs on her father's arm. "She looked like a little cherub," Katy recalled. Twain was very quiet before the ceremony, but during the reception he talked and laughed and bragged contentedly about his new son-in-law.[23]

———

The myth of total bleakness in Twain's last years needs to be put to rest. He continued to rail against the Ashcrofts for recreation and release. But he suddenly had a family again, where they all looked out for each other. Clara championed her sister's needs, urging her father to pay Jean a good salary for all the work she was doing as his secretary. "[S]he has always had a great desire to earn money," Clara told her father, "and is certainly doing it now poor child for there can't be a much more arduous task than writing letters and looking after accounts."[24] Clara never intended to fill that role in her father's life and was obviously impressed by her sister's competence.

Both Sam and Clara were impressed by another characteristic of Jean: her willfulness. It was a trait that ran in the family, and Jean returned the compliment. "For, although he is very good and generous," she commented about her father to her friend Marguerite, "when he has an idea in his head, it's like melting marble with a piece of ice to make him change his mind!!" The irony of Jean's comment is that her father had changed his mind—about her. "You can't imagine what a darling she was," he told Clara, "& how *fine,* & good, & sweet, & noble—& *joyful,* thank Heaven!—and how intellectually brilliant." He could admit now, "I had never been acquainted with Jean before, I recognized that."[25] At age seventy-three, Mark Twain discarded his long-held stereotype of Jean's epileptic temperament and became acquainted with her at last. Marble had been melted, not by ice, but by love.

CHAPTER 20

The End of
My Autobiography

TWAIN'S CONSTANT SMOKING finally caught up with him. In the summer of 1909 he began to experience more frequent chest pains.[1] His health was also not improved by the nerve-shattering betrayal of his closest confidants. Dr. Quintard advised less smoking and diminished exercise. Predictably, his patient followed only one-half of Quintard's counsel.

After finishing the Ashcroft-Lyon manuscript in September, however, Twain was lighthearted and full of plans. According to Paine, his face was "as full of bloom as at any time during the period I had known him." Clemens's sense of humor was also full of bloom. "I have always pretended to be sick to escape visitors," he admitted. "[N]ow, for the first time, I have got a genuine excuse. It makes me feel so honest." Once, after being told that he had a caller in the living room, he replied, "Jean, I can't see her. Tell her I am likely to drop dead any minute and it would be most embarrassing." He amused himself by playing billiards and discussing astronomy, to him a constant source of wonder. "He was always thrown into a sort of ecstasy by the unthinkable distances of space," Paine remembered, "—the supreme drama of the universe." He was also writing to entertain himself. He had all the fame and money he needed and, with his family back, he was content to let his mind play and his pen follow. He was unofficially retired even before the *New York Times* announced it to the world in late December.[2]

In October, he returned to an old theme with "Letters from the Earth," a series of eleven letters composed by Satan, an immortal visitor on this planet, to friends in a remote part of the universe. Since he never intended publication, he felt free to let his imagination roam at will. He took plea-

sure in reading the letters to Paine as he finished them. "[W]e laughed ourselves weak over his bold imaginings," Paine remembered. Clemens never
tired of poking fun at humanity. He loved to mock the popular Christian
images of Heaven with their singing, praying, and harp playing, but no
sex. He contrasted the conceit of brotherly love in heaven with the vicious
prejudice and racial hatreds on earth. He found man's self-admiration
laughable, especially in thinking himself the center of the universe.[3]

Though "Letters from the Earth" was not autobiography, one of
Satan's meditations in Letter VIII seems highly suggestive. Commenting upon the biblical commandment against adultery, Satan is especially amused by the prohibition's injustice to women. "During 27 days
in every month (in the absence of pregnancy) from the time a woman is
seven years old till she dies of old age, she is ready for action, and *competent*. As competent as the candlestick is to receive the candle. Competent every day, competent every night," Satan confidently declaims.
What is more, "she *wants* that candle—yearns for it, longs for it, han-
kers after it, as commanded by the law of God in her heart."[4] Twain's
high estimate of female sexuality—"that no woman ever sees the day
that she can't overwork, and defeat, and put out of commission any *ten*
masculine plants that can be put to bed to her"—surely reflects, in some
measure, Livy's passion, Isabel Lyon's determination, and Sam's experience.

Twain's opinion of male sexuality is, by contrast, fairly gloomy. "But
the man is only briefly competent; and only then in the moderate measure applicable to the word in *his* sex's case. He is competent from the
age of sixteen or seventeen thenceforward for thirty-five years. After 50
his performance is of poor quality, the intervals between are wide, and
its satisfactions of no great value to either party; whereas his great-
grandmother is as good as new. There is nothing the matter with her
plant. Her candlestick is as firm as ever, whereas his candle is increasingly softened and weakened by the weather of age, as the years go by,
until at last it can no longer stand, and is mournfully laid to rest in the
hope of a blessed resurrection which is never to come."[5] Twain's pessimism about man's candle and his mournful acceptance of masculine
sexual limitations is a mocking assault on male sexual pretensions, perhaps including his own.

Through the voice of Satan, Twain enthusiastically approved of female
lust. The law of God is that women are made to enjoy "unlimited adul-

tery," Satan observes, yet she "is robbed" of this enjoyment everywhere in the world. Only a woman is competent to satisfy a harem, he warns, yet men have arranged it "exactly the other way."[6] Twain expressed confidence in female sexual capacity at any age while he was equally certain of male sexual decline. This was surely a satiric response to Victorian gender stereotypes and a humorous gloss on the double standard, as well as another comment on his own sexual vanity and decline.

————

Deciding to escape the winter chill, Clemens invited Paine to join him for a month in Bermuda, departing on November 18. They drove the length of the island, soaking up the colors of the sea—"turquoise, emerald, lapis-lazuli, and jade." They also walked along the shore, appreciating the variegated water and the coral reefs—the quiet beauty of paradise. And he talked, pretty much nonstop. Clemens also celebrated his seventy-fourth birthday in Bermuda, happily ensconced by a fire at the home of his friends, the Allens. He played hearts, read passages from *Tom Sawyer* at the request of his hosts' daughter Helen, smoked cigars, and talked. "Once, in the course of his talk," Paine remembers, "he forgot a word and denounced his poor memory: 'I'll forget the Lord's middle name some time,' he declared, 'right in the midst of a storm, when I need all the help I can get.'"[7]

Eventually, he decided to return to Stormfield to spend his first Christmas in three years with his youngest daughter. Jean met him, along with reporters, when he arrived back in New York on December 20. "I am through with work for this life and this world," Twain announced, when asked if he would lecture for the cause of woman suffrage, which he supported. "The state of my health will not permit it. The fact is I am through with work. I have no new books in contemplation."[8]

Back at Stormfield Jean was in a flurry of Christmas preparations. She was trimming a Christmas tree with silver foil and intended to light it up in the evenings with candles, following the custom she had observed in Germany. Busily shopping for everyone, she sent photographs of herself and gifts to friends. She was planning to give her father something special, a globe of the world, which he had always coveted.[9] Possessed by a deeply generous spirit, Sam's daughter could at last express her feelings materially.

"Last night Jean, all flushed with splendid health, and I the same," her father wrote on December 24, 1909, "strolled hand in hand from the dinner table and sat down in the library and chatted, and planned, and discussed, cheerily and happily (and how unsuspectingly!) until nine—which is late for us—then went up-stairs, Jean's friendly German dog following. At my door Jean said, 'I can't kiss you good night, father: I have a cold, and you could catch it.' I bent and kissed her hand. She was moved—I saw it in her eyes—and she impulsively kissed my hand in turn. Then with the usual gay 'Sleep well, dear!' from both, we parted.

"At half past seven this morning I woke, and heard voices outside my door. I said to myself, 'Jean is starting on her usual horseback flight to the station for the mail.' Then Katy entered, stood quaking and gasping at my bedside a moment, then found her tongue:

"'*Miss Jean is dead!*'

"Possibly I know now what the soldier feels when a bullet crashes through his heart," Twain wrote.[10]

Jean had a grand mal seizure and drowned in her bath on the morning of Christmas Eve, 1909. Her father sent a number of telegrams that day with the message: "I thank you most sincerely, but nothing can help me."[11]

If there was no external source of comfort that could offer him relief, Mark Twain still had one place he could turn for solace. Writing was his bulwark, and it once again sustained him. The desolate author worked for two days on what would be his last piece for print, "The Death of Jean." He had vowed, after his wife's death, that he would never watch another loved one lowered into the ground. Remaining at Stormfield while his daughter's body was sent to its final earthly destination, he attended the funeral and stood at Jean's graveside in Elmira only in his imagination, which was enough.[12]

"I have finished my story of Jean's death," Twain told Paine and his wife on the evening of December 26. "It is the end of my autobiography. I shall never write any more. I can't judge it myself at all. One of you read it aloud to the other, and let me know what you think of it. If it is worthy, perhaps some day it may be published." According to both Paine and Clara, he never attempted any further writing for publication. Paine did publish Twain's last essay in *Harper's,* scarcely more than a year later, in a slightly sanitized form. Paine's version appeared again in a volume of miscellaneous sketches in 1927 and has also been anthologized in two modern editions of Twain's autobiographical writings.[13]

For its intimacy, power, and significance as his last work, Twain's description of his daughter's death deserves to be read exactly as it left his pen. It is reprinted here for the first time in its original form. Reading this essay is the best way to take the measure of the man at the end of his life, to see clearly that he was scarcely the bitter and uncaring figure that he has sometimes been portrayed.[14]

————

CLOSING WORDS
OF MY AUTOBIOGRAPHY
Stormfield, Christmas Eve, 11 a.m., 1909.

Jean is dead!

And so this Autobiography closes here. I had a reason for projecting it, three years ago: that reason perishes with her.

The reason that moved me was a desire to save my copyrights from extinction, so that Jean & Clara would always have a good livelihood from my books after my death. I meant that whenever a book of mine should approach its 42-year limit, it should at once be newly issued, with about 10,000 words of Autobiography added to its contents. This would be copyrightable for a term of 28 years & would practically keep the whole book alive during that term. I meant to write 500,000 words of Autobiography, & I did it.

That tedious long labor was wasted. Last March Congress added 14 years to the 42-year term, & so my oldest book has now about 15 years to live. I have no use for that addition (I am 74 years old), poor Jean has no use for it now, Clara is happily and prosperously married & has no use for it.

Man proposes, Circumstances dispose.

————

Has anyone ever tried to put upon paper all the little happenings connected with a dear one—happenings of the twenty-four hours preceding the sudden & unexpected death of that dear one? Would a book contain them? Would two books contain them? I think not. They pour into the mind in a flood. They are little things that have been always happening every day, & were always so unimportant &

easily forgettable before—but now! Now, how different! How precious they are, how dear, how unforgettable, how pathetic, how sacred, how clothed with dignity!

Last night Jean all flushed with splendid health, & I the same, from the wholesome effects of my Bermuda holiday, strolled hand in hand from the dinner table & sat down in the library & chatted & planned, & discussed, cheerily & happily (& how unsuspectingly!) until 9,—which is late for us—then went up stairs, Jean's friendly German dog following. At my door Jean said, "I can't kiss you good-night, father; I have a cold, & you could catch it." I bent & kissed her hand. She was moved—I saw it in her eyes—& she impulsively kissed my hand in return. Then with the usual gay "Sleep well, dear!" from both, we parted.

At half past 7 this morning I woke, & heard voices outside my door. I said to myself, "Jean is starting on her usual horseback flight to the station for the mail." Then Katy entered, stood quaking & gasping at my bedside a moment, then found her tongue:

"Miss Jean is dead!"

Possibly I know now what the soldier feels when a bullet crashes through his heart.

In her bathroom there she lay, the fair young creature, stretched upon the floor & covered with a sheet. And looking so placid, so natural, & as if asleep. We knew what had happened. She was an epileptic: she had been seized with a convulsion & could not get out of the tub.

There was no help near, & she was drowned. The doctor had to come several miles. His efforts, like our previous ones, failed to bring her back to life.

It is noon, now. How lovable she looks, how sweet & how tranquil! It is a noble face, & full of dignity; & that was a good heart that lies there so still.

In England, thirteen years ago, my wife & I were stabbed to the heart with a cablegram which said "Susy was mercifully released to-day." I had to send a like shock to Clara, in Berlin, this morning. With the peremptory addition, "You must not come home." Clara & her husband sailed from here on the 11th of this month. How will Clara bear it? Jean, from her babyhood, was a worshipper of Clara.

———

Four days ago I came back from a month's holiday in Bermuda in perfected health; but by some accident the reporters failed to perceive this. Day before yesterday, letters & telegrams began to arrive from friends & strangers which indicated that I was supposed to be dangerously ill. Yesterday Jean begged me to explain my case through the Associated Press. I said it was not important enough; but she was distressed & said I must think of Clara. Clara would see the report in the German papers, & as she had been nursing her husband day & night for four months & was worn out & feeble, the shock might be disastrous. There was reason in that; so I sent a humorous paragraph by telephone to the Associated Press denying the "charge" that I was "dying," & saying "I would not do such a thing at my time of life."

Jean was a little troubled, & did not like to see me treat the matter so lightly; but I said it was best to treat it so, for there was nothing serious about it. This morning I sent the sorrowful facts of this day's irremediable disaster to the Associated Press. Will both appear in this evening's paper?—The one so blithe, the other so tragic.

———

I lost Susy thirteen years ago; I lost her mother—her incomparable mother!—five & a half years ago; Clara has gone away to live in Europe; & now I have lost Jean. How poor I am, who was once so rich! Seven months ago Mr. Rogers died—the best friend I ever had, & the nearest perfect, as man & gentleman, I have yet met among my race; within the past four weeks Gilder has passed away, & Laffan—old, old friends of mine. Jean lies yonder, I sit here; we are strangers under our own roof; we kissed hands good-bye at this door last night—& it was forever, we never suspecting it. She lies there, & I sit here—writing, busying myself to keep my heart from breaking. How dazzlingly the sunshine is flooding the hills around! It is like a mockery.

Seventy-four years old, twenty-four days ago. Seventy-four years old yesterday. Who can estimate my age to-day?

———

I have looked upon her again. I wonder I can bear it. She looks just as her mother looked when she lay dead in that Florentine villa so long ago. The sweet placidity of death! it is more beautiful than sleep.

I saw her mother buried. I said I would never endure that horror again; that I would never again look into the grave of any one dear to me. I have kept to that. They will take Jean from this house tomorrow, & bear her to Elmira, New York, where lie those of us that have been released, but I shall not follow.

Jean was on the dock when the ship came in, only four days ago. She was at the door, beaming a welcome, when I reached this house the next evening. We played cards, & she tried to teach me a new game called "Mark Twain." We sat chatting cheerily in the library last night, & she wouldn't let me look into the loggia, where she was making Christmas preparations. She said she would finish them in the morning, & then her little French friend would arrive from New York—the surprise would follow; the surprise she had been working over for days. While she was out for a moment I disloyally stole a look. The loggia floor was clothed with rugs & furnished with chairs & sofas; & the uncompleted surprise was there: in the form of a Christmas tree that was drenched with silver films in a most wonderful way; & on a table was a prodigal profession of bright things which she was going to hang upon it to-day. What desecrating hand will ever banish that eloquent unfinished surprise from that place? Not mine, surely. All these little matters have happened in the last four days. "Little." Yes—*then*. But not now. Nothing she said or thought or did, is little, now. And all the lavish humor!—what is become of it? It is pathos, now. Pathos, & the thought of it brings tears.

All these little things happened such a few hours ago—& now she lies yonder. Lies yonder, & cares for nothing any more. Strange—marvelous—incredible! I have had this experience before; but it would still be incredible if I had had it a thousand times.

———

"Miss Jean is dead!"

That is what Katy said. When I heard the door open behind the bed's head without a preliminary knock, I supposed it was Jean coming to kiss me good morning, she being the only person who was used to entering without formalities.

And so—

I have been to Jean's parlor. Such a turmoil of Christmas presents for servants & friends! They are everywhere; tables, chairs, sofas, the

floor—everything is occupied, & over-occupied. It is many & many
a year since I have seen the like. In that ancient day Mrs. Clemens and
I used to slip softly into the nursery at midnight on Christmas Eve &
look the array of presents over. The children were little, then. And
now here is Jean's parlor looking just as that nursery used to look. The
presents are not labeled—the hands are forevermore idle that would
have labeled them to-day. Jean's mother always worked herself down
with her Christmas preparations. Jean did the same yesterday & the
preceding days, & the fatigue has cost her her life. The fatigue caused
the convulsion that attacked her this morning. She had had no attack
for months.

———

Jean was so full of life & energy that she was constantly in danger
of overtaxing her strength. Every morning she was in the saddle by
half past 7, & off to the station for the mail. She examined the letters
& I distributed them: some to her, some to Mr. Paine, the others to the
stenographer & myself. She dispatched her share & then mounted her
horse again & went around superintending her farm & her poultry the
rest of the day. Sometimes she played billiards with me after dinner, but
she was usually too tired to play, & went early to bed.

Yesterday afternoon I told her about some plans I had been devising
while absent in Bermuda, to lighten her burdens. We would get a
housekeeper; also we would put her share of the secretary-work into
Mr. Paine's hands.

No—she wasn't willing. She had been making plans herself.
The matter ended in a compromise. I submitted. I always did. She
wouldn't audit the bills & let Paine fill out the checks—she would
continue to attend to that herself. Also, she would continue to be
housekeeper, & let Katy assist. Also, she would continue to answer
the letters of personal friends for me. Such was the compromise. Both
of us called it by that name, though I was not able to see where any
formidable change had been made.

However, Jean was pleased & that was sufficient for me. She was
proud of being my secretary, & I was never able to persuade her to
give up any part of her share in that unlovely work. I paid her this
compliment of saying she was the only honest & honorable secretary
I had ever had, except Paine. It is true that Jean had furnished me no

statements, but I said I hadn't ever wanted them from her, for she was honest, & the lack of them had never caused me any uneasiness.

Oh, that unfortunate conversation! Unwittingly I was adding to her fatigues, & she was already so tired. Before night she suspended her Christmas labors, & drew up a detailed statement for November, & placed it in my hands. I said, "Oh, Jean, why did you do it? didn't you know I was only chaffing?"

But she was full of the matter, & eager to show me that her administration had been care-taking & economical. The figures confirmed her words. In the talk last night I said I found everything going so smoothly that if she were willing I would go back to Bermuda in February & get blessedly out of the clash & turmoil again for another month. She was urgent that I should do it, & said that if I would put off the trip until March she would take Katy & go with me. We struck hands upon that, & said it was settled. I had a mind to write to Bermuda by tomorrow's ship & secure a furnished house & servants. I meant to write the letter this morning. But it will never be written, now.

For she lies yonder, & before her is another journey than that.

————

Night is closing down; the rim of the sun barely shows above the skyline of the hills.

I have been looking at that face again that was growing dearer & dearer to me every day. I was getting acquainted with Jean in these last nine months. She had been long an exile from home when she came to us three-quarters of a year ago. She had been shut up in sanitariums, many miles from us. How eloquently glad & grateful she was to cross her father's threshold again!

Would I bring her back to life if I could do it? I would not. If a word would do it I would beg for strength to withhold the word. And I would have the strength; I am sure of it. In her loss I am almost bankrupt, & my life is a bitterness, but I am content: for she has been enriched with the most precious of all gifts—that gift which makes all other gifts mean & poor—death. I have never wanted any released friend of mine restored to life since I reached manhood. I felt in this way when Susy passed away; & later my wife; & later Mr. Rogers. When Clara met me at the station in New York & told me Mr. Rogers had died suddenly that morning, my thought was, Oh, favorite of fortune—fortunate all his long & lovely life—fortunate to his latest moment! The reporters said there were tears of sorrow in my eyes. True—but they were for *me,* not for him. He had suffered no loss. All the fortunes he had ever made before were poverty compared with this one.

———

Why did I build this house two years ago? To shelter this vast emptiness? How foolish I was. But I shall stay in it. The spirits of the dead hallow a house, for me. It was not so with other members of my family. Susy died in the house we built in Hartford. Mrs. Clemens would never enter it again. But it made the house dearer to me. I have entered it once since, when it was tenantless & silent & forlorn, but to me it was a holy place & beautiful. It seemed to me that the spirits of the dead were all about me, & would speak to me & welcome me if they could: Livy, & Susy, & George, & Henry Robinson, & Charles Dudley Warner. How good & kind they were, & how lovable their lives! In fancy I could see them all again, I could call the children back & hear them romp again with George—that peerless black ex-slave & children's idol who came one day—a flitting stranger—to wash windows, & stayed eighteen years. Until he died. Clara & Jean would never enter again the New York hotels which their mother had frequented in earlier days. They could not bear it. But I shall stay in this house. It is dearer to me tonight than ever it was before. Jean's spirit will make it beautiful for me always. Her lonely & tragic death—but I will not think of that, now.

———

Jean's mother always devoted two or three weeks to Christmas shopping, & was always physically exhausted when Christmas Eve came. Jean was her very own child—she wore herself out present-hunting in New York these latter days. Paine has just found in her desk a long list of names—fifty, he thinks—people to whom she sent presents last night. Apparently she forgot no one. And Katy found there a roll of bank notes, for the servants. Also two books of signed checks which I gave her when I went to Bermuda. She had used half of them.

Her dog has been wandering about the grounds to-day, comrade-less & forlorn. I have seen him from the windows. She got him from Germany. He has tall ears & looks exactly like a wolf. He was educated in Germany, & knows no language but the German. Jean gave him no orders save in that tongue. And so, when the burglar alarm made a fierce clamor at midnight a fortnight ago, the butler, who is French & knows no German, tried to interest the dog in the supposed burglar. He remembered two or three of Jean's German commands (without knowing their meaning), & he shouted them to the eager dog. "Leg' Dich!" (lie down!) The dog obeyed—to the butler's distress. "Sei ruhig!" (be still!) The dog stretched himself on the floor, & even stopped batting the floor with his tail. Then Jean came running, in her night clothes, & shouted "Los!" (Go! fly! rush!) & the dog sped away like the wind, tearing the silences to tatters with his bark. Jean wrote me, to Bermuda, about the incident. It was the last letter I was ever to receive from her bright head & her competent hand. The dog will not be neglected.

Paine has come in to say the reporters want photographs of Jean. He has found some proofs in her desk—excellent ones, & evidently not a fortnight old. This is curiously fortunate, for she has not been photographed before for more than a year.

———

There was never a kinder heart than Jean's. From her childhood up she always spent the most of her allowance on charities of one kind or another. After she became secretary & had her income doubled she spent her money upon these things with a free hand. Mine too, I am glad & grateful to say.

She was a loyal friend to all animals, & she loved them all, birds, beasts & everything—even snakes—an inheritance from me. She knew all the birds: she was high up in that lore. She became a member of various humane societies when she was still a little girl—both here & abroad—& she remained an active member to the last. She founded two or three societies for the protection of animals, here & in Europe.

She was an embarrassing secretary, for she fished my correspondence out of the wastebasket & answered the letters. She thought all letters deserved the courtesy of an answer. Her mother brought her up in that kindly error.

She could write a good letter, & was swift with her pen. She had but an indifferent ear for music, but her tongue took to languages with an easy facility. She never allowed her Italian, French & German to get rusty through neglect.

Her uncarned & atrocious malady—epilepsy—damaged her disposition when its influence was upon her, & made her say & do ungentle things; but when the influence passed away her inborn sweetness returned, & then she was wholly lovable. Her disease, & its accompanying awful convulsions, wore out her gentle mother's strength with grief & watching & anxiety, & caused her death, poor Livy! Jean's—like her mother's—was a fine character; there is no finer.

The telegrams of sympathy are flowing in, from far & wide, now, just as they did in Italy five years & a half ago, when this child's mother laid down her blameless life. They cannot heal the hurt, but they take away some of the pain. When Jean & I kissed hands & parted at my door last, how little did we imagine that in twenty-two hours the telegraph would be bringing me words like these!

"From the bottom of our hearts we send our sympathy, dearest of men & dearest of friends."

For many & many a day to come, wherever I go in this house, remembrancers of Jean will mutely speak to me of her. Who can count the numbers of them?

She was an exile so long, so long! There are no words to express how grateful I am that she did not meet her fate in the house of a stranger, but in the loving shelter of her own home.

———

"*Miss Jean is dead!*"

It is true. Jean is dead.

A month ago I was writing bubbling & hilarious articles for magazines yet to appear, & now I am writing—this.

———

Christmas Day. Noon. Last night I went to Jean's room at intervals, & turned back the sheet & looked at the peaceful face, & kissed the cold brow, & remembered that heart-breaking night in Florence so long ago, in that cavernous & silent vast villa, when I crept down stairs so many times, & turned back a sheet & looked at a face just like this one—Jean's mother's face—& kissed a brow that was just like this one. And last night I saw again what I had seen then— that strange & lovely miracle—the sweet soft contours of early maidenhood restored by the gracious hand of death! When Jean's mother lay dead, all trace of care & trouble, & suffering, & the corroding years had vanished out of the face & I was looking again upon it as I had known it & worshipped it in its young bloom & beauty a whole generation before.

———

About 3 in the morning, while wandering about the house in the deep silences, as one does in times like these, when there is a dumb sense that something has been lost that will never be found again, yet must be sought, if only for the employment the useless seeking gives, I came upon Jean's dog in the hall down stairs, & noted that he did not spring to greet me, according to his hospitable habit, but came slow & sorrowfully; also I remembered that he had not visited Jean's apartment since the tragedy. Poor fellow, did he know? I think so. Always when Jean was abroad in the open he was with her; always when she was in the house he was with her, in the night as well as in the day. Her parlor was his bedroom. Whenever I happened upon him on the ground floor he always followed me about, & when I went up stairs he went too—in a tumultuous gallop. But now it was different: after petting him a little I went to the library—he remained behind; when I went upstairs he did not follow me, save with his wistful eyes. He has wonderful eyes—big, & kind, & eloquent. He can talk with them. He is a beautiful creature, & is of the breed of the New York police-dogs. I do not like dogs, because they bark when there is no occasion for it: but I have liked this one from the beginning, because he belonged to Jean, & because he never barks except when there is occasion—which is not oftener than twice a week.

In my wanderings I visited Jean's parlor. On a shelf I found a pile of my books, & I knew what it meant. She was waiting for me to come home from Bermuda & autograph them, then she would send them away. If I only knew whom she intended them for! But I shall never know. I will keep them. Her hand has touched them—it is an accolade—they are noble now.

And in a closet she had hidden a surprise for me—a thing I have often wished I owned: a noble big globe. I couldn't see it for the tears. She will never know the pride I take in it, & the pleasure. To-day the mails are full of loving remembrances for her; full of those old, old kind words she loved so well, "Merry Christmas to Jean!" If she could only have lived one day longer!

At last she ran out of money & would not use mine. So she sent to one of those New York homes for poor girls all the clothes she could spare—and more, most likely.

———

Christmas Night. This afternoon they took her away from her room. As soon as I might, I went down to the library, & there she lay, in her coffin, dressed in exactly the same clothes she wore when she stood at the other end of the same room on the 6th of October last, as Clara's chief bridesmaid. Her face was radiant with happy excitement then; it was the same face now, with the dignity of death & the peace of God upon it.

They told me the first mourner to come was the dog. He came uninvited, & stood up on his hind legs & rested his forepaws upon the trestle, & took a long last look at the face that was so dear to him, then went his way as silently as he had come. *He knows.*

At mid-afternoon it began to snow. The pity of it—that Jean could not see it! She so loved the snow.

The snow continued to fall. At six o'clock the hearse drew up to the door to bear away its pathetic burden, Payne playing Schubert's "Impromptu," which was Jean's favorite. Then he played the Intermezzo; that was for Susy; then he played the Largo; that was for their mother. He did this at my request. Elsewhere in this Autobiography I have told how the Intermezzo & the Largo came to be associated, in my heart, with Susy & Livy in their last hours in this life.

From my windows I saw the hearse & the carriages wind along the road & gradually grow vague & spectral in the falling snow, & presently disappear. Jean was gone out of my life, & would not come back any more. The cousin she had played with when they were babies together—he & her beloved old Katy—were conducting her to her distant childhood home, where she will lie by her mother's side once more, in the company of Susy & Langdon.

———

December 26. The dog came to see me at 8 o'clock this morning. He was very affectionate, poor orphan! My room will be his quarters hereafter.

The storm raged all night. It has raged all the morning. The snow drives across the landscape in vast clouds, superb, sublime—& Jean not here to see.

———

2:30 p.m. It is the time appointed. The funeral has begun. Four hundred miles away, but I can see it all, just as if I were there. The scene is the library, in the Langdon homestead. Jean's coffin stands where her mother & I stood, forty years ago, & were married; & where Susy's coffin stood thirteen year's ago; & where her mother's stood, five years & a half ago; and where mine will stand, after a little time.

———

Five o'clock. It is all over.

———

When Clara went away, two weeks ago, to live in Europe, it was hard, but I could bear it, for I had Jean left. I said *we* would be a family. We said we would be close comrades and happy—just we two. That fair dream was in my mind when Jean met me at the steamer last Monday; it was in my mind when she received me at this door last Tuesday evening. We were together; *we were a family!* The dream had come true—oh, preciously true, contentedly true, satisfyingly true! and remained true two whole days.

And now? Now, Jean is in the grave!

In the grave—if I can believe it. God rest her sweet spirit!

Mark Twain
End of the Autobiography

———

The closing of Twain's autobiography, his private funeral service in words, displays the man in the raw: his uncommon dignity, his intensity of feeling, his sensitivity to the telling detail, his biting irony; and most of all, his honesty, even as he gazed at Jean's corpse. While he rejoiced in the special intimacy they had shared before she died, he did not pretend that it was long-lived. "I said *we* would be a family. We said we would be close comrades and happy—just we two.... We were together; *we were a family!* The dream had come true—," he wrote with a guilty but defiant exultation—"and remained true two whole days." The gibe told of his pain. Her death extinguished the dream of family that was closest to his heart. Yet he also felt relief that she was no longer vulnerable to the accidents and suffering he had feared might come to her through epilepsy. "[N]ow she is free," he wrote a friend, "& harm can never come to her more."[15]

Clara had gone to live in Europe with her new husband little more than a month before the shocking news arrived. She was less sanguine than her father. "[T]here are many glimpses into the past that turn my heart sick & almost bury me in remorse," she told her cousin Julia. Distressed that no one was near when Jean drowned, Clara was relieved to learn that Katy and another servant were in fact close by and neither heard the distinctive cry that Jean usually made during a seizure.[16] "So nothing could have been done to prevent it," Clara concluded thankfully.

Twain also felt gratitude—he had Jean back for eight months, and he tasted deeply the joys of paternal love. "I don't know why you should love me, I have not deserved it;" he confessed to Clara, "& the love Jean manifested for me astonished me daily; I recognized its sincerity but could not divine the source of it, nor what had bred it & kept it alive.... But I was deeply grateful to Jean for that unearned love," he wrote mindfully, "& I am deeply grateful to you for yours. More than once I have been humiliated by my resemblance to God the Father: He is always longing for the love of His children & trying to get it on the cheapest & laziest terms He can invent."[17]

His witty comparison to God the Father had a savage dimension that he accentuated in "Letters from the Earth," which remained unpublished until 1962. "The best minds will tell you," Satan observed, "that when a man has begotten a child he is morally bound to tenderly care for it, protect it from hurt, shield it from disease, clothe it, feed it, bear with its waywardness, lay no hand upon it save in kindness and for its own good, and never in any case inflict upon it a wanton cruelty." Twain follows this eloquent summary of good parenting with a striking contrast: "God's treatment of his earthly children, every day and every night, is the exact opposite of all that."[18]

"Letters from the Earth" is, for the most part, a blistering indictment of God the Father—as presented by orthodox Christianity. Twain excoriated "Our Father in Heaven" for his moral bankruptcy, Old Testament cruelty, hypocrisy, jealousy, lack of mercy and justice, as well as his mistreatment of Adam and Eve and their descendents. Some of the venom directed against God in "Letters from the Earth" clearly originates from Twain's frustration and anger at his own failings as a father, as he made explicit in saying to Clara: "More than once I have been humiliated by my resemblance to God the Father."

Another parallel was also operating in "Letters from the Earth." God cruelly mistreats his earthly children, Satan observed, yet those same children condone His crimes, "excuse them, and indignantly refuse to regard them as crimes at all, when *he* commits them."[19] Jean had also excused her father, perhaps even refusing to regard his actions as "crimes at all." He was amazed by Jean's generosity, he confessed to Clara, recognizing that he had not deserved her love.

In the time they had together, however, he attempted to make amends. For eight months he related to his daughter Jean in a new way—more attentive, open, and respectful than before her exile. Much to his surprise, he discovered that she was like her "incomparable" mother, he wrote to several friends after her death. "So fine, so admirable, so noble," was how he described her to his friend Joe Twichell. "Jean had a fine mind, and most competent brain," he insisted vehemently. "That shit said she was insane!" he railed bitterly at the memory of his secretary's betrayal. "She & her confederate told that to everybody around here."[20]

But then Twain remembered something even more important about his daughter. "Jean's last act, Thursday night, was to defend her [Lyon] when I burst out upon her! It makes me proud to remember that.... O blessed Jean, and precious!" Without Jean he was, as Joe Twichell described him, "the lonesomest man in the world."[21]

———

After Jean's death, Twain remained at Stormfield for ten days, but eagerly anticipated his return to Bermuda on January 5. On the night before he sailed, he saw his friend William Dean Howells for the last time. They reminisced but they also continued to speak of the vital subjects of the day. Howells recalled that their last meeting was "made memorable" by Twain's defense of labor unions as the "sole present help of the weak against the strong."[22]

Paine did not escort Twain to Bermuda this time. Thus, with Clara in Europe, he was the only family intimate to read the Sunday *New York Times* in early February 1910. Perusing an article on Twain's *Tom Sawyer,* Paine discovered a letter, reprinted in the *Times,* that was signed by "I. V. Lyon," followed by the abbreviation for "secretary." The letter summarized Twain's response to charges that the plot of *Tom Sawyer, Detective* was plagiarized from a Danish story by Steen Blicher. Clemens was not familiar with Danish, his secretary reported, and had never read any translation or adaptation of Blicher's work. The problem was that the secretary's letter was dated Dec. 9, 1909, eight months after Twain had fired Lyon from her position.[23]

Paine was furious, sending this ditty to Clemens on the same day that the *Times* article appeared: "Who feeds on bromide and on Scotch / To keep her nerves at highest notch? / Who makes of business-books a botch? / *The Bitch.*" A week later, Paine was still fuming. "Is there no way to shut your people off?" he angrily wrote the publisher of the *Times.* "'Was Tom Sawyer Danish or American' is mere Sunday filling & does not matter," he lectured, "but what does matter is the letter.... That date must have been deliberately changed, somewhere, if the letter is genuine."[24]

Fortunately, Twain was cut off from the latest shenanigans of his former confidants. With his butler functioning as aide-de-camp, he was content to enjoy life on the island, summarizing his feelings in a letter to Paine as "good times, good home, tranquil contentment all day & every day without a break." He stayed at the home of the Allens and was surrounded by a bevy of admirers and friends, including Woodrow Wilson, who played miniature golf with him for several hours. But there was no substitute for the one he had lost. "I miss Jean so!" he wrote to Clara. "She was utterly sweet & dear those last days; & so wise, & so dignified, & so good."[25]

Clemens made no mention of his illness in letters to Paine, but on March 25 he wrote that he had booked passage home because he did not want to die in Bermuda. "I am growing more and more particular about the place," he told Paine, and he disliked the idea of his corpse lying in a dark, dank undertaker's cellar on the island while waiting to be shipped home. On April 1 letters arrived from both Clemens and his host which indicated that his condition was critical. Paine hurriedly sailed for Bermuda and arrived to find him surprisingly vital and enjoying a short period of calm before the final storm. But his chest pains came again—severe attacks that no one thought he could survive.[26]

He sailed for home on April 12 in serious distress. At first his breathing was difficult, then impossible. He could not lie down, or even recline, as he fought for air in the humid Gulf Stream. He changed positions over and over in an attempt to get comfortable; first sitting on the couch, then being helped to his feet by Paine, then lurching back to his berth. But he would relax only to be jerked to attention by the absence of air. The tortures of suffocation were so great, he did not think he would make it back to Redding. When Paine told him he must hold on for Clara, who was steaming across the Atlantic to join him, Sam responded: "It is a losing race; no ship can outsail death."[27]

But he sailed his ship just fast enough to see Clara again. She arrived at Stormfield with her husband on April 17, only to find her father cheerful and talkative. Two days later he asked her to sing for him, which she found the strength to do. Soothed and comforted by her voice, "he bade her good-bye," Paine recalled, "saying he might not see her again." He called for Paine close to the end and asked him to throw away two unfinished manuscripts. "I assured him that I would take care of them," Paine wrote, "and he pressed my hand. It was his last word to me." On his final day of life, he took Clara's hand, looked steadfastly into her eyes and faintly murmured, "Good bye, dear." Dr. Quintard thought he added, "If we meet—"[28]

Clemens died with dignity. "There was not a vestige of hesitation," Paine insisted, "there was no grasping at straws, no suggestion of dread." In the shadow of death, according to Paine's eyewitness account, Clemens was "never less than brave."[29]

More than a dozen years preceding his death, a reporter had come to interview the Clemens family about a report that the author was seriously ill. Clemens, in good health, walked into the parlor unexpectedly, and the reporter showed him the orders he had received by cablegram: "If Mark Twain very ill, five hundred words. If dead, send one thousand." Twain never skipped a beat. "You don't need as much as that. Just say the report of my death has been grossly exaggerated."[30] On April 21, 1910, the exaggeration ended. Mark Twain was dead, and the world would need more than a thousand words to contain its loss.

How Little One May Tell

How little one may tell of such a life as his!
ALBERT BIGELOW PAINE,
Mark Twain: A Biography

THERE WAS NO ONE, not even Mark Twain's surviving daughter, who grieved more than Katy Leary over his death. "It almost cut my heart in two when I looked at him for the last time," she remembered fifteen years later. "I felt like my life ended then! That I had lost the best friend I'd had in the world."[1] To the devoted servant, in times of trouble, fell the work of a Clemens family burial and the painful aftermath of tidying up. In 1896 she had packed away Susy's belongings for good; eight years later she gathered the small treasures of her dead mistress; too soon it was Miss Jean's turn to receive her ministrations. And now at last she was picking through the litter of Mr. Clemens's room. Cigars, pencils, matches, pins, and whiskey—the defining effluvia of his intimate habits.

"Oh, it was awful!" Katy remembered. "Every morning while I was putting the things in order, I always locked the door so nobody could come in, because I would cry over everything I picked up—every single thing—because I knew he never would use it again. It was so terrible to think he wouldn't be ever any more in that room." It took Katy more than a week to bring order to Mr. Clemens's room because she could only work in brief intervals before breaking down. Although the desolation of Stormfield was partially dissipated in the summer with the birth of Clemens's grandchild, Nina, still, Katy was not assuaged. "It didn't seem right to have summer come without him, and I was glad to go away from there."[2]

Clara and her husband had decided to return to Germany to live. "I would have loved to have taken care of her and the baby," Katy admitted. "But I couldn't. I wasn't able. So we made up our minds we'd part." Katy was left behind, officially retired from the Clemenses' family service after thirty years. Her last day at Redding she inspected the entire house, saving her boss's room for the final moment. "I went in and locked the door—and stood there all alone," she remembered, "and I looked around and I smelled his tobacco just the same as when he used to be there. Then I said good-by to it all—forever."[3]

Katy opened a boarding house in New York City, but she did not need to generate much income. The generosity of Sam and Clara meant that she could retire without financial worries. What gave her most comfort, however, was the furniture Clara had given her. "I used to look and look at them," she said, referring to the chairs and table, "and tried to feel I was with the family again, and try to imagine the old days once more." She recalled that early in her service, Livy had selected her reading and strictly supervised her social life. "Yes, Mrs. Clemens, she was wonderful and kind—," Katy announced, "but I could have had a great deal better time going out, if she didn't take *quite* such good care of me!"[4] Her recollections were shrewd but guileless. She confessed to a "natural" fondness for wine, an inability to be nice to the people she disliked, and an unabashed enjoyment of a risqué book she once discovered by accident in Sam's billiard room. But she made no comments about the woman who had tried to take Livy's place, and her complete silence about Miss Lyon seems oddly out of character.

Katy's memoir was told to Mary Lawton and was published in 1925. Her recollections of the old days blossomed under the careful tending of Lawton—who almost certainly excised any remarks about the secretary. Lawton did not, however, invent this strategy of omission; it originated with Clara, Lawton's dearest friend. Elizabeth Wallace, a professor of Romance languages at the University of Chicago, wrote a book on Mark Twain in Bermuda, where she had met and become friends with both Clemens and Lyon. Before the book was published in 1913, she was given a special warning by Paine: Clara would not look kindly on any references to Miss Lyon. The year before, Paine himself had published his biography of Twain—1,587 pages in three volumes, with only a single reference to the secretary and one to the business manager. This was a stunning act of literary amputation. And in her 1931 memoir, *My Father, Mark Twain,* Clara followed her own dictum and Paine's example and referred once each to her father's secretary and business manager.[5] With Paine's advice and help, Clara's blackout worked surprisingly well. Following his radical surgery, almost fifty years of deliberate silence surrounded Lyon and Ashcroft.

———

Lyon and Ashcroft were undoubtedly aware of the quarantine that surrounded them. But whatever their frustrations with Clara, they had to cope with their own problems, which unfortunately included their marriage. Not unexpectedly, at least from their former boss's perspective, the marital relationship turned out badly. "By this time," Twain mused less than three months after the pair had set up housekeeping together in Brooklyn, "they loathe each other." His brag that he would be avenged by their matrimonial misery proved prescient.[6]

The Lioness's judgment at age eighty-four was emphatic. She told Clemens's great-nephew, Samuel Webster, that her marriage "was a mistake." Eight years earlier she had been even more forthright, telling a private detective posing as a literary agent that "she had taken a husband without loving him." Lyon blamed Ashcroft, confiding to the undercover detective that her husband had "proceeded to make her life a living hell." It is easy to believe, however, that the marriage was unpleasant for both partners. They moved to Canada in 1913 and divorced in 1926. Ashcroft, who stayed in Canada, remarried in 1927 and had a successful career in advertising.[7]

Lyon returned to New York and remained single. She eventually found her way to a small basement apartment in Greenwich Village, where she lived the lifestyle of a "new woman"—cultured, independent, freethinking, and salaried. In public she smoked a thin cigar, and in her apartment, a pipe. She worked as a secretary for the rest of her life, and probably had few material advantages, sustaining herself with memories of the glory days with Twain.[8]

During all those years that Clara successfully shut her out of the story of Twain's life, she was not entirely passive. After her divorce, she conceived a plan to revise her diary. "Some day the penalty for having such perfect living will come," Lyon had written in ink on January 15, 1905, referring to her life with Twain. "After 28 years—Jan 3/33—," she inserted in pencil, "No penalty attaches itself to perfect living—No penalties ever attach themselves to joys—[.]" At least two other notations indicate that she probably revisited her chronicles of daily life with Twain throughout the 1930s. She did more than annotate her diaries at another stage of life, however. Over the years, Lyon altered a number of entries in her original diaries, making revisions on top of, in the margins, and alongside her initial accounts. Her revisions are easily detected. Often in a different color of ink or pencil, they were clearly superimposed upon or added to the original text. She usually made no attempt to disguise her alterations to the original.[9]

These "open revisions" might suggest that Lyon's purpose was personal and spontaneous were it not for the discovery of a duplicate diary that she copied in longhand. Referred to by its archival location as the Austin diary, this "work" quietly incorporated Lyon's changes to the original text. By exactly copying her revised text in longhand, she created a *new* diary. The existence of this duplicate diary in longhand, beginning on January 3 and ending on June 22, 1906, is crucial. It suggests that Lyon intended to edit her original diaries, recopy them by hand, and bequeath those copies to history. It seems likely that she meant to destroy her originals, with their obvious evidence of superimposed revisions. The handwritten copy, standing on its own, could now be substituted for the original.[10] But the switch was never made. Even with all the intervening years, somehow she failed to finish the job. She continued to be employed into her eighties, which may have been a factor in her aborted copying scheme.[11] Probably the task of hand copying proved daunting—not least because she continued to drink heavily.

When she was eighty-four, Lyon granted Twain's great-nephew, Samuel Webster, an interview. "I wouldn't try to drink her under the table if I were you," Webster joked with a renowned Twain scholar, "as I don't think you have quite the capacity. But maybe I misjudge you. I understand there's a college course for advanced students & they give you a degree." Despite Lyon's own "advanced degree" in alcohol consumption, which Webster and his wife, Doris, recorded in their observations after an evening with her, she remained in full possession of the charm and persuasive skills that had mesmerized Twain. She soon became their friend and confidante. She gave them her original diaries with all her superimposed revisions, perhaps with publication in mind.[12] Doris Webster produced a typescript copy that, for the most part, adhered to Lyon's alterations of the original text—and resulted in still another variant of the original diaries.

————

Lyon's interview with Samuel and Doris Webster took place on March 5, 1948. Webster's mother was Mark Twain's niece; his father ran Twain's publishing house, Charles Webster and Company, until he retired out of sheer exhaustion at thirty-seven, a victim of his own vanity and Twain's errant and expansive financial schemes. Two years before the interview with Miss Lyon, Webster had published a book defending his father's honor against attacks in the published portions of Twain's autobiography.[13] Despite the abuse of his father's reputation, Webster still expressed affection and admiration for his great-uncle.

"She was a charming old lady who seems bright as a hawk," Samuel Webster began the notes of their interview. "She has charm & intelligence & it seemed to us complete sincerity," his wife agreed. They took dinner at the apartment of a mutual friend, and Lyon told them she "had never talked so freely before." Doris Webster believed Lyon opened up because of her husband's intimate knowledge of Twain. In her conversation with the Websters, Lyon created the impression that her relationship with Twain had been like that of an exemplary daughter—helpful, observant, deferential, and devotedly attached. Whether spontaneous or deliberate, the persona of the caring daughter played well and perhaps became her last version of their life together. "There was positively no question of romance," Doris informed a friend five years later, after becoming Lyon's friend. "He was an old man to Isabel, who must have been an exceedingly attractive young woman."[14]

In reality, of course, Isabel Lyon had been deeply enthralled by Mark Twain's body as well as his mind and yearned to become his wife. "Such a beautiful man he is," she wrote in 1907, after he slipped into her room "with just his silk underclothes on."[15] Doris Webster retyped those lines from the original diary, along with countless others that contradicted Lyon's claims. Her romantic desires were inscribed in every nook and cranny of the chronicles of her life with Twain. Yet Doris and her husband found the "caring daughter" persona totally convincing. Lyon's ability to imagine herself into other people's expectations continued to be irresistible.

That her "good daughter" persona prevailed over a mountain of contrary evidence aided Lyon's effort to promote a "bad daughter" image for Jean. She told them "a good deal about Jean's illness," and the Websters, who shared the still-common, though mistaken, association of epilepsy with violence, had no trouble believing that Jean "was really dangerous." It was here the accusation that Jean had made "homicidal attacks" on Katy Leary originated. The Websters eventually read Lyon's diary entry for January 27, 1906, in which she wrote, "In a burst of unreasoning rage she [Jean] struck Katie a terrible blow in the face. . . . She knew she couldn't stop—she had to strike—and she said that she wanted to kill." Lyon also claimed that Jean had made an earlier murderous attack, on November 26, 1905. The date had such clarity, she told the Websters, because she had recorded it in her journal in a simple code. The entry read: "Jean. 3—pm 8 *PM* <u>Katie</u>," with the word "Katie" underlined twice. "This refers to an attack on the maid Katie Leary, that Miss Lyon told me about," Webster noted on the typescript of the journal and continued, "Jean was getting dangerous, and the doctor told Miss Lyon never to let Jean get between her and the door, and never to close the door." Significantly, Lyon actively campaigned against Jean, depicting her as a dangerous person "when one of these attacks was on."[16] Almost forty years after Twain's death, she was still anxious to cast herself as his protector and guardian angel.

She also managed to convince the Websters that Paine was jealous of Jean, an idea so lacking in corroboration as to be absurd, but perhaps a revealing projection of her own feelings. Paine had wanted to remove Jean from the Redding house, Lyon told the gullible duo, and replace her with his wife. She was obviously campaigning against Paine too in 1948, attempting to construct him as the selfish, manipulative schemer and herself as the high-minded person who saved his job as biographer.[17]

The pattern that Lyon established in her 1948 interview with the Websters reflects the changes that she made to her original diaries, most likely in the 1930s. Paine and Jean were prime targets. She sometimes deleted favorable remarks or added negative comments in entries about Paine, such as "Old Fraud!" On two occasions, she made revisions to strengthen the impression of Jean as a homicidal killer. In the entry for January 27, 1906, she added these lines in a penciled revision: "and was sorry she hadn't—to her mind, it doesn't seem right not to finish any job you have begun and she had wanted to kill Katie." She also crossed out the parenthetical phrase in that entry, "(She is distressed poor child)"—only five words, but their deletion is substantial. In the same entry she noted that "now she has done what I...feared she would do," a clear indication that this was the "first" attack, while in the entry for September 29, 1906, she inserted a strikingly contradictory comment that the doctors feared the "violence may come in time."[18] She was striving to create a narrative in which she was the innocent heroine, working hard to protect her famous boss (and his household) from the dangerous menace within. Lyon clearly wanted to be remembered as Twain's defender, and therefore as justified in her treatment of Jean.

Surprisingly, Clara, who had once been her pet, received minimal attention in Lyon's revisions as well as in her interview with the Websters. Though she told them that Clara "took a dislike" to her and got her dismissed, Lyon did not appear to dwell on Clara's shortcomings. In her seventies and eighties, the daughter who still troubled her was Jean.

Lyon was also occasionally troubled by the specter of Mark Twain. She must have suspected, though she had no concrete evidence, that he had written something quite negative about her.[19] Perhaps fearing his condemnation in writing that would surface someday, she took the precaution of excising an especially revealing passage about him in her diary. As a rule, she only lightly edited descriptions of Twain's behavior, character, conversation, or writing. But there is a glaring exception. "I often think that if the value of his approval is great, then the value of his disapproval is greater," she wrote in her original 1906 entry about Twain, "with his loveliness and depth of character he can see and overlook many weaknesses, human weaknesses—but where his [sic] really condemns—you won't ever find any condemnation juster." She concludes, "He has temporary prejudices, thousands of them, but you learn the differences between those and the things he really condemns." This entire passage is missing from her Austin diary, which she rewrote by hand.[20]

Lyon strove to vindicate herself in her own eyes as well as the eyes of the world. That she succeeded in the world's eyes is no small triumph, even if she did not live to savor her victory. But for all her anxiety about her future reputation, she surely would never have expected, or even wanted, to be a heroine at Twain's expense. The shrine she kept to his memory into her eighties speaks of her attachment to him as a fundamental part of her self-image.[21]

————

A new neighbor, not knowing Lyon's absolute dread of hospitals, called an ambulance when she fell in her apartment. While the attendants were lifting her into the vehicle, Isabel Lyon had a heart attack that ended her life. She was almost ninety-five.[22] If Clara let herself believe with Lyon's death in 1958 that her family history was safe, she would have been deceived. Her protective strategy was on the verge of collapse when she herself died four years later.

In 1960 Caroline Harnsberger published an idiosyncratic, unreliable account of Twain's family life that featured a heroic portrait of Clara. Ironically, Harnsberger, an enthusiastic admirer of Twain's ever-vigilant daughter, was the first to break her code of silence. Harnsberger cobbled together a collection of lies and half-truths about Twain's last years from Ashcroft's newspaper accounts and interviews. Jean was depicted as quarrelsome and antisocial, but the rest of Clemens's family was blameless, and she portrayed the Ashcrofts as innocents.[23] Once again Ralph's expertly crafted public relations job had protected his image and that of his wife.

Harnsberger got one thing right. Clara had been contentedly married to Ossip Gabrilowitsch. But Harnsberger, eager for the happily-ever-after ending, was undeterred by the fact that Gabrilowitsch died of cancer in 1936. After Clara remarried, Harnsberger rhapsodized that she "entered 'a multifarious strata of rainbowism.'" Unfortunately, the pot of gold at the end of Clara's rainbow was a whopping $351,154.97 in promissory notes borrowed by her second husband, Jacques Samossoud, an unemployed orchestra conductor whose serious gambling habit brought Mark Twain's only surviving child to the brink of financial ruin. She was reduced, in the late 1950s and early 1960s, to borrowing money from her friends, including Harnsberger. Clara even signed a promissory note for $13,950.03 to her secretary.[24]

Ironically, just as Clara had challenged the financial stewardship of Lyon and Ashcroft, so her daughter, Nina Gabrilowitsch, contested the fiscal conduct of her stepfather, whom she accused of fraud and undue influence after her mother died. A settlement was reached, but only after Nina's lawyer filed a civil suit asking for repayment of the promissory notes, followed by a motion requiring Clara's second husband to produce all communications concerning his wife's estate. Nina, who received no inheritance under the terms of her mother's will, settled out of court for more than one-third of the income from her grandfather's royalties. In January 1966, Nina died alone in a motel room strewn with pills and liquor bottles. Her unfinished autobiography was sadly titled "A Life Alone."[25]

Mark Twain's last descendent died the same year that Justin Kaplan published *Mr. Clemens and Mark Twain,* which won critical acclaim and a Pulitzer Prize. Kaplan's account of Twain in his old age was perceptive, albeit cautiously abridged. Only once did he seem to ratify Twain's point of view about Ashcroft and Lyon, observing that he "had grounds enough to charge them with mismanagement and possibly larceny." This was probably the line that brought the threat of a lawsuit from Ashcroft's relatives in Canada. Although they ultimately realized they did not have legal grounds to sue, the Ashcrofts eventually had their revenge from a different source.[26]

After Lyon died in 1958, her diaries and notebooks remained in the care of Samuel and Doris Webster. Lyon had stipulated that they were not to be made available to researchers until after Clara's death. Eventually they were deposited at the Mark Twain Papers at the University of California, Berkeley. In 1973 Hamlin Hill published *God's Fool,* crowning the Ashcrofts as innocent martyrs, victims of one vicious daughter, Clara; one homicidal daughter, Jean; and a vain forgetful old man who created the corruption of his loyal servants in his own mind. Hill triumphantly broke through the wall of censorship that had so obscured Twain's late years. Although he had access only to excerpts from Jean's diaries, he read the Ashcroft-Lyon manuscript and all the accompanying materials as well as all versions of Lyon's diaries except the Austin version. And he chose to trust the secretary and mock the boss—letting Isabel Lyon's diaries define his facts and shape his interpretation of Twain's family life.[27]

Mark Twain is a household word; his secretary's name has been known to few outside the world of Twain scholars, yet she won the battle over the narrative of the last years of her boss's life. Twain wrote the Ashcroft-Lyon manuscript to wipe her off the field of battle, but the literary establishment (with some exceptions) bought her version of Twain's life, culled from her edited diaries. Twain's autobiography has been condemned or disparaged by all but a few of the scholars who have examined it.[28] Thus in a striking irony of American letters, an obscure social secretary triumphed over one of the greatest writers in American literature—until now.

———

After many years, it is time for prejudice and prevarication to give way to an honest and compassionate story. Surely Jean deserves better than to be characterized by her seizures. Doubtless Twain would have raged at the gullible establishment. He would have laughed at his failure to convince them that his most humiliating confessions were true. He would have railed at the damned human race—in which he almost always included himself—yet he would have understood the biographer's difficulty in sorting out the truth.

His was not in the end an old age of weakness, of helpless failure, or of fear. He was a more fortunate, less tragic Lear, who betrayed his own daughter but got her back—almost miraculously. In the end he lost her not to his folly but to a cruel fate. For this he was grateful—and in genuine humility he wrote her valedictory, "The Death of Jean." He was appalled at his secretary's meanness and, yes, angry at the cost his family had paid for his colossal selfishness. But Mark Twain did not die a forlorn man. He knew, to a depth that most human beings never plumb, that he had not deserved his daughters' love, and yet they gave it anyway. He understood that this was his grace and he took it to his grave.

———

Twain also knew how difficult it is to read a text. Therefore, the last word belongs to him in a short fable he wrote in June 1906 and read aloud to Jean and her friend Nancy Brush that summer in Dublin. Among the writings of his late years, this little piece may be obscure, but it is a coda on historical evidence—his gently imaginative and deeply moral judgment on all who grapple with the past.[29]

A FABLE

Once upon a time an artist who had painted a small and very beautiful picture placed it so that he could see it in the mirror. He said, "This doubles the distance and softens it, and it is twice as lovely as it was before."

The animals out in the woods heard of this through the housecat, who was greatly admired by them because he was so learned, and so refined and civilized, and so polite and high-bred, and could tell them so much which they didn't know before, and were not certain about afterward. They were much excited about this new piece of gossip, and they asked questions, so as to get at a full understanding of it. They asked what a picture was, and the cat explained.

"It is a flat thing," he said; "wonderfully flat, marvellously flat, enchantingly flat and elegant. And, oh, so beautiful!"

That excited them almost to a frenzy, and they said they would give the world to see it. Then the bear asked:

"What is it that makes it so beautiful?"

"It is the looks of it," said the cat.

This filled them with admiration and uncertainty, and they were more excited than ever. Then the cow asked:

"What is a mirror?"

"It is a hole in the wall," said the cat. "You look in it, and there you see the picture, and it is so dainty and charming and ethereal and inspiring in its unimaginable beauty that your head turns round and round, and you almost swoon with ecstasy."

The ass had not said anything as yet; he now began to throw doubts. He said there had never been anything as beautiful as this before, and probably wasn't now. He said that when it took a whole basketful of sesquipedalian adjectives to whoop up a thing of beauty, it was time for suspicion.

It was easy to see that these doubts were having an effect upon the animals, so the cat went off offended. The subject was dropped for a couple of days, but in the mean time curiosity was taking a fresh start, and there was a revival of interest perceptible. Then the animals assailed the ass for spoiling what could possibly have been a pleasure to them, on a mere suspicion that the picture was not beautiful, without any evidence that such was the case. The ass was not troubled; he was calm, and said there was one way to find out who was in the right, himself or the cat: he would go and look in that hole, and come back and tell what he found there. The animals felt relieved and grateful, and asked him to go at once—which he did.

But he did not know where he ought to stand; and so, through error, he stood between the picture and the mirror. The result was that the picture had no chance, and didn't show up. He returned home and said:

"The cat lied. There was nothing in that hole but an ass. There wasn't a sign of a flat thing visible. It was a handsome ass, and friendly, but just an ass, and nothing more."

The elephant asked:

"Did you see it good and clear? Were you close to it?"

"I saw it good and clear, O Hathi, King of Beasts. I was so close that I touched noses with it."

"That is very strange," said the elephant; "the cat was always truthful before—as far as we could make out. Let another witness try. Go, Baloo, look in the hole, and come and report."

So the bear went, when he came back, he said:

"Both the cat and the ass have lied; there was nothing in the hole but a bear."

Great was the surprise and puzzlement of the animals. Each was now anxious to make the test himself and get at the straight truth. The elephant sent them one at a time.

First, the cow. She found nothing in the hole but a cow.

The tiger found nothing in it but a tiger.

The lion found nothing in it but a lion.

The leopard found nothing in it but a leopard.

The camel found a camel, and nothing more.

Then Hathi was wroth, and said he would have the truth, if he had to go and fetch it himself. When he returned, he abused his whole subjectry for liars, and was in an unappeasable fury with the moral and mental blindness of the cat. He said that anybody but a near-sighted fool could see that there was nothing in the hole but an elephant.

MORAL, BY THE CAT

You can find in a text whatever you bring, if you will stand between it and the mirror of your imagination. You may not see your ears, but they will be there.

NOTES

The following abbreviations are used throughout the notes:

ABP   Albert Bigelow Paine

ABP, *Biography*   Albert Bigelow Paine. *Mark Twain: A Biography*. New York: Harper & Brothers, 1912.

AL   Mark Twain's 1909 handwritten narrative of his years with Isabel Lyon and Ralph Ashcroft, referred to as the Ashcroft-Lyon manuscript; unpublished; MTP, also ME.

AL File   Loose documents related to the AL manuscript; located in Boxes 48 and 49, MTP, also ME.

AL "To the Unborn Reader"   Introduction added to the completed AL manuscript; separately paginated as pp. 1–4; MTP, also ME.

CC   Clara Clemens

CFP   Clemens Family Papers, HEH.

Cooley, ed.   John Cooley, ed. *Mark Twain's Aquarium: The Samuel Clemens–Angelfish Correspondence, 1905–1910*. Athens: University of Georgia Press, 1991.

DQ   Dorothy Quick

HEH   Henry E. Huntington Library, San Marino, Calif.

HHR   Lewis Leary, ed. *Mark Twain's Correspondence with Henry Huttleston Rogers*. Berkeley: University of California Press, 1969.

Hill   Hamlin Hill. *God's Fool*. New York: Harper and Row, 1973.

IVL   Isabel Van Kleek Lyon

IVL Journal / Daily Reminder / Datebook / Stenographic Notebook   Original and ph. diaries, 1903–8; and five original stenographic notebooks kept 1906–8; MTP. The original diaries have superimposed editing done at a later date by IVL in black and red pencil and ink of various colors (see Epilogue). Included are Daily Reminder 1903, ph. (original at Vassar College, Poughkeepsie, N.Y.); Journal 1903–4 (also contains entries through Sept. 18, 1905); Antenne-Dorrance Daily Reminder 1905, ph. (appointment notes); Daily Reminders 1905, 1906; Datebook 1907; Daily Reminder 1908.

Two revised versions are also at MTP: IVL Journal 1906, ph. of IVL's hand-copied edited entries drawn from her original Daily Reminder 1906 for Jan. 3–June 22 (original at University of Texas, Austin; referred to as the Austin version); and Samuel and Doris Webster's ts. copy of most of the original diaries, which often silently incorporates the editing IVL had marked in them and presents 1905 entries that were originally written in the 1903–4 journal as if they came from the 1905 Daily Reminder. This ts. was done with IVL's approval.

IVL MT Notes   File of later notes, fragments, etc., applicable to IVL's relationship with SLC and his family; MTP.

JC   Jean Clemens

JC Diaries   Diaries for 1900, 1905–7 (1907 only through Feb. 28); CFP, Box 1.

JCE Diary   JC's Excelsior Diary, a small datebook in which she jotted short descriptive notes throughout 1907.

JC to Nancy Brush letters, ph.   Photocopies of correspondence, read at MTP; originals located in Archives of American Art, Smithsonian Institution, Washington, D.C.

Kaplan   Justin Kaplan. *Mr. Clemens and Mark Twain: A Biography.* New York: Simon and Schuster, 1966.

Kiskis, ed., *MT's Autobiography*   Michael Kiskis, ed. *Mark Twain's Own Autobiography: The Chapters from the "North American Review."* Madison: University of Wisconsin Press, 1990.

Lifetime   Mary Lawton. *A Lifetime with Mark Twain.* New York: Harcourt, Brace, and Co., 1925; Katy Leary's memoir of her thirty years of service to the Clemens family, as told to Mary Lawton, a friend of Clara Clemens. Note that I have used the spelling of Leary's first name as it appears in this memoir, although the Clemens family often used "Katie."

Macnaughton   William R. Macnaughton. *Mark Twain's Last Years as a Writer.* Columbia: University of Missouri Press, 1979.

ME	Microfilm edition of Mark Twain's Manuscript Letters now in the Twain Papers, the Bancroft Library, University of California, Berkeley; microfilm edition of Mark Twain's literary manuscripts available in the Mark Twain Papers, the Bancroft Library, University of California, Berkeley; and microfilm edition of Mark Twain's previously unpublished letters (Berkeley: Bancroft Library, 2001).
MMT	William Dean Howells. *My Mark Twain: Reminiscences and Criticisms.* Edited by Marilyn Austin Baldwin. Baton Rouge: Louisiana State University Press, 1967; orig. pub. 1910.
MTHL	Henry Nash Smith and William Gibson, eds. *Mark Twain–Howells Letters: The Correspondence of Samuel L. Clemens and William D. Howells, 1876–1910.* Cambridge, Mass.: Harvard University Press, 1960.
MTP	Mark Twain Papers, Bancroft Library, University of California, Berkeley. All material written by or to SLC, CC, and JC is located here, unless otherwise indicated.
My Father	Clara Clemens. *My Father, Mark Twain.* New York: Harper & Brothers, 1931.
OLC	Olivia (Livy) Langdon Clemens
ph.	photocopy
RWA	Ralph W. Ashcroft
SLC	Samuel Langhorne Clemens, known as Mark Twain
SLC Probate	Probate report: To the Court of Probate of and for the District of Redding [Conn.], October 18, 1910. Estate of Samuel L. Clemens, Deceased; MTP.
ts.	typescript
WDH	William Dean Howells
Webster Notes on IVL	"Notes by Samuel C. & Doris Webster on talk with Mrs. [sic] Lyon March 5 1948" (also includes a few undated pages); actually a memorandum to Dixon Wecter dictated by Sam Webster to his wife, Doris, who added her impressions. IVL MT Notes.

PREFACE

1. Louis J. Budd calls Hal Holbrook's show "the strongest popularizing influence since around 1960," in *Our Mark Twain: The Making of His Public Personality* (Philadelphia: University of Pennsylvania Press, 1983), 237.

2. See Hill, xxvii. Although Jean's diaries were unavailable to Hill in 1973, he did have access to a 23-page typescript of selected extracts from the diaries that had been transcribed in 1951.

3. AL, 71. In ME.

CHAPTER 1

1. *Mark Twain's Notebooks and Journals,* ed. Robert Pack Browning, Michael B. Frank, and Lin Salamo (Berkeley: University of California Press, 1979), 3: 238.

2. On Livy, Kenneth R. Andrews, *Nook Farm: Mark Twain's Hartford Circle* (Cambridge, Mass.: Harvard University Press), 89. On the marriage, see Dixon Wecter, ed., *The Love Letters of Mark Twain* (New York: Harper & Brothers, 1947), hereafter cited as *Love Letters;* also Susan K. Harris, *The Courtship of Olivia Langdon and Mark Twain* (New York: Cambridge University Press, 1996), esp. chapter 5. OLC to SLC, Dec. 2, 1871, *Love Letters,* 166–69. SLC to OLC, Jan. 7, [1872], *Love Letters,* 171–72.

3. Van Wyck Brooks, *The Ordeal of Mark Twain* (New York: E. P. Dutton & Co., 1920), 145–55; quote at 145; "infantile" at 155. See Laura Skandera-Trombley, *Mark Twain in the Company of Women* (Philadelphia: University of Pennsylvania Press, 1994), for a discussion of Brooks's influence on Twain criticism and biography, 1–23; she also provides an excellent critique of the stereotypes of Livy as prude and helpless victim of Victorian conventions, 58–62. Kiskis, ed., *MT's Autobiography,* 24. *My Father,* 85.

4. MMT, 11, 28, 13–14. *Lifetime,* 236, 240–41. When Twain's eldest daughter Susy was five, she informed a visitor that "she had been in church only once, and that was the time when [her sister] Clara was 'crucified' (christened)." Albert Bigelow Paine, ed., *Mark Twain's Autobiography* (New York: Harper & Brothers, 1924), 1: 52.

5. MMT, 64. Kiskis, ed., *MT's Autobiography,* 47–48.

6. *My Father,* 26, 203; I have added the narrative frame here, but the dialogue quotations are exact.

7. SLC to Mother [Mary Mason Fairbanks], Feb. 20, 1868, in Dixon Wecter, ed., *Mark Twain to Mrs. Fairbanks* (San Marino, Calif.: Huntington Library, 1949), 18–19; see also Wecter's introduction for Fairbanks's influence on *Innocents,* xxv. Mary Mason Fairbanks to OLC, Apr. 1, 1872, CFP.

8. MMT, 18.

9. Kiskis, ed., *MT's Autobiography,* 49; also see *My Father,* 68, for more on Twain's positive attitude toward his wife's editing.

10. *Lifetime,* 18, 22, 36; see 19–42 for Katy's descriptions of the dinner parties and guests.

11. *Lifetime,* 84–87, 110–11. Again, I have added a narrative frame to Katy's conversational quotes.

12. Kiskis, ed., *MT's Autobiography*, 63, 27.

13. *My Father*, 85, 154. ABP, *Biography*, 682.

14. On deferring to Livy, see MMT, 11–12. Kiskis, ed., *MT's Autobiography*, 30–31.

15. *Lifetime*, 7–10, 18, 236. On Clemens sitting with the children at lunch, *My Father*, 56.

16. *My Father*, 60–61.

17. Kiskis, ed., *MT's Autobiography*, 28, 30, 178, 124, 163–64. *My Father*, 6.

18. Kiskis, ed., *MT's Autobiography*, 177–78.

19. *My Father*, 188; *Lifetime*, 82; Andrew Hoffman, *Inventing Mark Twain: The Lives of Samuel Langhorne Clemens* (New York: William Morrow & Co., 1997), 337. Paine, ed., *Mark Twain's Autobiography*, 2: 63–64.

20. Paine, ed., *Mark Twain's Autobiography*, 2: 64. Kiskis, ed., *MT's Autobiography*, 170–71.

21. *My Father*, 76–77.

22. Kiskis, ed., *MT's Autobiography*, 178.

23. Kiskis, ed., *MT's Autobiography*, 178, 176. *My Father*, 25. Caroline Harnsberger, *Mark Twain: Family Man* (New York: Citadel Press, 1960), 21.

24. Kiskis, ed., *MT's Autobiography*, 178, 35, 51, 38–40; Twain quotes comments from Susy's *Papa* at 51, 40.

25. Kiskis, ed., *MT's Autobiography*, 190, 58.

26. *Lifetime*, 4, 49–50.

27. *Lifetime*, 49, 112, 54, 339.

28. *Lifetime*, 7, 75–77.

29. *Lifetime*, 27–28, 59.

30. *Lifetime*, 12–15. Again, I have added a narrative frame, but the dialogue quotes are exact.

31. *Lifetime*, 17.

32. *Lifetime*, 69–70, 272.

33. *Lifetime*, 154, 152.

34. *Lifetime*, 339–40, 60, 298–99, 333.

35. *Lifetime*, 348, 274.

36. JC Diary, July 9, 1906.

37. Webster Notes on IVL, undated, and Mar. 5, 1948. Lyon told Doris Webster that she met Clemens "about ten years before she became his secretary." This would mean that the meeting occurred sometime in the early 1890s, or maybe in the late 1880s—certainly before their departure from Hartford in June 1891.

38. Kaplan, 280–306, 327–32.

39. Charles Neider, Introduction to Susy Clemens, *Papa: An Intimate Biography of Mark Twain,* ed. Neider (New York: Doubleday & Co., 1985), 12, 19, 14–30.

40. Grace King, *Memories of a Southern Woman of Letters* (New York: Macmillan Co., 1932), 173. Neider, Introduction, 13–14. The nature of Susy's relationship with Louise Brownell remains ambiguous. In his introduction to *Papa*, Charles Neider includes portions of Susy's love letters to Louise. He resists the conclusion that they had a physical relationship, maintaining that although they clearly kissed and caressed and slept together, their physical expression did not necessarily mean that either woman intended a life-long commitment to same-sex relationships. Andrew Hoffman quotes letters from Susy to Louise (374) that are more passionate than Neider's examples and claims that Susy was taken out of Bryn Mawr because her parents did not approve of her romantic attachment to Louise Brownell; *Inventing Mark Twain*, 367–68. Though possible, I think the bits and pieces of evidence suggest otherwise, especially Clemens's warm response to Brownell after she named one of her daughters in memory of Susy. (SLC to Mrs. [Louise Brownell] Saunders, Oct. 16, 1906, in Neider, Introduction, 39–40.) Neider concludes (42), and I would concur, that it is unlikely Clemens knew the nature of the young women's relationship.

41. Kaplan, 310–12. *Lifetime,* 123. *My Father,* 87.

42. *My Father,* 90–94.

43. See Hoffman, *Inventing Mark Twain,* 373–80; Kaplan, 314–16; Everett Emerson, *Mark Twain: A Literary Life* (Philadelphia: University of Pennsylvania Press, 2000), 208–14.

44. Neider, Introduction, 16–18. King, *Memories,* 176–77, 173.

45. Olivia [Susy] Clemens to Louise Brownell, [late July or early Aug., 1893], in Neider, Introduction, 18–19. *Lifetime,* 130.

46. Hoffman, *Inventing Mark Twain,* 374–76.

47. Harnsberger, *Family Man,* 103–5. *My Father,* 128.

48. Kaplan, 317–33. *My Father,* 121.

49. OLC to SLC, July 31, 1894, in *Love Letters,* 381.

50. OLC to SLC, July 31, 1894, in *Love Letters,* 308–10. OLC to SLC [undated]. *My Father,* 109.

CHAPTER 2

1. For Twain's debt, see Jan. 15, 1894, notebook entry as quoted in Everett Emerson, *Mark Twain: A Literary Life* (Philadelphia: University of Pennsylvania Press, 2000), 204. Kaplan, 330. Charles Neider, Introduction to Susy Clemens, *Papa: An Intimate Biography of Mark Twain,* ed. Neider (New York: Doubleday & Co., 1985), 34–35. *Lifetime,* 130.

2. ABP, *Biography,* 1002.

3. *My Father,* 138–39.

4. *My Father,* 159.

5. M. Allen Starr, M.D., to Susan Langdon Crane, Feb. 29, 1896, CFP. Also see SLC, Aug. 5. Saturday [1899]. *Jean*, ms. pages +1 through +10, at ms. +2; hereafter cited as SLC, "Jean's Illness." (This was apparently an addition to SLC, "Diary of a Kellgren Cure," 170 ms. pages. Albert Bigelow Paine created a typescript copy of the "Diary of a Kellgren Cure," incorporating "Jean's Illness" into his typescript. Citations from the typescript copy [tp.] will be distinguished from manuscript citations [ms.]. I believe these titles—"Jean's Illness," "Diary…"—are Paine's.) On epilepsy, see Richard Lechtenberg, *Epilepsy and the Family* (Cambridge, Mass.: Harvard University Press, 1984).

6. M. Allen Starr, M.D., to Susan Langdon Crane, Feb. 29, Mar. 19, Apr. 16, and May 26, 1896, CFP.

7. These conclusions are based on the letters Dr. Starr wrote to Susan Langdon Crane cited above. While some of Starr's phrasing is ambiguous, Jean's improvement is clearly indicated in the last two extant letters.

8. *My Father*, 170. It was the royalties from *Following the Equator*, not the $30,000 that Twain cleared from the lecture tour, that allowed him to pay off all his debts by the end of January 1898. Emerson, *A Literary Life*, 222–27.

9. *Lifetime*, 130–37. Kiskis, ed., *MT's Autobiography*, 25–27. Andrew Hoffman, *Inventing Mark Twain: The Lives of Samuel Langhorne Clemens* (New York: William Morrow & Co., 1997), 411–12.

10. Neider, Introduction, 43–47.

11. *My Father*, 170–71. Kiskis, ed., *MT's Autobiography*, 27. SLC to OLC, Aug. 1896, in Dixon Wecter, ed., *The Love Letters of Mark Twain* (New York: Harper & Brothers, 1947), 320–21; hereafter cited as *Love Letters*.

12. *Papa*, 54. *My Father*, 171.

13. *Lifetime*, 138–39. Actually, Susy was unconscious for two days before she died. What Katy remembers was in fact Susy's last day of consciousness. Though Katy may have confused the time line in her retelling, hers is the only eye-witness account of Susy's demise. I have therefore preferred hers on details of Susy's death to either Clara's memoir or Twain's autobiography.

14. *My Father*, 64, 179. *Lifetime*, 135–37. SLC, "Jean's Illness," ms. +3. If Clara's claim to ignorance of her parents' favoritism in childhood is believed, then she must have discovered their partiality to Susy sometime in early adulthood. She does not date this painful realization. It might have occurred earlier, of course, but I am guessing that Susy's death brought home the point. Also see *Lifetime*, 140; JC Diary, May 29, 1906.

15. SLC, "Jean's Illness," ms. +3, +4. Jean's doctor sailed for Europe on July 1, 1896. "I will try to find Mr. Clemens if I go to London," Starr wrote Susan Crane in his May 26, 1896, letter. Either he connected with the Clemenses in England before Livy sailed for America or in the States during the brief interval after Susy's death when Livy was there.

16. SLC, "Jean's Illness," ms. +3, +4.

17. Carl Dolmetsch, *"Our Famous Guest": Mark Twain in Vienna* (Athens: University of Georgia Press, 1992), 105–6. *Lifetime*, 82–84, 188, 162.

18. SLC, "Jean's Illness," ms. +4 (in ME), +6 (in ME), +5.

19. SLC, "Jean's Illness," ms. +5 to +6. In ME.

20. SLC, "Jean's Illness," ms. +1, +5.

21. SLC, "Jean's Illness," ms. +7. In ME.

22. Emerson, *A Literary Life*, 222–27. *My Father*, 212–13. *Lifetime*, 163.

23. *My Father*, 193. CC, "Penalties of a Father's Fame," *The London Express*, June 3, 1908, as quoted in Caroline Harnsberger, *Mark Twain: Family Man* (New York: Citadel Press, 1960), 240–41. I have used Harnsberger to reconstruct early aspects of Clara's musical career because this is probably the strongest aspect of her narrative. Her treatment of Jean is unreliable, and in general her book should be used with caution.

24. *My Father*, 201–2.

25. Kiskis, ed., *MT's Autobiography*, 178. *My Father*, 65, 74.

26. *My Father*, 214. Harnsberger, *Family Man*, 183. SLC, "Jean's Illness." SLC, "Diary of a Kellgren Cure," Aug. 11, 1899, ts., 18.

27. SLC, "Diary of a Kellgren Cure," ms. 18, 9G, 9H. In a satirical letter dated "Hell, July /99," Clemens also mocked his experience at the Kellgren sanitarium. See *My Father*, 214–15.

28. SLC, "Diary of a Kellgren Cure," ms. 6. SLC, "Jean's Illness," insert following ms. +2, ms. +9. *My Father*, 214. SLC, "Diary of a Kellgren Cure," Aug. 7 and 11, 1899, ts., 7–8, 18.

29. SLC, "Diary of a Kellgren Cure," Aug. 7, 11, 27, 1899, ts., 7–8, 18, 31.

30. JC Diary, Nov. 10, 1900. Throughout her extant diaries (for 1900, 1905, and 1906) Jean makes intermittent comments about being friendless.

31. Jade L. Dell, "Social Dimensions of Epilepsy: Stigma and Response," in Steven Whitman and Bruce P. Hermann, eds., *Psychopathology in Epilepsy: Social Dimensions* (New York: Oxford University Press, 1986), 191–92.

32. Ellen Dwyer is one of the few contemporary social historians working on the topic of epilepsy. See her outstanding article, "Stories of Epilepsy, 1880–1930," in Charles E. Rosenberg and Jane Golden, eds., *Framing Disease: Studies in Cultural History* (New Brunswick, N.J.: Rutgers University Press, 1992), 256. JC Diary, Nov. 20, Oct. 27, 1900. If she was cured and still found no one to love her, Jean wrote, the "fair reason for suicide" would actually increase.

33. Both Clara and Albert Bigelow Paine believed that the source of Clemens's "deep-seated pessimism" was Susy's death. See *My Father*, 176; ABP, *Biography*, 1021–22. See SLC, "Jean's Illness"; at ms. +3, and ms. +6. Clemens originally wrote that Jean's epilepsy had begun in summer 1896, then corrected that to spring 1896.

34. SLC, "Diary of a Kellgren Cure," Aug. 11, 1899, ts., 18. In ME.

35. Livy quoted in ABP, *Biography,* 1102. On "The Chronicle of Young Satan," see Emerson, *A Literary Life,* 248–51, 253; and William M. Gibson, ed., *Mark Twain's Mysterious Stranger Manuscripts* (Berkeley: University of California Press, 1969), 5–7, 14–19.

36. ABP, *Biography,* 1110. *My Father,* 216–17.

37. *My Father,* 217–20. MTHL, 725–27.

38. Macnaughton, 142–43, 149–57, 160–62. See also Philip S. Foner, *Mark Twain: Social Critic* (New York: International Publishers, 1958), 280–81.

39. Harnsberger, *Family Man,* 186–89.

40. JC Diary, Oct. 24–Nov. 28, 1900.

41. JC Diary, Nov. 5, 9, 1900.

42. Leila Zenderland, *Measuring Minds: Henry Herbert Goddard and the Origins of American Intelligence Testing* (Cambridge: Cambridge University Press, 1998), 266. Dwyer, "Stories," 251.

43. JC Diary, Nov. 10, 1900. On families and stigma, see Dell, "Social Dimensions of Epilepsy," 185–210, esp. 186; Dwyer, "Stories," 250; and Nicky Britten, Michael E. J. Wadsworth, and Peter B. C. Fenwick, "Sources of Stigma Following Early-Life Epilepsy: Evidence from a National Birth Cohort Study," in Whitman and Hermann, eds., *Psychopathology in Epilepsy,* 223–44, esp. 228; Robert J. Mittan, "Fear of Seizures," in Whitman and Hermann, eds., *Psychopathology in Epilepsy,* 90–119, esp. 90–99; Patrick West, "The Social Meaning of Epilepsy: Stigma as a Potential Explanation for Psychopathology in Children," in Whitman and Hermann, eds., *Psychopathology in Epilepsy,* 250, 198 (hereafter cited as West, "Stigma"). Stigma is a negative cultural attitude directed toward physical and behavioral differences among people. It is a deeply discrediting response that most often creates intense shame in sufferers. Strategies used by families to cope with the stigma of epilepsy in the last half of the twentieth century parallel the reported behaviors of Jean's mother found in JC diaries.

44. WDH to SLC, July 31, 1901, in MTHL, 728. "The United States of Lyncherdom," in Justin Kaplan, ed., *The Great Short Works of Mark Twain* (New York: Harper & Row, 1967), 198–200. Macnaughton, 173. I think Twain's reputation among his contemporaries was actually more secure than he recognized. But even his friend Howells, one of the most astute critics of the period, had doubts about the persistence of Twain's public acclaim. See ABP, *Biography,* 1111–12.

45. MTHL, 730 fn. 3, 732–33 fn. 1. WDH to Thomas Bailey Aldrich, Dec. 8, 1901, in MTHL, 735 fn. 2. SLC to Thomas Bailey Aldrich, Sept. 11, 1902, in MTHL, 745 fn. 2.

46. SLC to WDH, Jan. 3, 1902, in MTHL, 736–38; MMT, 66–68, and SLC Probate, 3–4. Harnsberger, *Family Man,* 190.

47. MMT, 74; *Lifetime,* 220. Emerson, *A Literary Life,* 261–63.

48. SLC to Henry Rogers, July 7, 1902, in HHR, 489–90.

49. JC Diary, Nov. 27, 1900. Hill, 20.

50. SLC to Henry Rogers, July 7, 1902, in HHR, 489.

51. SLC to Henry Rogers, July 7, 1902, in HHR, 490, and Aug. 7, 1902, in HHR, 496.

52. MTHL, 745 fn. 2. SLC to WDH, dated Sept. 23 [actually written Sept. 24], 1902, in MTHL, 744–45. WDH to Thomas Bailey Aldrich, Nov. 18, 1902, in MTHL, 747 fn. 1. MTHL, 745 fn. 2, and SLC to WDH, June 6, 1904, in MTHL, 785. Biographer Justin Kaplan described Livy's illness as "hyperthyroid heart disease." See Kaplan, 369. More surprising was biographer Hamlin Hill's medical diagnosis, rejecting heart disease in favor of "nervous breakdown." The Clemenses had a sick family, he suggested, controlled by Livy through her illness. See Hill, 46–48.

53. SLC to WDH, Dec. 26, 1902, in MTHL, 757–58. Dwyer, "Stories"; Lechtenberg, *Epilepsy,* 3. Hill, 56.

54. MMT, 7, 63. *My Father,* 227.

55. SLC, as quoted in *My Father,* 227–28.

56. OLC quoted in *My Father,* 230. SLC quoted in Hoffman, *Inventing Mark Twain,* 449. See also *Lifetime,* 221; *My Father,* 231–35.

57. Emerson, *A Literary Life,* 264–67. Mark Twain, "Christian Science," *North American Review,* Dec. 1902, 768, and January 1903, 7. Commentators have generally missed that there were four installments in the *North American Review,* citing only the December 1902 and January 1903 issues. Actually the "Christian Science" series continues in February 1903 (pp. 173–84) and concludes in April 1903 (pp. 505–17) with "Mrs. Eddy in Error." The book version, *Christian Science,* was published in February 1907.

58. Sholom J. Kahn, *Mark Twain's Mysterious Stranger: A Study of the Manuscript Texts* (Columbia: University of Missouri Press, 1978), 91–94.

59. AL, 8–18 (in ME), 39–44. Hill, 93. Jennifer L. Rafferty, " 'The Lyon of St. Mark': A Reconsideration of Isabel Lyon's Relationship to Mark Twain," *Mark Twain Journal* 34 (fall 1996): 43–44.

60. CC's letter of Dec. 10, 1902, quoted in Rafferty, " 'The Lyon of St. Mark,' " 44–45.

61. SLC to Joseph Twichell, July 21, 1903, in ABP, ed., *Mark Twain's Letters* (New York: Harper & Brothers, 1917), 2: 741–42. Hill, 56–58; Kaplan, 369–70. *Lifetime,* 222. ABP, *Biography,* 1209–11.

62. Hill, 72–74. *My Father,* 241–46. *Lifetime,* 223.

63. *Lifetime,* 224–25; Hill, 73. *My Father,* 246. See also SLC to Joseph Twichell, Jan. 7, 1904, as quoted in ABP, *Biography,* 1211–12.

64. Gibson, *Mysterious Stranger Manuscripts,* 491, 9–10, 405. Emerson, *A Literary Life,* 272–74. Kahn, *Mysterious Stranger,* 94–96.

65. Macnaughton, 195–200, 61. IVL Journal 1903–1904 ts., Feb. 28, July 28, 1904. Webster Notes on IVL, undated. For a perspective on Lyon as "pseudo-

analyst" during the autobiographical dictation sessions, see Jennifer L. Zaccara, "Mark Twain, Isabel Lyon, and the 'Talking Cure': Negotiating Nostalgia and Nihilism in the Autobiography," in Laura E. Skandera-Trombley and Michael J. Kiskis, eds., *Constructing Mark Twain: New Directions in Scholarship* (Columbia: University of Missouri Press, 2001), 101–21.

66. AL, 39. On Lyon's duties, note appended to IVL Journal 1903–1904 ts. by the Websters, under June 5, 1904, entry. IVL Journal 1903–1904, Feb. 28, June 16, 20, 22; May and June 1904 entries refer to her mother's presence.

67. Harnsberger, *Family Man,* 207–8. *Lifetime,* 226–27; MMT, 75. SLC to Joseph Twichell, June 8, 1904, in *Love Letters,* 348–49. Twain had not entirely lost his humorous touch, though perhaps it was tinged with melancholy: after Clara's concert he noted, "Yes, I am passing off the stage, and now my daughter is the famous member of the family"; Harnsberger, *Family Man,* 208.

68. *Lifetime,* 227. SLC to Joseph Twichell, June 8, 1904, in *Love Letters,* 348.

69. *Lifetime,* 228–29. On Jean's seizure, Hill, 75, quoting from SLC's notebook #37, ts., p. 12. The exact timing of Jean's grand mal is unclear, but it occurred soon after her mother's death.

70. *Lifetime,* 231–32. JC Diary, June 4, 1905. IVL Journal 1903–1904 ts., July 18, 1904.

71. *Lifetime,* 233.

72. *Lifetime,* 233–34. WDH to SLC, June 7, 1904, in MTHL, 786.

73. SLC to Susan Crane, July 25, 1904. In ME. SLC to Joseph Twichell, July 28, 1904. In ME. *My Father,* 174–75, 251, 254.

74. *Lifetime,* 234. ABP, *Biography,* 1224. IVL Journal 1903–1904 ts., July 22, 1904. *My Father,* 256.

75. IVL Journal 1903–1904, written under the July 28, 1904, entry date but obviously postdated from at least the time of the accident, July 31, 1904; SLC to Samuel E. Moffett, Aug. 6, 1904.

76. *My Father,* 256. IVL 1903–1906 Journal ts., Aug. 2, 5, 1904.

77. *Lifetime,* 245–46. Harnsberger, *Family Man,* 213. Opinion differs on whether Clara helped decorate the Fifth Avenue house in fall 1904 or 1905 or both.

78. Hill, 98; *Lifetime,* 246. See Macnaughton, 202–11. Emerson, *A Literary Life,* 276–77.

79. IVL 1903–1904 Journal ts., Nov. 30, 1904. Harnsberger, *Family Man,* 214–17. JC Diary, May 15, 1905. *Lifetime,* 233–34. AL, 39. ABP, *Biography,* 1228–29. SLC Probate, 6. Clemens grew so attached to the Orchestrelle that he later shipped it to his summer home in Dublin, N.H.

CHAPTER 3

1. Paul Fatout, ed., *Mark Twain Speaks for Himself* (West Lafayette, Ind.: Purdue University Press, 1978), 198–99.

2. *Lifetime,* 248–49. In her account, Katy confuses the Brushes for the Thayers.

3. *Lifetime,* 248–49.

4. *Lifetime,* 249. In Jean's speech, I have changed "them snowshoes," as Katy tells it, to "those snowshoes," a more likely usage for Jean.

5. IVL Antenne-Dorrance Daily Reminder, Apr. 5, 1905. Carolyn Harnsberger, *Mark Twain: Family Man* (New York: Citadel Press, 1960), 217.

6. JC Diary, May 8, 15, 1905. (Jean's extant diary picks up again on May 7, 1905, after a four-year hiatus.) IVL Journal 1903–1904, May 16, Aug. 12–13, May 1, 4–5, 1905. (Lyon's original 1903–1904 journal contains entries through September 18, 1905.) See also Fatout, *MT Speaks,* 199.

7. JC Diary, May 20, 29, June 9, May 19, June 15, 1905.

8. JC Diary, May 8, 21, June 1, 1905. *Lifetime,* 277–78.

9. JC Diary, May 3, July 21, 1906, in which Jean refers to the previous summer. IVL Daily Reminder, Oct. 7, 1905, Mar. 27–28, 30, 1906; JC to Nancy Brush, Jan. 11, 1906, ph.

10. SLC to CC, June 11, 1905. Fatout, *MT Speaks,* 200. IVL Journal 1903–1904, May 10, 18, 1905. Macnaughton, 225–26. On SLC's readings, see IVL Antenne-Dorrance Daily Reminder, May 22, 24, 25, 31, and June 15, 1905.

11. Everett Emerson, *Mark Twain: A Literary Life* (Philadelphia: University of Pennsylvania Press, 2000), 272. After deciding to keep chapters 8–25, Twain destroyed another 125 pages he had written in Florence. See chapters 26–32 in William M. Gibson, ed., *Mark Twain's Mysterious Stranger Manuscripts* (Berkeley: University of California Press, 1969), 353–400. Twain probably did not know exactly where he was in his composition at this time; see Sholom J. Kahn, *Mark Twain's Mysterious Stranger: A Study of the Manuscript Texts* (Columbia: University of Missouri Press, 1978), 97. "Eve's Diary," in Louis J. Budd, ed., *Mark Twain's Collected Tales, Sketches, Speeches, and Essays, 1891–1910* (New York: Library of America, 1992), 707. Macnaughton, 218–19.

12. IVL Daily Reminder, Oct. 4, 1905; Emerson, *A Literary Life,* 284. IVL Antenne-Dorrance Daily Reminder, Oct. 5, 1905. IVL Journal 1903–1904, July 1, 1905.

13. Fatout, *MT Speaks,* 199. SLC to CC, Aug. 3, 1905. In ME.

14. *Lifetime,* 252–53. IVL Antenne-Dorrance Daily Reminder, Sept. 19, 1905. Katie Leary to SLC, Oct. 18, 1905. IVL Daily Reminder ts., Nov. 1, 1905.

15. Harnsberger, *Family Man,* 221–22. IVL Daily Reminder ts., Jan. 6, Feb. 28, Mar. 2, 13, 17, 21, 24, 1906.

16. SLC to Lilian Aldrich, Sept. 16, 1905. In ME.

17. For Jean's seizures, see IVL Daily Reminder, Nov. 14, 20, 26, Dec. 15, 25, 1905. JC to Nancy Brush, Jan. 11, 1906, ph.; IVL Daily Reminder, Mar. 27–28, 30, Jan. 5, 1906.

18. SLC, "Closing Words of My Autobiography" in Autobiographical Dictations File, Dec. 24, 1909, Folder no. 252, hereafter cited as "Closing Words."

This was published in slightly altered form as "The Death of Jean," *Harper's Monthly Magazine,* Jan. 1911, 210–15. SLC to CC, Oct. 20, 1905. In ME.

19. Ellen Dwyer, "Stories of Epilepsy, 1880–1930," in Charles E. Rosenberg and Jane Golden, eds., *Framing Disease: Studies in Cultural History* (New Brunswick, N.J.: Rutgers University Press, 1992), 254.

20. SLC, "Jean's Illness," ms. +2. In ME.

21. Nicky Britten, Michael E.J. Wadsworth, and Peter B.C. Fenwick, "Sources of Stigma Following Early-Life Epilepsy: Evidence from a National Birth Cohort Study," in Steven Whitman and Bruce P. Hermann, eds., *Psychopathology in Epilepsy: Social Dimensions* (New York: Oxford University Press, 1986), 228. See JC Diary, Nov. 10, 1900.

22. SLC to CC, Oct. 20, 1905. In ME.

23. IVL Journal 1903–1904, Apr. 23, 1905.

24. IVL Journal 1903–1904, Dec. 14, 1904.

25. SLC to CC, June 8, 1905 (in ME), emphasis Twain's. AL, 39–44, (in ME), 132; see also Lewis Leary, ed., *Mark Twain's Letters to Mary* (New York: Columbia University Press, 1969), Aug. 25, 1906, 45–46, and fall 1907, 106–7; hereafter cited as *Letters to Mary.* These are letters to his friend Mary Rogers, who was married to Henry H. Rogers's son Harry.

26. IVL Daily Reminder, Jan. 11, Feb. 3, 1906.

27. IVL Daily Reminder, Feb. 25, 1906. In the typescript version "She" has been substituted for "The little rascal," and other cosmetic changes have been made.

28. IVL Daily Reminder, Jan. 27, 1906. For a discussion of the many changes later made to this entry, the dating of this event, and the allegation that there was a second attack, see the Epilogue.

29. See *Lifetime,* 262, 293.

30. On Sam's trip, IVL Daily Reminder, Jan. 25, 30, 1906; on her talk with Quintard, Feb. 2, 1906. AL, 81. Dr. Quintard believed Lyon completely.

31. For Lombroso, see Steven Whitman, Lambert N. King, and Robert L. Cohen, "Epilepsy and Violence: A Scientific and Social Analysis," in Whitman and Hermann, eds., *Psychopathology in Epilepsy,* 284–302. Journals quoted in Dwyer, "Stories," 256–57.

32. See Dwyer, "Stories," 265; Ellen Dwyer, "Stigma and Epilepsy," *Transactions and Studies of the College of Physicians of Philadelphia* 13 (Dec. 1991): 410. The popular prejudice persists. Epilepsy was used as a defense in homicide trials at least twenty times between 1977 and 1984, and 25 percent of adults in a 1977 survey still believed in a link between epilepsy and violence. See Whitman, King, and Cohen, "Epilepsy and Violence," 286–90, 295, and Jade L. Dell, "Social Dimensions of Epilepsy: Stigma and Response," in Whitman and Hermann, eds., *Psychopathology in Epilepsy,* 193. Scores of scientific studies over the past quarter-century have found no increased aggression in those suffering

from epilepsy. The empirical evidence is overwhelming: directed violence is *not* triggered by a seizure, nor does aggression increase after a seizure. Yet this stereotype has remained stubbornly alive.

33. Dwyer, "Stigma and Epilepsy," 408. Supporting evidence for this statement can be found in Dwyer, "Stories," 260–261.

34. See Emily Abel, *Hearts of Wisdom: American Women Caring for Kin, 1850–1940* (Cambridge, Mass.: Harvard University Press, 2000), chapter 10. Abel generously shared her work in manuscript.

35. IVL Daily Reminder, Jan. 3, 1906; ABP, *Biography,* 1260. IVL Daily Reminder, Jan. 9, 1906; see also ABP, *Biography,* 1260–62. The referral story is a little more complex in Paine's retelling, which basically hinges on the urging of a friend, Charles Harvey Genung, who sat next to him at the Players Club dinner honoring Twain.

36. ABP, *Biography,* 1263–64. See also IVL Daily Reminder, Jan. 6, 9, 1906.

37. IVL Daily Reminder, Jan. 6, 9, 1906; ABP, *Biography,* 1262–67.

38. ABP, *Biography,* 1267. IVL Daily Reminder ts., Jan. 9, 1906.

39. ABP, *Biography,* 1268. Emerson, *A Literary Life,* 286.

40. ABP, *Biography,* 1272–80, 1291.

41. IVL Daily Reminder, Feb. 20, 1906. This whole passage was deleted in her revised Austin diary entry. On Paine's welcome, see IVL Daily Reminder, Jan. 12, 14, and 19, 1906.

42. IVL Daily Reminder, Jan. 23, 1906. This line was also deleted from her revised Austin diary entry but appears in the Webster ts. See the Epilogue for an explanation of the process.

43. WDH to SLC, Apr. 26, 1903, in MTHL, 768.

44. MTHL, 798–99.

45. MMT, 77.

46. IVL Journal 1903–1904, June 26, 1905. Webster Notes on IVL, Mar. 5, 1948.

47. IVL Journal 1903–1904, Mar. 14, 1905, and see for example, May 21, 1905.

48. This is found on a loose-leaf page of notepaper, dated October 12, with no indication of the year. Although it was inserted into Lyon's 1906 Daily Reminder between the pages headed October 11 and October 12, there is no certain evidence when these lines were actually written.

49. IVL Journal 1903–1904, May 19, 1905.

50. Lyon probably added "No one suspected it" sometime in the 1930s. At that time she may have been referring to Albert Bigelow Paine or even to her former husband, Ralph Ashcroft, toward whom she expressed some animosity in later life. (See the Epilogue for a brief discussion of Lyon's attitude toward Paine after Clemens died.) But when she recorded the original parable in her diary, she did not know Paine and had only a superficial acquaintance with Ashcroft. It was more than half a year *later* that Paine joined Clemens's inner

circle. In my reading, her original parable fit her own situation, although she may not have been intentionally describing herself in such a negative light. I also believe the added comment may have been a subconscious reference to her service to the King, though again I doubt she meant to convey a sense of manipulation about herself. Whatever Lyon's level of conscious application to her own situation, the parable is revealing.

CHAPTER 4

1. Louis J. Budd, *Our Mark Twain: The Making of His Public Personality* (Philadelphia: University of Pennsylvania Press, 1983), 234.

2. See Arthur G. Pettit, "Mark Twain and His Times: A Bicentennial Appreciation," in Louis J. Budd, ed., *Critical Essays on Mark Twain, 1910–1980* (Boston: G. K. Hall, 1983), 202–13, esp. 210, 212. Hyatt Howe Waggoner, "Science in the Thought of Mark Twain," in Louis J. Budd and Edwin H. Cady, eds., *On Mark Twain: The Best from American Literature* (Durham, N.C.: Duke University Press, 1987), 1. Hill, 272–75.

3. Macnaughton attacks the myth of despair in Twain's late work with interpretive skill and a mountain of evidence. See esp. 6 fn. 8, 95, 130. See also Edward Wagenknecht, *Mark Twain: The Man and His Work,* 3rd ed. (Norman: University of Oklahoma Press, 1967), 204–8; Wagenknecht swings back to the myth after arguing against it.

4. John S. Tuckey, "Mark Twain's Later Dialogue: The 'Me' and the Machine," in Budd and Cady, eds., *On Mark Twain,* 127–37, esp. 127.

5. Macnaughton, 33, 130, 167.

6. Macnaughton, 6–7, 84; see also chapter 18 below.

7. Macnaughton, 14–17, 24.

8. *Lifetime,* 282–83. SLC to Emilie Rogers, Nov. [5?] 1906, HHR, 619–20. IVL Datebook, June 20, 1907. ABP, *Biography,* 1415–17. Clara was initially upset about Twain's leaving the English hotel in his robe and slippers, but her father subsequently convinced her that this was a common practice there; see *My Father,* 270.

9. IVL Daily Reminder, May 31, 1906.

10. IVL Daily Reminder, June 7, July 8, 12, 1906.

11. ABP, *Biography,* 1308, and JC Diary for the summer of 1906. See also IVL Daily Reminder ts., June 13, Aug. 13, Sept. 22, 1906, for references to Clara in New York.

12. ABP, *Biography,* 1308–12.

13. SLC to CC, June 7, 1906. In ME. ABP, *Biography,* 1315, 1317. IVL Daily Reminder, June 2, 7–8, 10, 1906.

14. JC Diary, Aug. 8, 1906.

15. JC Diary, June 22, Aug. 1, 8, 1906.

16. Twain was away from Dublin from June 26 to July 25, 1906. See IVL Daily Reminder 1906 during this period and JC Diary, June 26, 1906.

17. JC Diary, May 15–16, 1906. *Lifetime,* 281–82.

18. SLC to Thomas Bailey Aldrich, Oct. 2, 1906, HHR, 617–18 fn. 2.

19. JC Diary, July 26, 1906; for a general description of their games, see JC Diary, Sept. 15, 1906.

20. JC Diary, Sept. 15, 16, 1906.

21. JC Diary, Sept. 8, Aug. 9, 1906; IVL Daily Reminder, Aug. 9, 1906.

22. JC Diary, July 15, Aug. 13, 1906.

23. JC Diary, May 22, Aug. 5, 1906.

24. JC Diary, Sept. 3–4, 1906.

25. JC Diary, June 4, 15, July 10, 30, Oct. 6, 14, 23, 1906.

26. JC Diary, June 4, July 25, Sept. 5, 27, 1906.

27. JC Diary, June 15, 4, Oct. 5, 1906.

28. JC Diary, May 7, 1906.

29. Patrick West, "The Social Meaning of Epilepsy: Stigma as a Potential Explanation for Psychopathology in Children," in Steven Whitman and Bruce P. Hermann, eds., *Psychopathology in Epilepsy: Social Dimensions* (New York: Oxford University Press, 1986), 250.

30. "I have felt for a long time that I really ought to tell those four best friends and at last, I have," Jean recounted. JC Diary, July 22, 1906; also see JC Diary, June 16, 1906.

31. JC Diary, May 1, 1906.

32. JC Diary, May 14–15, 30, 1906.

33. JC Diary, May 18, July 28, 1906.

34. JC Diary, May 30, 1906. This frequency is an average based on a day-by-day survey of Jean's diary from May 1 through September 30, 1906.

35. JC Diary, June 6, 13, 12, 16, 1906.

36. JC Diary, May 10, June 7, 8, July 23, 1906.

37. JC Diary, July 1, Sept. 3, 1906.

38. See IVL Daily Reminder, Feb. 5, 1906. Lyon accompanied Jean on the first visit to Dr. Peterson.

39. On Peterson and early-twentieth-century views, Ellen Dwyer, "Stories of Epilepsy, 1880–1930," in Charles E. Rosenberg and Jane Golden, eds., *Framing Disease: Studies in Cultural History* (New Brunswick, N.J.: Rutgers University Press, 1992), 258–59, 251–55. On late-twentieth-century views, Jade L. Dell, "Social Dimensions of Epilepsy: Stigma and Response," in Whitman and Hermann, eds., *Psychopathology in Epilepsy,* 191–92.

40. See JC Diary, May 1, 15, June 19, 21, Sept. 15–16, June 17, 1906.

41. JC Diary, Sept. 24, July 3, 1906.

42. JC Diary, June 24, 28, July 22, Sept. 4, 1906.

43. JC Diary, Sept. 8, June 19, 1906.

44. ABP, *Biography*, 1308. JC Diary, Oct. 1, 1906. IVL Daily Reminder, Apr. 7, 1906.

45. JC Diary, May 1, 6, 1906.

46. JC Diary, May 30–31, June 22, 26, 1906.

47. JC Diary, July 3, 21, 1906.

48. JC Diary, Aug. 9, 14, 15, 1906.

49. JC Diary, July 4, 1906.

50. See Leila Zenderland, *Measuring Minds: Henry Herbert Goddard and the Origins of American Intelligence Testing* (Cambridge: Cambridge University Press, 1998), 147–50, 186–87, 222–23, 226–27.

51. JC Diary, July 4, June 27, 1906.

52. JC Diary, Oct. 14, 4, June 28, July 4, 1906.

53. IVL Journal 1903–1904, March 30, 1905, and IVL Daily Reminder, Jan. 8, 1908. JC Diary, July 22, 1906.

54. JC Diary, June 30, 25, 1906.

55. IVL Daily Reminder, May 30, 1906; she deleted "So wonderful is he— that all others are bleak" from the Austin version; the phrase is not deleted from the typescript, though "So wonderful" is crossed out in the original.

56. IVL Daily Reminder, May 17, 31, 1906. The first phrase in the latter quote, ending in "marvel" was eliminated in the Austin version.

57. IVL Daily Reminder, June 12, 1906. This passage is completely excised from the Austin version.

58. IVL Daily Reminder, July 5, 1906. Crossed out in slashing pencil lines in the original. Included in the typescript with a notation "I.V.L. crossed out." For Paine's whereabouts, see IVL Daily Reminder, June 28, 1906.

59. IVL Daily Reminder, Apr. 10, 1906. JC Diary, Oct. 5, 1906.

60. JC Diary, July 4, 28, 1906.

61. JC Diary, July 6, 1906.

62. IVL Daily Reminder, July 6, 1906.

63. IVL Daily Reminder, Mar. 19, 1906.

64. IVL Daily Reminder, Mar. 19, 1906. Lyon cut this line in her revisions to the original diary, but it remained in the typescript with a notation, "omitted by IVL." More unexpectedly, she also excised the seemingly innocuous discussion of property in Redding from her Austin version.

65. SLC Probate, 1–2.

66. JC Diary, July 16, 1906.

67. See, for example, IVL Daily Reminder, Sept. 22, 1906.

68. IVL Daily Reminder, Aug. 13–14, 18, 1906; JC Diary, Aug. 20–21, 1906.

69. IVL Daily Reminder, Aug. 6, 1906.

70. AL, 405; Clemens only learned about this incident well after the fact.

71. IVL Daily Reminder, June 7, 21, 25, 1906.

72. IVL Daily Reminder, June 26–27, 29, July 8–9, 1906.

73. IVL Daily Reminder, July 17–18, 1906.

74. IVL Daily Reminder, July 21, 1906. IVL Datebook, July 19, 1907. See, for example, comments in IVL Daily Reminder, July 27, Aug. 6, 1906.

75. Lyon makes no mention of the Redding house in her diary entries around this time. See, for example, IVL Daily Reminder, Sept. 12–14, 1906. All the house information comes from JC Diary, Sept. 11, 15, 1906. The first usage of "Lioness" I could find occurred on July 3, 1906, in JC Diary.

76. JC Diary, July 26, Sept. 15, 1906.

77. Caroline Harnsberger, *Mark Twain: Family Man* (New York: Citadel Press, 1960), 225–27; the music critic is quoted at 227. IVL Daily Reminder, Sept. 16, 1906. JC Diary, Sept. 16, 20, 23, 28, 1906. Jean did occasionally suffer two attacks on a single day. Ultimately that September, she had single attacks on three days, Sept. 16, 20, 23, and a double on Sept. 28, but the September total of five seizures was equal to her experience in June.

78. JC Diary, Sept. 26, 1906. IVL Daily Reminder, Sept. 14, 24, 1906. JC Diary, Sept. 24, 1906.

79. See IVL Daily Reminder, June 29, 1906, quoted in this chapter, where she spoke of "giving birth to something" and continued that she doesn't know "what shall be born," but it will be "greater than I."

CHAPTER 5

1. JC Diary, Sept. 26, 1906.

2. JC Diary, Sept. 27, 1906. Lyon must have accomplished this in person before Twain left Dublin on September 15 or by telephone later.

3. JC Diary, Sept. 26, 1906. Clearly, Jean voluntarily went into the sanitarium. Hill (152, 154) states that Peterson recommended "that Jean be committed to an institution," though Lyon's diary contains only a one-line notation: "Letter from Dr. Hunt containing cablegram from Dr. Peterson," written above her Oct. 11, 1906, entry heading.

4. JC Diary, Sept. 27, 1906.

5. IVL Daily Reminder, Sept. 28, 1906. Note that Lyon wrote to Peterson only after procuring the assent of Jean, her father, and Dr. Stowell to the sanitarium idea. Ellen Dwyer, "Stories of Epilepsy, 1880–1930," in Charles E. Rosenberg and Jane Golden, eds., *Framing Disease: Studies in Cultural History* (New Brunswick, N.J.: Rutgers University Press, 1992), 258–59.

6. IVL Daily Reminder, Sept. 28, 1906. JC Diary, Sept. 28, 1906.

7. JC Diary, Sept. 29, 1906.

8. IVL Daily Reminder, Sept. 29, 1906.

9. See IVL Daily Reminder, Sept. 29, 1906. The asterisk that marks where Lyon intended to add her insert is written in a faded, far lighter ink than the original sentence. But the insert itself, squeezed crosswise into a margin of the

text, appears to be penned in similar ink to the original. Therefore it is difficult to determine with certainty at what point this insert was added, but whenever it was written, it was certainly an afterthought. See the Epilogue for a fuller discussion of Lyon's revisionist safari through her original diary.

10. IVL Daily Reminder, Oct. 1, 1906; Lyon crossed out this phrase in the original, and it was not included in the Webster typescript.

11. JC Diary, Oct. 1, 1906.

12. JC Diary, Oct. 11, 1, 5, 1906.

13. JC Diary, Oct. 16, 17, 1906.

14. JC Diary, Oct. 18–20, 22–23, 1906.

15. JC Diary, Oct. 20, 15, 1906.

16. IVL Daily Reminder, Oct. 25, 1906.

17. SLC to Mary Rogers, Oct. 12, 1906, in Lewis Leary, ed., *Mark Twain's Letters to Mary* (New York: Columbia University Press, 1969), 69–75; hereafter cited as *Letters to Mary*. The specific cause of Sam's jubilation was censored by the author before he mailed his letter. "I have been editing this letter with the scissors—" he wrote, "for I had put into it the very dismalness which I had spared you in that recent note." I believe the "dismalness" refers to Jean's epilepsy.

18. SLC to Emilie Rogers, Oct. 24, 1906, in HHR, 618. IVL Daily Reminder, Oct. 27, 1906.

19. JC Diary, Oct. 25, 1906.

20. SLC to Emilie Rogers, Nov. [5?], 1906, in HHR, 619–20. My guess is that the letter was actually written in December; see JC Diary, Dec. 5, 1906.

21. IVL Daily Reminder, Oct. 27, 1906.

22. SLC to JC, Oct. 29, Nov. 8, 13, 1906; SLC to Mary Rogers, Nov. 7, 1906, in *Letters to Mary*, 84–86; IVL Daily Reminder, Oct. 31, 1906.

23. ABP, *Biography*, 1324–26.

24. The first trip began on Jan. 2, 1907. Lyon and Clemens sailed again for Bermuda on March 16 and returned March 21, 1907. See IVL 1907 Datebook for confirmation of these dates.

25. IVL Stenographic Notebook #1, Jan. 4, 1907.

26. AL, 46–47. In ME.

27. AL, 403. In ME.

28. See AL, 47. There is a mountain of contextual evidence to support Clemens's painful admission, not least of which were his belief in the epileptic temperament and his secretary's animus toward Jean. Moreover, he would have had no reason to confess falsely to such a despicable act.

29. IVL Daily Reminder, Oct. 8, 1906. SLC to JC, May 14, 1907. Also see Kaplan, 380.

30. Kaplan, 380.

CHAPTER 6

1. JC Diary, Oct. 22 (Jean went to preview her sanitarium three days before her actual relocation), Oct. 26–Nov. 1, Nov. 3, 1906.

2. JC Diary, Nov. 2, Dec. 11, 23, 1906, Jan. 1, 1907, Nov. 27, 1906.

3. JCE Diary, May 16, 1907, and for ordering chocolate, Mar. 31, May 13, June 10, Oct. 29, 1907. A comparison of her diary and the Excelsior datebook (JCE) for early 1907 suggests that Jean was in the habit of taking short notes in a datebook and then using them as a memory prod for her larger journal entries. The diary entries for 1906 and for the first two months of 1907 were recorded in larger journals where she could write more expansively and reflexively. She may have stopped keeping a more extensive journal at the end of February 1907, but it is also possible that the remaining large-format journals for 1907 were lost or destroyed. No extant diaries have surfaced for the years 1908 and 1909.

4. JC Diary, Nov. 3, 6, 9, 22, 1906.

5. JC Diary, Jan. 19, 1907 (woodcarving), Nov. 10, 1906 (language lessons).

6. JC Diary, Nov. 21, 25, 1906. JCE Diary, Apr. 5, 1907.

7. JCE Diary, Aug. 7, 1907; JC "To the Editor of *The New York Times,*" March 29, 1909. *Lifetime,* 293. On the dishonorable discharges, JC Diary, Nov. 23, 1906; see John D. Weaver, *The Brownsville Raid* (College Station: Texas A&M University Press, 1992), for a full account of the national controversy.

8. JCE Diary, Aug. 20, 1907 (Sharp responded by moving the valet, who was a patient's servant, to another table); and see JC Diary, Jan. 11, 1907. JC to SLC, Aug. 28, 1907, CFP.

9. JCE Diary, Apr. 17, May 21, 1907. On the distance to Katonah, see JC Diary, Oct. 22, 1906. I could find only one recorded instance when Clemens talked to a doctor; see IVL Datebook, May 21, 1907.

10. SLC to JC, Jan. 11, 1907. In ME.

11. JC Diary, Jan. 14, 1907.

12. JC Diary, Oct. 26, 1906.

13. JC Diary, Nov. 26, 1906.

14. JC Diary, Dec. 3–4, Nov. 1, 19, Dec. 26, 1906, Jan. 3, 1907.

15. JC Diary, Dec. 8, 1906.

16. JC Diary, Dec. 8, 11, 14, 19, 1906.

17. JC Diary, Dec. 20, 1906.

18. For an example of her temper, see JC Diary, Dec. 23, 1906.

19. JC Diary, Jan. 2, 1907.

20. JC Diary, Oct. 4, 1906.

21. JC Diary, Dec. 23, 19, 1906.

22. JC Diary, Dec. 15, 19, 1906.

23. JC Diary, Dec. 25, 1906, Jan. 14, 1907, Dec. 17, 1906.

24. JC Diary, Dec. 9, 16, 1906. JCE Diary, Jan. 9, 1907.

25. JC Diary, Dec. 22, 1906; Feb. 2, 1907. JCE Diary, Nov. 10, 17, 1907.

26. JC Diary, Feb. 2, 1907.

27. JC Diary, Dec. 25–27, 1906. Sharp's initial unwillingness to confront her was explained by Dr. Hibbard as the result of her having a famous father and the fact that she paid more for her room and board than the other patients. Hibbard said that she had a better room.

28. JC Diary, Dec. 27, 1906. Not all the patients at Katonah were persons with epilepsy. One of the sanitarium clients, for example, was being treated for alcoholism. See JCE Diary, April 18–19, 1907.

29. JC Diary, Jan. 20, Dec. 31, 1906.

30. JC Diary, Dec. 29, 1906, Jan. 5, 1907.

31. JC Diary, Jan. 14–16, 1907.

32. JC Diary, [Jan. 18, 1907]. The date page is torn out of this partially censored entry, but because of the context and the fact that it is wedged between the Jan. 17 and Jan. 19 entries, this is the most likely date.

33. JC Diary, Jan. 16, [18], 20, 22–24, 30, 1907. Quote at Jan. 24.

34. JC Diary, Jan. 14, 1907.

35. JC Diary, Jan. 14; JCE Diary, July 22, 1907.

36. JC Diary, Jan. 10 ("Father has been here and gone," JC noted), 12, Feb. 4, 1907.

37. JC Diary, Feb. 4, 1907.

38. JC Diary, Feb. 3–5, Jan. 17, 26–28, 1907.

39. JC Diary, Feb. 10, 11, 18, 27, 1907.

40. JC Diary, Feb. 18, 1907.

41. JC Diary, Feb. 15, 1907; JCE Diary, Apr. 8–9, 1907.

42. JCE Diary, Apr. 13, 8, 15, 1907.

43. JCE Diary, May 4, Apr. 5, May 15–16, 1907.

44. JC to SLC, June 24, 1907, CFP.

45. JC to SLC, July 23, 1907, CFP.

46. JC to SLC, July 23, 1907, CFP.

47. JCE Diary, July 22, 25, 30, Aug. 2, 5, 1907.

48. JCE Diary, Aug. 2, 19, 1907.

CHAPTER 7

1. AL, 34–35, 269, 394–95. In ME.

2. Hill, 156. Also IVL Daily Reminder 1906 ts., Mar. 28, Apr. 6, 11, June 15, 1906.

3. IVL Daily Reminder, Oct. 22–24, 1906; actually recorded on a loose-leaf paper inserted in the diary between pages headed Oct. 21 and Oct. 22, 1906. Lyon does not mention Johnson by name.

4. Most of the specific information about this incident comes from Charlotte Teller Johnson's "Foreword" to a privately printed collection of letters, "S.L.C. to C.T.," as cited in Hill, 156. Lyon never mentions that Clemens asked Johnson to move.

5. See IVL Datebook, May 22, 1907, for another report of a rumor spread by Lyon about Charlotte Johnson marrying Clemens. Lyon denied the charge in this case. Clemens also enjoyed flirting with Henry Rogers's daughter-in-law, Mary Rogers, with whom he maintained a regular correspondence. See Lewis Leary, ed., *Mark Twain's Letters to Mary* (New York: Columbia University Press, 1969); hereafter cited as *Letters to Mary*.

6. Hill, 156. Even her champion, the biographer Hamlin Hill, attributes her breakdown to the gossip over her boss and the young playwright, but he believes the root cause is Lyon's fear that a marriage rumor might be turned upon her.

7. Hill, 155–56. SLC to Mary Rogers, Nov. 28, 1906, in *Letters to Mary*, 92–94. IVL Daily Reminder, Dec. 10, 4, 1906. The quoted comment was written in pencil (the entries that preceded and followed were in pen) and could have been added later. It was untouched in the original but was crossed out with instructions to omit in the Webster ts.

8. IVL Daily Reminder, Dec. 12, 1906. ABP, *Biography*, 1342–50. IVL Daily Reminder, Dec. 13, 1906.

9. IVL Stenographic Notebook #1, Jan. 4, 1907.

10. IVL Datebook, Jan. 29, Mar. 10, 9, 15, 1907.

11. IVL Datebook, June 7, Jan. 13, June 1, 1907.

12. IVL Datebook, May 4–5, 29, 1907. Macnaughton, 202–3. On dictations, see ABP, *Biography*, 1405, and Everett Emerson, *Mark Twain: A Literary Life* (Philadelphia: University of Pennsylvania Press, 2000), 286. Twain did seventy dictations in 1907.

13. IVL Datebook, May 29, 1907.

14. IVL Datebook, May 13, 25, 30, June 3, 4, 1907.

15. IVL Datebook, June 20, 22, 1907. Twain and Ashcroft sailed for England on June 8, 1907. The degree was awarded June 26, and they sailed for home on July 13. See ABP, *Biography*, 1380–1404.

16. AL, 395–96. In ME.

17. AL, 396. IVL Datebook, July 26, 1907.

18. See IVL Datebook, July 25, 1907, ts. insert 264 ½, for Samuel Webster's handwritten comment reporting Lyon's verbal claim that Charlotte Johnson had threatened, "I'll get even with you for this!" Lyon began talking with the Websters in the late 1940s. Her original diary contains no report of an explicit threat by Johnson during this encounter, though she did write: "I think we'll hear from her again"; IVL Datebook, May 22, 1907. For Twain's alleged concurrence, IVL Datebook, July 25, 1907.

19. AL, 397–98. In ME. The brackets are Twain's choice of punctuation for his commentary. Although Twain did not remember whether this conversation took place before or after Lyon planted the marriage rumor, it must have followed, since he was in England when the story started to circulate.

20. AL, 399 (in ME.), 394–95. The friends included Mrs. Henry H. Rogers, and Mr. Broughton and Mr. Benjamin, both sons-in-law of Rogers.

21. AL, 395 (in ME), 393. In ME.

22. AL, 73. In ME.

23. IVL Daily Reminder, Dec. 29, 1906; Hill, 153; also AL, 38. By comparison to the Clemens family's "only $25,000 a year," in 1906 a postal employee earned 38 cents per hour; a public school teacher made $409 per year, and jobs in finance and insurance might pay about $1,085 per year. Scott Derks, ed., *The Value of a Dollar: Prices and Incomes in the U.S., 1869–1999* (Lakeville, Conn., Grey House Publishing, 1999), 74–75.

24. See Hill, 172. The first mention of the gift is in IVL Datebook, June 13, 1907, and see AL, 13. JCE Diary, May 21, 1907. May 7, 1907, Power of Attorney to Isabel V. Lyon, AL File. See chapter 14, note 27, for a later irony involving a second, disputed power of attorney.

25. JCE Diary, June 8, 1907.

26. AL, 45–55. In ME.

27. JCE Diary, June 28, July 27, Aug. 12, 1907.

28. JCE Diary, Sept. 18, 1907.

29. SLC to JC, Jan. 11, 1907. In ME.

30. JC to Nancy Brush, Oct. 2, 1907, ph.

31. JCE Diary, Sept. 20, 22, 28, 1907.

32. JCE Diary, Sept. 26, 30, 1907.

33. JCE Diary, Oct. 2, 3, 1907.

34. IVL Stenographic Notebook #4, Oct. 5, 1907.

35. Lyon often had good intuition about how far she could push people. See Twain's later comment in AL, 292.

36. AL, 251, 1. SLC to CC, Mar. 11, 1909. IVL Datebook, Oct. 23, 1907.

37. Hill, 184–85.

38. CC to SLC, Aug. 13, 26, 1907, CFP.

39. CC to SLC, Sept. 1, 1907, CFP.

CHAPTER 8

1. JC to Nancy Brush, Jan. 16, 1907 [misdated and misfiled; actually 1908], ph.

2. IVL Datebook, Oct. 2, 1907. According to Hill Lyon "rushed" to Katonah to meet with Dr. Peterson; 185–86. JCE Diary, Oct. 7, 1907.

3. SLC to JC [early Oct. 1907] (in ME); this survives as a typescript included in "The Ashcroft's [sic] Defense in Suit against S. L. Clemens," RWA to John

B. Stanchfield, July 30, 1909, in AL File, and is hereafter cited as SLC to JC [early Oct. 1907]. In ME.

4. SLC to JC [early Oct. 1907]. In ME.

5. JC to Nancy Brush, Mar. 10, 1908, ph. On the theory that a fall had caused Jean's epilepsy, as noted in chapter 2, see SLC, Aug. 5. Saturday [1899], "Jean's Illness," insert following ms. +2; *My Father,* 214.

6. Macnaughton, 230–31.

7. IVL Datebook, Oct. 2, 1907.

8. SLC to JC [early Oct. 1907]. In ME.

9. JC to Nancy Brush, Oct. 2, 31, 1907, ph. (my emphasis).

10. JCE Diary, Oct. 5, 7, 13, 12, 1907.

11. JCE Diary, Aug. 30, Dec. 3, 1907.

12. JCE Diary, Nov. 1, Dec. 11, 1907.

13. JCE Diary, Nov. 4, Dec. 11, 1907.

14. JCE Diary, Oct. 13, 1907. ABP, *Biography,* 1445. IVL Datebook, Oct. 22, 1907; see also IVL Datebook, ts., Oct. 27, 1907; JCE Diary, Oct. 28, 1907.

15. JCE Diary, Nov. 2, 1907.

16. JC to Nancy Brush, Oct. 31, 1907, ph. See IVL Datebook, ts., Oct. 27, 1907, for Lyon's cautiously optimistic assessment. By the end of the year, Lyon could be certain that this money would not be lost. See IVL Daily Reminder, Jan. 2, 1908: "Depositors will get back everything full value in 2 yr., 4 mos." Also IVL Steno Notebook #3, Jan. 17, 1908.

17. JC to Nancy Brush, Dec. 9, 1907, ph.

18. Hill, 153, 191; SLC to CC, Aug. 3, 1906. Clemens's figure is, however, undoubtedly too high.

19. JCE Diary, Dec. 7, 9, 15, 22, 1907.

20. JCE Diary, Dec. 15, 11, 25, 15, 1907.

21. JC to Nancy Brush, Jan. 16, 1907 [misdated and misfiled, actually 1908], ph. JCE Diary, Dec. 25, 1907.

22. *Lifetime,* 282, 310.

23. IVL Stenographic Notebook #2, Jan. 16, 1907.

24. IVL Daily Reminder ts., Oct. 18, 1905. Lyon makes no mention of pincushions in the summer of 1906. Twain notes dryly that she stopped making pincushions after he gave her check-signing privileges; AL, 11–12.

25. See AL, 39–44; SLC to CC, June 8, 1905; and IVL Daily Reminder, Feb. 25, 1906.

26. *Lifetime,* 341. AL, 29–30. In ME. IVL Datebook ts., Aug. 30, 1907.

27. Hill, 62–63, 101–4.

28. AL, 417–20, and AL File, one-page description of RWA (in ME), ph., original at University of Wisconsin, Madison. This piece was written in SLC's hand but is undated and has no attribution of author.

29. See an enclosure titled "In the Supreme Court of Fair Play S. L. Clemens, Presiding Judge," in RWA to SLC, Sept. 16, 1904; also AL, 8–9; IVL Antenne-Dorrance Daily Reminder, Jan. 9, Apr. 26, 1905. Ashcroft called on Clemens twice in the first half of 1905.

30. On Plasmon, AL, 8–9. (Twain apparently lost another $25,000 by investing in a new version of Plasmon, the Milk Products Co. See SLC reply to letter from Charles Lark to ABP, Aug. 10, 1909, 11–13, in AL File.) On hairpins, safety pins, and insoles, RWA to SLC, Sept. 19, 1904, June 23, 1905; HHR, 623–24, fn. 1. And see chapter 16.

31. Hill, 155. ABP, *Biography*, 1325–26.

32. See HHR, 623–24 fn. 1; two letters cited, RWA to SLC, Nov. 10 and 25, 1906, are not in the collection of letters to SLC at MTP. SLC Probate, 4.

33. AL, 234. Twain dates the initiation of Lyon and Ashcroft's friendship to the latter half of 1906 and their "excessively friendly & sociable" relationship from the beginning of 1907. I have found no evidence in the first six months of Lyon's 1907 Datebook to support this latter contention.

34. Hill, 188, 183, 191–92.

35. AL, 82–83, 279–80.

36. IVL Datebook, Oct. 1, 13, 1907. She later edited "sweet" out of the original Oct. 1 entry with red pencil.

37. IVL Daily Reminder, Jan. 9, 5, 10, 1908. It appears that Ashcroft did attempt to learn billiards but never became much of a player; Clemens commented to one of his Angelfish, "And he [Ashcroft] plays good billiards now. Not as good as Col. Harvey or Mr. Paine, but better than formerly"; SLC to DQ, Aug. 10, 1908, in Cooley, ed., 198.

38. IVL Daily Reminder, Jan. 12, 1908. The Bermuda trip lasted twelve days, Jan. 25–Feb. 6, 1908. See IVL Daily Reminder, Jan. 23, 1908.

39. See, for example, AL, 38.

40. IVL Daily Reminder, Feb. 22, 1908.

41. IVL Daily Reminder, Jan. 23, 1908.

42. IVL Daily Reminder, Jan. 24, 1908.

43. SLC to WDH, Jan. 22, 1908, in MTHL, 828. WDH to SLC, Feb. 4, 1908, in MTHL, 829–30.

44. ABP to IVL, Jan. 28, 1908, AL File.

45. ABP to Mrs. Lyon (IVL's mother), July 21, 1909, AL File; see also ABP to IVL, Jan. 28, 1908, AL File.

46. WDH to SLC, July 8, 1908, in MTHL, 830. WDH to ABP, July 8, 1908, Albert Bigelow Paine Collection, HEH.

47. IVL Daily Reminder, July 26, 1908. According to *The Oxford Companion to Medicine,* Phenacetin is an aspirin-like analgesic that was introduced in 1887. Widely used in the past, it is no longer recommended because it can cause serious kidney damage.

48. See AL, 36, 38. IVL Daily Reminder, Oct. 6, 1908; emphasis in the original. Twain dates the rise of Ashcroft's financial influence from the beginning of 1907, but I believe it began no earlier (and probably later) than the Knickerbocker Trust collapse in late October 1907. See AL, 234, and IVL Datebook, Oct. 24, 1907.

49. Charles Lark to Bernard DeVoto, Aug. 28, 1940, attachment, "Report of Miss X," 2, ph., DeVoto Papers, Stanford, Calif.

CHAPTER 9

1. See JCE Diary, Nov. 5, 1907, for Jean's first mention of the sisters; and JCE Diary, Dec. 22, 1907, where Jean learns of the plan for her release. Lyon mentions the Cowleses in her Daily Reminder, June 17, 27, 1903, ph.

2. JCE Diary, Dec. 6, 25, 1907. Lyon confirmed the plan by phone on December 25. Jean later reports that she had caught Edith eavesdropping; JC to IVL, Aug. 5, 1908.

3. IVL Stenographic Notebook #4 1907 & 1908, Feb. 16, 1908. This is apparently a draft or copy of a letter Lyon wrote to Gra Thayer.

4. On the Cowleses, JCE Diary, Dec. 6, 1907; JC to IVL, Aug. 1, 1908. On Dr. Peterson, JCE Diary, Dec. 25, 1907. On moving day, IVL Daily Reminder, Jan. 9, 1908. On Marguerite Schmitt, JCE Diary, Oct. 14, Dec. 6, 29, 1907. Though Jean never states her name, she describes a young French woman, about twenty years of age, whom Peterson started bringing along on his sanitarium visits in mid-October and with whom she enjoyed the chance to speak and listen to good French. Both her age and the diminutive "little" Jean uses to describe her, as well as her French nationality, fit the profile of Marguerite Schmitt (born about 1887) when she is identified in Jean's later letters.

5. JC to Nancy Brush, June 29, 1908, ph.; JC to Nancy Brush, Aug. 5, 1908, ph. See JC to IVL, Aug. 1, 1908.

6. JC to Nancy Brush, Feb. 17, 1908, ph.

7. JC to Nancy Brush, Feb. 23, 1908, ph.

8. JC to Nancy Brush, Mar. 2, 1908, ph.

9. See JC to Nancy Brush, June 29, July 23, 1908, ph. Jean reports she has been ordered to go sailing frequently by the local doctor; she was also swimming regularly.

10. JC to Nancy Brush, Mar. 29, 1908, ph. SLC to JC, June 14, 1908. It is possible that Clemens took Jean back to New York with him on that April visit and that they spent an hour or two at 21 Fifth Avenue in violation of Peterson's prohibition before she returned to Greenwich. See IVL Daily Reminder, Apr. 24, 1908, and SLC to Helen Allen, Apr. 25, 1908, in Cooley, ed., 144. Lyon states categorically that Clemens and Ashcroft went to Greenwich on April 24,

and Clemens wrote, "My youngest daughter came yesterday, but she could only stay an hour or two, then hurry away."

11. Frederick Peterson to IVL, Mar. 26, 1908.

12. SLC to JC, Mar. 23, 1908. In ME. Frederick Peterson to IVL, Mar. 26, 1908.

13. JC to Nancy Brush, Mar. 29, 1908, ph. "Some" appears to be crossed out with "the" written above it.

14. SLC to JC, May 20, 1908. In ME. JC to Nancy Brush, June 29, 1908, ph. JC to IVL, Aug. 4, 1908. SLC to JC, May 20, 1908. In ME.

15. JC to SLC, May 26, 1908, CFP.

16. SLC to JC, May 20, 1908. In ME. SLC to JC, [May 21, 1908]. In ME.

17. SLC to JC, [May 21, 1908]. In ME.

18. SLC to JC, June 14, 1908. In ME. SLC to JC, [June 19, 1908]. In ME.

19. SLC to JC, [June 19, 1908]. In ME.

20. George de Forest Brush to SLC, Aug. 25, 1908.

21. IVL Stenographic Notebook #4 1907 & 1908, Feb. 16, 1908. After "misunderstood," a full parenthesis encloses two question marks—"(??)"—in the original text. I have excised the question marks from the quote. Lyon may be indicating her difficulty deciphering the word, or she may be editorializing.

22. IVL Stenographic Notebook #4 1907 & 1908, Feb. 16, 1908.

23. AL, 52.

24. SLC to DQ, Aug. 9, 1907, in Cooley, ed., 49. SLC, autobiographical dictation, Apr. 17, 1908, in Cooley, ed., 137–41.

25. See IVL to DQ, Aug. 31, 1907, in Cooley, ed., 59–60. On meeting the children's trains, see in Cooley, ed., SLC to DQ, Aug. 9, 1907, 49; SLC to Dorothy Sturgis, May 9, 1908, 151. On photographs, see, for example, in Cooley, ed., IVL to DQ, Oct. 7, 1907, 75; Dorothy Sturgis to SLC, May 21, 1908, 159. On tea, IVL Datebook, Aug. 5, 26, 1907. Although Lyon makes a negative comment about Dorothy Quick in her Sept. 9, 1907, Datebook entry, while on a six-week vacation with Clemens in Bermuda in 1908, she offers no overt criticism of his behavior with children.

26. IVL Datebook, Aug. 7, 9, 1907. And see in Cooley, ed.: IVL to DQ, Aug. 31, 1907, 59–60; DQ to SLC, Aug. 26, 1907, 55–56; Irene Gerken to SLC, Mar. 13, 1908, 121; Dorothy Sturgis to SLC, Apr. 14, 1908, 135.

27. IVL Daily Reminder, April 1, 1908. On Angelfish, Cooley, ed., 94. SLC, autobiographical dictation, Feb. 12, 1908, as quoted in Cooley, ed., xvii.

28. Hill, xxvii. Hill also made a more specific accusation. On the basis of hearsay circulated in a letter by a party twice-removed from the source, he speculated that Clemens might be guilty of an act of sexual impropriety with Helen Allen, a Bermuda Angelfish; 260–61. Two scholars who have studied the evidence in detail dismiss this conjecture. See especially Laura E. Skandera-Trombley, *Mark Twain in the Company of Women* (Philadelphia: University of Pennsylvania Press, 1994), 181–83, 194, footnote 10, which indicates that Helen

Allen's mother did not support the allegation. And John Cooley, who is most familiar with the Angelfish letters, has flatly asserted, "[T]here is no evidence to suggest real impropriety or scandal in connection with any of the angelfish"; 285.

29. See the photographs in Cooley, ed., 44, 50, 77, 112, 126, 187, 190, 201, 213.

30. ABP, *Biography,* 1440; IVL Daily Reminder, Jan. 14, 1908.

31. Skandera-Trombley, *In the Company of Women,* 183. Cooley, ed., 282–83; Albert E. Stone, *The Innocent Eye: Childhood in Mark Twain's Imagination* (New Haven, Conn.: Yale University Press), 1961.

32. IVL Daily Reminder, Feb. 6, 28, 1908; see also SLC, autobiographical dictation, Feb. 13, 1908, in Cooley, ed., 104–6.

33. In Cooley, ed.: SLC, autobiographical dictation, Apr. 17, 1908, 141; photograph, 196; SLC to Frances Nunnally, June 20, 1908, 180; SLC to Margaret Blackmer, July 7, 1908, 185–86.

34. Cooley suggests that soon after Clara returned from Europe, the Clemens household stopped saving Angelfish letters, perhaps because of her disapproval; 177–78.

35. In Cooley, ed.: SLC to Helen Allen, Apr. 25, 1908, 144; SLC autobiographical dictation, Apr. 17, 1908, 137–41; and see 176.

36. SLC to Helen Allen, Apr. 25, 1908, in Cooley, ed., 144. As noted above, Clemens went to Greenwich on April 24 and may have brought Jean back to the city for a brief visit.

37. Cooley, ed., 95. During the spring and summer of 1908, Clemens's letters to his Angelfish totaled more than half of his entire correspondence.

38. SLC to DQ [late July 1907], in Cooley, ed., 45; the list of Angelfish as constituted in June 1908 can be found on p. 165. IVL to DQ, Sept. 2, 1907, in Cooley, ed., 61.

39. IVL Daily Reminder, Feb. 8, 1908.

CHAPTER 10

1. IVL Daily Reminder, June 7, 21, 28, Aug. 18, 13, 1906. Clemens continued to purchase property in Redding as late as April 1909; see SLC Probate.

2. SLC to CC, Aug. 3, 1906, and Hill, 153. IVL Datebook, Aug. 5, 1907; JC Diary, Sept. 15, 1906. CC to SLC, Aug. 6, 1907, CFP. Clemens authorized Clara and John Howells to spend $15,000 and allowed another $5,000 or $6,000 as a reserve. The architect's estimates were in the neighborhood of $25,000 to $30,000, but he assured Clemens that it was possible to design a house for any sum. See John Howells to SLC, Sept. 19, 1906.

3. IVL Datebook, May 23, 1907; Hill, 172.

4. Hill, 182. John Howells to IVL, May 29, 1907; John Howells to SLC, May 29, Aug. 3, 1907. Though Clara was intimately involved in the initial design,

once she approved Howells's plans for the house on March 27, 1907, the project fell to Lyon. Later, however, a loggia was added on Clara's account.

5. IVL Datebook, Apr. 9, 1907. *Lifetime,* 289.

6. IVL Daily Reminder, May 2, 1908.

7. IVL Datebook, June 15, 1907; and see IVL Datebook, June 22–24, 1907.

8. IVL Daily Reminder, Jan. 8, 1908. IVL to ABP, loose notes, undated, written around Jan. 23, 1908, and inserted into her 1908 Daily Reminder.

9. JCE Diary, Dec. 7, 1907. SLC Probate. AL, 9–10.

10. AL, 10 (in ME); also see Twain's reply to a letter from Charles Lark to ABP, Aug. 10, 1909, 10, in AL File.

11. Statements and Accounts / Ashcroft-Lyon / 1907–1909, "Statement submitted in behalf of Mrs. Ashcroft at the request of Mr. Stanchfield, in which are classified (E. & O. E.) the cash disbursements made by Mrs. Ashcroft for Mr. Clemens during the two years ending February 28, 1909," folder 2, in AL File, hereafter cited as IVL Statement of Accounts. See also Accountants' Statements and Schedules / Ashcroft-Lyon Affair / March 1907–Feb. 28, 1909, schedule #5, in Folder 1, AL File; hereafter cited as Auditor's Report.

12. IVL Daily Reminder, May 2, 4, 1908.

13. *Lifetime,* 282, 303. Charles E. [Will] Wark to IVL, June 24, 1908.

14. CC to IVL, June 24, 1908.

15. IVL Statement of Accounts. AL, 24–25. In ME.

16. AL, 337–39.

17. Mark Twain, *Extract from Captain Stormfield's Visit to Heaven* (New York: Oxford University Press, 1996), 43–54. The work remains incomplete and exists in several different versions; see James Miller, "Afterword," in *Stormfield,* 1. See also Everett Emerson, *Mark Twain: A Literary Life* (Philadelphia: University of Pennsylvania Press, 2000), 40, 54, 126.

18. SLC to JC, Oct. 2, 1908. *My Father,* 276–77.

19. IVL Datebook, Aug. 5, 1907. Undated note in IVL Statement of Accounts, folder 2, in AL File; see also AL, 280–81, 388. AL, 292. See Hill for a flat denial that any extant evidence supports the statement that Jean could never come home; 215.

20. In Cooley, ed.: SLC to Margaret Blackmer, July 7, 1908, 185; SLC to Frances Nunnally, June 20, 1908, 180–81; SLC to DQ, July 16, 1908, 188; Clemens described the loggia as a "fish market" for his Angelfish in Cooley, ed., 192. SLC to JC, June 19, 1908. In ME.

21. The difficulty of where Clemens was to stay may have helped squelch the planned visit. JC to SLC, May 26, 1908, CFP; SLC to Frances Nunnally, June 3, 1908, in Cooley, ed., 167; SLC to JC, June 19, 1908. In ME.

22. ABP, *Biography,* 1455. AL, 53. JC to Nancy Brush, Jan. 16, 1907 [misdated and misfiled; actually 1908]. No other letter Jean wrote to friends in 1908 gives any indication that she was having seizures. Though her letters are not as reli-

able evidence as her diary, because they do not give a daily record of events, they still provide a rough approximation of her health, which she was frankly divulging to her Dublin friends.

23. AL, 54–55. In ME.

24. AL, 52–53. SLC to JC [July 2, 1908]. In ME. Two months earlier, Lyon had managed to locate a "dear old house" on a 70-acre farm for Zoheth and Sheba Freeman. See IVL Daily Reminder, May 1, 1908. Mr. Freeman was a well-known banker and one of the executors of Mark Twain's will.

25. JC to Nancy Brush, letter fragment [circa July 1908], ph. I have corrected one use of the verb tense "had" to "have."

26. On Jean's thought of Germany instead of Dublin, see JC Diary, Oct. 21, 1906 (the first page of this entry is torn out of the journal). JC to Nancy Brush, Aug. 1, 1908, ph. Frederick Peterson to IVL, Aug. 15, 1908. JC to IVL, Aug. 1, 1908. See Hill, 199, for the claim that it was Clemens who devised the plan to send Jean to Berlin.

27. JC to Nancy Brush, July 23, 1908, ph. JC to IVL, Aug. 1, 1908. JC to IVL, Aug. 4, 1908. Jean's sympathy did not extend to a reprieve for the sisters. After watching their maneuvers with the local doctor's wife, she lobbied Lyon to ensure their swift departure. On August 4, Dr. Peterson ordered the sisters to vacate the Gloucester cottage as soon as possible. Jean stayed on with Marguerite Schmitt and various servants until her departure for Germany. See JC to IVL, Aug. 5, 1908.

28. JC to IVL, Aug. 5, 1908.

29. JC to Nancy Brush, Aug. 1, 1908, ph.; AL, 49. (John Stanchfield was also one of Twain's lawyers.) JC to IVL, Aug. 5, 1908. Frederick Peterson to IVL, Aug. 18, 1908; Prof. Hofrath von Renvers to IVL, Sept. 16, 1908.

30. IVL Daily Reminder, Aug. 8, 6, 1908. See also ABP, *Biography*, 1458–59. IVL to Harriet Whitmore, Aug. 17, 1908, Mark Twain Memorial, Hartford, Conn. Paine later said that doctors told him this dizzy spell was probably the first indication of "a more serious malady." Paine dated the incident after Clemens returned from Sam Moffett's funeral on August 5, while Lyon claimed Paine told her on August 6 that Clemens had had the "fainting spell" while playing billiards ten days earlier. In this case, I follow Lyon's timeline rather than Paine's because hers was constructed at the time of Clemens's sickness.

31. IVL Daily Reminder, Aug. 8, 1908; ABP, *Biography*, 1459. IVL Daily Reminder, Sept. 9, 1908.

32. IVL Daily Reminder, Oct. 15, Sept. 10, 1908.

33. AL, 16–17. In ME. ABP to Mrs. Lyon (IVL's mother), July 21, 1909, AL File. ABP to IVL, Jan. 28, 1908, AL File. IVL Daily Reminder, Aug. 8, 1908.

34. ABP to Mrs. Lyon, July 21, 1909.

35. ABP, *Biography*, 1328, 1324–32. On invitations to ABP to play billiards at Stormfield, see IVL Daily Reminder, Aug. 29, 1908, and SLC to JC, [June 19, 1908].

36. ABP, *Biography*, 1324, 1327–29, 1330, 1332.

CHAPTER 11

1. IVL Daily Reminder, Aug. 4, 1908. AL, 36, 425–26. See report titled "Employees, S. L. Clemens" in Folder 2, Statement and Accounts, 1907–1909, AL File.

2. AL, 86–90, 284–85; quote at 88. In ME.

3. AL, 279, 25. In ME.

4. AL, 73. IVL Daily Reminder, Mar. 22, 1908.

5. AL, 12, 122–26; quotes at 125, 126. In ME. IVL to SLC, Apr. 12, 1909 [a 6-page letter included in AL manuscript, all pages numbered 122].

6. IVL to SLC, Apr. 12, 1909, in AL, 122. AL, 123–24 (quote at 123), 92, 12, 73. In ME. Lyon stated that Clara's offer of a clothing supplement came in 1907 while Jean was emphatic that her sister's permission was given in the winter of 1908. See "Jean's Narrative," in AL, 323–24. (See chapter 15 for an explanation of this narrative.)

7. AL, 12, 73. In ME. IVL Datebook, Mar. 6, Apr. 7, 13, June 9, July 10, 29, 1907.

8. AL, 126 (in ME), 232, 262, 351.

9. The departure date is Hill's, 213. Clemens's letter of Sept. 30, 1908, to Louise Paine would indicate Sept. 29 instead; Cooley, ed., 210. On Marguerite Schmitt, JC to IVL, Dec. 11, 1908. On Jean's finances, JC to IVL, Aug. 1, Oct. 19, 1908; AL, 50; JC to IVL, Oct. 20, 1908; JCE Diary, Accounts Rec'd and Paid, Jan.–Dec. 1907.

10. JC to IVL, Oct. 27, 1908.

11. JC to IVL, Oct. 27, 1908. JC to IVL, Dec. 11, 1908. Jean self-consciously underlined the word "successfully" in referring to the narration. See JCE Diary, Accounts Rec'd and Paid, Jan.–Dec. 1907; in that year Jean's dividends totaled $300.

12. SLC to JC, Dec. 17, 1908, telegram. AL, 49–50. In ME.

13. JC to Marguerite Schmitt, Oct. 19, 1909; all letters to Schmitt are typescripts in English translated from the French originals owned by Hamlin Hill. Hill has a different interpretation. "Nothing in the surviving record indicates that Miss Lyon was instrumental in keeping father and daughter apart," he states flatly, "and if that were her intention, she would surely not have vetoed Jean's plea to stay in Berlin"; 215. Hill is also mystified by Clemens's claim that he did not know about Jean's plea to stay in Germany. I believe that Peterson, not Lyon, ordered her home. (Peterson might have been less censorious if he

had chosen the German doctor.) Clearly the plan to send Jean abroad was Lyon's.

14. IVL Daily Reminder, Dec. 30, 1908; Hill, 214–15.

15. JC to SLC, Mar. 5, 1909.

16. JC to SLC, Mar. 5, 1909; SLC, "Closing Words of My Autobiography" in Autobiographical Dictations File, Dec. 24, 1909, Folder no. 252, ms. 27.

17. AL, 3. In ME.

18. See Accountants' Statements and Schedules/Ashcroft-Lyon Affair/Mar. 1907–Feb. 28, 1909, schedules #4 and #5 for Miss Clara Clemens, in Folder 1, AL File. On schedule #4 Clara's total expenditure for the year ending Feb. 29, 1908, was $11,233.61; her total for the following year, ending Feb. 28, 1909, was $11,669.64. On schedule #5, only $100.00 cash is credited to Clara but another notation for Santa (Clara's nickname) of $250.00 adds up to a total of $350.00 in the year ending Feb. 28, 1909. Note that these totals include both verifiable and unverifiable cash payments. I posit that Clara received all the C.C. cash in both years, unlike her father, who believed that some C.C. cash was stolen by Lyon.

19. See AL, 25. In ME. IVL Daily Reminder, Sept. 9, 1908.

20. IVL Daily Reminder, Oct. 26, 1908.

21. IVL Daily Reminder, Oct. 18, 26, 1908.

22. AL, 3. In ME.

23. On Clara's whereabouts, see *My Father*, 257, 266; IVL 1903–1904 Journal ts., Nov. 30, 1904; IVL Datebook, June–July 1907; SLC to Emilie Rogers, Nov. [5?], 1906, in HHR, 619–20; SLC to JC, June 19, 1908; IVL Daily Reminder, Oct. 6, 1908. Clara returned from her western concert tour on March 28, 1907; see IVL Datebook 1907. She was in Europe from May 16 to Sept. 9, 1908; see IVL Daily Reminder 1908.

24. AL, 26. In ME.

25. SLC dictation, Oct. 21, 1909, "Miss Lyon's habits," 1–4, quote at 3 (in ME); AL, 405; see also AL, 342. Lyon's huge capacity for alcohol consumption was confirmed almost forty years later by Sam and Doris Webster, despite the fact that they were favorably disposed toward Lyon from their initial meeting and became fast friends. See Webster notes on IVL.

26. ABP to Mrs. Lyon (IVL's mother), July 21, 1909, AL File.

27. IVL Daily Reminder, Oct. 1, 20, 1908. AL, 107–8.

28. On Ashcroft, see AL, 234, 347, 417–20, and AL File, one-page description of RWA, ph., original at University of Wisconsin, Madison. At AL 426, Clemens offered the modified opinion that Lyon was already a small thief before she met Ashcroft, who turned her into a large one. On Clemens's wealth, see SLC Probate.

29. AL, 280. In ME. IVL Daily Reminder, Sept. 3, 1908.

30. AL, 25 (in ME), 123, 127, 3 (in ME), 4 (in ME).

31. AL, 3–4. In ME.

32. IVL Daily Reminder, Jan. 24, Feb. 12, Jan. 25, 1908.

33. AL, 27, 28. In ME.

34. AL, 26, 34. In ME.

35. AL, 27 (in ME), 403–5, 406, 25.

36. See IVL Datebook, Apr. 12, 19, June 2, 15, Sept. 26, 1907; IVL Daily Reminder, Jan. 4, Feb. 12, Apr. 15–23, Sept. 28–29, 1908; AL, 73. But Lyon did enjoy a 6-week vacation in Bermuda from March 1 to April 11, 1908. See Hill, 202–3, and Cooley, ed., 93, 117–18.

37. AL, 36–38, 200–210.

38. IVL Datebook, June 7, July 27, Sept. 11, 16, Oct. 10, 1907. AL, 132.

39. AL, 225–30, 85. In ME.

40. AL, 223–28.

41. AL, 229–30.

42. AL, 217. See Michael L. Closen, Glen-Peter Ahlers, Robert M. Jarvis, Malcolm L. Morris, Nancy P. Spyke, *Notary Law and Practice: Cases and Materials* (Chatsworth, Calif.: National Notary Association, 1997), 218–19, which states that "With respect to notarial acts in particular, numerous uniform laws and state statutory provisions have declared that notarial acts are entitled to interstate recognition"; for example, *Nicholson v. Eureka Lumber,* 1912, cited at 223–26. Interestingly, Nickerson's authority was uncontested throughout this period. In fact, he notarized Twain's Probate Inventory after his death. Later, one newspaper, *The American,* reported that the two men who had purportedly witnessed Clemens's signature, "when shown the document, said positively they had never seen it before." The newspapers printed a host of lies, half-truths, and factual errors in their accounts of this affair. Thus I cite this claim only as a possibility within a larger pattern of evidence. See AL File.

43. IVL Daily Reminder, Nov. 10–11, 12–14, 1908; quote at Nov. 11.

44. AL, 216–25; Exhibit A / Copy of the Ashcroft-Lyon Power of Attorney, AL File.

45. AL, 71. In ME.

CHAPTER 12

1. AL, 292, 45, 47 cont., 25. Clemens was far from isolated, however. Close to twenty guests per month were providing him with pleasant diversion at Stormfield. See AL, 73.

2. AL, 17. In ME.

3. AL, 71 (in ME), 420 (in ME), and see 417–20. IVL to SLC, Feb. 25, 1909, in AL File.

4. AL, 81 (in ME), and see 420–21, 81–83.

5. AL, 400–401; Twain gives no specific dates but it seems likely this began sometime in the winter of 1908–9.

6. Everett Emerson, *Mark Twain: A Literary Life* (Philadelphia: University of Pennsylvania Press, 2000), 294; Leslie Fiedler, "Afterword," in Mark Twain, *1601 and Is Shakespeare Dead?* (New York: Oxford University Press, 1996), 9.

7. Twain, *Is Shakespeare Dead?*, 127–28. Paine is absolutely convinced that Twain thought Bacon wrote Shakespeare's plays, and Twain does appear to have held that belief. But the point of his essay is much more complex. See ABP, *Biography*, 1478–81, 1486.

8. This insight about the autobiographical nature of *Is Shakespeare Dead?* came from Fiedler's "Afterword," 14.

9. *Is Shakespeare Dead?*, 144. The word count is Emerson's in *A Literary Life*, 286.

10. AL, 58, 400–401, 22–24. SLC to DQ, Cooley, ed., 251–52. Also see Hill, 221, and ABP to Mrs. Lyon (IVL's mother), July 21, 1909, AL file; ABP, *Biography*, 1480.

11. AL, 60, 61, 63, 33, 30–31. As noted in chapter 11, Paine had already informed Clemens about Lyon's use of bromides, which he ignored; see ABP to Mrs. Lyon, July 21, 1909. Clemens probably recognized her cocktail habit because it was a daily exercise.

12. AL, 32–33, 62. In ME.

13. AL, 35–36, 61–65; SLC to JC, Mar. 3, 1909. See also Hill, 218; IVL to Hattie Whitmore Enders, Feb. 16, 1909.

14. This scene is drawn from Clemens's account in AL, 65–70. In ME. In order to present it as dialogue, I have adapted some of Clemens's indirect discourse, excerpting only portions of the conversation, summarizing one of Ashcroft's colloques, changing pronouns and verb tenses, and using "and" in place of ampersands. Such paraphrases are indicated by the use of single quotes. Exact quotations are in double quotes.

15. AL, 69–71.

16. AL, 28, 127–28.

17. AL, 68, 97–98 (in ME), 72, 96–97.

18. "Report of Miss X," ph., DeVoto Papers, Stanford, Calif. The detective was hired by the Clemenses' family lawyer to investigate whether Lyon might have any Twain manuscripts in her possession.

19. See AL, 58 (in ME), 68.

20. IVL to SLC, undated [early March 1909].

21. AL, 421, 59. In ME.

22. AL, 57–58, 157–59.

23. AL, 127–28. In ME.

24. AL, 77, 81. In ME.

25. SLC to CC, Mar. 11, 1908, in AL, 245–56.

26. SLC to CC, Mar. 11, 1908, in AL, 250–52. In ME.

27. SLC to CC, Mar. 11, 1908, in AL, 253–55. In ME.

28. AL, 77, 86, 244.

29. AL, 78–79. Twain notes that without specific mention of compensation, the first contract was nonbinding. He was incorrect: a paper exchange of one dollar was acknowledged in the contract that made Ashcroft his business manager. See AL File, Folder 2.

30. AL, 79–81, quote at 81. In ME.

31. AL, 77–85, 279–80.

32. AL, 86, 87. In ME.

33. SLC to CC, Mar. 14 postscript to Mar. 11, 1908, letter, in AL, 257–58. In ME.

34. AL, 262.

35. AL, 91, 90½. In ME.

36. AL, 93–94, In ME.

37. AL, 86. In ME. And see, for example, AL, 244, where Clemens wrote of the contracts as a "diarrhea" and a "spectacular flux"; also AL, 173–74 and 279–80, where he characterized them as "impertinent."

38. AL, 182; May 7, 1907 Power of Attorney to Isabel V. Lyon, AL File. See also SLC, one-page outline for "Ashcroft-Lyon Ms.," in AL File.

39. AL, 139, 182, 214, 98. In ME.

40. AL, 98. In ME.

CHAPTER 13

1. AL, 97, 378–79; quote at 379. In ME.

2. AL, 426.

3. AL, 98.

4. AL, 161. In ME.

5. AL, 162–63. In ME.

6. AL, 161, 163. In ME.

7. AL, 163.

8. Horace Hazen to SLC, [Apr. 26, 1909], in AL, 147–48. AL, 155.

9. Hill, 222. Horace Hazen to SLC, [Apr. 26, 1909], in AL, 149, 150. AL, 141.

10. AL, 142, 99–102, quote at 100. In ME.

11. AL, 101–2. In ME. The quoted speeches in this dialogue are exact, although I have excerpted only a portion of the conversation.

12. Horace Hazen to SLC, [Apr. 26, 1909], in AL, 146–52.

13. AL, 102. In ME. Clemens's parenthetical remarks about Ashcroft's silence are excluded from this exchange.

14. AL, 102–3. In ME. In this dialogue, I have again excerpted only a portion of the conversation, though the speech quoted here is verbatim.

15. AL, 104–5. In ME. In early April, at the time this incident occurred, Twain was merely confused. Later he observed that this was one of "the smallest & shabbiest" dishonesties that had ever been practiced upon him; see AL,

304. He returned a third time to this incident, using it to prove that Ashcroft was a liar, traitor, sneak, and a would-be thief; AL, 416.

16. AL, 107–8.

17. AL, 108–9 (in ME), 137–38.

18. AL, 108 (in ME), 110. Clemens wrote (at 110) that he saw Clara on April 7 and she made an appointment with Peterson for four o'clock the next day. But in an outline for the AL manuscript, Clemens dates her appointment three days later, on April 11. Given the specificity of the date on the outline and the fact that this document was probably written closer in time to the actual event, I prefer April 11. SLC, Outline for "Ashcroft-Lyon Ms.," in AL File.

19. AL, 115–16, 81, 95. It appears likely that the decision to fire Mrs. Ashcroft was made on April 7 when Clemens saw Clara, although it may have been a day or two later. Clearly Twain had decided before he went to New York on April 12.

20. AL, 109–10.

21. AL, 111. In ME.

22. AL, 111–12. See chapter 10, n. 22, for a discussion of the evidence that led me to this conclusion.

23. SLC, Outline for "Ashcroft-Lyon Ms."

24. AL, 112.

25. AL, 113, 116; SLC, Outline for "Ashcroft-Lyon Ms."; AL, 112–13. In ME.

26. AL, 116–18. Twain thought, but wasn't absolutely certain, that he had this conversation with Ashcroft on April 14.

27. IVL to SLC, Apr. 15, 1909, in AL, 136 ½.

CHAPTER 14

1. AL, 140, 173–75; quote at 174. In ME.

2. AL, 118, 174, 175. In ME.

3. AL, 173–77 (in ME), 82–83, 280.

4. AL, 169, 173–76.

5. Henry Rogers to SLC, Apr. 23, 1909, in AL, 165.

6. AL, 176–78. In ME. Clara harbored strong suspicions that leaving Lyon's trunks untouched may have been a mistake for reasons other than carnelian beads. See "Report of Miss X," ph., and Bernard DeVoto to Mr. Andrews, Oct. 14, 1946, DeVoto Papers, Stanford, Calif. After Twain's death in 1910, Ashcroft put the original manuscript of *Is Shakespeare Dead?* on the market in New York City, and Charles Lark, one of the lawyers handling Twain's estate, bought it back for a "nominal consideration," in his words. Avoiding an outright charge of piracy, he noted carefully that "we did not know that he had the same or claimed any right thereto." See note by Charles Lark, Feb. 28, 1911, AL File.

7. ABP to Mr. Lark, June 7, 1909, in AL, 179–81.

8. AL, 181, 179, 114, 167.

9. SLC to JC, Apr. 19, 1909. In ME. SLC, "Closing Words of My Autobiography" in Autobiographical Dictations File, Dec. 24, 1909, Folder no. 252, hereafter cited as "Closing Words," ms. 22.

10. AL, 64, 113–14. Ashcroft bought the farm in the last week of February, and the deed was recorded on April 8, 1909. See SLC Probate.

11. See JC to Marguerite Schmitt, Nov. 7, 1909, English ts. of French original. Not every day was the same, but Jean was nearly always occupied. The day she described in detail in this letter to her friend is the basis for my description of her routine.

12. SLC to CC, July 18, 1909. In ME.

13. SLC to CC, July 18, 1909. As far as I know, he bestowed this praise—"like her mother"—on no one else. SLC, "Closing Words," ms. 31, 22.

14. AL, 210, 141–43 (quote at 141; in ME), 155.

15. RWA to SLC, Apr. 29, 1909, in AL, 171.

16. RWA to SLC, Apr. 29, 1909, in AL, 172.

17. AL, 5 [written May 2, 1909]. In ME. Neither Clara nor Jean ever approached the power Isabel Lyon wielded over their father.

18. AL, 185–86.

19. AL, 186–87. In ME. The auditor's report confirms Lounsbury's figures: Lyon spent a total of $3,435.24. See Accountants' Statements and Schedules / Ashcroft-Lyon Affair / Mar. 1907–Feb. 28, 1909, Schedule #2, in Folder 1, AL File; hereafter cited as Auditor's Report.

20. AL, 189–91; quote at 187. In ME.

21. Auditor's Report, Schedule #12, Notes and Comments. AL, 264, 266. This early example of Lyon's revisionist work seems analogous to her later practice of altering her diary to suit her version of history. See the Epilogue.

22. AL, 196, 198–99, 186–87; see Auditor's Report, Schedule #2.

23. AL, 264–65, 129–30. In ME. See chapter 15, note 19, for a more detailed discussion of house money.

24. AL, 213 (in ME), 214.

25. AL, 215–16; quote at 216 (in ME); also see chapter 11. ABP, *Biography*, 961–79, 983–87, 1017, 1021; Caroline Harnsberger, *Mark Twain: Family Man* (New York: Citadel Press, 1960), 213. AL, 223. In ME.

26. Hill, 231–32.

27. ABP, *Biography*, 1432–33, 1442–44, 1456, 1464–69. Twain may have been careless about the exact boundaries of legal documents that he signed. For example, he acknowledged giving Isabel Lyon the power to sign checks for him in 1907. Although he was fully cognizant of signing that document and of his assignee (see AL, 214), he apparently did not realize that this was a comprehensive, not a restricted, power of attorney—that is, it was not limited to check-signing privileges, but already granted the wide range of power Lyon and

Ashcroft "acquired" in the later, suspect power of attorney. I do not think Twain, Lyon, or Ashcroft ever understood this irony; they all assumed that Lyon had check-signing privileges *only*. In fact the two forms contained virtually identical boilerplate copy. See both power of attorney documents in AL File. Please note that Clemens did have one documented memory lapse in late July or early August 1908, which was discussed in chapter 10; see ABP, *Biography*, 1458–59; IVL Daily Reminder, Aug. 6, 1908. For a more negative view of Twain's mental capacities, see Hill, 194–95.

28. AL, 139, 233–36 (in ME).

29. "Report of Miss X."

30. AL, 236, 237. In ME. In fact at his death Twain's estate came closer to half a million; see SLC, Probate.

31. See Charles T. Lark to Mr. A. B. Payne [*sic*], Aug. 10, 1909, in AL File. Lark described a long itemized statement that Ashcroft presented to him "as to services rendered Mr. Clemens beginning with May 1903 with the alleged value of each service detailed." Lark listed a number of the items in Ashcroft's memo along with their dollar amounts.

32. Memo by SLC to Mr. Lark, undated (in ME), and memo by SLC to Mr. Lark, Aug. 15, 1909, 5–6 (in ME), both attached to Charles Lark to Mr. Payne (sic), Aug. 10, 1909, AL File. AL, 238–39. Revocation of November 14, 1909, Power of Attorney to Ralph W. Ashcroft and Isabel V. Lyon, June 1, 1909, AL File.

33. AL, 205 (in ME); 190, 139. In ME. (Twain was an excellent speller but he missed on "potato," which I have corrected silently here.)

CHAPTER 15

1. AL, 113. In ME. SLC to CC, July 18, 1909. In ME.

2. See AL, 114, 167, 308–9. The latter pages were written sometime in July 1909. On Jean's seizures, JC to Nancy Brush, Jan. 16, 1907 [misdated and misfiled; actually 1908], ph.

3. RWA to SLC, Apr. 29, 1909, in AL, 172.

4. AL, 240, 261–62. RWA to SLC, June 3, 1909, AL File. Unused interview prepared by SLC on June 8, 1909, 5, AL File. Charles Lark to ABP, June 12, 1909 in AL, 241.

5. AL, 263, 267–68. Clara blamed the leak to the press on the Bridgeport notary; see AL, 366.

6. *New York American* newspaper clipping, "Twain Charges False, Declares Mrs. Ashcroft," in AL, 267.

7. See AL, 210, where Twain asks similar questions.

8. AL, 275–76. Newspaper articles such as the one in *The Evening Telegram*, July 13, 1909, reveal the story that Mrs. Ashcroft was telling herself.

9. Lyon's statement in *The Evening Telegram,* July 13, 1909, in AL, 276. See additional newspaper clippings in AL, 288–89, 282, 276. Each daughter was fingered in at least one account. One paper reported that Mrs. Ashcroft declined to name the culprit.

10. *The Evening Telegram,* July 13, 1909, in AL, 276. And see applicable newspaper clippings in AL, 267, 276, 282, 288–89. On Clemens's reckonings, AL, 217–18; the figures were verified in the final auditor's report.

11. AL, 305–8; quote at 308 (in ME); ABP to Mr. Lark, July 13, 1909, AL File.

12. AL, 310. In ME. I have changed "she" to "you."

13. "Jean's Narrative," in AL, 311–12. Jean's handwritten 24-page report, which Twain titled "Jean's Narrative," is placed in its entirety in AL, as pp. 311–34.

14. "Jean's Narrative," in AL, 312–13.

15. "Jean's Narrative," in AL, 314–15.

16. "Jean's Narrative," in AL, 316–17.

17. "Jean's Narrative," in AL, 318, 314, 321–22.

18. "In a year & ten months she drew nearly ten thousand dollars house-money!" Twain announced in June 1909; AL, 265. But the final auditor's report clearly indicates that house money "claimed to have been paid" for the two-year period totaled only $5,575: $2,950 in the year ending Feb. 29, 1908, and $2,625 in the year ending Feb. 28, 1909. See Accountants' Statements and Schedules / Ashcroft-Lyon Affair / Mar. 1907–Feb. 28, 1909, Schedule #12 Notes and Comments, in Folder 1, AL File; hereafter cited as Auditor's Report.

19. AL, 264–65. In ME. The Clemens camp was confused about the exact figure. Paine incorrectly notes that Miss Lyon spent $4,000 "house money" in 1907, less than $1,000 of which was used for the purpose of paying servants' wages in cash. He adds that similar conditions prevailed in 1908. He estimates that half of the remainder was misappropriated. See ABP to Mr. Lark, July 13, 1909, in AL File. Twain's numbers differ from Paine's, which differ from Lark's, who said she stole $4,000. See "Jean's Narrative," in AL, 321. Luckily the final auditor's report stands as an arbiter of the conflicting claims. Note the last line in Auditor's Report, Schedule #12 Notes and Comments: "There are some receipted invoices which have not been traced to checks, and these presently account for part of the currency obtained by means of cashed checks" (in other words, some house money was used for legitimate purposes).

20. AL, 324–25.

21. "Jean's Narrative," in AL, 325–26. Dialogue enclosed in single quotes paraphrases the original by changing pronouns and verb tenses.

22. "Jean's Narrative," in AL, 326–27.

23. "Jean's Narrative," in AL, 322–23, 328.

24. "Jean's Narrative," in AL, 327–29.

25. "Jean's Narrative," in AL, 328.

26. "Jean's Narrative," in AL, 330–31.

27. "Jean's Narrative," in AL, 332.

28. AL, 308.

29. SLC to CC, July 18, 1909. In ME.

CHAPTER 16

1. AL, 351–52.

2. AL, 345–46. In ME.

3. The quotes that follow are taken from Clara's handwritten report, which Twain labeled "Clara's Narrative" and inserted in AL, 354–73; Clara recorded the conversation as direct dialogue.

4. Clara said that Mrs. Lyon repeated here her earlier remark about faithful devotion, so I have repeated that quotation at this point.

5. "Clara's Narrative," in AL, 374–75. Although Clara is vague about the exact timing of Lounsbury's observation of Mrs. Ashcroft at her window, it seems reasonable that he saw her around this time.

6. Again, all quotes are taken directly from "Clara's Narrative" in AL, 354–73.

7. AL, 375–76. My thanks to Sally Gordon for her legal perspective on this interaction.

8. See "Clara's Narrative," in AL, 364–65; AL, 234–35; "Report of Miss X," ph., DeVoto Papers, Stanford, Calif.

9. AL, 424–26.

10. AL, 388, 72.

11. AL, 78–79. See also RWA, "Memorandum for Mr. Rogers re. Clemens' Matter," AL File; RWA to Mr. Stanchfield, July 30, 1909, titled "The Ashcroft's Defense in Suit against S. L. Clemens," AL File. On the contract Clemens signed on Clean-Up Day, see chapter 12.

12. SLC's reply to Charles Lark to ABP, Aug. 10, 1909, 2 (in ME), AL File, hereafter cited as "SLC reply." SLC Probate, 4. In the summer of 1909, Clemens reckoned his investments in hairpins and safety pins at $12,000. It is unclear whether this figure included the earlier sum of $4,500 he had invested in 1904 (see chapter 8). Also see one-page summary of the settlement with the Ashcrofts dated Sept. 10, 1909, AL File.

13. "SLC reply," 10. In ME.

14. "SLC reply," 11–13; also AL, 8–9. Note that the original Plasmon investment was Twain's own doing. At his death, Twain owned 400 stock shares and 32 bonds in the American Mechanical Cashier Company, all worthless; 375 shares of the Plasmon Milk Products Company, "which stock is practically worthless," according to his probate inventory; and 345 shares of the Koy-lo (hairpin) Company, again worthless according to probate records. See SLC Probate.

CHAPTER 17

1. See RWA to Mr. Stanchfield, July 30, 1909, titled "The Ashcroft's Defense in Suit against S. L. Clemens," AL File; hereafter cited as "The Ashcrofts' Defense." Despite its title, the letter constituted a settlement offer, or rather a list of demands, not a legal action.

2. RWA to Mr. Whitmore, Aug., 1909, Mark Twain Memorial. "The Ashcrofts' Defense."

3. "The Ashcrofts' Defense."

4. AL, 380.

5. "Ashcroft Accuses Miss Clara Clemens," *New York Times,* Aug. 4, 1909, in AL 382–83.

6. AL, 264–65; and see SLC's reply to Charles Lark to ABP, Aug. 10, 1909, 2, AL File.

7. See Accountants' Statements and Schedules / Ashcroft-Lyon Affair / Mar. 1907–Feb. 28, 1909, Schedule #4 for Miss Clara Clemens, in folder 1, AL File. In the two-year period from February 28, 1907 to February 28, 1909, Clara went through a whopping $22,903.25; see note 18 to chapter 11. Five of the six checks paid to the Lincoln National Bank were for unverifiable cash or credit, according to the auditor's notation of an uncertain deposit. This untraceable cash totaled $1,165. For all other checks either there was a specific payee or the auditor noted that there was some evidence that "this ck was deposited to order of CC."

8. SLC to JC, [early Oct. 1907]; see chapter 8, at notes 3–4. AL, 389. In ME.

9. AL, 391.

10. AL, 408–9. In ME.

11. See AL, 77–95, which was probably written between June 27 and 29, 1909 (see p. 77 for confirmation of the June 27 date). The discussion of the promissory notes on Clean-Up Day is at AL, 86–87. See AL, 409–10, for Clemens's later reaction to his discovery of the forgery.

12. AL, 412–16, 384, and "The Ashcrofts' Defense."

13. AL, 139.

14. AL, 391. In ME.

15. Edna Ashcroft to Mr. Frederick Anderson, Oct. 26, 1968, AL File.

16. Clipping of "Mark Twain Suits All Off," *New York Times,* Sept. 13, 1909, attached to SLC to Mr. Ochs, undated [approx. Sept. 15, 1909], AL File; Ochs was the editor and publisher of the *New York Times.*

17. On the date of the property gift, see unused interview prepared by SLC, 2–3, AL File; IVL Datebook, June 13, 1907.

18. "Mark Twain Suits All Off," *New York Times,* Sept. 13, 1909. SLC to Mr. Ochs, AL File. I could find no extant legal document to support Ashcroft's claim of a loan nor any reference in any letter written to Twain's lawyers nor any evidence in the remaining correspondence.

19. "Mark Twain Suits All Off," *New York Times,* Sept. 13, 1909.

20. See SLC to Mr. Ochs, 4–6; this letter was probably never mailed. Also see loose one-page summary of the settlement by Twain dated Sept. 10, 1909, AL File.

21. Kaplan, 386. Edna Ashcroft to Mr. Frederick Anderson, Oct. 26, 1968, and Robert Ashcroft to Simon and Schuster, Publishers, Nov. 2, 1968, AL File.

22. SLC to Mr. Ochs, 1–2. In ME.

23. SLC to Mr. Ochs, 8, 2. In ME.

24. AL, 387. In ME. Given that Ashcroft became an intimate of Lyon in early 1908, his involvement did not span the three-year period Jean was exiled. In all likelihood, Ashcroft was never an initiator of actions toward Jean.

25. AL, 388 (in ME), 53–55.

26. AL, 292, 349. In ME.

CHAPTER 18

1. George Bernard Shaw to SLC, July 3, 1907, as quoted in ABP, *Biography,* 1398; the line is from Shaw's play *John Bull's Other Island,* act 2.

2. Macnaughton, 32–33, 173.

3. AL, "To the Unborn Reader," 9. In ME. Twain dated only the first and last of the thirty-two sections of the manuscript. For a while he numbered sections following the first one, but then dropped that convention as well and used spaces to indicate breaks in the text. Whenever possible I have dated these un-dated sections through internal clues. See also AL, 4–5.

4. See Hill, 229–32. According to Hill, the Ashcroft-Lyon manuscript be-came publicly known "for the first time" in 1970. Many scholars have followed Hill's lead, characterizing the manuscript as "malicious," "laughable," "petty," "unfair," and in certain respects, a complete fabrication. See Allan Gribben, "Autobiography as Property," in Sara de Saussure Davis and Philip Beidler, eds., *The Mythologizing of Mark Twain* (University, Ala.: University of Alabama Press, 1984), 44; Laura E. Skandera-Trombley, *Mark Twain in the Company of Women* (Philadelphia: University of Pennsylvania Press, 1994), 177–81. Others have described Twain as "floundering in fantasy during his closing year" and veering into a "dead-end despair." See Louis Budd, "A 'Talent for Posturing': The Achievement of Mark Twain's Public Personality," in Davis and Beidler, eds., *Mythologizing,* 97; Arthur G. Pettit, "Mark Twain and His Times: A Bi-centennial Appreciation," in Louis J. Budd, ed., *Critical Essays on Mark Twain, 1910–1980* (Boston: G. K. Hall and Co., 1983), 210. Everett Emerson has de-scribed the manuscript as "a sad document"; *A Literary Life* (Philadelphia: University of Pennsylvania Press, 2000), 294–95.

5. WDH to SLC, Feb. 14, 1904, in MTHL, 781.

6. See AL, 45–55; quote at 47. In ME.

7. AL, "To the Unborn Reader," 3. In ME. AL, 155.

8. AL, 134, In ME. 4–5, 65. In ME.

9. See AL, 10, 1 (in ME), 2 (in ME), 17–18. Twain refers to his financial disasters with Elisha Bliss, his first publisher; James Paige, the inventor of the mechanical typesetter; and Charles Webster, publishing partner and business manager. Also see the excellent essay on Twain's humorous devices by John C. Gerber, "Mark Twain's Use of the Comic Pose," in Louis J. Budd, ed., *Critical Essays on Mark Twain, 1910–1980* (Boston, Mass.: G.K. Hall and Co., 1983), 131–43.

10. AL, 20.

11. AL, 35, 30–31, 350–51, 43 (in ME), 44. In ME.

12. AL, 47. In ME.

13. AL, 52–56. In ME.

14. AL, 58–61, 71. In ME.

15. AL, 114. In ME.

16. On the firing, AL, 135–37. On bill-paying habits, AL, 36–38, 200–210; quote at 207. In ME.

17. AL, 170, 42 (in ME), 234, 347. It was later that Clemens revised this opinion, deciding that Lyon was already a small thief before Ashcroft turned her into a large one; see AL, 426.

18. AL, 280–81. In ME.

19. AL, 277, 295.

20. AL, 388. "Ashcroft Accuses Miss Clara Clemens," *New York Times,* Aug. 4, 1909, in AL, 382.

21. AL, 395. In ME.

22. AL, 393 (in ME), 394–95. In ME.

23. AL, 418. In ME.

24. AL, 398–401. In ME.

25. AL, 402. In ME.

26. AL, 406. In ME.

27. AL, 407. In ME.

28. AL, 399, 421.

29. H.M. Bernheim, "De la Suggestion et de Ses Applications à la Thérapeutique," in Maurice M. Tinterow, M.D., ed., *Foundations of Hypnosis: From Mesmer to Freud* (Springfield, Ill.: Charles Thomas, 1970), 454. And see Theodore R. Sarbin, "Attempts to Understand Hypnotic Phenomena," in Leo Postman, ed., *Psychology in the Making: Histories of Selected Research Problems* (New York: Alfred A. Knopf, 1962), 745–85, quote at 766.

30. Dr. Frederik Van Eeden, "Curing by Suggestion," *The World's Work,* Sept. 1909, 11993–99, esp. 11997.

31. Van Eeden, "Suggestion," 11997.

32. Van Eeden, "Suggestion," as cited in AL, 422.

33. Van Eeden, "Suggestion," as cited in AL, 422.

34. For the theoretical and experimental foundations of learned helplessness, see Judy Garber and Martin E. P. Seligman, *Human Helplessness: Theory and Applications* (New York: Academic Press, 1980); also Rebecca Curtis, ed., *Self-Defeating Behaviors: Experimental Research, Clinical Impression, and Practical Implications* (New York: Plenum Press, 1989). The literature applying the concept to various social, psychological, and educational problems is extensive. For insight into the social conditions that create and maintain dependency in old age, see Margret M. Baltes, *Many Faces of Dependency in Old Age* (Cambridge: Cambridge University Press, 1996).

35. AL, 53, 417–20. In ME.

36. *Lifetime,* 234.

37. See, for example, *My Father,* 179–80; also see Macnaughton, 21–22, for two of Clemens's hare-brained financial schemes that Livy helped quash.

38. AL, 34–35, 132. In ME.

39. AL, 418. In ME.

40. Norman Maclean, *Young Men and Fire* (Chicago: University of Chicago Press, 1992), xiii.

41. AL, 423.

CHAPTER 19

1. Hill, 231.

2. James Martin Miller, ed., *Discovery of the North Pole* (Chicago: J. T. Moss, 1909), editor's preface, unnumbered, and 124–25. This book contains Cook's autobiographical account of how he supposedly reached the North Pole on April 21, 1908, as well as the story of Peary's discovery of the Pole on April 6, 1909.

3. AL, 428. In ME.

4. AL, 429. In ME.

5. Miller, ed., *Discovery,* 425, 259, 267.

6. Charles Coulston Gillispie, ed., *Dictionary of Scientific Biography* (New York: Scribner's, 1970), 1: 53–54. As Twain indicates, the bolder scientist, Le-verrier, whose published calculations were used for the actual observation of Neptune, was given credit for the planet's discovery in 1846, even though he began his investigation later than Adams.

7. Hon. Simeon Davidson Fess, "The North Pole Aftermath," Speech in the House of Representatives, Mar. 4, 1915, including excerpts from the report of the Congressional Committee of Investigation issued Jan. 21, 1911, 1–27 (pamphlet, U.S. Government Printing Office).

8. See Fess, "Aftermath," 19–24. Cook managed to get on the Chautaqua circuit, a highly regarded public lecture platform, after he was discredited by the scientific community.

9. ABP, *Biography,* 1517.

10. AL, "To the Unborn Reader," 3. In ME.

11. AL, "To the Unborn Reader," 2. In ME.

12. AL, "To the Unborn Reader," 2. In ME.

13. Anthony J. Ouellette, "The Paston Letters," in *Dictionary of Literary Biography* (Detroit: Gale Research Inc., 1994), 146: 420–25.

14. AL, "To the Unborn Reader," 4. In ME.

15. SLC to CC, Feb. 21, 1910. JC to Marguerite Schmitt, Nov. 7, 1909, English ts. of French original. JC to Nancy Brush, Nov. 10, 1909, ph. JC to Marguerite Schmitt, Oct. 19, 1909, English ts. of French original.

16. JC to Marguerite Schmitt, Oct. 19, 1909, English ts. of French original. *My Father,* 212–13. *Lifetime,* 309.

17. CC to SLC, July 9, 1909.

18. SLC to Mr. Stone, Sept. 14, 1909. In ME. ABP to Adolph Simon Ochs, Feb. 14, 1910, Albert Bigelow Paine Collection, HEH. "Mark Twain Done with Work," *New York Times,* Dec. 21, 1909, 1.

19. SLC to Joseph Twichell, Sept. 19, 1909, ph., Beinecke Rare Book Library, Yale University, New Haven, Conn. [SLC] memo, Sept. 10, 1909, loose in AL File. SLC to Mrs. Whitmore, Dec. 28, 1909 (in ME), ph., Mark Twain Memorial, Hartford, Conn.

20. Mark Twain, "The Turning Point of My Life," in Louis J. Budd, ed., *Mark Twain: Collected Tales, Sketches, Speeches, and Essays, 1891–1910* (New York: Library of America, 1992), 931–36; quotes at 932, 936.

21. IVL, Aug. 16, [1909]. This was written on a separate card that was stuck in her 1908 diary and thus preserved. No extant copy exists, so far as I know, of her 1909 diary.

22. SLC form letter to Coe, Duneka, Enders, Paine, Starr, Sunderland, Wayland, among others, ca. Oct. 7, 1908, Mark Twain Memorial, Hartford, Conn. ABP, *Biography,* 1522.

23. *My Father,* 280–81. *Lifetime,* 311–13.

24. CC to SLC, July 9, 1909.

25. SLC to CC, Dec. 28, 1909. JC to Marguerite Schmitt, Dec. 21, 1909, English ts. of French original. SLC to CC, Dec. 29, 1909. In ME.

CHAPTER 20

1. ABP, *Biography,* 1503–5.

2. ABP, *Biography,* 1528–29, 1509; also note 8 below.

3. ABP, *Biography,* 1532. See Mark Twain, "Letters from the Earth," in Louis J. Budd, ed., *Mark Twain: Collected Tales, Sketches, Speeches, and Essays, 1891–1910* (New York: Library of America, 1992), esp. 885–90.

4. "Letters from the Earth," 914–15.

5. "Letters from the Earth," 915.

6. "Letters from the Earth," 915–16.

7. ABP, *Biography*, 1543–45.

8. "Mark Twain Done with Work," *New York Times,* Dec. 21, 1909, 1.

9. On the Christmas tree, JC to Marguerite Schmitt, Dec. 21, 1909, English ts. of French original. On Jean's gifts, see, for example, Emma Thayer to SLC, Dec. 25, 1909; Joe and Harmony Twichell to SLC, Dec. 25, 1909. On the globe, ABP, *Biography,* 1548.

10. Mark Twain, "The Death of Jean," *Harper's Monthly Magazine,* Jan. 1911, 210–15.

11. SLC to Ethel Newcomb [and others], Dec. 24, 1909. In ME.

12. "Closing Words," Dec. 24, 1909, Autobiographical Dictations file, folder no. 252, 10–11. He repeated his reasons in a deleted paragraph (41) that posed the question "Why did I not go?" ABP, *Biography,* 1549.

13. Twain quoted in ABP, *Biography,* 1552. See ABP, *Biography,* 1555; *My Father,* 286. "The Death of Jean" appears in Henry Seidel Canby, ed., *Harper Essays* (New York: Harper & Brothers, 1927), 146–59; Charles Neider, *The Autobiography of Mark Twain* (New York: Harper & Brothers, 1959), and Kiskis, ed., *MT's Autobiography,* 245–52.

14. Mark Twain, "Closing Words of My Autobiography," *Stormfield, Christmas Eve,* 11 a.m., 1909, in Autobiographical Dictations file, Dec. 24, 1909, folder no. 252. This autobiographical essay by Mark Twain is by Richard A. Watson and The Chase Global Private Bank as Trustees of the Mark Twain Foundation, which reserves all reproduction or dramatization rights in every medium. It is published here with permission of the University of California Press and Robert H. Hirst, General Editor of the Mark Twain Project. For a perceptive reading of this essay, see Michael J. Kiskis, "Mark Twain and the Tradition of Literary Domesticity," in Laura E. Skandera-Trombley and Michael J. Kiskis, eds., *Constructing Mark Twain: New Directions in Scholarship* (Columbia: University of Missouri Press, 2001), 221.

15. SLC to Mrs. Coe, Dec. 27, 1909 (in ME), Mark Twain Memorial, Hartford, Conn. In this letter Clemens speaks of his dream of family.

16. *My Father,* 282. CC to Julia Langdon, Jan. 23, 1910.

17. SLC to CC, Feb. 21, 1910. In ME.

18. "Letters from the Earth," 895.

19. "Letters from the Earth," 895.

20. SLC to Joe and Harmony Twichell, Dec. 27, 1909, ph., Beinecke Rare Book Library, Yale University, New Haven, Conn.; and see SLC to Mrs. Coe, Dec. 27, 1909, Mark Twain Memorial, Hartford, Conn.

21. SLC to Joe and Harmony Twichell, Dec. 27, 1909 (in ME), ph., Beinecke Rare Book Library, Yale University, New Haven, Conn. Joseph & Harmony Twichell to SLC, Dec. 25, 1909.

22. MMT, 84; ABP, *Biography,* 1556–57.

23. "Was 'Tom Sawyer' Danish or American?" *New York Times,* Feb. 6, 1910, 7.

24. Paine's ditty is found in a letter he sent to SLC on Feb. 6, 1910, and is quoted in Hill, 268. ABP to Adolph Simon Ochs, Feb. 14, 1910, Albert Bigelow Paine Collection, HEH.

25. ABP, *Biography,* 1560. SLC to CC, Mar. 24, 1910. In ME.

26. ABP, *Biography,* 1562–63, 1568.

27. ABP, *Biography,* 1570–73.

28. ABP, *Biography,* 1575–78; *My Father,* 290–91.

29. ABP, *Biography,* 1573. Admittedly, Paine was capable of drastic omissions and elisions in his work. He also intended to show the admirable side of Mark Twain, which dovetailed neatly with the filters Clara wanted applied to her father. Nonetheless his account of Clemens's deathbed courage strikes me as authentic.

30. *My Father,* 183–84.

EPILOGUE

1. *Lifetime,* 331.

2. *Lifetime,* 335–36.

3. *Lifetime,* 338, 337.

4. *Lifetime,* 339, 50–58, quote at 54.

5. ABP to Elizabeth Wallace, Mar. 9, 1912, MTP. ABP, *Biography,* 1379, 1446. *My Father,* 257, 270. Lawton described Clara as "the best beloved of all my friends" in her introduction to *Lifetime,* xiii. On the origin of her book, see xi–xv.

6. AL, 114–15. In ME.

7. Webster Notes on IVL, Mar. 5, 1948, 6. "Report of Miss X," ph., DeVoto Papers, Stanford, Calif. Jennifer L. Rafferty, " 'The Lyon of St. Mark': A Reconsideration of Isabel Lyon's Relationship to Mark Twain," *Mark Twain Journal* 34 (fall 1996): 53. On Ashcroft, see *Who's Who In Canada,* 412.

8. "Report of Miss X." In the report, the detective remarked that Lyon's gowns were almost twenty years out-of-date. Also see Webster Notes on IVL, Mar. 5, 1948, 7, for a brief description of her memorabilia table. Lyon worked for the Home Title Company in Brooklyn.

9. In addition to this dated foray back into her original diaries, there are excursions marked "1936" and "June 1937." The exact timing of others would be helpful, but what is essential has been established by these three notations. See IVL Daily Reminder, Jan. 15, 1905; IVL Datebook, Oct. 12, 1907; IVL Steno Notebook #2, Oct. 23, 1906. Of course, not every diary is a private confessional. Although it is at odds with our tendency to think of diaries as the pro-

tected and privileged records of intimate feelings and events, writing a diary for public consumption is not unusual. Rewriting already completed entries with a public in mind increases the level of complexity. Revisions of an unpublished novel or short story are expected, and highly conventional, and the "original" is what is finally published, however many revisions precede the work in print. Yet reworking an unpublished diary is rewriting history to one's own purpose. Perhaps because there is no expected benchmark of publication, diary revisions made weeks, months, or even years later violate the form's crucial frame of immediacy: the date of entry. If an entry is presented on a date in 1906 and then secretly revised thirty years later that frame is shattered.

10. Laurie Lentz, "Mark Twain in 1906: An Edition of Selected Extracts from Isabel V. Lyon's Journal," *Resources for American Literary Study* 11 (spring 1981): 10–11. Unavailable to Hill, this autographic copy was purchased by the University of Texas, Austin, in 1975 and was made available to scholars in 1976; a copy was given to the Mark Twain Papers at Berkeley in 1976 as well. Lyon actually made one telling slip of the pen that might have given her away even if she had destroyed the original diary. She mistakenly dated an entry May 30, 1946, rather than 1906, perhaps indicating the year (or at least the decade) in which she was actually working on her hand recopy—although this could, of course, merely be a random numerical error. See Austin diary, May 30, 1946.

11. On March 5, 1948, Doris Webster wrote that Lyon was "80 years old and only just retired." She was actually eighty-four at that date.

12. Webster Notes on IVL, Mar. 5, 1948, 3; Webster was addressing Dixon Wecter. See Doris Webster to Dr. Smith, Dec. 5, 1958, for a sense of the Websters' long-lasting friendship with Lyon. See John Seelye to Fred [Anderson], Mar. 18, 1977, IVL MT Notes, for the hint on publication. The Websters were not always faithful to Lyon's wishes, however, retaining whole entries that she had clearly intended to excise. See IVL ts., June 28, July 5, July 6, 1906, all accompanied by the notation, "I.V.L. crossed out."

13. Samuel Charles Webster, *Mark Twain, Business Man* (Boston: Little, Brown and Company, 1946); see Kaplan, 289–92. It is possible Lyon believed, on the strength of his book, that Webster held a grudge against Twain and would therefore be sympathetic to her version of events.

14. Webster Notes on IVL, Mar. 5, 1948. Doris Webster to Rachel Varble, Oct. 25, 1953.

15. IVL Datebook, June 3, 1907; also, refer to the first half of chapter 7.

16. IVL Daily Reminder, Jan. 27, 1906, Nov. 26, 1905. Webster's note is on an insert to the typescript, 110. Webster Notes on IVL, Mar. 5, 1948, 2. See the discussion of the common folklore of epilepsy and the attitudes of family members in chapter 3.

17. Webster Notes on IVL, Mar. 5, 1948, 1–2. Twain's testimony, Paine's letters, and corroborating evidence in the secretary's own diary demonstrate that she worked ceaselessly to alienate her boss from the biographer and his project.

18. See IVL Daily Reminder, June 28, 1906, for the negative comment on Paine. Lyon also crossed out "Oh, it is so wonderful!," which referred to the story of Paine's life. IVL Daily Reminder, Jan. 27, 1906. Hill quoted Lyon's revised entry for Jan. 27 without comment; 120–21. See also Laura Skandera-Trombley, *Mark Twain in the Company of Women* (Philadelphia: University of Pennsylvania Press, 1994), esp. 16, but also 177–81, and 194 fn. 6; Lentz, "Mark Twain in 1906," 1–36. In the Austin version, which was not available to Hill, Lyon added even more emphasis, changing "terrible blow" to "heavy blow," for example. But note that the January 27 entry contradicts Lyon's claim to the Websters that Jean's first attack had occurred the previous November. For a discussion of the ambiguities of dating the insert for Sept. 29, 1906, see note 9 to chapter 5.

19. See Doris Webster to Mr. Smith, Nov. 1, 1954, IVL MT Notes.

20. IVL Daily Reminder, Mar. 20, 1906; Austin version, Mar. 20, 1906. (Katy shared a similar view of Twain's loyalty and sense of justice; see *Lifetime*, 278.) Lyon did *not* delete this passage in her revisions to the original diary; consequently it remains intact in the Webster typescript. This is another notable inconsistency. One explanation might be the time that lapsed between her revisions to the original diaries and her Austin diary rewrite. Another might be the variable of alcohol consumption during any given period of revision.

21. Webster Notes on IVL, Mar. 5, 1948.

22. Doris Webster to Dr. Smith, Dec. 5, 1958, IVL MT Notes.

23. Caroline Harnsberger, *Mark Twain: Family Man* (New York: Citadel Press, 1960), 220, 228, 252–55. It was Jean's animosity toward Miss Lyon, according to Harnsberger, along with her frequent seizures and highly critical nature, that forced Twain to place her in a sanitarium for proper treatment and supervision.

24. Harnsberger, *Family Man,* 269. Isabelle Budd, "Clara Samossoud's Will," *Mark Twain Journal* 23 (spring 1985): 17–19.

25. Budd, "Clara's Will," 18–19. "Rites for Mark Twain's Last Descendent Set," *Los Angeles Times,* Jan. 19, 1966, II, 2.

26. Justin Kaplan to Mr. Ashcroft, June 18, 1968, AL File; this is Kaplan's defense after a letter objecting to his portrayal of the Ashcrofts was sent to him by the family in early June. Kaplan, 373, 386. Robert E. Ashcroft to Simon and Schuster, Publishers, Nov. 2, 1968, AL File. Edna Ashcroft to Frederick Anderson, Oct. 26, 1968, AL File.

27. Hill, 269, xxvi–xxvii, 230–32. Four years later, John Seelye published a condensed version of Hill's narrative in *Mark Twain in the Movies: A Meditation with Pictures* (New York: Viking Press, 1977), giving it wider circulation. For a different view of Hill's reliance on Lyon's diaries, see Laura E. Skandera-Trombley and Gary Scharnhorst, "'Who Killed Mark Twain?' Long Live Samuel Clemens," in Laura E. Skandera-Trombley and Michael J. Kiskis, eds., *Constructing Mark Twain: New Directions in Scholarship* (Columbia: University of Missouri Press, 2001).

28. See note 4 to chapter 18 for the critics. Boldest among the defenders of the Ashcroft-Lyon manuscript, Andrew Hoffman credited Twain's charges of embezzlement as "a certainty" and insisted that the autobiography "tells the truth in many places." But he has left it to others to define what that truth is. See Andrew Hoffman, *Inventing Mark Twain: The Lives of Samuel Langhorne Clemens* (New York: William Morrow & Co., 1997), 491–92. William Macnaughton also did not condemn the Ashcroft-Lyon manuscript, though his comments are very brief; 236. Jennifer Rafferty, in " 'The Lyon of St. Mark,' " claimed that the Ashcroft-Lyon manuscript was convincing, but she split the difference, blaming Ashcroft and exonerating Lyon; 52.

29. IVL Daily Reminder, June 11, 1906. Mark Twain, "A Fable," *Harper's Monthly Magazine*, Dec. 1909 , 70–71.

INDEX

ABBREVIATIONS

CC	Clara Clemens
JC	Jean Clemens
OLC	Olivia (Livy) Langdon Clemens
SC	Olivia Susan (Susy) Clemens
SLC	Samuel Langhorn Clemens
(nn)	Subject referred to but not named

Adams (carpenter), 195
Adams, John Couch, 235, 318n7
Aldrich, Lilian, 49
Aldrich, Thomas Bailey (husband of above), 63, 139–40, 187–88
Allen, Helen, 301–2n28
Allen, Mr. and Mrs. William H. (parents of above), 245, 261
American Board of Commissioners of Foreign Missions, 31
American Journal of Insanity, 54
American Mechanical Cashier Company, 118, 206, 314n14
Amundsen, Roald, 236
Angelfish. *See* Clemens, Samuel Langhorn: and his Angelfish
Anti-Imperialist League of New York, 30
Ashcroft, Edna (sister-in-law of Ralph), 215

Ashcroft, Ralph
    and CC: battle over control of SLC's money and household, 114, 122, 135–38, 151–53, 154, 160, 162–63, 164, 166–67, 169, 172–75, 176, 183–85, 187, 191, 193, 204, 207–9, 210–13, 224, 225, 228, 239, 306nn18,28, 309–10n15, 312n5, 313n9 (nn), 315n7; and her demand to inspect Lyon's trunks, 178, 180, 310n26 (nn); and her fear that SLC would marry Lyon, 226; on her lack of care for SLC, 207; lends her money, 135–36; and his and Lyon's attacks on via interviews, 209, 214, 215, 239; and his scheme to topple her as housekeeper, 172–75, 183, 224, 309–10n15
    financial skullduggery of, xii–xiii, 157–58, 166–70, 172, 184–90, 192, 201–5, 207–8, 211, 224, 240, 241, 306n28, 307n42, 309nn29,37,38, 311n19, 311–12n27, 315n11; controversy with SLC over charges against Lyon, 207, 208–12, 213–15, 226, 239; defends himself and Lyon against SLC's charges, xiii, 192–93, 202, 207–8, 209–15, 216, 218

Ashcroft, Ralph (continued)
    (nn), 225–26, 239, 312nn5,6,8,
        313nn 9,10, 315nn1,16; and
        fraudulent powers of attorney,
        106, 158, 187, 188–89, 201, 204,
        224, 297n24, 311–12n27; and
        independent audit of SLC's
        finances, xii–xiii, 160, 166,
        167, 180, 183–84, 192, 207–8;
        as protagonist in SLC's auto-
        biographical exposé, xii–xiii,
        218, 221, 224–25; scheme of to
        topple CC as housekeeper,
        172–75, 183, 224, 309–10n15
    and JC, 125, 183–84, 207, 216,
        300–301n10, 316n24
    later life of, 265
    and Lyon, 103, 118–20, 122, 135,
        152, 154, 155, 204, 205, 222,
        288–89n50, 299n33, 306n28;
        marriage to and divorce from,
        163–66, 171, 205, 239, 265; her
        nickname for, 122
    and Paine: attempts to discredit
        Paine with SLC, xiv, 120–22,
        135, 140, 143–44, 159, 268,
        322n17, 323n18; discrediting of
        with Lyon, 121–22
    and SLC: effect of Clean-Up Day
        contracts on, 168–70, 205,
        309nn29,37, 314n11; effect of
        marriage to Lyon on, 169; gift
        to Lyon of land in Redding,
        Conn., 147, 214; SLC's total
        dependence on him and Lyon,
        140, 159–60, 207–8, 223, 224,
        228–30, 231; as SLC's unpaid
        traveling companion and
        servant, 103–4, 117–20, 143, 159,
        160, 167–68, 169, 190, 205, 221,
        230, 296n15, 299n37; SLC's
        view of as trickster and liar,
        117, 162, 167–68, 172, 183, 184,
        207, 208, 210–15; and sale of
        SLC's MS of "Is Shakespeare

Dead" after SLC's death,
        310n6; as SLC's self-appointed
        business manager: and invest-
        ment advice for SLC, 117–18,
        122, 135–36, 137, 138, 157–58,
        189, 205–6, 213, 300n48,
        303n11; "In the Supreme Court
        of Fair Play S.L. Clemens,
        Presiding Judge," 299n29; and
        Mark Twain Company, 118,
        157–58, 168, 172, 189, 212,
        214–15, 224, 316n20 (nn); and
        money from SLC's invest-
        ments and Clean-Up Day
        contracts, 205–6, 314n11;
        purchase of Redding, Conn.,
        farm for SLC, 181, 311n10
    as viewed by twentieth-century
        scholars, 219 (nn), 271–72,
        323n26
Ashcroft, Robert (nephew of Ralph),
    215–16, 271
Associated Press, 249
Atlantic Monthly, 5
Austen, Jane, 8

Bacon, Francis, 161, 308n7
Barbi, Alice, 25
Barnum, P. T., 1
Benchotte, Claude (SLC's butler), 153,
    175, 261
Benjamin, Mrs. (patient at Katonah), 97
Benjamin, William E., 297n20
Bernheim, Hippolyte, 229, 317n29
Binet, Alfred, 229
Blackmer, Margaret, 132, 133
Blicher, Steen, 261
Bliss, Elisha, 317n9
Breckenridge, Marjorie, 133
Brookes, Mr. (patient at Katonah), 97–98
Brooks, Van Wyck: The Ordeal of Mark
    Twain, 2, 278n3
Broughton, Urban H., 297n20
Brownell, Louise, 16, 17, 20,
    279–80n40

Browning, Robert, 1, 8

Brush, George de Forest (artist; father of Nancy and Gerome), 62–63, 69; and JC, 66, 69, 111, 124–25, 129

Brush, Gerome (Gerry; friend of JC in Dublin, N.H.), 47, 64, 66, 290n30; JC's attempt at romance with, 70–73, 82, 83, 84, 91, 92

Brush, Nancy (friend of JC in Dublin, N.H.), 47, 49, 64, 65, 66, 112, 272

Brush (youngest daughter of George Brush), 129

Brush family, 285n2

Bryn Mawr College, 16, 279–80n4

Bynner, Witter, 33

Cabot, Anna, 70, 71

Carroll, Lewis, 1

Charles Webster and Company, 267

Cherubini, Teresa (maid at Stormfield), 155–56, 175, 180

Christian Science, SLC's written attacks on, 37, 284n57

Churchill, Winston, 1

Clean-Up Day, 168–70, 205–6, 309nn29,37,38, 314n11, 315n11

Clemens, Clara (CC)
    and Alice Barbi, 25
    birth and childhood of, 7, 9, 10, 278n4
    character of, 8, 10, 18, 72, 75, 109, 162–63, 270
    and construction of Stormfield, 75–76, 77, 134, 135, 136, 138, 302n2, 302–3n4
    and Ossip Gabrilowitsch, 26, 31, 34, 239, 240–41, 247, 263, 270
    death of, 270, 271
    foreign travels of, 16–18, 20–21, 22, 23, 24, 26–30, 38–41, 61, 143, 152, 289n8, 306n23
    as guardian of the Clemens family story, xiv, 264–65, 270, 271
    health problems and sanitaria stays of, 44, 46, 47, 90, 109, 152

    and JC, 92, 99, 241, 248; on chaperones for, 64–65; and JC's death, xiv, 248, 249, 258, 259; and JC's exile, 84, 85, 90, 92, 93, 94, 95–96, 99, 114–15, 130, 150, 175–77, 223, 310n18; and JC's horse-riding accident, 43

    and Lyon and Ashcroft, 38, 39, 72, 75, 105–6, 109, 122, 135–37, 151–53, 154, 159, 178, 204, 209, 211, 221, 264; Ashcroft's house-keeping scheme, 172–76, 183, 224, 309–10n15; attacks by the Ashcrofts in newspaper, 209, 214, 215, 239; battle for control of SLC's money and house-hold, 114, 122, 135–38, 151–53, 154, 160, 162–63, 164, 166–67, 169, 172–75, 176, 180, 183–85, 187, 191, 193, 204, 207–9, 210–13, 224, 225, 228, 239, 306nn18,28, 309–10n15, 312n5, 313n9 (nn), 315n7; on character and appearance of Lyon, 38, 204; "Clara's Narrative" on meeting with Lyon's mother and attorney Lark in re farmhouse, 199–204, 211, 225, 312n5, 314nn3–5; and marriage of Ashcroft and Lyon, 164, 165, 166; and money for Lyon's clothes, 148, 170, 201, 305n6; and money/allowance from SLC, xiv, 94–95, 109, 114, 122 (nn), 135–38, 151, 159, 160, 162, 164, 166–67, 209, 306n18; and OLC's missing carnelian beads, 178, 180–81, 203, 310n6; pet names between CC and Lyon, 72, 75; and Lyon's rela-tionship with SLC, xiv, 104, 159, 226, 227, 232, 311n17
    marriage of to Jacques Samossoud, 270

Clemens, Clara (*continued*)
    musical studies of, 9, 18, 23, 25, 26,
        27, 34, 40, 285n67
    in New York City, 31–32, 42–43,
        48, 78, 152, 175
    and Paine's biography of SLC, xiv,
        321n29
    personal expenditures of (1907–9),
        209–10, 306n18, 315n7
    relationships of: with Katy Leary,
        9, 25, 26, 31, 115–16, 136,
        154–55, 166–67, 239, 241,
        264; with OLC, xiv, 36, 37,
        40, 41, 42–43, 115, 253; with
        SC, 24, 108–9, 154, 281n14;
        with Will Wark, 109, 136,
        165, 209
    and SLC, 3, 42, 49, 92, 180, 247,
        311n17; and his Angelfish, 133,
        302n34; battles with Lyon and
        Ashcroft, 167–68, 174, 175,
        180; and his celebrity, xiv,
        26–27, 49, 108–9, 282n23; and
        his final illness and death, xiv,
        23, 262; and her first flirta-
        tion, 16–17; *My Father Mark
        Twain* (1931), xii–xiv, 264–65,
        321n5; as mistress of SLC's
        households after OLC's death,
        42–43, 128, 152, 159, 170, 171,
        174–75, 285n77; and OLC, 3,
        42; and her singing career, 78,
        177, 285n67; and her wedding,
        241
    singing career of, 31, 49, 78, 109,
        116, 152, 177, 241, 306n23
Clemens, Jean (JC)
    and Ashcroft, 125, 183–84, 207,
        216, 300–301n10, 316n24
    birth of, 7
    "causes" of (animal and human
        rights), 10, 48, 54, 88, 89, 93, 254
    character and intelligence of, ix,
        10–11, 64–65, 91–92, 96, 142,
        182, 198, 241–42, 245, 254, 255,
        311n13, 323n23

    her Christmas preparations at
        Stormfield (1909), 245,
        250–51, 253
    and Cowles sisters, 123–24, 141,
        149, 300nn1,2, 4, 304n27
    death, funeral, and burial of, 247,
        248, 249–50, 257, 258
    described, 70, 125, 255–56
    diaries of, x, ix, xiii, 53, 130, 277n2,
        286n6, 294n3
    and Dublin, N.H., life and
        friends, 45–47, 49, 61, 64–65,
        72, 75, 78, 80, 83, 85, 92, 125,
        129, 303–4n2
    and family travels abroad, 16–18,
        28–30, 38–39
    and her farm in Redding, Conn.,
        140–41, 181–82, 191, 217, 238,
        311nn10,11
    and her German dog, 151, 246,
        248, 254, 256, 257, 258
    as horsewoman and outdoor-sports
        devotee, ix, 10, 18, 43, 46–47,
        61, 64–65, 69, 88, 91, 96–97,
        125, 191, 238, 246, 248, 251,
        285n75, 300n9
    loneliness/yearning of, 29, 70–71,
        91–92, 107, 115, 253, 282n30
    non-epileptic illness of, 37
    and OLC's illness and death, 36,
        41, 107, 115, 249–50, 253,
        285n69
    organ as gift from SLC, 44, 285n79
    social life of in New York, 31–32
    visit to Gilders' farm, Tyringham,
        Mass., 42–43
    as woodcarver, 24, 46, 65–66, 83,
        88, 113
    care facilities and sanitarian for
        epilepsy treatment: in Babylon,
        Long Island, N.Y., 150; in Ger-
        many (Sept. 1908–Jan. 1909),
        141, 142–43, 149–50, 304n26; in
        Gloucester, Mass., 126–27, 140,
        141, 149, 304n27; in Green-
        wich, Conn., 123–24, 125–26,

140, 142, 300nn1,4; in Katonah, N.Y. (*see* Clemens,
Jean: at Katonah, N.Y.,
sanitarium); at Kellgren
treatment center, Sanna, Sweden, and London, 27–29; in
Montclair, N.J., 150–51, 159

and CC, 43, 64–65, 92, 95–96, 99,
150, 241, 248; JC's part in her
wedding, 241, 257; JC's visit
to CC at Miss Mullhall's
sanitarium, 90; negotiations
to end JC's exile, 175–77, 223,
310n18; visits to JC at Katonah, 84, 85, 90, 92, 93, 99

and epilepsy: effect of on her
family and friends, 28, 32, 34,
66, 68, 71, 72, 111, 115, 231,
290n30; her frustrations in re
and dreams about, ix, 29, 64,
69, 99, 282n32; Lyon's supervision of at home, 38, 46, 54,
64, 65, 73–74, 81–82, 156 (*see
also* Clemens, Jean: exile of by
Lyon); physical effects of, 26,
53, 55, 66–68; seizures, 21, 22,
24–26, 41, 46, 49, 50, 53, 64,
66–67, 78, 81, 82, 93, 140,
176–77, 191, 248, 251, 281n7,
285n69, 286n17, 290n34,
292n77, 303–4n22, 312n2;
theory about cause of, 28, 111,
298n5; treatments for, xiii,
21–22, 24–26, 27–28, 29–30,
51, 69, 80–81, 83, 142; vs.
hopes for romance and
marriage, 65, 69, 70–72, 92, 95

exile of, x, 54, 80–81, 110, 115,
129–30, 137, 138–39, 141, 143,
150, 159, 181, 191, 204, 216–17,
222, 223, 225, 232, 303n19,
304n26, 316n24, 323n23; and
alleged attack on Katy Leary,
xi, 53–54, 83, 217, 268; communication with SLC, 88, 89,
90, 98, 99, 110, 113, 127–29,

150, 175; Lyon's control over
correspondence with SLC,
86–87, 88, 98–99, 113, 145, 156,
182, 217, 222, 228; and Lyon's
control over doctors, 107–8,
110, 112, 114, 125–26, 128–29,
139, 140, 150, 156, 175–76, 223,
238, 297n2, 303n21, 310n18;
Lyon's deception of SLC in re,
115, 125–26, 128, 220, 223, 232,
240; visits with family and
friends, 84, 85, 90, 92–93, 98,
99, 107, 114, 124–26, 139–40,
177, 300–301n10

financial affairs of: and SLC's
money problems, 94–95, 126,
241; and Lyon's strictures in re
extra money for her, 105,
106–7, 114–15, 137, 147, 148;
money problems of on trip to
Germany, 142, 149, 305n9;
monthly allowance from SLC,
149

at Katonah, N.Y., sanitarium:
activities and outdoor life at,
88, 89, 91, 96–97, 98, 112;
attempts to leave, 92, 107–8,
110, 112, 115; friendships at, 93,
97, 98, 112, 113; homesickness
at, 92, 98, 99; preview visit
and arrival, 84, 85, 292n3,
294nn1,9; regimen and
treatment, 88–90, 91, 93–94,
112, 113–14, 127, 295nn27,28

and Katy Leary, 54, 61, 89, 98, 246,
248, 250, 253, 255 (nn), 257,
259, 263; JC's alleged attack
on, xi, 53–54, 83, 268

and Lyon, 38, 46, 64, 69, 72,
73–74, 76, 81–83, 110, 114, 219,
323n23 (*see also* Clemens, Jean:
exile of); her fear that SLC
would marry Lyon, 104, 226,
227; JC's nickname for, 77,
292n75; Lyon's characterization of as "crazy," xii, 139,

Clemens, Jean (continued)
17, 260, 268–69; on Lyon's
nervous condition, 81–82; on
Lyon's misappropriation of
SLC's funds, 192–93, 194–98,
225, 313n13
relationships of: with Paine, 64,
70, 241, 268; with her family,
32, 35, 36, 55, 72, 95; with
George de Forest Brush, 66,
69, 111, 124–25, 129; with
Gerry Brush, 47, 64, 66,
70–73, 82, 83, 84, 91, 92; with
Gra Thayer, 47, 66, 72–73, 129,
290n30; with Dr. Hibbard,
90–92, 93, 94, 95, 97, 113,
295n27; with Marguerite
Schmitt, 114, 149, 150, 300n4,
304n27, 305nn9,13
and SLC, ix, xi, 10–11, 51, 69, 72,
92, 110, 115, 149, 242, 245, 249,
250, 259, 260; acknowledges
his part in her exile, xii, 220,
223, 225; billiards with, 182,
251; her death and his
"Closing Words of My
Autobiography," 246–59; and
her epilepsy, ix, 49, 50–51, 69,
92, 255; gift of Redding,
Conn., farm to, 181, 217,
311n10; at Katonah, N.Y.,
sanitarium, 95–96, 98–99,
107, 294n9; their last day together, 245–46, 248; and
OLC's death, 49, 50; as his
secretary and housemistress,
39, 181, 182, 192, 238, 241,
251–52, 254–55; and Stormfield, 75, 77–78, 96, 139,
181–82, 191–92, 223, 238, 242,
250, 251–52, 254, 292n75
Clemens, Langdon, 6–7, 37 (nn)
Clemens, Olivia (Livy) Langdon (OLC)
carnelian beads of found in Lyon's
trunk, 178, 180–81, 203, 310n6

children of, 6–7, 9
Christmas preparations of, 251, 253
description and character of, 2–4,
42, 278nn2,3
and family travels abroad, 16–18,
20–23, 24, 26–30, 38–41
final illness, death, and burial of, x,
36–37, 41, 42–43, 60, 129, 219,
249–50, 252, 253, 255–56, 263
(nn)
illnesses of, 3, 17, 19, 35–37, 38, 39,
40–41, 115, 129
and JC's epilepsy, 22, 24–26, 29,
32, 35, 49, 50, 55, 65, 107, 231,
255
marriage of, 2, 6, 258, 278n2
pet name for SLC, 4, 36
relationships of: with CC, xiv, 36,
37, 40, 41, 42–43, 115, 253;
with Katy Leary, 11, 12, 13, 14,
41, 42, 115, 230, 263; with
Lyon, 38, 40; with SC, 11, 22,
23–24, 26, 42, 105; with SLC,
2–5, 13, 19, 36–37, 40–41, 42,
278n2
role of in Clemens family, 2, 7–8,
11, 12, 19, 42, 226, 230, 231,
278n14
as SLC's editor and censor, 2–3, 4,
5, 8, 278nn3,9
and SLC's financial problems, 19,
231, 318n37
Clemens, Olivia Susan (Susy; SC):
birth, childhood, and early
adulthood of, 6, 7, 9, 16, 128,
278n4, 279–80n40; at Bryn Mawr,
16, 279–80n40; and CC, 24,
108–9, 154, 281n14; character of, 7,
8, 9, 10, 11; and family travels in
Europe, 16, 17–18, 30; as favorite
child, 8, 11, 24, 26, 27, 281n14;
illness and death of, 22–24, 29, 37,
42, 59, 115, 248, 249, 252, 253,
281n13, 282n33; and Louise
Brownell, 16, 17, 20, 279–80n40;

and Mental Science, 22–23, 37; and
OLC, 11, 22, 23–24, 26, 42, 105;
Papa (her biography of SLC), 11,
279n24; and SLC, 8, 26, 132; and
SLC's fame, 16, 17; vocal studies of,
16, 17–18, 22
Clemens, Samuel Langhorn (SLC)
and his Angelfish, 60, 130–33, 146,
301nn25,27, 302nn34,37,38;
Cooley on, 301nn25,27,
301–2n28
and Ashcroft. *See* Ashcroft, Ralph
Ashcroft-Lyon MS of, xii, 187
(nn), 218–33, 237, 316nn3,4;
parable of North Pole and
Neptune discoveries in,
234–36; preface of "To the
Unborn Reader," 236–37;
public release of, 220, 237,
238, 316n4; reasons of for
writing, 211, 219, 220–21, 228,
232–33; scholarly criticism and
interpretation of, xii–xiii, 219,
220, 232, 234, 271, 272, 316n4,
324n28; as series of letters to
Howells, 219, 221; vs. Lyon's
diaries, xii–xiii
autobiographical dictations of, 40,
56, 61–62, 103, 119, 162,
284n65, 296n12
and billiards, 7, 60, 63, 76, 85–86,
113, 119, 132, 143, 145, 146, 182,
187, 220, 243, 251, 299n37,
305n35
and cats, 7, 9, 10, 11, 62, 135
causes and social concerns of:
American imperialism and
foreign policy, 1, 30–31; animal
rights, 48; artificial hierarchy
of society, 14; astronomy, 243;
atrocities in Belgian Congo,
43–44; Bacon as author of
Shakespeare's plays, 161–62,
308n7; Boxer Rebellion, 31;
Christian Science, 37, 284n57;

copyright laws, 1, 19, 87, 101,
167, 247; determinism, 111–12;
ex-slaves, their children, and
lynchings, 33; labor unions,
261; post-Civil-War reconstruction, 60; racial prejudice,
244; Russian revolution,
100–101; spiritualism, 22
celebrity and fame of, ix, 1–2,
26–27, 30, 33, 56–57, 60–61,
162, 277n1, 283n44, 285n67,
289n8
character and personality of, 3, 29,
36, 60, 63, 132, 184, 220, 240,
242, 243, 244–45, 282n33
and Charlotte Teller Johnson,
100–101, 104, 295n3,
296nn4,5,18
and CC. *See* Clemens, Clara (CC)
and Countess Masiglia, 39; death
of, xiv, 23, 262, 307n42
on deaths of family and friends,
249, 252–53, 257
and death of son Langdon, 6–7, 37
(nn)
despair after death of SC, 29, 59,
282n33
and Dublin, N.H., summer home,
45, 48, 60, 62, 74
family life of (*see* Clemens family:
home life and diversions of)
and funds for Redding, Conn.,
public library, 240–41
Harper's seventieth birthday party
for, 57
honorary degrees of, 33, 103,
296n15
illnesses of, 16, 17, 28, 34, 43,
85–86, 143, 243, 249, 282n27,
304n30
inner circle of and parallels with
King Lear, xii, 158, 223, 225,
232, 238, 272
and JC: chaperones for, 64–65; on
her character and disposition,

Clemens, Samuel Langhorn (cont'd)
9, 50–51, 55, 69, 127, 182, 242–42,
255, 311n13; and her death,
249–50, 255–56, 257, 259, 261;
"The Death of Jean," 246,
272, 287n18; and her German
dog, 151, 246, 248, 254, 256,
257, 258; her horse-riding accident, 43, 285n75; and her last
days, 246, 248–49; and her life
and friends in Dublin, N.H.,
64–65, 69, 83, 98; money for,
94–95, 106–7, 114, 137, 147,
148, 241; and Redding, Conn.,
land and farmhouse for,
140–41, 181; relationship with,
ix, xi, 10–11, 51, 69, 72, 108–9,
110, 115, 181, 182, 191–92, 238,
242, 245, 249, 250, 252, 257,
258, 259, 260; requests her to
join Lark in settlement
negotiations with Lyon, 194
and JC's epilepsy: abdication of
parental role in re to Lyon,
86–87, 111, 128, 129–30, 191, 217,
227, 293n28; and her
alleged homicidal attack on
Katy Leary, xi; attitude
toward, 25–26, 29–30, 34–35,
50, 51, 69, 86, 111–12, 142, 177,
191, 216–17, 255, 259, 293n28;
chronicle of her illness ("Jean's
Illness"), 29, 282n33; and the
epileptic temperament, 90, 111,
112, 127, 182, 217, 242, 293n28;
exile of JC for treatment, 81,
84–85, 95–96, 113, 123, 125,
128–29, 292n5, 323n23; and
Lyon's characterization of JC as
"crazy," xi, xii, 217, 260; and
Lyon's control of correspondence, 86–87, 88, 98–99, 113,
145, 156, 182, 217, 222, 228; and
Lyon's control over doctors,
107–8, 110–11, 112, 114, 125–26,

128–29, 139, 140, 141, 150,
175–76, 177, 216–17, 223, 238,
248, 249–50, 257, 258, 294n9,
297n2, 305n13; plans for and
end of her exile, 140–41, 175–77,
181, 310n18; during her exile, 85,
90, 92–93, 95–96, 98, 99,
125–26, 139, 140, 294n9, 295n36,
300–301n10; and her seizures,
22, 24–25, 34–35, 49, 141, 246
and John Howells, 33, 75–76,
77–78, 134, 302n2
and Katy Leary, 12–14, 63, 264,
323n20
and learned helplessness syndrome,
230–31
as lecturer, 1, 20–21, 22, 56–57,
187–88
and Louise Brownell, 279–80n40
and Lyon. See Lyon, Isabel Van
Kleek
and Mary Mason Fairbanks, 4–5,
278n7
and Mary Rogers, 84–85, 102,
287n25, 293n17, 296n5
mental faculties of (1908), 187–88,
311–12n27
and money matters, 118, 224,
317n16; bad investments of, 15,
33–34, 113, 117–18, 167, 205–6,
299nn29,30, 314nn12,14,
317n9, 318n37; bankruptcy of,
2, 18–19, 20, 26, 280n1, 281n8;
his income (1907), 114,
298n18; and Knickerbocker
Trust Co. default, 114, 135, 189,
298n16; wealth of (1908), 154,
306n28 (see also Ashcroft,
Ralph: financial skullduggery
of; as SLC's self-appointed
business manager; see also
Lyon, Isabel Van Kleek:
business and financial
arrangements with SLC; as
SLC's check signer and

budget keeper; *see also* Rogers,
Henry Huttleston)
nicknames of, 4, 36, 57
old age of, x, 128, 229–30, 232–33;
scholars' views of, x, xii–xiii,
59, 219, 289n3
and OLC: as his editor and censor,
2–3, 4, 5, 8, 278nn3,9; and his
financial problems, 19, 231,
318n37; illness, death, and
burial of, x, 36–37, 41, 42–43,
60, 129, 249–50, 252, 253,
255–56, 263 (nn); marriage of
to OLC, 2, 6, 258, 278n2;
memories of, 61, 62, 105;
relationship with, 2–5, 13, 19,
36–37, 40–41, 42, 278n2
and religion, 3, 13–14, 33, 44, 62,
244, 259–60, 278n4
retirement of, 239, 243, 319n18,
320n8
and SC. *See* Clemens, Olivia Susan
(Susy; SC)
seventy-fourth birthday of, 245,
249
as a smoker, 101–2, 243
Stormfield, house of in Redding,
Conn.: and JC, 139, 140–41;
plans for, construction of, and
cost of: 75–76, 77–78, 85,
134–35, 137, 185, 302nn1,2;
names for, 133, 137, 138
travels of: abroad with family,
16–18, 20–21, 22, 23, 24,
26–30, 38–41, 61, 289n8; to
Bermuda, 86, 102, 119, 120,
131, 132, 136, 245, 252, 260,
261–62, 293n24, 299n38,
301n25; to Hannibal, Missouri
(1902), 37; to Oxford for
honorary degree (1907),
103–4, 118, 296n15
white suits of, 87
and William Dean Howells (*see*
Howells, William Dean)

and Paine. *See* Paine, Albert
Bigelow
writings of: censorship of by OLC
and by himself, 2–3, 4–5; early
vs. later, x, 59–60, 246; for
himself, 218, 243; regimen, 4,
7, 8, 12, 47–48; techniques and
devices, 2, 34, 48, 221, 317n9;
as therapy, 43–44, 249. *See also*
Twain, Mark works of
Clemens family
in the Adirondacks, 33
animals and pets of, 7, 9, 10, 11
at the Gilder farm, Tyringham,
Mass., 42
and JC's epilepsy, 32, 35, 36,
55, 95
and Katy Leary, 11–14, 44, 45–46,
86, 146, 251, 264, 285n2
and SLC's Angelfish, 133
travels abroad of, 16–18, 20–21, 22,
23, 24, 26–30, 38–41, 61,
289n8
yearly income of, 105, 297n23
home life and diversions of, xii, 2,
3, 5–11, 46, 48, 61, 241–42, 119,
250, 251, 259–60, 278n10,
279n15; card games, 32, 44,
157, 250; charades and plays,
8, 9, 62–63, 69; dinner parties,
5–6, 8, 31; music, 8, 9, 44;
poetry reading, 73
houses and summer residences of:
Dublin, N.H., 45–48, 61–76,
285n79; Hartford, Conn., 2,
5–6, 7–8, 15, 16, 30, 43,
279n15; New York City (14
West 10th St.; 21 Fifth Ave.),
30, 31, 33, 34, 43, 48–49, 61,
77–78, 84, 114, 285n77;
Quarry Farm, Elmira, N.Y., 5,
8, 10, 20, 38; Riverdale, Bronx,
N.Y., 33, 34, 36; Stormfield,
17, 75–76, 77, 96, 134, 135, 136,
138, 139, 153, 158, 172–75, 176,

Clemens family *(continued)*
  302n2, 302–3n4, 303n20, 307n1;
  Tuxedo Park, N.Y. (summer 1907),
  99, 102–3; York Harbor, Maine, 34,
  35
Cleveland, Grover, 1
Congo Reform Association, 44
Cook, Frederick, 234–36, 318nn2,7,8
Cooley, John, *Mark Twain's Aquarium*,
  301nn25,27, 301–2n28
Cowles, Edith and Mildred, 123–24,
  141, 149, 300nn1,2,4, 304n27
Craig Colony for Epileptics, 68
Crane, Susan Langdon (sister of OLC),
  16, 20, 22, 281n7
Crane, Theodore (husband of above),
  8, 20

Darwin, Charles, 1
Dickens, Charles, 8
Duneka, Frederick, 166, 171–72

Eddy, Mary Baker, 37, 161, 284n57
Edward VII (king of England), as
  prince of Wales, 1
epilepsy: attitudes toward, xi, xiii,
  21–22, 28–29, 68, 71, 280–81n5,
  282n31; and the epileptic temperament, 28–29, 50–51, 81–82, 90,
  182, 242, 255, 293n28; family acceptance of, 32, 54–55, 72, 288n33,
  322n16; linkage of with mental illness and homicidal aggression, xi,
  54, 268, 287n31, 287–88n32,
  288n33, 290n39, 322n16; social/fa-
  milial stigma of, 32, 54–55, 66, 71,
  72, 282n32, 283n43, 288n33; vs.
  late-twentieth-century views of,
  290n39
Evening Telegram (New York City),
  312n8, 313nn9,10

Fairbanks, Mary Mason, 4–5, 278n7
Farrish, Miss (patient at Katonah), 97
Faulkner, Barry, 47

Fess, Simeon Davidson, 318n7
Foote, Mary (SC's governess), 22
Freeman, Zoheth and Sheba, 147,
  304n24

Gabrilowitsch, Nina (daughter of CC),
  263, 270–71
Gabrilowitsch, Ossip (first husband of
  CC), 26, 31, 34, 239, 240–41, 247,
  263, 270
Genung, Charles Harvey, 288n35
Gerken, Irene, 133
Gilder, Dorothea, 203
Gilder, Richard Watson, 41, 249
Gilder, Rodman, 43
Gillette, William, 6
Gordon, Miss (CC's nurse), 139
Grant, Ulysses S., 1, 61–62
Greene, Henry Copley, 45
Griffin, George (Clemens family
  butler), 6, 8, 9, 12 (nn), 253

Halsey, Dr. (CC's doctor), 109
Hardy, Father (Katy Leary's priest), 13,
  14
Harnsberger, Caroline, *Mark Twain:
  Family Man*, 270, 282n23,
  323n23
Harper & Brothers, Inc., 37, 57, 168
Harper's Bazaar, 240
Harper's Monthly Magazine, 43, 138,
  286–7n18
Harrington, Phyllis (CC's secretary), ix,
  270 (nn)
Harte, Bret, 1
Hartford Woman's Exchange,
  204–5
Hartley, Dr. (JC's doctor), 51
Harvey, Dorothy, 133
Harvey, Col. George, of Harper &
  Brothers, 57, 63, 143, 144, 299n37
Hazen, Horace (SLC's butler at
  Stormfield), 155, 173–75, 183, 224,
  309–10n15
Henderson, Hildegaarde, 64

Hibbard, Dr. (staff physician at Katonah), 90–92, 93, 94, 95, 97, 113, 295n27

Hill, Hamlin, *God's Fool*, x–xi (nn), 219 (nn), 271–72, 277n2, 284n52, 296n6, 301–2n28, 305n13, 316n4, 323n27

Hobby, Josephine, 56, 61, 146

Hoffman, Andrew, 279–80n40

Holbrook, Hal, ix, 277n1

Hosford, Mr. (patient at Katonah), 98

Howells, John (architect and designer of Stormfield), 33, 75–76, 77–78, 134, 302n2

Howells, Mildred ("Pilla"), 31–32

Howells, William Dean: friendship with SLC, 5, 6, 30, 33–34, 57, 260–61, 283n44; nickname of for SLC, 57; and OLC, 3–4, 35–36, 42; and SLC's Ashcroft-Lyon MS as series of letters to, 219, 220; and SLC's letters to, 120–21

Hull (plumber), 195

Hunt, Dr. Frederick (JC's doctor at Katonah), 88, 93, 107, 292n3; Lyon's manipulation of, 84, 96, 99, 107

Iles, Harry, 142

Irving, Henry, 6

James, William, 1

Johnson, Charlotte Teller, 100–101, 104, 295n3, 296nn4,5,18

Journal of Nervous and Mental Disease, The, 54

Kaplan, Justin, *Mr. Clemens and Mark Twain*, 215, 271, 284n52, 323n26

Katonah, N.Y., sanitarium of Dr. Peterson. *See* Clemens, Jean: at Katonah, N.Y., sanitarium

Kellgren, Jonas Henrik, treatment centers of in Sweden and London, 27–30, 280–81n5

King, Grace, 16, 17

Knickerbocker Trust Co., 114, 135, 189, 298n16

Koy-lo (hairpin) Company, 314n14

Kipling, Rudyard, 1

Laffan, William M., 249

Langdon, Charley (brother of OLC), 23

Langdon, Jervis (cousin of CC), 257 (nn)

Langdon family homestead, Elmira, N.Y. *See* Quarry Farm, Elmira, N.Y.

Lark, Charles (SLC attorney), 311n6; and farmhouse in Redding, Conn., 210–11, 213 (nn), 214, 315n18 (nn); and SLC finances, 189, 192, 196, 312n31, 313n19; in settlement negotiations with Lyon et al., 193–203, 207, 208–9, 212, 213, 216 (nn)

Larkin, John (SLC's business lawyer), 172

Lawton, Mary: as editor of *A Lifetime with Mark Twain*, xiv, 264, 321n5; friendship of with CC, 228, 321n5

learned helplessness syndrome, 230–31, 318n34

Leary, Katy

on Clemens family life, 3, 5–6, 46, 48, 278n10

and JC, 54, 61, 89, 98; JC's alleged homicidal attack on, xi, 53–54, 83, 268; JC's death, 246, 248, 250, 253, 255 (nn), 257, 259, 263

A Lifetime with Mark Twain, xiv, 264, 321n5

and OLC's death, 41–42

and relationships of: with CC, 9, 25, 26, 31, 115–16, 136, 154–55, 166–67, 239, 241, 264; with Lyon, 86, 116, 117, 153, 154–55, 159, 166–67, 264; with OLC, 11, 12, 13, 14, 41, 42, 115, 230, 263; with SLC, 12–14, 63, 264, 323n20

Leary, Katy *(continued)*
　role of in Clemens household,
　　11–14, 44, 45–46, 86, 146, 251,
　　264, 285n2
　and SC's final illness and death,
　　22–24, 263, 281n13
　and SLC's granddaughter Nina,
　　263–64
　and trips to Europe with
　　Clemenses, 16, 17, 18, 38, 39,
　　136
Leschetizky, Theodore, 25, 26
Leslie, Elsie, 10
Leverrier, Urbain, 235
Liberty National Bank, New York City,
　187
Littell's Living Age, 62
Logan, Mrs. (patient at Katonah), 95,
　98
Lombroso, Cesare, 54, 287n31
Lounsbury, H. A. (general contractor):
　on Lyon's drinking problem, 76;
　on Lyon as surrogate for SLC in re
　JC, 140, 156, 228; at meeting of
　CC and Lark with Mrs. Lyon, 199,
　202, 314n5; and renovation of
　Lyon's farmhouse, 184–85, 195, 196,
　218 (nn), 311n19
Lounsbury, Harry (son of above), 186,
　224
Lyon, Charles H., Sr. (father of Lyon),
　141–5
Lyon, Mrs. Charles H. (mother of
　Lyon), 33, 38, 40, 75, 148, 163, 186,
　193, 285n66; and CC's inspection
　of her daughter's trunks, 203; Lyon
　as sole supporter of, 148, 186, 196;
　and her daughter's settlement with
　SLC, 194–98, 199–204, 314n5
Lyon, Isabel Van Kleek (later Mrs.
　Ralph Ashcroft)
　and Ashcroft, 103, 118–20, 122, 135,
　　152, 154, 155, 204, 205, 222,
　　288–89n50, 299n33, 306n28;
　　and financial skullduggery,
　　xii–xiii, 157–158, 166–70, 172,

184–90, 192, 201–5, 207–8, 211,
224, 240, 241, 306n28, 307n42,
309nn29,37,38, 311n19,
311–12n27, 315n11; marriage to
and divorce from, 163–66, 171,
205, 239, 265, 321n7; and *New
York Times* letter and interviews,
xiii, 192–93, 207–8, 209–15,
216, 218 (nn), 225–26, 239, 261,
312nn5,6,8, 313nn9,10, 315n16,
321n23; her nickname for, 122;
SLC's list of grievances in re,
213–14; and SLC's parable in
re, 235
business/financial arrangements
with SLC: Ashcroft's memorandum of her services and
SLC's compensation for,
169–70; audit of finances after
her dismissal, xiii, 183, 184,
185, 210, 211, 311n19, 315nn7,11;
Clean-Up Day contracts with
SLC, 168–70, 178, 309n37;
fraudulent powers of attorney,
106, 158, 187, 188–89, 201, 204,
224, 297n24, 309n38,
311–12n27; SLC's offer of
royalties from edition of his
letters, 118, 168–69, 179–80;
wages of and SLC's offer to
increase, 146, 166–67, 169,
170, 186, 196, 201
character of, 46, 74, 122, 204, 217
diaries, daybooks, and journals of,
xi, xii–xiii, 58, 266, 268, 271,
286n6, 288n48, 322nn10,12;
her later alterations to, xi, 185,
265–66, 268–69, 287nn27,28,
288nn41,42, 291nn55–57,64,
292–93n9, 296n7, 311n21,
321–22n9, 322–23n10,
223nn18,20
drinking and drug problems of,
73, 76, 79, 121–22, 138, 153,
163, 203, 299n47, 306n25,
308n11

early life of, 14–15

emotional collapses of, 78–79, 82, 101, 136–37, 153, 154, 158, 163, 173, 203, 222, 266, 292n79, 296n6, 308n11, 323n20

and Father Stiattisi, 40, 41

and JC: as her chaperone in SLC's absence, xi–xii, 38, 46, 64, 69, 72, 73–74, 76, 80, 81–82, 83, 156, 219; characterization of JC as "crazy," xii, 139, 217, 260, 268–69; control of JC/SLC correspondence, 86–87, 88, 98–99, 113, 145, 156, 182, 217, 222, 228; control over doctors, 107–8, 110, 112, 114, 125–26, 128–29, 139, 140, 150, 176, 177, 223, 238, 248, 249–50, 257, 258, 297n2; exile of JC, x, xii, 54, 80–84, 90, 92–93, 94, 107–8, 115, 129–30, 137, 138–39, 141, 142, 143, 150, 156, 159, 181, 191, 204, 216–17, 222, 223, 232, 240, 292nn2,3,5, 292–93n9, 297n35, 303n19; financial strictures on JC, 104, 106–8, 114–15, 137, 142, 147, 148; influence on SLC's and JC's relationship, xii, 65, 105–6, 110–12, 128, 139, 140–41, 181, 240; and JC's alleged homicidal attack on Katy Leary, xi, 53–55, 83, 217, 268; and JC's Dublin, N.H., friends, 129–30, 301n21 (nn); and JC's epilepsy, xi–xii, 49–50, 54, 55, 78, 81–83, 91–92, 108, 110–11, 112, 129–30, 142, 177, 217

and Katy Leary, 86, 116, 117, 153, 154–55, 159, 166–67, 264

and land/farmhouse in Redding, Conn.: misappropriation of SLC's money, 146–47, 184–86, 193, 205, 311n19, 313nn10,18,19; SLC's attachment of, 192, 195, 197–98, 203–4, 225, 312n5;

SLC's deed of to Lyon, 74–76, 106, 117, 147, 157–58, 193, 214, 291n64, 297n24, 315n17; settlement negotiations in re, 192–93, 194–98, 225, 312n5, 313n13

life of after SLC, 265, 266, 321n8, 322n11

her nicknames, 75, 77, 160

obsession with clothes and furnishings, 147–48, 166–67, 170, 186, 196, 305n6

and OLC, 38, 40

relationships of: with CC: 38, 39, 72, 75, 105–6, 109, 122, 135–37, 151–53, 154, 159, 178, 204, 209, 211, 221, 264 (see also Clemens, Clara: battle over control of SLC's money and household); with Katy Leary, 86, 116, 117, 153, 154–55, 159, 166–67, 264; with Dr. Peterson, 81, 107–8, 110, 112, 114, 125–26, 128–29, 139, 140, 142–43, 150, 175–76, 177, 216, 223, 238, 292n5, 297n2, 305–6n13, 310n18; with Samuel and Doris Webster, 153, 265, 266–67, 268, 269, 272, 296n8, 322nn12,13

and Paine, xiv, 57, 73–78, 119–22, 135, 140, 162, 171, 268, 288n50; attempts of to discredit Paine with SLC, xiv, 120–22, 135, 143–44, 159, 268, 322n17, 323n18

and SLC: and Ashcroft's business arrangements with SLC, 168–69; attempted reconciliation, 179–80, 193; autobiographical dictations sessions, 40, 56, 284n65; his belief in her, 208, 110–11, 167, 179, 210; as buffer between SLC and the world, 128, 157, 159; and Clean-Up Day contracts, 168–70, 171, 179–80, 309n37;

Lyon, Isabel Van Kleek (continued)
her control over SLC, xiv, 79, 133,
140, 152, 155, 156, 159–60, 184,
188, 207–8, 223, 227, 228, 230,
231, 232, 311n17; effect of her
marriage to Ashcroft on, 155,
163–66, 169, 171, 176, 179, 239,
269; her first meeting with
SLC, 15, 279n37; her flattery
of, 52, 61; as friend and
Clemens family member, 116,
159, 205; her nickname for
SLC, 57, 58, 288–89n50; her
obsession with SLC, xi, xiv,
51–52, 57–58, 73, 76, 100,
101–2, 103–4, 105, 116, 132, 138,
226–27, 160, 166, 226–27, 267,
269, 296n18, 297n19; after
OLC's death, 51–53; as protagonist in SLC's autobiographical exposé, 218–33; and "Report
of Miss X," 122, 165, 188, 204,
300n49, 308n18, 310n6, 321n8;
her shrine of to SLC's memory,
58, 269–70; and SLC's An-
gelfish, 130–31, 132, 133, 301n25;
and SLC's catalogue of her fall,
239–40; and SLC and Clemens
family travels, 38–40, 41, 76,
85, 101, 103, 136, 157, 227,
307n36; on SLC's character,
184, 269; and SLC's conflicted
feelings toward, 199, 217,
221–22, 224, 225, 231, 239–40;
and SLC's construction of
Stormfield, 75–76, 77–78, 85,
96, 134–35, 136, 137, 154, 185,
292n75, 302nn1,2, 302–3n4;
SLC's disenchantment with,
xiii, 163, 176, 177–178, 179–80,
190, 212, 218, 224, 310n19,
317n16; as SLC's housekeeper
and hostess, 117, 143, 146,
153–57, 159, 171, 175, 176; and
SLC's relationship with Charlotte Teller Johnson, 100–101,
104, 295n3, 296nn4,5,18; as

SLC's secretary, 38, 40, 44, 52,
180, 285n66; and SLC's sexuality, 226–27; as SLC's surrogate
wife, 105, 132, 138, 143, 166, 186;
and SLC as victim of "learned
helplessness syndrome,"
230–31, 318n34; vs. OLC, 226
as SLC's check signer and budget
keeper, 105, 170, 171, 224,
317n16; and audit wars with
CC, 160, 162–63, 166–67, 168,
223, 307n5; and her case
against SLC, 203–4; failure to
distinguish between SLC's
money and hers, 106, 116, 122,
146, 147–48, 159, 163, 166–67,
170, 186, 196, 298n24,
311–12n27; "house money"
misappropriated by, 146,
147, 184–86, 196, 311n23,
313nn18,19; pre-SLC financial
deceptions of, 204–5, 306n28;
SLC suspects her of stealing,
209–10, 315n7; and SLC's
threatened legal action against,
185, 193, 196–97, 204, 225,
313n9

McAleer, Patrick, 47, 49
McKinley, William, 30
McKittrick, Tom, 47, 64–65
Malibran, Maria Felicita, 43–47
Marchesi, Blanche, 17–18, 20, 27
Mark Twain Company, 157–58, 167–68,
172, 189, 212, 214–15, 224, 316n20
(nn)
Masiglia, Countess, 39
Mental Science, 22
Moffett, Samuel E. (SLC's nephew),
143, 304n30
Mullhall, Miss, sanitarium of, 90
Munro, David, 55

National Cash Register Company, 118,
206
Neider, Charles, introduction to SC's
Papa, 279n39, 279–80n40

Neptune (planet), SLC parable of, 235, 318n6

New York American, 312n6

New York Times: "Mark Twain Done With Work," 239, 243, 319n18, 320n8; publication of Lyon-Ashcroft interviews, xiii, 208, 209–15, 216, 218 (nn), 225–26, 239, 315n16; "Was 'Tom Sawyer' Danish or American?" 261, 321n23

Nickerson, John (SLC's notary public), 187, 197–98, 202 (nn), 307n42

North American Review, xii, 37, 44, 284n57

North Pole (SLC parable on), 234–36, 318nn2,7,8

Nunnally, Frances, 133

Ochs, Adolph Simon (publisher of the *New York Times*), 216, 239, 315n16

O'Conners, George (JC's groom), 65, 74, 96–97, 142

old age, stereotypes of SLC's, x, xii–xiii, 59, 219, 289nn1–3

Paige, James, 317n9

Paine, Albert Bigelow, 55, 74, 83, 251
  and JC, 64, 70, 241, 268; and her death, 246, 253, 254, 257; and her epilepsy, 280–81n5
  and Lyon and Ashcroft's attempt to alienate SLC, xiv, 120–22, 135, 143–44, 159, 268, 322n17, 323n18; and Lyon's drinking and drug problems, 153, 261; and Lyon's misappropriation of SLC's money, 184, 185–86, 196, 313n19; and plot to keep SLC under their control, 140; his relationship with Lyon, xiv, 57, 73, 74–75, 76–77, 78, 119, 120, 121–22, 135, 162, 171, 288n50
  and SLC, 62, 76, 128, 143, 243, 251; and Bacon as author of Shakespeare's plays, 308n7; and

billiards sessions with SLC, 76, 86, 119, 145, 187, 220, 299n37, 305n35; on cause of SLC's despair, 282n33; and financial oversight, 119–20, 251; as part of Clemens family inner circle, xiv, 57, 143, 288n41, 288–89n50; and SLC's Angelfish, 131; and SLC's dizzy spell (1908), 143, 304n30; as SLC's emissary to the *New York Times*, 239; and SLC's final illness and death, 262; on SLC's *Letters from the Earth*, 244; and SLC's purchase of Redding, Conn., property, 74–75, 76, 134, 145; and SLC's settlement in re Redding farmhouse, 194, 198, 212; and trip to Bermuda (1909), 245
  as SLC's biographer: and Howell's letters from SLC, 120–21; his proposal to SLC in re, 55–56, 288n35; publication of *Mark Twain: A Biography*, xiii, xiv, 144, 264, 321n29; and his removal of SLC biographical material, 121, 144; retraces SLC's steps in *The Innocents Abroad*, 162; and SLC's and CC's strictures on, xiv, 144, 264, 321n29; and SLC's autobiographical dictations, 40, 56, 61–62, 103, 119, 162, 284n65, 296n12
  wife and children of, 74–75

Paine, Louise (daughter of above), 131, 133

Paston Letters, SLC on value of, 237

Peary, Commander Robert, 234–36, 318nn2,7,8 (nn)

Peterson, Dr. Frederick (JC's doctor): and Mr. Brush, 11, 125; and CC's and SLC's insistence that JC come home, 175–76, 177, 181, 310n18; and JC's move from Katonah, 112,

Peterson, Dr. Frederick (continued)
113, 123–24, 125, 126, 128–29, 139,
300n4, 304n27; and JC's trip to
Germany, 141, 142–43, 149–51,
305–6n13; manipulation of by
Lyon, 31, 107–8, 110, 112, 114,
125–26, 128–29, 139, 140, 150,
175–76, 177, 216, 223, 238, 292n5,
303n21, 310n18; treatment of JC's
epilepsy, 68–69, 71, 80, 81, 83, 85,
238, 290nn38,39, 292nn2,3
Plasmon Milk Products Company, 33,
117–18, 167, 206, 299nn29 (nn)
and 30, 314n14
Players, The (private men's club), 55
Pumpelly, Raphael, 47

Quarry Farm, Elmira, N.Y. (Langdon
family homestead); Clemens family
visits to, 5, 8, 10, 20, 22 (nn), 38; as
site of SLC family weddings and
funerals, 2, 41 (nn), 258
Quick, Dorothy, 108–9, 130–31, 132, 133,
301n25
Quintard, Dr. Edward (Clemens family
doctor), 243, 262; blows whistle on
Lyon and Ashcroft, 16, 160; and
JC, 44, 54, 177, 223, 287n30; lends
CC money, 135–36

Rice, Dr. Clarence (SLC's doctor), 31
Roberts, Miss (patient at Katonah), 93
Robinson, Gov. and Mrs. George, 6
Robinson, Henry, 253
Rogers, Emilie (wife of Henry
Huttleston Rogers), 85–86, 104
(nn), 297n20
Rogers, Harry, 102, 287n25
Rogers, Henry Huttleston (SLC's
financial advisor), 18–19, 31, 34–35,
63, 173, 287n25, 290n16; death of,
180, 185, 207, 249, 252–53; and
independent audit of SLC
finances, 160, 166, 167, 180,
183–84, 192, 207–8, 213, 306n18;
with SLC in Bermuda (1908), ill.

Rogers, Mary (wife of Harry Rogers),
84–85, 102, 287n25, 293n17,
296n5
Roosevelt, Theodore, 89
Rosa (Clemens family German nurse),
10
Rubaiyat of Omar Khayyam, The, 73

St. Nicholas Magazine, 55
Samossoud, Jacques (CC's second husband), 270, 271
Schmitt, Marguerite (Bébé), friend and
companion of JC, 124, 149, 150,
250 (nn), 300n4, 304n27,
305nn9,13
Scott (JC's horse). See Clemens, Jean:
as horsewoman and outdoor sports
devotee
Shakespeare, William: Bacon
controversy and SLC, 161–62,
308n7; King Lear and SLC, xii,
158, 223, 225, 232, 238, 272
Sharp, Dr. (director of Katonah, N.Y.,
sanitarium), and his wife, 89, 93,
94, 95, 97, 112, 295n27
Shaw, George Bernard, 218
Society for the Prevention of Cruelty to
Animals, 18
Society of Craftsmen, New York City, 88
Stanchfield, John (SLC's lawyer), 205;
and attachment of Lyon's
farmhouse, 210–11, 213 (nn); and
independent audit of SLC
finances, 185, 311n19; recommends
German doctor for JC, 142,
304n29; and SLC's negotiations
with Lyon and Ashcroft, 185, 197,
212, 216 (nn), 304n29
Stanley, Sir Henry, 6
Starr, Dr. M. Allen, treatment of
JC's epilepsy, 21–22, 24,
281nn7,15
Sterritt, Anna (JC's maid at Katonah and
in Germany), 67, 81, 84, 89, 149
Stiattisi, Don Raffaello (Catholic
priest), and Lyon, 40, 41

Stoker, Bram, 1

Stowe, Harriet Beecher, 1

Stowell, Dr. Sarah (JC's gynecologist), 80, 292n5

Stuck, Hudson, 236

Sturgis, Dorothy, 133

Tenant, Dorothy, 6

Thayer, Abbot, 45

Thayer, Emma Beach (wife of above), 107

Thayer, Galla, friend of JC, 47, 66, 98

Thayer, Gerald (Gra; friend of JC), 47, 66, 72–73, 129, 290n30

Thayer, Robert (friend of JC), 64

Thayer family, Dublin, N.H., 45–46, 64, 80

Twain, Mark, works of: *The Adventures of Huckleberry Finn*, 1, 7, 60; *The Adventures of Tom Sawyer*, ix, 1, 7, 13; Ashcroft-Lyon MS (*see* Clemens, Samuel Langhorn, Ashcroft-Lyon MS of); *Christian Science*, 37, 284n57; "The Chronicle of Young Satan," 30, 38, 282n35; "Closing Words of My Autobiography" (published as "The Death of Jean"), 247–58 (text of), 286–87n18, 320n14; *A Connecticut Yankee in King Arthur's Court*, 7, 13–14, 60; "The Czar's Soliloquy," 43–44; "The Death of Jean," as edited by Paine for *Harper's Monthly Magazine*, 246, 272, 286–87n18, 320n10; "Diary of a Kellgren Cure," 280–81n5, 282n27; "Eve's Diary," tribute to OLC, 47–48; "Extract from Captain Stormfield's Visit to Heaven," 138; "A Fable," 272–74 (text of); *Following the Equator*, 22, 281n8; "The Golden Arm," 149; "A Horse's Tale," 48; *The Innocents Abroad*, 4, 162, 240, 278n7; *Is Shakespeare Dead?*, 161–62, 308nn7,8, 310n6; "Jean's Illness," 29, 282n33; "King

Leopold's Soliloquy," 44 (nn); *Letters from the Earth*, x, 243–44, 259–60; *Life on the Mississippi*, 7; MS about Huck Finn at age sixty (later destroyed), 37; *No. 44, The Mysterious Stranger*, x, 38, 39, 47, 60, 286n11; *Personal Recollections of Joan of Arc*, 17; *The Prince and the Pauper*, 7; *Puddn'head Wilson*, 17; "The $30,000 Bequest," 39; "Three Thousand Years Among the Microbes," 47; *Tom Sawyer Abroad*, 17; *Tom Sawyer, Detective*, 261, 321n23 (nn); "To My Missionary Critics," 31; "To the Person Sitting in Darkness," 30; "The Turning Point of My Life," 240; "The United States of Lyncherdom" (unpublished), 33, 283n44; "The War Prayer," 44; *What Is Man?*, 111; *Which Was It?*, 34

Twichell, Harmony, 6

Twichell, Joseph (Clemens family minister and husband of above), 6, 41, 86, 102, 220, 260, 293n24 (nn)

Van Eeden, Dr. Frederik, "Curing by Suggestion," 229

Von Renvers, Dr. Hofrath (JC's doctor in Germany), 142, 143, 149, 150

Wallace, Elizabeth, *Mark Twain and the Happy Island*, 264

Wark, Will (CC's accompanist), 109, 136, 165, 209

Warner, Charles and Susan, 6, 22, 253

Watson, Miss (Rogers' secretary), 184

Webster, Charles (SLC's nephew), 267, 317n9

Webster, Samuel (SLC's great nephew), and wife Doris, 265, 296n18; attitude of towards epilepsy, 268, 322n16; interview with Lyon (1948) and transcription of her diaries, 266–67, 268–69, 271, 322nn11,12;

Webster, Samuel *(continued)*
on Lyon's drinking problem, 153,
266; on Lyon's engagement and
marriage, 265, 296n18; *Mark
Twain, Business Man*, 267, 322n13
Whistler, James, 1

Whitmore, Mr. and Mrs. Franklin, 15,
38, 205, 208
Wilson, Woodrow, 261

Young Men's Christian Association,
New York City, 57

Compositor:	Impressions Book and Journal Services, Inc.
Text:	Adobe Garamond
Display:	Adobe Garamond
Printer and binder:	Edwards Brothers, Inc.